The History of the Colonial Expanison and North-South Relations in the 20th Century

edited by Gao Dai

translated by Xiang Xinni and Jiang Ping

CANUT INTERNATIONAL PUBLISHERS

Istanbul - Berlin - London - Santiago

The publication is authorized by Jiangxi People's Publishing House Limited Liability Company, China.

The publication is funded by "B&R Book Program".

The History of the Colonial Expansion and North-South Relations in the 20th Century

Edited by Gao Dai

Translated by Xiang Xinni, Jiang Ping

Original Title: 战殖民擴張與南北關係 / ISBN: 978-7-210-04741-4

Copyright © Jiangxi People's Publishing House, October, 2011.

Canut International Publishers

Canut Intl. Turkey, Teraziler Cad. No.29. Sancaktepe, Istanbul, Turkey

Canut Intl. Germany, Heerstr. 266, D-47053, Duisburg, Germany

Canut Intl. United Kingdom, 12a Guernsay Road, London E11 4BJ, UK

Copyright © Canut International Publishers, 2018

ISBN: 978-605-9914-70-3

Printed in UK

Lightning Source Ltd. UK

Chapterhouse, Pitfield Kiln Farm

MK11 3LW

United Kingdom

www.canutbooks.com

Scholars home and abroad, however, differ in their view on the formation and development of the North-South relationship within this system. Researchers in Europe and the U.S., from the classical economists in the 19th century to contemporary scholars, believe there exists a mutually beneficial relationship, especially in the economic field, between countries and regions of "the North" which are in the core and their counterparts of "the South" in the periphery within the world system because an open world market benefits both parties. In order to fully discuss and elaborate on colonial expansion and the course of the North-South relationship, we have made new explorations into the style and structure of the whole book. The whole book is divided into two parts. The first part covers chapter I to chapter IV and the second part from chapter V to chapter IX.

Part I of the book mainly includes an overall and theoretical description of the process of colonial expansion before the WWII and the development of the North-South relationship. It points out that since the 15th and 16th century with the development of capitalism in Western Europe and the great geographical discovery, colonial expansion has become an important instrument of primitive accumulation of capital by numerous colonial countries of the North, while coercing these countries and regions into an asymmetrical world political and economic system.

Since the 18th and 19th century, with the further development of capitalism in the countries and regions of the North, they have further destroyed the social and economic structure of their counterparts of the South, making use of their economic advantages and cheap products as an important economic instrument in the process of their overseas expansion, which caused the natural economy of traditional agricultural civilizations and handicrafts to disintegrate. Under the direct control of colonial powers, many big dynasties of the latter, China, Ottomans, Persian and many others with long historical and cultural traditions were partially or totally paralyzed.

Countries and regions of the South suffered in various degrees from colonial expansion and made strong reactions accordingly. At the early stage, they usually took direct military actions against the colonial expansion of countries of the North or rose in revolt against the colonial rule and its local rulers. By the mid-19th century, after the successive independence of many Latin American colonies, countries and regions of the South began to assimilate some positive political and economic elements of metropolitan states and modernize some economic sectors. As a result, many modern economic sectors of these countries and regions have developed greatly, especially between the two world wars. The emergent progressive forces took national independence as their main task and gained increasing political influence, which had laid a solid foundation for the independence of their national politics and economy but also created favorable conditions to gain a proactive position and state in the developing process of the North-South relationship after the WW II.

Acknowledgments

The History of the Colonial Expansion and the North-South Relations in the 20th Century is one component part of the "International Relations Volumes" published by Jiangxi Publishing House under the title of Comprehensive World History which includes 39 volumes. The book in your hands, the fourth part of the "International Relations Volumes" series probes into the analysis of the relations between North and South since the formation of this division. The North-South relationship as one product of North-South division is not only the product of contemporary world society, but also a product of relatively gradual historical course closely related with European colonial expansion.

The book categorizes European metropolitan states, including the US and Japan, into the scope of the North, while refer to those Asian, African and Latin American colonies and semi-colonies as the South, preferring the terminology and conception of Humanities instead of Economics.

Scholars home and abroad understand colonial expansion and the formation and development of the North-South relationship basically in the same way. That is, the world was composed of regions far apart which tended to develop their economies independently till the 16th century. But it was since this period that Europeans cleared away territorial borders, broke through geographical barriers, and unite Asia, Africa, Latin America, some of the Pacific islands, and European countries into a whole by means of their advanced navigation technology, ever-increasing military power, economic power which took shape in this period, and colonial expansion throughout the world. As a result, the former mutually divided world was transformed into a world system dominated by Europe (including the U.S. after the WW II).

Part II of the book discusses systematically the development of the North-South relationship after the WW II by tracing the postwar development of international relations. After a relatively clear exposition on some major events and key points in the development process of the North-South relationship, it points out the postwar North-South relationship has undergone a process of dialogue, confrontation, and co-operation and the South-South co-operation after the war plays an increasingly important role in contemporary international relations.

With the disintegration of the colonial system and the rapid development of national independence movements after the WW II, many countries and regions of the South gained political independence and the obvious colonial rule exited the historical stage. But due to the rivalry between the U.S. and the former Soviet Union after the WW II, the development of the North-South relationship was greatly influenced by the Cold War, and therefore a tortuous course has occurred. However, currently we observe 3 aspects in the relationship, North-South confrontation, North-South dialogue, and North-South co-operation. Although there are problems and difficulties in the co-operation, it suffices to show countries and regions of the South are confident and determined to co-operate and forge ahead in unity to sublate the unequal world system.

With the end of the Cold War by the 1980s, the North-South relationship has undergone great changes mainly in two aspects: one is that the North-South relationship has been given greater prominence in international relations; the other is that the two parties are increasingly interdependent. The trend of the increasing regional co-operation between the South and the North has been a feature of the North-South relationship after the Cold War. We have reason to believe this paradigm of co-operation will exert important influence on the future development of world politics and economy.

Creation of this volume has been a cooperative work: The first, third, and fifth chapters of the book was written by Prof. Dr. Jin Hai and Prof. Dr. Jiang Nan respectively, and Prof. Dr. Zhou Rongyao has written the second, the fourth and the sixth chapters and provided conceptual design of the whole book and compiled the drafts written by the other colleagues and first draft of the complete book. We would like to extent our sincere gratitude to Prof. Dr. Gu Junli who reviewed and made valuable suggestions for the final draft and leaders of Jiangxi Publishing House who have enabled the realization of the book.

Zhou Rongyao,
Deputy Director-General,
Institute of World History, Chinese Academy of Social Sciences

Publisher's Note

This book is Volume 25 the of Comprehensive World History Series book project by the World History Institute of CASS, which was started in 2000s, which comprises 39 volumes, and 1.4 million Chinese characters altogether. China's most prominent 130 history scholars have contributed to this Project. The book is authored by Gao Dai, the renowned scholar in the Institute of World History attached to Chinese Academy of Social Sciences. Comprehensive World History Series is a pioneering project, which demonstrates the theoretical achievements of China's world history studies, and will certainly contribute to the international history academy.

The book series is published by Jiangxi Publishing House, in Nanchang. This is the 2nd book we have translated to English after the publishing of the Volume 27, "The History of Western Alliance After the World War II-1945-2005". The "International Relations Volumes" altogether include 8 volumes.

The North-South relations which include multiple aspects have become one major factor of the international relations after the World War II, alongside with the disintegration of the old colonial system and vigorous development of national independence movements. Numerous countries of the South have gained their political independence. But due to the intense rivalry between the US and the former Soviet Union after the WW II, the development of the North-South relationship was greatly affected by the Cold War, and therefore a tortuous course has occurred. However, currently we observe 3 aspects in the relationship, North-South confrontation, North-South dialogue, and North-South cooperation. The book with high academic value, offers a comprehensive historical review of the North-South relations, and abundant historical material.

Lastly, we present our cordial thanks to the editors of Jiangxi Publishing House and to translators Xiang Xinni and Jiang Ping, who have greatly contributed to the realization of the English version of the book.

Dennis Simon,
December 2017, Berlin

Contents

CHAPTER V

THE THIRD WORLD EMBRACING POLITICAL INDEPENDENCE

CHAPTER VI

THE MAKING OF THE NORTH-SOUTH POLITICAL STRUCTURE

CHAPTER IX

THE NORTH-SOUTH RELATIONS AFTER THE COLD WAR 319

Introduction

The North-South relationship is an important research area, which has gradually attracted great concern of researchers. However, the formation and development of the North-South relationship is not only the product of contemporary world society but also a relatively gradual historical course closely related with European colonial expansion. In order to clarify this course, we will categorize European metropolitan states, including the US and Japan, into the scope of the North, while refer to Asian, African and Latin American colonies and semi-colonies as the South. Although this classification is not precise enough, we will define the two words and use them as terms of Humanities instead of concepts of Economics, which is feasible academically.

Scholars home and abroad understand colonial expansion and the formation and development of the North-South relationship basically in the same way. That is, the world was composed of regions far apart which tended to develop their economies independently till the 16th century. But it was since this period that Europeans cleared away territorial hindrance, broke through geographical barriers, and unite Asia, Africa, Latin America, some of the Pacific islands, and European countries into a whole by means of their advanced navigation technology, ever-increasing military power, economic power taking shape in this period, and colonial expansion throughout the world. As a result, the former mutually divided world has been transformed into a world system dominated by Europe (including the U.S. after the WW II).

Scholars home and abroad, however, differ in their view on the formation and development of the North-South relationship within this system. Researchers in Europe and the U.S., from the classical economists in the 19th century to contemporary scholars, believe there exists a mutually beneficial relationship, especially in the economic field, between countries and regions of "the North" which are in the core and their counterparts of "the South" in the periphery within the world system because an open world market benefits both parties.

Not a few scholars at home and in Latin America, however, claim that the world political and economic system, dominated by countries of the North, is imposed on the nations of Asia, Africa, Latin America and the Pacific region, which is necessarily detrimental to the future development of these "peripheral" countries. Although at a certain historical phase, this system contributed to the economic growth of these countries and regions but they had to pay too high a price for such a growth. If countries and regions of the South could have developed naturally under their previous economic conditions, they would have reached a satisfying stage without being precipitated into such a frustrating political and economic plight after breaking away from colonial rule and having opportunities to develop independently.

In order to fully discuss and elaborate on colonial expansion and the course of the North-South relationship, we have made new explorations into the style and structure of the whole book. The whole book is divided into two parts. The first part is from chapter one to chapter four and the second is from chapter five to chapter nine.

Part one is mainly an overall and theoretical description of the process of colonial expansion before the WW II and the development of the North-South relationship. It points out that since the 15th and 16th century with the development of capitalism in Western Europe and the great geographical discovery, colonial expansion has become an important instrument of primitive accumulation of capital by many colonial countries of the North. The early colonial countries, like Portugal, Spain, the Holland, England and France, established successively their colonies and colonial settlements in some American, African, and Asian countries and regions, grabbing huge economic interests while coercing these countries and regions into an asymmetrical world political and economic system.

Since the 18th and 19th century, with the further development of capitalism in the countries and regions of the North, they have further destroyed the social and economic structure of their counterparts of the South, making use of their economic advantages and cheap products as an important economic instrument in the process of their overseas expansion, which caused the natural economy of traditional agricultural civilizations and handicrafts to disintegrate. Under the direct control of colonial powers, many great countries with long historical and cultural traditions were partially or totally paralyzed.

Countries and regions of the South suffered in various degrees from colonial expansion and made strong reactions accordingly. At the early stage, they usually took direct military actions against the colonial expansion of countries of the North or rose in revolt against the colonial rule and its local rulers. By the mid-19th century, after the successive independence of many Latin American colonies, countries and regions of the South began to assimilate some positive political and economic elements of metropolitan states and modernize some economic sectors. As a result, many modern economic sectors of these countries and regions have developed greatly, especially between the two world wars. The emergent progressive forces took national independence as their main task and gained increasing political influence, which had laid a solid foundation for the independence of their national politics and economy but also created favorable conditions to gain a proactive position and state in the developing process of the North-South relationship after the WW II.

Part two discusses systematically the development of the North-South relationship after the WW II by tracing the postwar development of international relations. After a relatively clear exposition on some major events and key points in the development process of the North-South relationship, it points out the postwar North-South relationship has undergone a process of dialogue, confrontation, and co-operation and the South-South co-operation after the war has been playing a more and more important role in contemporary international relations.

With the disintegration of the colonial system and the rapid development of national independence movements after the WW II, many countries and regions of the South gained political independence and the visible colonial rule exited the historical stage. But due to the rivalry between the U.S. and the former Soviet Union after the WW II, the development of the North-South relationship was greatly influenced by the Cold War, and therefore a tortuous and fluctuating course occurred in the postwar North-South relationship. However, generally speaking, North-South confrontation, North-South dialogue, and North-South co-operation constituted the North-South relationship in this period. Meanwhile, the co-operation between the South and the North has not only been put on the agenda after the war but also entered a phase of substantial development since 1980s. Although there are problems and difficulties in the co-operation, it suffices to show countries and regions of the South are confident and determined to co-operate and forge ahead in unity in the unequal world system.

With the end of the Cold War by the 1980s, the North-South relationship has undergone great changes mainly in two aspects: one is that the North-South relationship has been given greater prominence in international relations; the other is that the two parties are increasingly interdependent. The trend of the increasing regional co-operation between the South and the North has been a feature of the North-South relationship after the Cold War. We have reason to believe this paradigm of co-operation will exert important influence on the future development of world politics and economy.

Chapter I

On the North-South Economic Relationship

1.1. Concepts of South and North and the Relevant Debates

1.1.1. The Definition of the South and the North

Before the theoretical deliberation on the North-South relationship, it is necessary for us to have a rough understanding and definition of the concepts of the South and the North.

The concept of Northern countries, with its counterpart of Southern countries, is defined from their geographical locations. Developing countries are referred to as Southern countries because most of them are south of the equator. Northern countries normally refer to industrialized countries located at the north of the equator[1]. In view of Development Economics, despite their disparate population, size, natural resources, history, culture and religion, the South composed mainly by developing countries share some common features in social economy, mainly in the following aspects: 1. low per capita income, huge gap between the rich and the poor, and low living standards; 2. low labor productivity, high unemployment, and ineffective use of labor force; 3. high

---

1 Yan, Xiaofei. *An Introduction to Development Economics*. Beijing: Economic Science Press, 2000: 2.

growth rate of population and great support burden; 4. binary or dual structure of the society, economy, and culture; 5. passive position in international economic relations. According to the classification of World Development Report issued by the World Bank in 1995, the Southern countries and regions, according to their geographical locations, can be roughly divided into the following categories: the first is the 39 countries in Sub-Sahara, the second is the 15 countries in East Asia and Pacific region, the third is the 7 countries in South Asia, the fourth is the 30 countries in Europe and Central Asia, the fifth is the 16 countries in the Middle East and North Africa, and the sixth is the 23 countries in the regions of Latin America and the Caribbean Sea[2]. According to the classification, the South is, in effect, an umbrella term for developing countries.

In our research into international relationship, the concepts of the South and the North are in fact not precisely defined just as those of the East and the West, "the core" and "the periphery", "developed" and "underdeveloped", "the first world", "the second world", and "the third world". In terms of the common concepts of the West and the East, although the West referred mainly to the Christian World distinct from Asian, African, and Latin American countries and regions since modern times, it has become another name for industrialized countries in the world with the rise of the U.S. and Japan in the 20th century. Meanwhile, although people are accustomed to considering the South as underdeveloped countries and regions and the North as developed industrialized countries, countries like Australia and New Zealand have moved into the ranks of developed countries despite their location in the southern hemisphere. Therefore, the South and the North are relative concepts. For the sake of discussion, we generally put European metropolitan states, the U.S., and Japan into the category of the North, while Asian, African, and Latin American colonies and semi-colonies into the South. Although this categorization is not precise enough, we will, after clarifying and defining them, use them as terms of Humanities instead of Economics, which is feasible in an academic sense.

According to the celebrated British historian D.K. Fieldhouse, the concept of the North was first "adopted by the Brandt Commission Report of 1980"[3]. As to when the term of the South was first employed, we need further research. Nevertheless, as early as the 19th century, high attention had been paid to the economic relationship between the metropolitan states and (semi)-colonies, i.e., the North-South economic relationship in our terminology, with focus on two questions: one is whether countries and regions of the South have benefited or suffered from the economic relationship that the South has forged with the North; the other is whether countries and regions of the South would have enjoyed better development, if they had kept a distance from countries and regions of the North and been alert to their interventions. On these two questions, divergent conclusions have been made and controversies are thereof inevitable.

---

2   Ibid.: 3-9.
3   Fieldhouse, D.K. *The West and the Third World: Trade, Colonialism, Dependence and Development*. Oxford: Wiley-Blackwell, 1999:1.

1.1.2. From Mutual Segregation to Union into a Whole

As to the formation and development of the North-South relationship, both classical economists and modern dependency theorists basically have similar understanding, i.e. the world was composed of regions far apart which developed their economies independently till the 16th century. But it is also in this period when Europeans broke through territorial barriers, cleared away geographical hindrance, and united Asia, Africa, Latin American, Pacific Islands, and European countries into a whole by means of their advanced navigation technology, ever-increasing military power, and economic power formed in this period so that the previously divided world was transformed into a wheel-like world system dominated by Europe. Within this system, Europe became the hub while other countries and regions the tire linked by the spokes and the hub. Consequently, they constituted the world system mapped out by Immanuel Wallerstein, which was composed of "the core" and "the periphery", and between them was the "semi-peripheral" area. Thereafter, with the rise of the U.S. and Japan, some changes occurred to the geographical connotations of "the core" with the U.S. became part of the hub[4].

1.1.3. How to Treat the North-South Relationship

Although it is agreed that the South and the North have been incorporated into a world system of capitalism after their mutual division, they dispute about the role of the historical course, mainly concerning whether the process is beneficial or detrimental to the economic development and social progress of countries and regions of the South, after they have broken away from their original economic patterns and became parts of the world system,.

7

For more than a hundred years, specialists and scholars of various historical periods have voiced their opinions, which, according to Fieldhouse, fall into two categories: the first can be designated as optimistic with classical economists, like Adam Smith and David Ricardo, as its representatives, who hold that the creation of a single world economic system has been beneficial to both the Northern countries at the core and the Southern countries and regions in the periphery, because an open international market is in the best benefits and interests for both parties; the second is pessimistic with dependency theorists as its representatives, who argue that any international politico-economic system dominated by the Northern countries and imposed upon countries in Asia, Africa, Latin America, and the Pacific region will necessarily tend to be detrimental to the future development of such so-called peripheral countries. Although it might promote the economic development of some countries and regions, they have to pay too high a price in a long term. If these Southern countries and regions could have develop naturally under their former economic patterns, they might have probably reached a satisfying state instead of

---

4   As to the elaborate analysis of "the wheel-like world system dominated by Europe", see Stavrianos, L. S. *Global Rift: The Third World Comes of Age*. New York: William Morrow & Co,1981. trans. Chi Yue, et al. Beijing: The Commercial Press, 1993: 5.

struggling in a frustrating situation worse than before[5], which we will discuss in details in the following chapters.

1.2. Classical Economists' View on the Influence of the World Market

1.2.1. Comparative Advantages Theory

Classical economists in the 19th century generally believe that both individuals and societies can obtain huge profits if they are free to produce and consume without artificial intervention. This, in turn, requires an open market for selling and buying, based on which is created a world system of production and exchange. Every component of this system can gain maximum economic interests out of it.

To reach this end, the early classical economists provide two closely related answers: specialization of function and comparative advantage. Both Adam Smith and J. S. Mill claim that an open market is the basis of increasing national wealth and specialization is the precondition of all economic progress. Adam Smith makes clear in An Inquiry into the Nature and Causes of the Wealth of Nations: "The greatest improvement in the productive powers of labour, and the greater part of the skill, dexterity, and judgment with which it is anywhere directed, or applied, seem to have been the effects of the division of labour"[6]. Taking the production of pins as an example, he further points out that the division of labor and specialized production based on capital accumulation and technological advance has greatly improved labor productivity of workers. When the similar division of labor is applied to a certain community or country, it will greatly improve their production capacity, which in turn will promote the development of business and the formation of markets. Therefore, all commerce, be it inland, regional, or international, is of a great significance. In terms of the world market, commercial activities facilitate associated countries and regions to develop their specialized production, improve trade, and enhance economic development by means of their own resources and advantages.

Every country, in this sense, should produce what it is in their greatest advantages, products of best qualities or most competitive commodities, while purchase all the other commodities from other countries and regions. In the words of Adam Smith: "It is the maxim of every prudent master of a family never to attempt to make at home what it will cost him more to make than to buy…. What is prudence in the conduct of every private family can scarce be folly in that of a great kingdom. If a foreign country can supply us with a commodity cheaper than we ourselves can make it, better buy it of them with some

5   Fieldhouse, D.K. *The West and the Third World: Trade, Colonialism, Dependence and Development*. Oxford: Wiley-Blackwell, 1999: 4-6.
6   Smith, Adam. *An Inquiry into the Nature and Causes of the Wealth of Nations*. vol. 1. New York: Modern Library, 1964: 4.

part of the produce of our own industry employed in a way in which we have some advantage."[7]

What commodity is, then, the product that a country has the greatest advantages or most worthwhile to produce in a specialized way? An answer was provided by David Ricardo in his concept of "comparative advantage". His classic example was the trade between Britain and Portugal. In 1703, Britain and Portugal signed a commercial treaty, which stipulates that wine produced by Portugal can be sold to Britain under a tariff one third lower than that of French wines. In return, British wools can be sold in Portugal free from duty. Ricardo suggested that Portugal needed to spend 80 hours on each unit of wine and 90 hours on each cloth, whereas Britain needed to devote 120 hours per unit of wine and 100 hours per unit of cloth. That might suggest that Portugal had an absolute advantage in both categories.

But Ricardo argued that, after comparison and analysis, it was clear hat since Portugal had an advantage of 80 to 120 against Britain on wine but only of 90 to 100 on cloth. Therefore, the Portuguese should concentrate on producing and exporting wine while Britain should specialize in making and selling cloth. In this way a Portuguese brewer could obtain 20 hours in his exchange of a unit of wine for a unit of British cloth, but could lose 10 hours if he exchanged his unit of wine with a unit of Portuguese cloth because it took the Portuguese 90 hours to produce a unit of cloth[8]. Generalizing from this model, Ricardo concluded that: "Under a system of perfectly free commerce, each country naturally devotes its capital and labour to such employments as are most beneficial to each.... It is this principle which determines that wine shall be made in France and Portugal, that corn shall be grown in America and Poland, and that hardware and other goods shall be manufactured in England."[9] According to Ricardo's theory of comparative advantage, a country which correctly judges its priorities and specialize in its production will occupy a vantage point in world trade.

A problem, however, lied in Ricardo's theory, i.e. it assumed that each country engaged in specialization of production following the principle of comparative advantage were supposed to employ fully its resources like land, labor, and capital to meet the demand of the market. It had, therefore, to make a choice how best to allocate these resources. But when Ricardo put forward his theory, few countries and regions were up to this standard whose resources were not already fully committed, labor forces unreasonably allocated, capital limited and improperly distributed.

---

7   Smith, Adam. *An Inquiry into the Nature and Causes of the Wealth of Nations*. vol. 1. New York: Modern Library, 1964: 401.
8   Fieldhouse, D.K. *The West and the Third World: Trade, Colonialism, Dependence and Development*. Oxford: Wiley-Blackwell, 1999: 11.
9   Ricardo, David. *Principles of Political Economy and Taxation*. 1817 ed. London: M. P. Fortarty, 1969: 81.

America and Poland at that time fell into this category while some industrial sectors in Britain and France were in a similar state. There is a considerable gap between countries and regions in the rest of the world and the demand. How, under this circumstance, these countries and regions as well as certain British industrial sectors entered the international market and became part of the world economic system? The answer provided by J. S. Mill was commonly known as the "vent-for-surplus" theory to supplement "comparative advantage" theory.

1.2.2. "Vent-for-Surplus" Theory

"Vent-for-surplus" theory assumes that some countries and regions, owing to their not fully committed resources, underdevelopment, and lack of overall coordination, produce more of certain types of goods, which are in their greatest advantages, than they can consume at home. As a result, the goods are overstocked and some of the positive economic elements are prevented (restricted) from full play. Under this condition, the best solution is to export the surplus domestic products to the international market to realize their value in the trade and exchange with other countries. As Smith wrote, "...the surplus must be sent abroad and exchanged for something for which there is a demand at home. Without such exportation a part of the productive labour of the country must cease....It is only by means of such exportation that this surplus can acquire a value sufficient to compensate the labour and expense of producing it"[10]. In addition, Smith further argued that, "Between whatever places foreign trade is carried on, they all of them derive two distinct benefits from it. It carries out that surplus part of the produce of their land and labour for which there is no demand among them, and brings back in return for it something else for which there is a demand. It gives a value to their superfluities, by exchanging them for something else, which may satisfy a part of their wants, and increase their enjoyments. By means of it the narrowness of the home market does not hinder the division of labour in any particular branch of art or manufacture from being carried to the highest perfection"[11].

Compared to "comparative advantage" theory, there lies a major problem in "vent-for-surplus" theory: trade among countries and regions means only to solve superfluities at home instead of relocation of resources, which will in the long run block the economic progress of these areas.

Whatever its theoretical defects as an economics, it seems to fit the conditions of many of the extra-European countries and regions. From the sixteenth century onward, with the great geographical discoveries and the union of the world, many countries and regions in Asia, Africa, Latin America, and the Pacific region have been drawn into the international economic system. Among these countries and regions, many were colonies occupied by European settlers, which had ample land, pleasant weather and rich resources, like North

---

10   Smith, Adam. *An Inquiry into the Nature and Causes of the Wealth of Nations*. vol. 1. New York: Modern Library, 1964: 333.
11   Ibid.: 392.

America, Australia, and New Zealand. It was, therefore, natural for the settlers to produce a "surplus" of agricultural products at a price which, even given the costs of sea transport, could not be matched in Europe. Thus, they were enabled to buy the necessary manufactured products by selling the surplus products without consuming huge economic resources. In this case, there were no real opportunities for the Extra-European colonies to relocate factors of production for more economic benefits. They were only two ways out of this plight: "either one exploited the land for exports, or one lived a very primitive Robinson Crusoe existence."[12]

1.2.3. "Complementarity" Theory

Based on "vent-for-surplus" theory, E.G. Wakefield, the prestigious British scholar on colonial studies, proposed a theory of "complementarity" in A View of the Art of Colonization (1849), claimed that colonies were naturally exporting communities since they had a large produce for exportation. Not only had they a large produce for exportation, but that produce was peculiarly suited for exchange with old countries. In consequence of the cheapness of land in colonies, the great majority of the people were owners or occupiers of land, which determined that they could employ the abundant land resources to produce food, and the raw materials of manufacture needed by old countries. On the other hand, old countries manufactured goods that the colonies needed but could not produce. The old country and the colony, therefore, were, naturally, each other's best customers. They were complementary in terms of economy[13].

11

This condition of complementarity fit not only early Spanish Latin America, 19th century Australia, New Zealand, and Canada but also Africa, Southeast Asia, and other regions in the world basically. They were directly influenced by European colonial expansion in the latter half of the 19th century. "As to many regions in Africa, although their native markets and regional trade were relatively prosperous, the inner markets are too limited to enhance productivity and promote the exportation of large items of commodity. The formation and development of overseas market contributes to the production of traditional agricultural produces like palm oil and peanuts as well as newly developed products like coco, rubber, and coffee, boosting the use and development of land and labour forces. (This situation also exists in Southeast Asia). Generally speaking, this kind of use and development which does not need drastic reform in the way of production and investment in new equipment is therefore cheap in cost and obvious in economic benefits. As to some countries and regions, they will pay a certain price if they no longer grow any foods and have to rely on the exportation of one or two crash crops to import foods"[14].

---

12   Fieldhouse, D.K. *The West and the Third World: Trade, Colonialism, Dependence and Development*. Oxford: Wiley-Blackwell, 1999: 12.
13   Wakefield, E. G. *A View of the Art of Colonization*. Oxford: Claredon Press, 1914: 83.
14   Ibid.: 14.

Thus it can be seen the classical economists believe that the development of international trade, the emergence of the world market, and the gradual formation of global economic system have a positive economic significance to all the members within the system. According to Mill in Principles of Political Economy, the positive economic significance lies chiefly in the following aspects: First, production specialized and meeting the market needs contributes to the improvement and advancement in, if not the fundamental transformation of, production skills; Second, the introduction of foreign goods will stimulate the needs of the local people and boost labour productivity; Third, new trends of thought will be propagated in the world in the process of commercialization; Fourth, the development of business and trade will result in the import of foreign capital even in regions like West Africa, which will accelerate the process of capital accumulation in these regions and countries. In particular, foreign capital invested in mining, manufacture, and railway accelerates capital accumulation.

In short, classical economists share the belief that the promotion of world trade under the guidance of "comparative advantage" theory and "complementarity" theory and in the way of specialized production and "the vent for surplus" will not only increase the national wealth of European metropolitan states but also give non-European countries and regions within the global economic system economic benefits, which have positive effects in uplifting the economic power and social welfare level in these countries and regions.

1.3. The Value and Influence of Laissez-faire

For the further development and improvement of the world market, whose formation has such positive influence on both sides of trade, classical economists stress the point that only if we insist on laissez-faire, decrease or exclude artificial intervention, and open bilateral markets can we promote mutual benefits. It seems to classical economists, like Adam Smith, David Ricardo, that any economic entity can gain more economic benefits under the guidance of specialized production, "comparative advantage" theory, and "vent of surplus" theory by means of direct participation in economic activities instead of exclusive commercial monopoly or other opportunistic intrigues.

The stress of classical economists on laissez-faire was closely related to the trade situation of European countries in the early 19th century, when trade between European metropolitan states and their colonies was restricted by all sorts of protective measures like tariffs and regulations, which caused serious influence on economic interests on both sides. Many European metropolitan states, including Britain, intended to dominate colonial markets, monopolize the colonies' exported goods, and act as the only transporter of sea trade between metropolitan states and colonies so as to gain maximum interests out of it.

Adam Smith made clear his firm objection to the system of monopoly in world trade, which he argued was totally detrimental to both sides of trade. "In order, however, to obtain this relative advantage in the colony trade, in order to execute the invidious and malignant project of excluding as much as possible other nations from any share in it, England, there are very probable reasons for believing, has not only sacrificed a part of the absolute advantage which she, as well as every other nation, might have derived from that trade, but has subjected herself both to an absolute and to a relative disadvantage in almost every other branch of trade"[15]. Only the implementation of laissez-faire can improve the world market and the development of bilateral economies. "The effect of the colony trade in its natural and free state is to open a great, though distant, market for such parts of the produce of British industry as may exceed the demand of the markets nearer home, of those of Europe, and of the countries which lie round the Mediterranean Sea. In its natural and free state, the colony trade, without drawing from those markets any part of the produce which had ever been sent to them, encourages Great Britain to increase the surplus continually by continually presenting new equivalents to be exchanged for it. In its natural and free state, the colony trade tends to increase the quantity of productive labour in Great Britain, but without altering in any respect the direction of that which had been employed there before. In the natural and free state of the colony trade, the competition of all other nations would hinder the rate of profit from rising above the common level either in the new market or in the new employment. The new market, without drawing anything from the old one, would create, if one may say so, a new produce for its own supply; and that new produce would constitute a new capital for carrying on the new employment, which in the same manner would draw nothing from the old one."[16] Therefore, Smith pointed out clearly that the monopoly practiced by metropolitan states impeded greatly global business trade and any artificial intervention into world market would necessarily influence the speed of economic development in the bilateral or multilateral trade parties.

13

Adam Smith's statement has been challenged since its publication. Scholars who do not believe in the implementation of laissez-faire as the sole condition for the operation of world economic system claim that once the markets in both metropolitan states and colonies are opened without reservation, some new industrial branches will be threatened and the interests of advantageous industries will be decreased greatly with the flowing of large quantities of cheap goods into their markets. Therefore, they consider it necessary to practice some form of protection and even monopoly to protect and promote the economic development of both metropolitan states and colonies. Hereto, Mill proposed infant industry of these countries as a solution to this problem and took it as an exception from the general principle of laissez-faire.

---

15 Luo, Rongqu, ed. *Selected Readings of Colonial Theories*. Beijing: Peking University, 1995: 28.
16 Ibid.: 33.

Mill argues that: "The only case in which, on mere principles of political economy, protecting duties can be defensible, is when they are imposed temporarily (especially in a young and rising nation) in hopes of naturalizing a foreign industry, in itself perfectly suitable to the circumstances of the country... But it cannot be expected that individuals should, at their own risk, or rather to their certain loss, introduce a new manufacture, and bear the burthen of carrying it on until the producers have been educated up to the level of those with whom the processes are traditional. A protecting duty, continued for a reasonable time, might sometimes be the least inconvenient mode in which the nation can tax itself for the support of such an experiment. But it is essential that the protection should be confined to cases in which there is good ground of assurance that the industry which it fosters will after a time be able to dispense with it; nor should the domestic producers ever be allowed to expect that it will be continued to them beyond the time necessary for a fair trial of what they are capable of accomplishing"[17].

James Mill's view on the necessity to protect infant industries is supported by not a few scholars and became gradually the theoretical basis of modern protectionism, especially in non-European colonies. Even if in Europe, as what a high-rank British colonial officer pointed out: "France, and possibly Germany and the United States in the future might become possible examples, which successfully protect their infant industries."[18]

14   In the discussion, whether laissez-faire contributes to bilateral or multilateral developments, the British Empire is argued as the perfect example to illustrate that this strategy promoted the economic development of non-European countries and regions. Indeed, as a superpower in the 19th century, free trade had been imposed on the whole empire, culminating in the abolition of preferences between 1846 and 1853. In the following decades, the empire began to practice "free-trading imperialism" in the world by means of its strong economic power, which stressed informal rule in addition to trade if appropriate and formal rule when necessary. The belief is that only by free trade can the economic levels of both metropolitan states and colonies and the global economic development in turn be enhanced.

New Zealand, for instance, submitted in 1876 a report to the Colonial Office via the Board of Trade to impose a temporary import duty on refined sugar imported from the UK in support of the manufacture of beet sugar. In view of infant industry proposed by scholars like Mill, this demand was reasonable. However, the reply from the Colonial Office is that "[if] an artificial stimulus is given to a particular industry in the hope of making it take root, the result is likely to be the loss of what is paid for the stimulus, the creation of a weak industry which will always need to be protected, and the diversion of industry and capital from enterprises which being more natural would be stronger and

17   Mill, J. S. *Principles of Political Economy*. London, 1898: 556.
18   Fieldhouse, D.K. *The West and the Third World: Trade, Colonialism, Dependence and Development*. Oxford: Wiley-Blackwell, 1999: 18.

more healthy. It may be doubted if there is any case on record of an industry having been successfully established by means of protective duties and then flourishing without the aid of such duties, and even if there had been such instances, there has been no attempt to prove that the communities affected are better off than they would be if they had left matters alone."[19]

Nevertheless, free trade policy of the UK was increasingly challenged in the late 19th century and the early 20th century. With the establishment of dominions in New Zealand, Canada, and Australia, the UK could not prevent them from protecting infant industries. Thus, New Zealand, Canada, and Australia took preferential measures to develop infant industries and imposed protectionist duties, which influenced greatly the UK and its colonies since these dominions played important economic roles within the British Empire. In fact, British itself began to slide away from free trade after 1914 and adopted fully-fledged protection for itself in 1932, implementing a very complicated system of imperial preference in its dominions and colonies. Britain provided either free or preferential entry for empire products and received the same for its exports to the empire. "It did so largely in response to the dramatic increase in protectionism in other countries, sparked off by the very high tariffs of 1922 and 1931 in the United States and intense protectionism throughout Europe. It seemed as if free-trade theory and practice had been destroyed by the economic crises of the post-war world"[20].

Free-trade, however, was revitalized in the 1930s. But it was the United States rising between the two world wars instead of the British Empire that played the leading role in practicing free trade. In the early 1930s as the recession of 1929 eased, the United States began to look for a general reduction of tariffs internationally to revitalize world economy: Congress passed a Reciprocal Trade Agreements Act which enabled the President to reduce tariffs by up to 50% on a reciprocal basis. After that, as the most powerful country in the world, the United States had been striving for the reduction of tariffs to clear barriers which blocked free trade. The major achievement was the General Agreement of 1947, which committed the signatory countries gradually to reduce tariffs for the promotion of multilateral economic development.

The United States set up in July 1944 International Monetary Fund (IMF) and Bank for Reconstruction and Development (The World Bank) on the recommendation of the Bretton Woods conference of 1944, which were committed to the objectives of reducing tariffs, clearing away clear barriers which blocked free trade, and removing protective measures and regulations among countries and regions by providing loans and investment into less-developed countries and regions.

15

---

19   Ibid.: 18.
20   Ibid.: 19.

In the later twentieth century, IMF and The World Bank became increasingly influential and were the main proponents of free-trade and other related policies especially in the less-developed countries and regions of the South. These two financial institutions both believed that one of the best ways to boost economic development for the less-developed world was to concentrate on production and export of those things in which they had a comparative cost advantage and not attempt to make things to which they were unsuited behind protective tariff and regulatory barriers. As what Fieldhouse points out, "the steps practiced by IMF and The World Bank on Third World countries almost precisely embody the principle of Adam Smith, David Ricardo and other classical economists. After two centuries the wheel had turned full circle."[21]

The revival and recognition of free trade and other related theories of specialization, comparative advantage, and complementarity made many postwar economists and politicians think highly of 19th-century classical economists' theories of world market and mutual influence. As to the less-developed countries and regions in the South, the best way to promote their economic development was to develop export trade and strengthen economic power under the guidance of theories of specialized production and comparative advantage. It was by means of international trade that the former colonies and semi-colonies gained at least the following real benefits:

First, international trade stimulated local producers who, under market pressure from international trade, improved production technology and acquired information to develop new products so as to increase the competitiveness of their products in the international market. Second, the introduction of foreign capital enhanced the development of export trade, which provided necessary credit for local producers and traders and helped them to accumulate capital in free trade. Third, international trade resulted in the establishment of better-developed monetary systems, financial and business institutions, ports, and inland transportation network which laid a solid foundation for further economic development. Moreover, international trade brought about the prosperity of home market because all kinds of cheap goods from home and abroad not only stimulated the demand of consumers but also promoted production as an important means to satisfy that demand.

Indeed, in the 19th and 20th centuries, countries and regions like Australia, New Zealand, Canada, and the Four Asian Tigers in the later 20th century advanced their economic development, accumulated substantial material wealth, and laid a solid foundation for their economic development by means of free trade under the guidance of classical economists' theories. However, we should also be clearly aware of that although there are successful cases of promoting one's own economical development under the guidance of classical economists' theories, it does not mean that these cases have a universal meaning. Other realities tell us that classical economists' theories based on free

21   Ibid.: 20.

trade have not achieved any positive effects in Sub-Sahara Africa, the South Asia Sub-Continent, and the Southeast Asia, which were colonies of the UK, Belgium, and Holland in the 19th century with exceptions of individual countries. Under colonial rule, they followed basically classical economists' theories, like principles of free trade and comparative advantage, to develop their economy by means of specialized production, set up market-oriented economic mechanism, and become indispensable components of world economic system. However, economy in these countries and regions had not been developed well until the mid-20th century. Apart from India, economically influential enterprises had not been set up in some countries and regions. Meanwhile, reliance on foreign capital, products, and international means of transportation reduced these countries and regions to an obviously inferior position in world economic system. Domestic economic developed stood still and international political status remained the same, which made clear that "the classical model had not worked, or had worked only up to a certain point."[22]

The reasons why these countries and regions practicing free trade had not achieved expected economic growth, according to some western scholars, are as follows:

First, in terms of business in these countries and regions, the trading system was largely controlled by expatriates, from the roots of commodity production to the ultimate overseas markets. In South Asia this was commonly through the managing agencies at the ports, leaving the inland operations in the hands of indigenous middlemen. In Black Africa, foreign-funded enterprises were deep-rooted and almost controlled the import-export trade in this region by such business institutions as United African Company. These trade companies were run solely by foreign-funded enterprises, where a few local people could be promoted into its top structure, let alone acquire management experience. In addition, their profits were largely exported and they seldom made reinvestment, which therefore made little or no contribution to the development of the host country. Even if these foreign-funded enterprises made reinvestment in the host country, their abundant capital left local businessmen incompetent to compete with them.

Second, in terms of production and marketing in these countries and regions, because the export production sector was highly specialized, it might constitute a partly insulated "enclave", particularly when in plantation or mines, detached from the rest of the local economy. Since the goods produced by the export production sector were almost exported to foreign countries, their technology had no direction connection with the local condition, which made it difficult to transfer technology or to gain necessary capital from the "enclave" to promote local economic growth. In the respect of selling, the dominance of foreign-funded enterprises enabled them to control and manipulate the production and price of commodities. In certain parts of Black Africa this might seriously affect

22   Ibid.: 22.

the benefits the indigenous people got from specialization in export production of primary commodities. Moreover, because ultimate selling prices were, and are, set by international market forces, which were subject to price fluctuations detrimental to primary export commodities, the producers following comparative advantage theory would be weak in gaining interests.

Third, in the respect of market, because under free trade the local market of these countries and regions was wide open to imported manufactures, some foreign manufacturers were able to defeat local competitors by selling cheap commodities. Meanwhile, because these countries and regions needed high technology which were too expensive, not only the local people but also the expatriates failed to set up enterprises to produce high-tech items so that they had to rely on the exportation of specialized primary commodities in exchange of the needed high-tech products, which rendered their own economy into a state of deindustrialization. In particular, when some countries and regions had to rely on the exportation of one or two products needed by the international market to import foods, their economic growth would be greatly influenced.

To sum up, classical economists claimed that under free trade the formation of an international market and world economic system would indeed accelerate the economic growth in the former colonies and semi-colonies and benefit both the South and the North by means of market economy. However, we should be aware that from the perspective of global economic growth and the economic prospect of both the South and the North, "even if the principles were and are sound, contingent factors which Smith, Ricardo, Mill and others did not foresee or take into account may have neutralized the benefits they predicted."[23]

1.4. Analysis on the Concept of Imperialism

After 1870, as the free trade theory was greatly challenged, western capitalist powers in Western Europe have increasingly began to attempt national interventions, tariff protection wars and imperial expansion policies. Therefore, it is significant in practice and theory to know and probe into the concept of "imperialism", which enables us to gain deep insight into the nature of the North-South relationship.

Like the French word colonialisme, imperialism was originally from French. Since the 1830s, imperialism and imperialist appeared frequently in French, which mainly referred to French Empire established by Napoleon I and the empire by Napoleon III. But it was the British who imbued the term with the connotation of colonial expansion since the 19th century when it referred mainly to the British Empire with its overseas colonies instead of French Empire on the European Continent.

23   Ibid.: 22-23.

Although since the 1860s the term imperialism has been constantly used by the British, it as a socio-historical concept which drew people's intense attention with the publication of J. A. Hobson's work *Imperialism: A Study* (1902).

1.4.1. Hobson on Imperialism

Hobson was a radical, not a socialist. As a correspondent, he experienced and was deeply impressed by the Anglo-Boer War at the end of the 19th century. In 1900 he published a book on this subject, The War in South Africa: Its Causes and Effects, in which he argued that rule of South Africa had fallen into the hands of a small group of financiers, "chiefly German in origin and Jewish in race"[24]. In his famous Imperialism: A Study, he elaborated this vision into a general theory of imperialism, and used the term imperialism to indicate the "expansion of Great Britain and of the major continental Powers"[25]. The word expansion referred to the fact that over the previous thirty years a number of European nations, Great Britain first and foremost, had "annexed or otherwise asserted political sway over vast portions of Africa and Asia, and over numerous islands in the Pacific and elsewhere"[26].

For Hobson the meaning of the word imperialism was very clear: it was the establishment of political control. He also deeply explored the forces behind it. Various people such as an "ambitious statesman, a frontier soldier and an overzealous missionary" might play some role in it, "but its final determination rests with the financial power"[27]. Thus Hobson offered us a definition from three aspects: imperialism is the expansion of political power of European countries over the non-European world; as a periodization, imperialism took place during the thirty years between 1870 and 1900; and an explanation: it was the result of the operations by financial powers[28].

In order to make a further analysis on imperialism, Hobson argued that, as a consequence of the capitalist system, the British economy suffered from underconsumption. As a result of this, surplus capital could no longer be invested profitably in England itself. Therefore, the capitalists were "seeking foreign markets and foreign investments to take off the goods and capital they cannot sell or use at home"[29].

As Hobson's theory implied a criticism of capitalism, it had a certain attraction for Marxist thinkers. As a result of this, a new Marxist theory of imperialism was born.

---

24 Hobson, J. A. *Imperialism: A Study*. London: Unwin Hyman, 1938: 189.
25 Ibid., 1938: 27.
26 Ibid., 1938: 15.
27 Ibid., 1938: 29.
28 Smelser, Neil J., and Paul B. Baltes. *International Encyclopedia of the Social & Behavioral Sciences*. Oxford: Elsevier, 2001: 7227.
29 Hobson, J. A. *Imperialism: A Study*. London: Unwin Hyman, 1938: 85.

1.4.2. Hilferding and Luxemburg on Imperialism

While originally Marx and Engels had considered capitalist expansion as an "objective" progressive force, some Marxist thinkers changed their opinion on capitalist expansion with the changes in its means and modes. Marxist theorists such as Karl Hilferding and Rosa Luxemburg scorned late nineteenth century imperialism as a form of exploitation and suppression. It is significant that for Luxemburg "it is the need to export goods and import raw materials, rather than the need to export capital, that is real stimulus behind capitalism. Briefly, because access to the markets and raw materials of the Third World was so crucial to the West, and because there was a finite supply of these assets, competition between the capitalist societies had evolved into imperialism"[30]. Therefore, Luxemburg points out that "it is precisely the unearned elements of income which tend towards an automatic process of accumulation, and which, by swelling the stream of surplus capital seeking markets of investment or markets for the surplus goods it helps to make, direct political forces into Imperialism"[31].

To Hilferding, since the middle of the 19th century the process of concentration of capitals had progressed very rapidly, industrial enterprises had coagulated to secure monopoly prices by eliminating competition. To finance their expansion, they had become close allies of the banks which resulted in the concentration of enterprises and capital into the hands of a few people so as to form "finance capital" and "monopoly capitalism". However, due to the finite domestic consumption, these monopolies enterprises had, therefore, to find overseas markets. In the first instance they cut prices to penetrate into the foreign markets. Second, these monopolies invested to set up overseas factories and manufactured inside tariff walls so that they could obtain a higher rate of profit. Therefore, each great capitalist state was determined to create its "national economic territory". "This was a primary explanation of the imperialism of the period."[32]

1.4.3. Lenin on Monopoly Capitalism and Imperialism

As a Marxist theorist and practitioner, Lenin made great efforts to elucidate monopoly capitalism and imperialism and studied other theories on imperialism in his master work *Imperialism: "The Highest Stage of Capitalism"* (1916), which is of great historical significance and established new paradigms in Marxist analysis of imperialism. Lenin stated that imperialism is a new and higher stage in the development of capitalism. When monopolies and finance capital established their dominant position, export of capital became increasingly important, international monopolies divided the world market, and Western capitalist states divided the world among themselves.

---

30   Fieldhouse, D.K. *The West and the Third World: Trade, Colonialism, Dependence and Development*. Oxford: Wiley-Blackwell, 1999: 48.
31   Luxemburg, R. *The Accumulation of Capital*. London: Routledge, 1951: 446.
32   Fieldhouse, D.K. *The West and the Third World: Trade, Colonialism, Dependence and Development*. Oxford: Wiley-Blackwell, 1999: 52.

Lenin's ideas of imperialism were mainly based on the works of Hilferding and Luxemburg, who in turn had been inspired by Hobson's theory. It was therefore understandable that there is a direct link between Hobson's and Lenin's theories, so much so that it became fashionable to speak of the "Hobson–Lenin thesis."

There are, however, essential differences between Hobson and Lenin. First, for Hobson the export of capital from the metropole to the overseas world was a consequence of the development of capitalism, but not a necessary consequence. That is to say, the development of capitalism would not necessarily lead to capital export. The origin of the problem, for Hobson, was under consumption. Briefly, the excess of production over consumption led to the overstocking of commodities and capital. Therefore, theoretically, if the problem of under consumption was solved, so would the problems of capital output and in turn imperialist expansion.

Hobson also believed that the way to solve the problem of imperialism in England was to implement some social improvement measures like increasing the purchasing power of the working class. He wrote in his Imperialism: A Study: that "if the consuming public in Great Britain raised its standard of consumption to keep pace with every rise of productive powers, there could be no excess of goods or capital clamorous to be used in imperialist expansion in order to find markets."

Second, Hobson and Lenin tried to explain two different things. Hobson, who wrote Imperialism: A Study during the South African War, wanted to explain the partition of the world, and more specifically of Africa, in the late nineteenth century. Lenin, who wrote *Imperialism: The Highest Stage of Capitalism* in 1916, tried to explain the repartition of the world of which the World War I was the most spectacular outcome. The word Africa hardly appears at all in Lenin's masterpiece.

Third, the period Lenin referred to was also different from the one dealt with by Hobson, whose focus was on the overseas expansion of European powers during 1870-1900 while Lenin mainly elaborated on their repartition of the world thereafter. For Lenin, imperialism was not the highest stage of colonialism but of capitalism.

On this subject, David Fieldhouse, a Cambridge professor and the most prominent expert on colonial studies, stated that Hobson differed from Lenin mainly in their ideas on the nature of domestic pressure under which imperial states underwent overseas expansion. "Hobson explained it in principles of underconsumption while Lenin believed that capitalism as a social system had entered into its last stage...which would give birth to proletarian revolution and socialism and bring about the end of capitalism."[33] Fieldhouse wrote: "Hobson illustrated through his theory the necessity of domestic social reform which might be able to eliminate the damages caused by 'underconsumption' while Lenin defined imperialism as an inherent and unavoidable stage of

33   Luo, Rongqu, ed. *Selected Readings of Colonial Theories*. Beijing, Peking University Press, 1995:75.

capitalism."[34] However, Fieldhouse also remarked that "as a prophet Lenin was not as successful as Hobson because he failed to notice that democratic system reform could make structural adjustment of capitalist society which precluded the existence of both capitalism and revolution"[35].

Although the capitalist theory of imperialism was not generally accepted by Western scholars, it exerted great influence with the success of the October Revolution and the establishment of the former Soviet Union. Some form of economic interpretation on the origin and development of imperialism became the standard explanation during the 1920s and 1930s.

Imperialism was considered as having originated from economic problems in Europe that were characteristic of the late nineteenth century, in particular the need to guarantee the flow of raw materials to the industrialized countries, and the protection of overseas markets for the sale of their industrial products.

After the World War II under the influence of decolonization and the rise of the American empire, alternative interpretations on imperialism were launched by scholars, who ceased to explain imperialism solely from the perspective of economy.

1.4.4. The Imperialism of Free Trade

After World War II, the impact of the new world political situation on the theory of imperialism was shown in the article "The Imperialism of Free Trade" published in The Review on Economic Studies in 1953 by two Cambridge historians, Jack Gallagher and Ronald Robinson, who developed the concept of "informal empire".

As Jiang Mengyin, a Chinese expert on British history points out, the concept of "Informal Empire" was first proposed by C.R. Fay in *The Cambridge History of the British Empire* (1940) to distinguish it from such formal empires as the ancient Roman Empire, the medieval Empire of Charlemagne, and the colonial empires of sword and mercantilism[36]. Gallagher and Robinson argued the British established a huge informal empire around the mid-Victorian period by means of its strong economic power. Therefore, the zenith of the British Empire was not to be found in the late nineteenth century but rather in the 1850s and 1860s. For Britain, the entire nineteenth century was one of outward expansion. It was an imperial century. Britain's imperial expansion manifested itself in various forms: emigration, trade, overseas investments, the establishment of naval bases, etc. Although political means were as important as economic policies in the process of expansion, the extension of political authority over foreign people was only one form of imperialism, and not even the most important one[37].

---

34   Ibid.:75.
35   Ibid.:75.
36   Jiang, Mengyin. *Collected Essays of Jiang Mengyin*. Nanjing: Nanjing University Press, 1995: 7.
37   Louis, Roger. *Imperialism*. New York: New Viewpoints, 1976: 54-58.

Gallagher and Robinson also argued that the British Empire in the 19th century was comparable to the informal American empire that came into being after 1945. It worked with informal mechanisms since that was the best way of doing things under different historical conditions. In fact, the maxim of British policy makers in the 19th century was: informal empire if possible, formal only if necessary. Due to the increasingly severe challenges which faced the British free trade policy in the lathe 19th century, however, the late Victorians were forced to formalize their Empire. Therefore, the formalization was the outcome of objective circumstances instead of subjective wishes[38].

While Gallagher and Robinson discovered that imperialism existed before the formal British Empire established by the end of the 19th century, other scholars also discovered that imperialism would continue to exist after the disintegration of the formal empire. This resulted not so much from a reflection on the rise of the American empire and the formal Soviet Union after the WWII, but from a reassessment of post-war decolonization. While after the World War I with the defeat of Germany and the partition of the Ottoman Empire the European powers had expanded their colonial territories. However, the situation was very different after the WW II. In Asia, the process of decolonization started immediately after the war and was followed quickly later in Africa. Thus, in the 1960s, most of the former colonies had become independent politically.

But political independence did not automatically bring an end to the social problems and the economic dependency of the ex-colonies. Some of the new states became even more dependent on the Western-dominated world system than they had been before independence. It was clear for many observers that the end of empire did not simply mean the simultaneous perishment of imperialism.

1.5. Dependency Theory on the North-South Economic Relation

In order to expound on the objective circumstances theoretically, some scholars proposed the theory of dependency. According to the dependency theorists, imperialism manifested not only in political rule but also in economic control, i.e. the establishment of the dependency of less developed parts of the world on developed countries. Formal Empire was only one form of imperialism, the outcome of the economic control by Western powers imposed on Asian and African colonies. Therefore, even if empires ceased to exist, the ex-colonies independent politically were still under imperialist control due to this dependency. "The trade and investment of developed capitalist countries only slowed down and held back the growth of underdeveloped countries which were mired in poverty and dependency."[39]

---

38   Ibid.: 64-70.
39   Gao, Dai, and Zheng Jiaxin. *General Introduction to Colonialism*. Beijing: Peking University Press, 2003: 310.

Dependency theoreticians stressed the role of external elements. They believed that western developed countries caused the dependency of underdeveloped countries and the persistence of imperialism after the end of empires by means of their advantage in economy, their dominance in world economic system and the unequal trade relations. To this influential view, many a scholars proposed their own points, including Gall Gallagher and Robinson. They argued in their famous book Africa and the Victorians (1961) that in most cases social changes in the non-Western countries rather than in the Western countries were directly responsible for the changes in the imperialist expansion policies and the ways and means of imperialist control. Egypt's economic crisis in the 19th century, for example, led to increasing foreign interference, and in turn to the rise of Egyptian nationalism, which plunged Egypt into political crisis and in turn to direct intervention and political control by the UK and France. They also argued that the discovery and mining of rare minerals in South Africa aggravated the contention of western powers over the region which led to change in the balance of power and in turn to the Boer War[40].

Robinson later proposed the so-called collaborationist theory based on the survey of the important role of the African and Asian partners of Western countries in the imperialist rule. He argued that imperialism could be conceived of as a partnership or a system of collaboration was established between Western countries and their colonial political partners before, during, and after colonial rule. He also claimed that the changing forms of imperialism could be considered as changing forms of collaboration that resulted from changes in the party politics in the ex-colonies and ex-metropolitan states[41].

Greatly differing from the dependency theory, Gallagher and Robinson believed that the persistence of imperialism in the ex-colonies after independence could not be solely attributed to such external elements as the imposition of dependency status upon the underdeveloped countries by the western developed ones by means of the unequal world economic system. It should also be noticed that the changes in the colonies were closely related to the future development of the emergent countries after independence.

Admittedly, Gallagher and Robinson's perspectives on imperialism is quite advisable. However, they were as limited as dependency theorists in that they considered it was the internal elements, i.e. the social changes in the colonies, which led to the persistence of imperialism after the end of empire. Thus, they ignored such a basic fact that the political and economic relations between colonies and metropolitan states were unequal since the very beginning so that it was impossible to establish an equal partnership. Therefore, I claim the Gallagher and Robinson's theories embody a misunderstanding on the concept of imperialism.

---

40   Smelser, Neil J., and Paul B. Baltes. *International Encyclopedia of the Social & Behavioral Sciences*. Oxford: Elsevier, 2001: 7228-7729.
41   Ibid.: 7229.

Dependency theorists are pessimistic about the North-South relationship. Generally speaking, they all believe that colonies and semi-colonies of the South seldom gained any positive economic benefits from their economic exchanges with the metropolitan states of the North since the formation of the world economic system in the 16th century. The advanced countries develop at the cost of the underdeveloped countries in the Third World, where the economic surplus has been exploited.[42]

Countries and regions in South Asia, Southeast Asia, and Sub-Saharan Africa did not fare better although they gained political independence after the WWII. If anything, they were even poorer and more dependent on countries of the North than ever before. For dependency theorists, if they were still under the control of western economic imperialism (neo-imperialism), they would continue to be poor[43]. This situation was mainly caused by the fact that "colonial empires transferred sovereignty into the hands of their local servants, the so-called 'compradors', who worked for their overseas masters in the name of nationalism. Therefore, the economy of ex-colonies was improved in the short term after decolonization but it would become stagnated very soon. People were still poor and in debt and therefore generally dissatisfied with the 'local elites'. Only through a revolution could the ex-colonies made the transition from capitalism to socialism and break away from international economic system so that they could get out of 'the plight of underdevelopment and gain real development'"[44].

As a radical branch of the sociology of development, dependency theory came into being at the late 1950s, whose early representatives included G. Myrdal, P. Baran, and R. Prebisch. Later, L. Furtado, A.G. Frank, I. Wallerstein, and A. Emmanuel have all made positive contribution to the enrichment and development of this theory, clarifying the reason why there is an increasing gap between the poor countries and the rich ones in the world. Their major theses include, first, the stress should be on the analysis of external elements, emphasizing the role of imperialism, foreign control powers, and neocolonialism in the economic backwardness of developing countries; second, the economic system of the core and periphery is detrimental in that countries in the North exploited rather than helped those in the South economically; third, because countries in the South are in a position of dependency in the unequal international economic system, their economic development will become even more backward, which not only make them unable to achieve modernization but also probably become bankrupt in the end.

---

42   Webster, Andrew. *Introduction to the Sociology of Development.* Hampshire: Macmillan, 1984: 55.
43   Ibid.: 55.
44   Gao, Dai, and Zheng Jiaxin. *General Introduction to Colonialism.* Beijing: Peking University Press, 2003: 311.

1.5.1. Myrdal on the North-South Relationship

Western scholars believe that dependency theorists made great achievements on the study of the North-South relationship in 1957, when Myrdal and Baran published their influential masterpieces on this problem. They both argued that the poverty of the southern developing countries should not be attributed to the export of surplus capital by the northern industrialized ones. Meanwhile, they sought to account for the underdevelopment of the South from new perspectives.

Mrydal, Nobel Laureate in economics, discounted in *Economic Theory and Underdeveloped Regions* the influence of the capital export of European powers on the dire poverty of. Rather, he made a full account of the process of a cumulative polarization between the earliest industrialized countries and regions and other parts of the world. Deploying an institutional, dynamic, and evolutional method to analyze the reasons for the poverty in underdeveloped countries and regions, Mrydal claims that in a dynamic process of socio-economic development, mutually influenced and interconnected elements interacted as both cause and effect, progressing in a circular and accumulative way. That is, the change in one element would trigger the corresponding secondary change in another, which strengthened the original elements and led to the imbalanced development of economy determined by the original elements[45].

Mrydal also remarked that a state of inequality would emerge if one region developed faster than another due to foreign impact even though these two regions were of the same development level at the beginning. Moreover, economic and non-economic forces tended to impel local development of the advantageous region at the cost or sacrifice of another, which worsened the socio-economic condition and slowed down the development of the disadvantageous region and in turn aggravated the original inequality. "Because this technical gap, the more developed countries were able to exploit the LDCs by destroying their handicrafts through cheaper imports, by removing their accumulated wealth by political power, and by restructuring their economies so as to provide the raw materials needed by foreign industry at prices held artificially by foreign capital."[46] Therefore, Myrdal contended that poor countries could not make any real economic progress due to such elements. "Only if the income was becoming equal, the consumption of the poor mass was increased to attract foreign capital, and savings were increased to make for capital formation through reforms in power relations, land relations, and education system…could they get out of the circular and accumulative plight of low income and poverty and step into a dynamic process of benign circulation, accumulation, and causality"[47].

45   Han, Jijiang, and Xing Hu, eds. *Economics of Development*. Beijing: China Agriculture University Press, 2003: 77.
46   Fieldhouse, D.K. *The West and the Third World: Trade, Colonialism, Dependence and Development*. Oxford: Wiley-Blackwell, 1999: 56.
47   Yan, Xiaofei. *An Introduction to Development Economics*. Beijing: Economic Science Press, 2000: 29.

1.5.2. Baran on the North-South Relationship

In the early 1950s, Baran was basically a traditional Marxist. As to the North-South relationship, he still held that colonial expansion by European powers interrupted the course of social development and deformed the social economy of Asian, African, and Latin countries and regions, which were reduced to raw material base, commodity markets, investment outlets for northern industrialized countries which were better off while many of their counterparts in the South were mired in poverty. However, Baran changed his view in *The Political Economy of Growth* was published (1957), in which he had a serious discussion on and new understanding of the reasons for the gap between developed countries and developing ones in Asia, Africa, and Latin America.

In order to have a better understanding of the views proposed by Baran in *The Political Economy of Growth* and the basic principles of dependency theories, we should first clarify such basic concepts as "economic development", "economic growth", and "underdevelopment". When development economics first became a discrete discipline, there was no clear distinction between "economic development" and "economic growth". However, with the gradual evolution of economic practice and development of development economics, distinctions were made between these two concepts. Generally speaking, "'economic growth' only refers to the increase of products manifested in the increase of GDP or national income while 'economic development' means all aspects of social economy changed for the better as a result of economic growth, which could be seen in transformations in input structure, output structure, general living standard, income distribution, consumption model, education, health care, public participation, and eco-environment. Therefore, economic growth is a means to the end of economic development; economic growth is the basis on which economic development could be achieved."[48] Meanwhile, we should also be aware that "there would be no development without growth while there was indeed growth without development. Developed countries [in the North] might evolve out of economic underdevelopment rather than underdeveloped economy, which the colonial expansion by western capitalism in Asian, African, and Latin American colonies whose original social economy was deformed by foreign commodities and capital. This is the common economic features of the Third World as well as the economic root of its dependency."[49]

Baran argued in *The Political Economy of Growth* that local trade companies controlled by foreign capital played the major role in the process of economically controlling and plundering the underdeveloped regions in Asia, Africa, and Latin America, where the northern developed countries did not gain many economic interests out of their capital export. In fact, because many underdeveloped southern countries were unable to attract much foreign capital due to

---

48 Tan, Chongtai, ed. *The New Development of Economics of Development.* Wuhan: Wuhan University Press, 2002: 631.
49 Stavrianos, L. S. *Global Rift: The Third World Comes of Age.* New York: William Morrow & Co, 1981. trans. Chi Yue, et al. Beijing: The Commercial Press, 1993: 4.

their own economic development conditions, there was only a small amount of capital input from the northern developed countries. Baran pointed out that "the increase of Western assets in the underdeveloped world is only partly due to capital exports in the strict sense of the term; it is primarily the result of the reinvestment abroad of some of the economic surplus secured abroad."[50] And the trade companies which could gain profit and made reinvestment in the region were monopolized by foreign capital which controlled the major economic sectors of these countries and regions by means of their advantageous position in the world economic structure, incomparable capital to the local people of property, and political support from their own government and the upper class of the host countries. "This control enabled the foreign firms to dominate the host economy without necessarily owing much of it. Above all it enabled them to control a substantial part of the 'economic surplus' all societies generate in the form of profits and send them abroad."[51] This is the major reason for the economic underdevelopment of many countries and regions in Asia, Africa, and Latin America after political independence.

Baran also argued meanwhile that economic growth in the underdeveloped world was closely related to the fair use of the surplus capital, the economic value of which can be maximized by making right economic plans under the planned economy or invested freely according to market rules under the market economy. However, in the underdeveloped southern countries and regions, no proper use could be made of the limited capital, only a minor part of which could provide some advantages for the national economic growth while the major part was not invested in the most profitable local economic sectors. As a result, the underdeveloped world was still poor with limited economic growth rather than development. Baran thought the reasons were mainly as follows: First, the surplus capital in these countries and regions was either grabbed by foreign-funded companies or squandered in the purchase of luxuries by the local middle and upper classes and the landed aristocrats. In short, the capital was not invested in the economic sectors which could make for the independent and sustainable growth and the overall development, which led to economic underdevelopment. Second, neither foreign capitalists nor home bourgeoisie lacked sufficient interest in making investment in these countries and regions due to the limited local needs, low labor productivity, and low wages in the traditional agricultural sector, so that there was a lack of necessary conditions to make for economic growth.

Furthermore, Baran pointed out economic sectors, which already took shape in the underdeveloped world and were run by foreign-funded companies or local petty bourgeoisie, were largely monopolized and well protected by tariff and other measures. As a result, the international monopoly capital could ensure their economic bulwarks established in the rest of the world without

---

50　Baran, P. *The Political Economy of Growth.* New York: Monthly Review Press, 1957: 179.
51　Fieldhouse, D.K. *The West and the Third World: Trade, Colonialism, Dependence and Development.* Oxford: Wiley-Blackwell, 1991: 57.

necessarily costing a huge amount of manpower and material to sustain a formal colonial empire to mire the southern countries and regions in the plight of persistent poverty. Baran argued that "they could be released only through the destruction of capitalism. Economic growth is always dependent on the use of this surplus. In a planned, Soviet-type economy it will be maximized by correct planning."[52] This was because "the impact of foreign capitalism was not to narrow but to widen the gap between the capitalist West and the pre-capitalist Third World, making underdevelopment a potentially permanent condition which expressed the 'structural' weakness of these economies."[53]

1.5.3. Latin American Scholars on the "Underdevelopment" of Latin America

Baran's masterpiece has a great impact on Western scholars. However, because his masterpiece lacks substantial economic data of southern countries and regions, his theories inevitably sound somewhat empty. In the following decade after the publication of The Political Economy of Growth, some scholars in Latin America Studies and theorists who have made abundant use of economic data of the South conducted in-depth inquiry into the reasons for the economic gap between the North and the South.

Latin America became an object of study mainly because as the ex-colonies of European powers it gained a relatively long and independent development in countries and regions after independence in the 1920s. During this period, some Latin American countries and regions were on the same level of economic development as such European settled colonies as Australia, Canada, and New Zealand. However, since the 1950s these Latin American countries and regions were caught in the dilemma of economic stagnation and serious social problems. Therefore, the practical problem facing these scholars was why Latin America was caught in such a condition and how to get out of it. The prominent Argentina economist Raúl Prebisch once contended that in the long process of the formation of the world market, "the world economy breaks into the core and the periphery: the core comprises industrialized countries while the periphery includes all the undeveloped countries which are engaged in agriculture and the specialized production of primary goods, on the dualistic structure rests the whole world."[54]

The so-called dualistic structure proposed by L. Furtado, one of the most influential Latin American economists, contained a "capitalist wedge" into the pre-capitalist economies which enabled only such sectors which could meet the needs of the core countries as mines, plantations, transportation system and banking institutions to develop while failed to influence or reform the other sectors and the whole society. "This resulted in a 'hybrid structure' and a 'static

52 Fieldhouse, D.K. *The West and the Third World: Trade, Colonialism, Dependence and Development*. Oxford: Wiley-Blackwell, 1991: 57.
53 Ibid.: 58.
54 Ye, Jingyi. *Economics of Development*. Beijing: Peking University Press, 2005: 175.

equilibrium' at a low overall level, because the capitalist wedge had very little impact on the rest of economy and because those who owned it transferred much of their profits overseas. This patter became ossified because it was not in the interests of those who benefited to change it."[55] Meanwhile, Furtado also pointed out it was more noteworthy in Latin America that these economic beneficiaries included not only those foreign capitalists and businessmen but also the local people who co-operated with them, especially those native industrialists, politicians, and big land owners. Due to the complicity of the vested interest group, "[t]he result was not a negative or transitional stage to the higher levels of capitalism, but a concrete and potentially permanent condition of 'underdevelopment'".[56]

The theories of Latin American scholars gained much support from the radicals in the 1960s an 1970s, including the well-known dependency theorist A. G. Frank who published a book Capitalism and Underdevelopment in Latin America on this problem in 1969. In this book, Frank argued that underdevelopment was not the outcome of modern capitalism but took shape when the Europeans began their settlement and expansion in Americas. "My thesis is that these capitalist contradictions and the historical development of the capitalist system have generated underdevelopment in the peripheral satellites whose economic surplus was expropriated, while generating economic development in the metropolitan centers which appropriate that surplus—and, further, that this process still continues"[57]. In addition, Frank pointed out that the economic development and underdevelopment were not merely relative concepts nor differently merely in quantities. Instead, there existed essential connections as well as differences between them, which were formed because of the differences in economic structures and would develop as the relation between them developed[58].

Another prominent dependency theorist T. Dos Santos also published in 1968 an influential paper entitled "The Crisis of Development Theory and Dependency Relations in Latin America"[59]. Santos claimed the economic development in Latin America was of a dualistic character, which neither permitted nor made for full development of capitalist relations but rather based itself on bonded labor or slavery. Therefore, dependency was in fact the outcome of the long or otherwise period of well-established colonization experienced by the southern countries and regions in the process of economic development. It was formed on the basis of international labor division, which allowed industries in some countries to develop while others to stagnate. In these countries,

---

55   Fieldhouse, D.K. The West and the Third World: Trade, Colonialism, Dependence and Development. Oxford: Wiley-Blackwell, 1991: 59.
56   Ibid.: 59.
57   Frank, Andre Gunder. Capitalism and Underdevelopment in Latin America. New York: Monthly Review Press, 1969: 3.
58   Ibid.: 8.
59   The English version of this essay was collected in Underdevelopment and Development, edited by H. Bernstein, et al. Harmondworth, 1973.

there was no development only growth, even if whose existence was in compliance with and yielding to the economic development in the core countries. For countries and regions in the South, it was impossible for them to secure any real economic development under such conditions. Therefore, "the only hope for these peripheral countries was to break off relations with the capitalist world altogether, as China had done, and to make their own way.... So 'the only solution would be [for a country] to change its internal structure—a course which necessarily leads to confrontation with the existing international structure'"[60].

With the evolution of dependency theories, scholars in the 1970s were no longer satisfied in illustrating the problem with Latin American data but elucidated their opinion from a global perspective with the aid of data on Asian and African colonies.

The French prominent sociologist P.P. Rey made a more comprehensive summary and interpretation on the dualistic economic structure in 1973 based on data collected in Congo. Rey argued that in many southern countries and regions the reason for underdevelopment was greatly related to the nature of local society. In the northern developed countries, the transition from feudalism to capitalism was made possible because many of the upper feudal lords were not opposed to it. But the feudalism in the southern countries and regions was not like that in the Western Europe. When a society was integrated into the international economic system by means of foreign trade and absorbing foreign capital, it only led to the strengthening of control by the local ruling class and their resistance to capitalist expansion, the most obvious outcome of which was the people under their rule were prevented from becoming proletariat. The foreign capital which they absorbed during the whole process of the colonial rule was mainly used in the production of raw materials and tropical products needed by developed countries rather than or impossible in the reform of domestic economic structure to stimulate the overall development of social economy. As a result, domestic economy was stagnant. Meanwhile, this also enabled European colonial empires to protect well their own interests after decolonization through alliance with local rulers. Therefore, Rey pointed out "[f] or the dependent country the only way out of this dead end was revolution and the simultaneous overthrow of the class structure and capitalism, to be replaced by socialism."[61]

1.5.4. Wallerstein on World System

Immanuel Wallerstein was undoubtedly a scholar of importance in furthering the development of dependency theory. Since the 1970s, he has published a series of works on the formation and development of capitalist world system, taking the history of capitalist expansion, i.e. the history of global rift

---

60   Fieldhouse, D.K. *The West and the Third World: Trade, Colonialism, Dependence and Development.* Oxford: Wiley-Blackwell, 1991: 60.
61   Ibid.: 61.

and the formation and development of the North-South relationship, as that of a world system, based on which an international school came into being. For Wallerstein, a world economic system comprises mainly three parts: the core states of the West, peripheral countries, and semi-peripheral countries. "The distinctions were created by history industrialized first and acquired a commanding advantage over the rest of the world. The peripheral states are those that serve the needs of the core and are deliberately prevented from developing the higher industrial skills. The semi-periphery is an intermediate category of states that could be moving in either direction....The whole system reflects an international division of labour and the transferring surplus from periphery to core."[62] In the first volume of The Modern World System, Wallerstein made it clear that "the capitalist world-economy was built on a worldwide division of labor in which various zones of this economy (that which we have termed the core, the semi-periphery, and the periphery) were assigned specific economic roles, developed different class structures, used consequently different modes of labor control, and profited unequally from the workings of the system."[63]

Wallerstein also pointed out the world system was by no means static but in constant changes. In the 16th and 17th century, its core was located in North-Western Europe while its periphery was expanded to Americas. But Asia and Russia were still outside of its circumference and its semi-periphery was mainly in Europe. Therefore, it could be only referred to as "European economic system" at the time, at best "Atlantic economic system".

Since the industrial revolution in Great Britain in the 18th century, however, this European economic system gradually developed into a world economic system, in which there was always full of oppression, exploitation, inequality, and some periodic upheavals. Nonetheless, this system was equipped with a self-adjustment mechanism, which enabled it to survive many crises in the course of five centuries. As Wallerstein points out in the Chinese preface to The Modern World System, "the creation of capitalism is a shame rather than a glory of culture.... We are not in a triumphant but a chaotically terminal stage of capitalism."[64] Therefore, this world system will inevitably be replaced by a new one with more efficient and rational allocation system. "The only alternative world-system that could maintain a high level of productivity and change the system of distribution would involve the reintegration of the levels of political and economic decision-making. This would constitute a third possible form of world-system, a socialist world government."[65] Nevertheless, Wallerstein did not make clear the nature of such a system or government. He only roughly proposes that "when capitalism gives way to successive systems (one or more)

62   Ibid.: 60.
63   Wallerstein, Immanuel. *The Modern World-System: Capitalist Culture and the Origins of the European World-Economy in the Sixteenth Century*. New York: Academic Press, 1974: 162. Trans. Dan Lv. Beijing: Higher Education Press, 1998:5.
64   Ibid.: 1.
65   Ibid.: 6.

in the mid of the 21st century, we shall see whether the successive systems will be more equal. We cannot predict what a system it will be but we can influence its outcome through our current political and moral activities."[66]

1.5.5 Other Scholars on the Reasons for the Relative Poverty of the South

When Wallerstein discussed the North-South relationship from the perspective of the world system, some other scholars made detailed analysis on the basis of Rosa Luxemburg's theories of the reasons for the relative poverty of the South, whose representative works included Arghiri Emmanuel's Unequal Exchange: A Study of the Imperialism of Trade, Samir Amin's Accumulation on a World Scale, and Frank's Dependent Accumulation and Underdevelopment. Although these scholars have accepted Wallerstein's proposition that the world system comprises core, periphery, and semi-periphery, the question they are really interested in is that why such structural division of labor has resulted in a permanent huge gap between the core economies and the peripheral ones rather than the outcome promised by the principle of comparative advantage proposed by the leading classical economist Ricardo.

For A. Emmanuel and other scholars, this result was mainly due to the "unequal exchange" in the process of commercial trade between the underdeveloped South and the developed North. In order to obtain imported goods of the same value, the South had to pay much more socially necessary labor time. For instance, it takes country A 1,000 hours of socially necessary labor time to produce a car with an international market price of 10,000 pounds by means of advanced technology. However, it takes country B in West Africa 20,000 hours of socially necessary labor time to produce cocoa with an international market price of 10,000 pounds. When country A exchanges the car with country B for the cocoa, it means that country A exchanges a socially necessary labor time of 1,000 hours with country B for a socially necessary labor time of 20,000 hours. As a result, 19,000 hours of socially necessary labor time of country B is possessed by country A in the exchange. Meanwhile, if the socially necessary labor time as the real source of the wealth produced by country B has not possessed by country A in the unequal exchanged, it might have been used to increase the wealth of country B[67]. Therefore, Emmanuel and other scholars believe that "'unequal exchange' is a main reason why the wealth gap exists and indeed widens. Thus the world is divided into two segments: the high-wage, high-value economies, and the low-wage low-value economies. The former exploit the latter, not by capital investment but through the terms of trade. The result is unequal development and a progressive widening of the gap between the two."[68]

33

66   Ibid.: 2.
67   Emmanuel, A. Unequal Exchange: A Study of the Imperialism of Trade. Trans. Brian Pearce. New York: Monthly Review Press, 1972: 367-368.
68   Fieldhouse, D.K. The West and the Third World: Trade, Colonialism, Dependence and Development. Oxford: Wiley-Blackwell, 1991: 64-65.

Emmanuel and other scholars also believe this pattern will not be changed in a short time. "Economic relations between more-and less-developed countries cannot be of any benefit to the LDCs once a technological gap had developed between the two. Trade will not be an engine for transmitting growth and affluence from the core to the periphery but rather a device for perpetuating the differentials and extracting value from the poor for the benefit of the rich."[69] Meanwhile, as most dependency theorists have thought, the only effective way to change the situation is autarky. Emmanuel, however, points out there are two ways to ameliorate the situation: "(a) the poor countries simply stop international trading, though possibly trading between themselves, so putting a tourniquet round the haemorrhage of 'unequal exchange'; or (b) the formation by LDCs of alliances or cartels in order to raise traded prices artificially, by export duties, or by monopoly pricing (as of oil by OPEC in and after 1973)."[70]

Throughout the theoretical deliberation on the North-South relationship by dependency theorists, we can see clearly:

First, dependency theorists are generally pessimistic about the North-South relationship. They believe in the formation of the world system the developed North taking advantage of their dominant position in the system has reduced the South to a state of economic dependency and underdevelopment. "Underdevelopment is not merely lack of development but the product of the failure of western capitalism to fulfill the functions Marx ascribed to it"[71]. Second, the peripheral countries and regions in the South in the economic relations between the core and the periphery are in a dependent position in the unequal international economic system, from which the South has not only been prevented from obtaining any benefit but also been caught in the plight of economic stagnation. This is like what some dependency theorists have pointed out "[t]he trade and investment of developed capitalist countries have slowed down and held back the growth of underdeveloped countries which are mired in poverty and dependency."[72] Third, dependency theorists believe the existing dependency and underdevelopment of the South will continue for a long time. This is of benefit to the developed industrialized countries in the North, which will enable them to secure considerable economic interests at a very low cost. In particular, those multinational companies under their support will gain abundant profits. Fourth, as to the solution to the problem, most dependency theorists believe only by cutting off the connection with the world economic system can the less-developed countries and regions in the South get out of the plight of poverty. However, with the change in international environment after the 1980s, new dependency theorists no longer stress on the socialist substitution. Some of them argue "the benefit of foreign-owned companies can coexist

34

---

69   Ibid.: 66.
70   Ibid.: 65.
71   Ibid.: 61.
72   Gao Dai, and Zheng Jiaxin. *General Introduction to Colonialism.* Beijing: Peking University Press, 2003: 310.

with domestic prosperity of the dependent country due to the emergence of multinational companies and the infiltration of foreign capital into developing countries"[73]. Perhaps, this reflects the new theoretical deliberation on the North-South relationship by dependency theorists.

73   Han, Jijiang, and Xing Hu, eds. *Economics of Development*. Beijing: China Agriculture University Press, 2003: 69.

Chapter II

The Eurasian Relationship before Colonial Expansion

2.1. Historical Golden Age of Intercontinetal Trade

2.1.1. Eurasian East and West Contact by Land

Before European colonial expansion, there was no North-South relationship in the modern sense. North and South were only used to denote the differences in the distribution of races and some plants, especially grains. After the last deglaciation (circa 20, 000 years ago), the rising water level of all oceans interrupted the contact between some races and isolated some species of plants and animals. The real isolation at that time was from east to south rather than from east to west (taking the equatorial belt as the virtual demarcation): the isolation between the Old World of Asia, Europe, and Africa and the New World of Americas. Atlantic and Pacific were wide enough to prevent the spreading of any bacteria or viruses carried by monsoons or migratory birds. Therefore, such terrible plagues as Black Death (pestis) and small pox which killed one third of Europeans did not give any deathly damage to the still unknown New World; likewise, syphilis and other diseases which spread over the new continent wreaked havoc only on the American continents.

Before 1492, there was hardly any contact between the Old World and the New World except occasional drifts. However, evaluating from the process of the development and evolution of human civilization, the unification of world civilizations from mutual isolation and the integration of five continents from segregation were first pushed from west to east or vice versa, and were in turn swept from north to south.

Human civilization, especially in its early stage, was pushed from east to west, mainly determined by the unsteady relations between the settled part and the still nomadic one of tribes of the east. The latter often plundered the former from time to time. Scholars categorized these two parts into "the sedentary world" and "the nomadic world" and summed up the attacks from the nomadic on the sedentary in history. But in other ways, the attacks in fact collision and fusion between civilizations of the nomadic and the sedentary, complementary in terms of communication rather than subordinate in economic structure, which, however, led to the change in racial distribution, variation in languages, dissemination of religions, communication of species, and the relative expansion of hoeing and plowing civilized areas.

Before the 16th centuries, the ways in which human beings obtained food underwent several mutations: the majority of world civilization secured food by means of hoeing and plowing, on the basis of which came into being sedentary civilizations which were great and dominant in the world at that time. Till 1492, the strongest force which is pushed from east to west was the military power of nomadic tribes, which, comprising horses and chariots, converged into blast waves of reinforced mobility hard to defend by the sedentary people attached to their lands. Before Emperor Wu of Han Dynasty (140-87 BCE), the hard-working Chinese peasants of Han were powerless to defend against the reckless plunder and slaughter by Hun horsemen. Only when Emperor Wu implemented new policies and sent Wei Qing and Huo Qubing with their chosen troops to drive away the Huns from Mobei, did Chinese peasants secure the minimum guarantee for their sedentary life.

The nomadic world in the north of Asia underwent several movements different in direction from and larger in scale than those by Indo-European nomadic peoples: the one was from north to south, into Egypt at the farthest; the other was from west to east, into Mongolian steppe at the farthest. Their common feature was that both possessed horses and chariots (two-wheeled in most cases) because the nomadic were adept at driving chariots in fighting. It was hundreds of years after the nomadic people had already mastered horsemanship and charioting when the sedentary nation could strike back, chanting "Let us ride the long chariots / To crush those mountain strongholds". Around 1,000 BC, the nomadic people had started to grasp horsemen tactics, one man riding on one horse with great ease. The tamed horses originated in central Asia. Henceforth, the impact from east to west was more frequent. The Huns, the Turks, and the Mongols pushed successively from east to west with their mighty cavalries. After repeated attacks, the settled attackers became the attacked in the ensuing attacks. However, history is not simply a cycle because the proportion of nomadic attackers entering the sedentary world by force was after all constantly decreasing while that of the settled farms was constantly increasing. Those settlers who had mastered agricultural production technology and been influenced by agricultural civilization survived in the long impact from east to west. The sedentary world was gradually expanded after repeated contending of many centuries. Agricultural production and handicraft technologies in Tang China and the Muslim Empire in the West Asia, the two most developed regions of the sedentary world, had reached a climax after the 7th century and lasted till the 15th century.

In his exploration into the history of the general relationship between the sedentary world and the nomadic world, Marx paid great attention to "a fact which at all events contributed to the process"[1]. With the violent plunder and killing, the nomadic forces took away technology and culture with them. After the Scythians and the Aryans had learned metal smelting technology (applied first to smithing harnesses, weapons, and ornaments) from the sedentary peoples, the nomadic forces of the Arabs plundered a large number of craftsmen of Tang Dynasty while the Mongols took away all the skillful craftsmen but slaughtered the rest of the inhabitants in Bagdad. In the process of the evolution of human history into world history, violence, despite its bloodiness, served as the involuntary tool of history against human will in the expansion and conquest from east to west. It brought advanced productivity into the nomadic world like plowing, canal irrigation (including Karez wells), gardening, smelting, and house construction. Meanwhile, it distributed different races, the carriers of productivity, into every corner of the world, which was more in line with the ecological law. The Mongoloids were living mostly in East Asia, Siberia, and parts of Central Asia and Southeast Asia while the Caucasoids (Indo-European race) were mainly found in Europe, North Africa, West Asia, and Indian Subcontinent. The Indian race isolated in the American Continent and the Australnoid race in Oceania 10,000 to 30,000 years ago remained almost the same.

The food crops bred by pre-historic human beings and the plants of the highest value, such as rice (in places like Hemudu in China), potatoes, sugarcanes, and bananas, were introduced from East Asia and Southeast Asia into the central and western parts of Eurasia, and North Africa with the migration of human beings from east to west. Of course, there were plants introduced from west into east, for example, wheat spread to east and then west from West Asia. The spread was at a rather low speed in whatever direction and influenced greatly by zonal arrangement of the cold zone, temperate zone, subtropical zone, and tropical zone, which manifest different natures.

---

1   Marx, Karl, and Fredrick Engels. *Collected Works*. Vol. 39. New York: International Publishers, 1983: 332.

The trace of migration from east to west could also been seen in the process of the taming and spreading of animals. There might be two origins of wild horses: Central Asia (Xinjiang in China) and Northern Steppe in the Black Sea. Bactrian camel originated in Central Asia while dromedary on the Arabian Peninsula. Horses, camels, sheep, and goats all scattered west, reaching the Sahara Desert. Only the donkey tamed from the wild donkeys in Africa scattered west and east over Eurasia.

Generally speaking, seeing from the intercontinental arrangement of Eurasia, the eastern and central parts of the continent were slightly more advanced than the western part because the major world civilizations mainly originated in the eastern and central parts of Eurasia and Chinese civilization in East Asia has continued for 5,000 years and exercised a great influence on its surrounding regions. Chinese civilization and Indian civilization had nurtured the largest population, where agriculture had an advanced development and GDP ranked top in the world till the end of the 18th century.

The intercontinental communication of Eurasia was sustained for thousands of years partly due to several overland channels of communication from east to west or otherwise. Richthofen the German first referred to these channels which had existed for more than 2,000 years as Seidenstrassen or the Silk Road in English. Richthofen's denomination is proper since the long-distance transportation of silk produced in China for sale in the West played an irreplaceable role in sustaining the intercontinental communication throughout Eurasia. This channel of communication was opened up since the 2nd century BC and ran basically from east to west, though some specific routes had undergone more or less alteration, turning south or southwest or north or northwest due to wars or the rise and fall of business roads. It started from Xi'an China (the eastern end of Eurasia from east Xi'an to Lianyunguang, Rizhao or Langxie County as the domestic business roads of China in the western Pacific rim was hardly ever blocked) at 109 degrees east longitude, through Weiwu, Jiuquang, and Dunhuang in the Hexi Corridor, out of Yumen Pass, to northwest Loulan in Lop Nor first, and then bifurcated north and south: the north road stretched westward from Kongqi River to Korla, and then westward through Kuqa to Kashgar; the south road stretched southwestward alongside Qiemo River, through Khotan and Shache to Kashgar also. Therefrom, it crossed Congling to Ferghana, turned westward across Samarkand and Bukhara, or Kabul and Herat in Afghanistan, through Tehran to the south of the Caspian Sea to Mesopotamia, and continued westward across Damascus to Alexandria on the southeast coast of the Mediterranean or to Antakya on the northeast coast. Therefrom, it continued on the sea by sailing boats westward to the Greek Peninsula or the Italian Peninsula.

The channels opened up with the westward expedition of the Mongols (AD 1218-1260) were the smoothest on the overland Silk Road. Under the protection of Mongolian horsemen, the business road across the northern steppe obstructed for centuries crossed over the north of the Caspian Sea to arrive at

Tana of the Black Sea (the Azov Sea), connected with Moscow, Novgorod, and Riga further north, and therefore joined with the North Sea business road of the Hanseatic League. In most cases, the business road to Europe stretched slightly southward from east to west through waterway transport: mostly across Tabriz northward to Trabzon on the southern coast of Black Sea, over the Black Sea by ship, through Constantinople, out of the Dardanelles Strait, into the Mediterranean, to Venice or Genoa, which was usually undertaken by Italian merchant ships.

The total freight through the Eurasian business road in the 13th and 14th centuries might be uncountable forever. In the early 15th century, i.e. 50 years after the business road fell from the prosperity at the mid-14th century, Ruy Gonzalez de Cavijo, the Spanish Ambassador, was directed to come eastward in A.D. 1403 to Khan Tamurlaine's court in Samarkand. Several months before his arrival in Samarkand in August 1404, came a great caravan from China, which had 800 camels carrying bulk cargo. Each camel could carry around hundreds of kilos of goods. Therefore, the caravan could carry a huge amount of goods[2]. Clavijo witnessed the prosperity of the biggest Central Asian market in Samarkand:

The city is also very rich in merchandize which comes from other parts. Russia and Tartary send linen and skins; China sends silks, which are the best in the world, (more especially the satins), and musk, which is found in no other part of the world, rubies and diamonds, pearls and rhubarb, and many other things. The merchandize which comes from China is the best and most precious that comes to this city, and they say that the people of China are the most skillful workmen in the world. They say themselves that they have two eyes, the Franks one, and that the Moors are blind, so that they have the advantage of every other nation in the world. From India come spices, such as nutmegs, cloves, mace, cinnamon, ginger, and many others which do not reach Alexandria[3].

There are many complex reasons for the great changes of Eurasian Passage in history, the dominant of which was the transformation of the relationship between the sedentary world and the nomadic world. Moreover, the rise and spread of some religions had great impacts on the changes in the business road. For example, the Central Asia, the Arabian coastal and inland cities which had much trade with India first or China afterwards declined one after another. Of course, there were also emergent cities, like Jeddah, Mecca, Yemen and Aden.

---

2 Clavijo, Ruy González de. *Narrative of the Embassy of Ruy González de Clavijo to the court of Timour, at Samarcand, A.D. 1403-6.* New York: Cambridge University Press, 2009: 95. Trans. Zhaojun Yang. Beijing: The Commercial Press, 1985: 159.
3 Ibid.: 157.

2.1.2. The Intercontinental Maritime Communication on the Eurasian Continent

The economic and cultural links which closely interrelated East Asia, South Asia and West Asia included not only the overland Silk Road extending to several kilometers but also the maritime Silk Road which was opened up around the 1st century B.C., which connected the trade and the shipping route on the Pacific and the Indian Ocean through the Red Sea or the Persian Gulf with those on the Mediterranean. This maritime channel had developed to a high level by the 13th and the mid-14th centuries. Sailing from east to west, Chinese and Arabian business ships, carrying a staggering amount of Chinese silk, Porcelain, ironware and spices, started off at Quanzhou Port, through the Strait of Malacca, over the Arabian Sea (joining the Indian caravans), into the Red Sea, by way of Egypt, and arrived at the Mediterranean port city Alexandria, or by way of Malacca, and arrived at Hormuz of the Persian Gulf, and then shipped to the Black Sea. On the voyage from west to east, Arabian ships, Indian ships, and the giant Chinese business ships on their way back to China were truly outstanding, which were fully loaded with spice, ivory, and occasionally exotic birds and beasts specifically for the Chinese court.

The eastern Mediterranean in the 15th century was one of the most prosperous world trade centers. Italian businessmen were active in the Mediterranean and the Black sea, transporting oriental goods to Southern Europe and Western Europe. However, since the 13th century the control of the trade in the Baltic Sea was in the hands of the German Hanseatic League, which was even tighter than that of Italian cities over the trade in the Mediterranean. This trapped Europeans in the dilemma of mutually impenetrable trade on the two seas.

Italian businessmen, however, had their own Achilles' heel: they could not surmount Suez Isthmus at the southern tip of the Mediterranean and could only sail along the shores of the Black sea in the north. The shrewd merchants of Venice could still not bypass a stretch of land route into the Red Sea, which, together with the Persian Gulf and the east Mediterranean, was dominated by Muslim merchants, Chinese merchants (except in the intervals) and Indian merchants.

Different from the Italian merchants impeded by geographical barriers, Chinese folk merchants were gravely repressed by the policy of stressing agriculture and restricting business implemented by the Ming Dynasty since the end of the 14th century and the beginning of the 15th century, which imposed restrictions on folk maritime business. As a result, they were beleaguered in the disadvantageous position of "fighting with two hands bound" in the international market and lost many great historical opportunities. After the Xuande period of the Ming Dynasty, the Emperors even gave away the sea power, sea route and market opened up by Cheng Ho's fleet on the expedition to the West from 1405 to 1433 so that the business from east to west dominated by China and expanded till the 15th century suffered irretrievable losses. Meanwhile, with the rise of the Ottoman Empire in West Asia, Muslim merchants also suffered great losses in internal strife. And the Indian Subcontinent, with an area of more than three million square kilometers, was increasingly divided by politics, religion, and caste and nearly reduced to a mere geographical term. Thus, when Mongol-Turk horsemen slacked their surveillance along the overland Silk Road and the giant ships of the Ming Dynasty retreated from the Indian Ocean, it seemed that the intercontinental communication on the Eurasian continent was maintained mainly by the historical inertial power.

2.2. Communication of Intercontinental Civilizations

2.2.1. Intercontinental Civilizations

The intercontinental bonds of Eurasian continent connected the most ancient human civilizations: Chinese civilization, Indian civilization, Persian civilization, Greek-Roman civilization (Byzantine civilization), and Arabian Muslim civilization. Since ancient times, these major civilizations made contact and cultural exchanges from near to far with other civilizations. The intercontinental cultural exchanges were colorful and influential, including not only personnel exchanges, resources transference, mutual influence in manners and habits of basic necessities and rites and rituals of weddings and funerals, but also the dissemination, imitation, and assimilation of thoughts, religions, literatures, arts, and languages. Diplomatic envoys, students to study abroad, religious men, merchants, craftsmen, escorting cavalry, seamen and sailors navigating the ships, and war prisoners drove camels, led horses, hoisted the sails, traveling day and night in the high mountains and lofting ridges, in the boundless West Asian desert, on the tumultuous Pacific and Indian Ocean, under the blazing sun on the Red sea, and in the winter rain of the Mediterranean. The communication between advanced civilizations was made possible in the long process of the collision and fusion of cultures in countries and regions.

Human civilization first came into being in the Mesopotamia, the Aegean, Indian and China[4]. The earliest human civilization probably originated in the Mesopotamian river valley 45 degrees of longitude, radiating into all directions. In the following thousands of years, it contributed brilliant and various inventions and creations to the whole world, among which oxcart transportation invented circa 3,200 B.C. played a great role in the subsequent intercontinental cultural communication. The nomadic tribes from the east circa 2,000 to 1,700 B.C. introduced the horse into the Mesopotamia. Henceforth, on the intercontinental route appeared wagons. Perhaps because the sun rises from the east and sets in the west, people on the long journey were more accustomed to walking east or west. Wagons and chaises which appeared later were driven more frequently on the intercontinental thoroughfares. Although cuneiform characters unique to the Mesopotamia had become the commonly used medium in the

---

4   Egypt as an ancient civilization of Nile is here incorporated into civilization on African continent. Note by the author.

business transactions in most parts of West Asia since 500 B.C., it was not disseminated to the farther east or west on the Eurasian continent possibly because it was not an alphabetic script nor had the ingenious functions of Chinese hieroglyphs. However, the Code of Hammurabi as the dominant ancient legal system in the Mesopotamia exerted an important impact on the subsequent legal systems of the whole world. The ancient Babylonians were more adept in mathematical calculations than the subsequent Greeks. The counting method of dividing the daily life of modern people into double 12 hours, an hour into 60 minutes, a minute into 60 seconds was derived from the mathematical achievements by the ancient Babylonians. The duodecimal counting method had a profound influence on Europeans after it had spread to the West.

The Hittites as one of the nomadic tribes migrating westward from the eastern steppe around the Caspian Sea might have gained most from the advanced West Asian civilization. Their mastery of metallurgy, light chariots, and laws enabled their empire to expand to the Anatolia plateau in the west, bordering the eastern coast of the Aegean Sea, which bridged the Mediterranean and the Black Sea on the Eurasia. However, most of the achievements of the ancient civilizations on the intercontinental routes had not been preserved, some of which had vanished with the passage of time. There were two great constructions in the neo-Babylonian period: Neo-Babylonian Walls and the Hanging Gardens, which had been included in The Seven Wonders of the World. However, Babylon was totally deserted around A.D. 200, buried by water flows and silts, vanished for more than 1,700 years on the intercontinental routes, and discovered till 1,900 years later. Although many inventions in the Mesopotamia had not still spread to other peoples, Europe nowadays believes it is the Mesopotamian inventions which have gradually brought about modern inventions[5].

The Persian Empire established in the 6th century B.C. played an intermediary role in the transnational trade and cultural exchanges on the intercontinental routes. West Asia became the center of the blending of civilizations because of its geographical connection with Europe while the formation of the Persian Empire promoted the communication of intercontinental civilizations because it drew the farther east into the vision of world history. The western border of the Persian Empire had reached Bactria, peeping through Pamir at China entering the Warring States period to the east of Taklimakan desert. Darius (521-486 B.C.) constructed the Imperial Road, which stretched from Ephesus by the Aegean Sea to Susa near the Persian Gulf, and then from Opis in the Mesopotamia straightly to the upstream of the Indus River. This was the first road to promote the trade and transportation from West Asia to East Asia. Herodotus (500 B.C.) once described the unimpeded journey on the intercontinental road of more than 2,500 kilometers: "neither snow nor rain nor heat nor gloom of night stays these couriers from the swift completion of their

5   Lerner, Robert E., Standish Meacham, and Edward McNall Burns. *Western Civilization: Their History and Their Culture*. New York: Norton, 1988. Trans. Juefei Wang, et al. Vol. 1. Beijing: China Youth Press, 2003: 51.

appointed rounds."[6] The Persian Empire at its zenith covered the Mesopotamia, Egypt and Indian, the three centers of civilizations, and reached the border Greece, the fourth center of civilization, while tapped on the door of civilization to the east of Pamir. Therefore, this road which traversed the Western Asian plateau had indeed provided premise and condition for the direct communication between civilizations in the east and west.

It was the expansion of the Persian Empire which contributed to the continuous development of the economic, military, political exchanges and cultural interactions between West Asia, North Africa, and the eastern Mediterranean, which paved the way for the Hellenization beginning since A.D. 400. In the middle of the first millennium B.C., the Greeks established eastward trade relations with West Asia, learned craftsmanship skills, metal handicraft skills, and writing from the Mesopotamia, adopted Phoenician language system and thus formed an alphabet with phonetic symbols for each vowel and consonant. The Greek letters are relatively simple and convenient, easy for people to learn and record in words. Because the Greek is easier for people to learn and use than any other West Asian scripts, it played a great role in the expansion of Hellenization in West Asia and Central Asia. Hellenization which started in 323 B.C. and lasted for four centuries was in fact the eastward expansion of Greek civilization factors and their fusion with those of Asian civilization in Egypt, West Asia, and parts of Central Asia. With the increase in the communication among all nations in Europe and Asia, some nomadic tribes joined the sedentary world successively, which contributed to great developments of astronomy, physics, mathematics, literature, arts, and architecture in Egypt, and many countries in West Asia and Central Asia. The migration of many Greeks to Egypt, West Asia and parts of Central Asia furthered the development of Hellenization, which was not only the Hellenization of West Asian civilization in Asia but also the Orientalization of Greek civilization so that the content of Greek civilization was made even more colorful and profound and thus shined gloriously in the history of world civilization.

Hellenization set a new stage for the intercontinental development and influence among Eurasian civilization, which made it clear: first, Eurasian civilizations were mutually influential and beneficial. On the basis of Sinai letters developed Phoenician letters, from which in turn were derived the Greek and the Aramaean. The former evolved into the Slavic, Latin, and many modern scripts of Western European countries while the latter not only evolved into Arabic in West Asia but also spread to South Asia and West Asia and exerted an indirect influence on Turkic, Kitan, and Mongolian scripts. Alphabetic scripts which originated in West Asia made enormous contributions to human civilizations. Likewise, Judaism of the Hebrews in Palestine was widely circulated and became one of the sources of the subsequent Christian thoughts. The Old Testament is an essential part of the Bible, which contained some principles and ideas of ancient Jewish religion and Christianity. The Macedonians, Greeks,

---

6 Ibid.: 141.

and Romans entered West Asia and parts of Central Asia, not only obtaining many resources and wealth from the east but also communicating directly and fusing with local cultures. Secondly, the interruption and termination of classical civilizations. After the Nile Valley civilizations, the Mesopotamia civilizations, and the Indus Valley civilizations, and the Aegean civilization declined, fell, and were interrupted successively, they were chiefly inherited by later generations as cultural heritages, and their scripts were in oblivion for 2,000 years. The evolvement track of classical civilizations was as follows: the strong advance from east to west began from the 8th century to the 6th century B.C., which led to the shift of the civilization center. The Greek classical period did not last for a long time after the Greek city state defeated the Persian Empire in the 5th century B.C. After the rapid rise of Macedonia, the Alexandrian Empire disintegrated into several Hellenized kingdoms in the late 4th century B.C. Parallel to Greek civilization, Roman civilization rose on the Italian Peninsula, whose westward expansion finally gave an end to the Hellenized period in the first century B.C.

When the Greek civilization spread to Asia and Africa in the 2nd century B.C., the great East Asian civilizations linked China in East Asia and near the Pacific with the Western world via the trans-Eurasian Silk Road. China's Yellow River civilization had been developing for more than 2,000 years and had hardly any communications with the Western civilization to the east of Pamir, when the latter had generally entered the Early Iron Age, China still continued its bronze culture but there was no interruption of civilization like what had happened to the latter. Chinese characters evolved from inscriptions on oracle bone, bronzes, and stone tablets to seal characters, became the standardized national characters, and later developed into clerical script and regular script, which had been used for thousands of years and played an indelible role in the uninterrupted development of Chinese civilization for 5,000 years.

2.2.2. The Silk Road Set Up the Strong Links for Intercontinental Communication

Before the 2nd century B.C., the leg to the east Pamir on the Eurasian intercontinental road had not been opened up because both the expedition of the Persian Empire and that of Alexander could only reach the upstream of the Indus River, unable to cross Pamir. At that time, the north and northwest of China were in the hands of the nomadic Hun people, who controlled business roads, extracted wealth, and invaded and harassed repeated the sedentary area to the south of the Yangtze River. Although it had made peace with the Han Dynasty by marriage and was bequeathed with lavish gifts by the latter, its more than 300,000 picked horsemen frequently plundered and looted down south by means of its strong military power. Peasants in the north suffered enormous losses, unable to live and work in peace. Emperor Wu of the Han Dynasty changed its policy of tolerance and decided to mount counterattacks and attacks and therefore to open up the road to the western regions and make up allies with the nomadic tribes driven away by the Huns like Darouzhi. Emperor Wu sent Zhangqian to the Western Regions in 138 B.C., who blazed the path which stretched from Chang'an and over Pamir to Central Asia and West Asia to the west of Pamir after numerous difficulties and perils[7]. Banchao was sent to the Western Regions in A.D. 97, who in turn dispatched the vice-envoy Ganying to the Persian Gulf to reopen and consolidate the path. This intercontinental path was later called the Silk Road, which connected China with West Asia and Europe and broadened the intercontinental economic and cultural exchanges on the Eurasian continent. The opening of the path to the east of Pamir extended the intercontinental road to the coast of the Yellow Sea, which became a real bridge on the Eurasian continent. Its historical significance has been increasingly recognized with the passage of time and its contribution to the human development will always occupy an important place in the history of world civilizations.

Some scholars hold that Chinese silk from around the 6th century to the 4th century B.C. entered the view of the Greek world through "the grasslands of the Silk Road"[8] in the north. Syrian craftsmen unravelled the silk again to weave into silk brocade as thin as cicada's wings. This novel silk cloth unique to China and deeply loved by the Greeks exerted a deep and profound influence on the style of sculpture, fashion of clothing, and pursuit of human body in Greek. Roman aristocrats' bent for silk luxuries also became a fashion in the upper society. Meanwhile, by way of this road, grapes, pomegranates, flax, and clover of Central Asia and West Asia were transplanted to China, and rare horses from Ferghana were introduced into China. Chinese silk, paper, and steel spread to India after the 2nd century B.C., when the economic and trade exchanges between China and India became frequent and countries in Central Asia could buy Chinese Qiong bamboo rods and Shu cloth[9] from India (called Yuan Du at that time). Indian Buddhism was introduced into China round the first century and localized from the 3rd to the 6th centuries, which became an important aspect and bond of cultural exchanges between China and many countries on the intercontinental road. Buddhism spread by way of the eastern extension of the Silk Road to the Korean Peninsula, and then from Baekje to Japan, where it has been worshiped for more than 1,000 years with distinct Chinese characteristics. Chinese characters spread to Japan and were used to transcribe Japanese pronunciations, which developed into two sets of kanas. Chinese characters were more broadly used as recording tools by Japan, Korea, and Vietnam for a long time. The Sassanian Persians arrived in China to do business by way of the Silk Road. Provinces in the northwest and north and even Guangdong province had traces of Persians, who introduced sericultural techniques to Europe.

---

7 "Biography of Great Yuan." *Historical Records.*
8 Dai, He, and Zhang Yingli. "The Export of Chinese Silk and the 'Wild' Silk." *History-Geography of Northwest* 1(1986).
9 "Biography of Zhang Qian." *History of the Former Han Dynasty.*

Confucianism spread to Korea around the first century, valued and propagated with all means by the ruling class of all dynasties, and emerged a group of prominent Confucian scholars. Confucianism spread to Japan around the 5th century and gradually became the essential education among its aristocrats and bureaucrats. Under the influence of Confucian thoughts came about Taika Reform which was an epoch-making event for Japan. Empress Koken decreed in 757 that every family should possess a Book of Filial Piety, and Confucianism was popularized to every social stratum. There emerged unprecedented centers of economic and cultural exchanges on the intercontinental road from the 7th to 10th centuries. Chang'an (Xi'an today) of the Tang Dynasty became the convergence of the whole world. Students from Korea and Japan and envoys to Tang China converged in this cosmopolitan city, disseminated Tang culture after they went back home, and became prominent figures in their own countries, such as Minabuchi no Shōan and Kibi no Asomi Makibi. There were also not a few persons from Central Asia, Arab (called Tazi at that time), and India who remained in China and became celebrities, like Li Yanshen the Tazik who obtain Tien Si in the highest imperial examination, Li Xun the Persian was one of the Tang ci poets. Central Asians and South Asians who were good at singing and dancing taught Chinese people many kinds of dances, like Huteng Dance, Huxuan Dance, Zhezhi Dance from Chacha (Tashkent) and Samarkand and Liguo Dance accompanied with music from Myanmar. Different religious beliefs like Zoroastrianism, Nestorianism, Manichaeism, and Islam spread to China. The Persians established Parsee Prayer Halls in Chang'an. Xuanzang and Yijing might be the Chinese who had travelled farthest on the intercontinental road (including seaway) for religious purpose. By way of this road, China's papermaking technique spread to Central Asia through Chinese craftsmen, and to Europe by way of Tazi, which exerted a great influence on the later Renaissance. China's block printing technique spread eastward to Japan around 770, and westward to Tazi several centuries later. China's silk brocade weaving technique spread to Arabian nations in the Tang Dynasty. Tang China as the center of intercontinental cultural exchanges displayed charms of an advanced society rare in history.

2.2.3. Arabian Culture Shone Brilliantly on the Intercontinental Road

Around the 4th century, the intercontinental road suffered from severe turmoil due to the eastward and southward migration and pillage and plunder of the nomadic tribes in the north. In the east of the intercontinental road, Tuoba, a branch of Xianbei, migrated southward and roughly settled in the 6th century. In the European part of the intercontinental road, the westward migration of the Huns caused a "catfish effect" among the Germans, Slavs, and Avars. The rising nomadic nations' temperament of aggression and desire of conquest found a vent in the westward invasion the sedentary world. Aside from wreaking havoc, they settled in the sedentary areas and infused all the vigorous and creative life into the sedentary society after all. In the 5th century, the Western Roman Empire fell and the remaining Eastern Roman Empire cowered in the south of the Balkan Peninsula by the end of the century, and the classical civilization vanished.

The Islamic empire which rose in the 7th century expanded beyond the boundaries of all previous empires. Its eastward and westward expansion surpassed the boundaries of all previous empires, reaching westward the Pyrenees in West Europe and eastward borders of China in Central Asia. Therefore, the civilization it shouldered was quite different from the previous ones because there were Arabs, Persians, Syrians, Egyptians, and people from many other nations living within its borders, which enabled it to create an Arabian-Islamic civilization on the basis of ancient West Asian civilizations, Persian civilization, Egyptian civilization, and Greek-Roman civilization it had assimilated. What was particularly valuable was that the caliphs asked for Greek classical works from Byzantine emperors and translated these masterpieces into Arabic, which made it possible for many great works, especially those by Aristotle forgotten by Europeans, to be preserved and shined again brilliantly during the Renaissance. The most advanced and sophisticated astronomical instruments like the astrolabe, the quadrant, and the zenith sector produced by the Arabs were not used by the Europeans until the 16th century. The astronomical tables authored by al-Khwarizmi (780-810) and al-Battani (circa. 858-929) successively became the blueprint for all astronomical tables in the east and west and had been translated into many Europeans languages. In the 9th century, Indian numerals and zero spread to Arab, and al-Khwarizmi first applied Indian numerals and zero to substitute the counting method with Arabic Alphabet. In the 12th century, Indian numerals were disseminated with al-Khwarizmi's masterpiece to Europe, designated as "Arabic numerals", adopted by the whole world, and promoted the development of counting science. On its basis, Arabs first created arithmetic, applied it to algebra, combined it with Greek geometry and trigonometry, making comprehensive developments in almost all the fields of mathematics. Canon of Medicine by Avicenna (980-1037) spread to Europe and became the textbook for all European universities by the 17th century. Arabian Nights is the gem of Arabic literature, whose content and realistic style had a profound impact on European literature. Several European literary masters during the Renaissance like Dante, Boccaccio, and Cervantes were all influenced by its writing techniques.

Before the 12th century, the western Europeans assimilated in the economic field many technological achievements from Muslims, such as irrigation techniques, cultivation of new crops, enology, and papermaking from China. It can be proved by the fact that the current English vocabulary still preserves a large number of words and phrases from Arabic language and Persian language, such as transport, tariff, magazine, alcohol, sugar, muslin and even admiral. In terms of techniques, there are also many loan-words, such as algebra, numeral, minimum, alembic, amalgam, alchemy, alkali, soda, almanac and names of many planets. Europeans at that time looked down upon Byzantium which saw it self as the embodiment of European civilization while had eyes only for Arabic civilization. Nevertheless, the northern European countries (taking Britain as an example) north of 45 degrees north latitude had been peripheral and relatively isolated and backward since they entered the era of civilization, unable to advance side by side with the civilized countries in the middle and east on Eurasian continent. Rome was still a slavery society in the first century B.C., whose writer Cicero once suggested that his Greek friends should not purchase slaves from Britain anyway, because they were very foolish, totally incompetent to receive education. Till the 11th century, the Spanish Muslims still looked down upon the Northern Europeans, claiming that "they are of great stature and of a white color. But they lack all sharpness of wit and penetration of intellect"[10]. In the middle ages, many Arabic-Islamic countries were undoubtedly in modern terms the "developed countries" in the eyes of Europeans with different religious beliefs.

2.2.4. The Intercontinental Trade Route and Cultural Exchanges during the Mongolian Empire

The Mongolian rulers put regions from the Baltic to the Pacific and from Siberia to the Persian Gulf on the Eurasian continent under the control of the largest empire ever in history, established order, achieved peace, and thus expanded greatly the range of the intercontinental road on the Eurasian continent and connected all civilizations otherwise isolated due to geography, politics, and economy. Envoys, businessmen, monks, foreign students, and travelers from everywhere had frequent contacts, and there were closer economic connections and cultural exchanges. In Song Dynasty, the overland road was blocked since the fall of north Xinjiang, Song government paid more attention to maritime transport. After the cross to the south, one fourth of shipping tax obviously became the bulk of the financial income, the rich in Fujian, Zhejiang, and Guangdong were mostly engaged in maritime business, focusing on the trade in daily commodities rather than gaining profits solely from exporting and importing luxuries practiced by previous generations. The production of porcelain and silk by domestic manual workshops laid a sound foundation for exportation. In Yuan Dynasty, both overland and maritime communication were highly developed, which reduced greater part of the Persian Gulf as "tributaries" of the Mongolians. The export goods loaded by Chinese ships setting sail from such ports as Quanzhou were mainly handicraft products and cultural goods, like porcelain, silk, books, stationaries, paintings (the last three items were mostly exported to Korea, Japan, and Philippines). The import goods were mainly quality timber, gems, spices, and ivory from Southeast Asia, and leather and horses from Central Asia. As can be seen from the varieties of export and import goods, China occupied an advantageous position in the economic and cultural exchanges on the intercontinental road, which was not further sustained in the following centuries.

10   Benedict, Ruth. *Race: Science and Politics*. Rev. ed. New York: Viking Press, 1943: 8.

China's three inventions, printing, gunpowder, and compass, and paper money first created in China were disseminated into Europe during this period when the intercontinental road was unimpeded and greatly expanded. English philosopher Francis Bacon commented on the three inventions in 1620 that their dissemination manifested obvious power, effect and outcome:

For these three have changed the appearance and state of the whole world; first in literature, then in warfare, and lastly in navigation: and innumerable changes have been thence derived, so that no empire, sect, or star, appears to have exercised a greater power and influence on human affairs than these mechanical discoveries.[11]

There were many other inventions from China that had spread to Central Asia, West Asia, and Europe on the intercontinental road (including maritime). The highly influential stern rudder (in the 12th century), stirrup, and chest harness exerted profound impacts on ways of transportation, farming, and fighting on horse. Moreover, Chinese fruits and unique plants and flowers also spread westward all over Europe, like tea, chrysanthemum, camellia, rhododendron, tea rose, China aster, lemon, and orange, which is still called "Chinese apple" in Holland and Germany.

Astronomy and calendar, mathematics, and medical knowledge from the wet of Eurasian continent were introduced into China with Persians and Arabs. Likewise, Chinese knowledge in these fields spread to the West. They were mutually enhanced. The Italian father and son of the Marco Polo family came to China, recording for the first time the interaction between Europeans and Chinese in details. Marco Polo lived in China for 17 years and authored The Travels of Marco Polo after his return home, which became the primary source for Europeans to know Asia and China in the following centuries. Marco Polo came overland to China while returned home by sea. Henceforth, Europeans had a concrete and detailed knowledge of the overland and maritime paths of the demystified intercontinental road on the Eurasian continent.

2.2.5. The Reasons for Easterners' Failure to Sustain Their Advanced Status

The golden era of the overland path came to an end with the rapid fall of Mongolian Empire, followed by Tamerlane Empire which made the business road continuously unimpeded by means of their horsemen escorts and the inherent enormous inertia power of the business road. In 1405, 800-camel caravans starting from the inland China still could arrive at the capital city of Samarkand after travelling thousands of kilometers. However, the road to Syria-Levant coast was impeded. The giant Muslim business ships in the eastern Mediterranean which could equal or compete previously with those of Venice had to retreat to the Red Sea in the end of the 14th century, giving up the whole Mediterranean and henceforth holding sway only on the southern

---

11   Bacon, Francis. *Novum Organum.* Book 1. 1620: 129.

seaway (the Indian Ocean). Arabs fell into anarchy since the end of the imperial era. They lacked a proper organization to get united and had to maintain temporary advantages in some areas by means of traditional business experiences. The Turkish empires (including the Ottoman Empire) which succeeded the Arab Empire failed to undertake any pace-keeping reforms in the crucial historical period. There were no fundamental changes in agriculture, industry, financial means or commercial organizations although the Ottoman Empire still expanded its boundaries westward in the 16th century.

It was a glorious achievement that Chinese drove the Mongolian rulers to the north of the Gobi in the latter half of the 14th century. However, the succeeding Ming Empire did not grab the great historical opportunity in the 14th and 15th centuries but rather put too much power in the north of the Great Wall, sparing no effort to guard against the counter-attack of the Mongolian horsemen. And in the eastern coastal areas and territorial seas, to prevent the hostile forces from shaking the rule of Ming Dynasty from the sea, rigorous policy of "no maritime business" was implemented, which departed from the opening policy of free trade on the sea since Song Dynasty and Yuan Dynasty. Ming Dynasty (1368-1644) and the succeeding Qing Dynasty (1644-1911) implemented the closed-door policy which banned maritime trade. Its deep cause was the self-sufficient and self-reliant agriculture-oriented economy, the basic policy goal of which was to maintain a solid economic community on the basis of self-sufficiency rather than foreign trade. Therefore, every Chinese government implemented the policy of stressing agriculture and repressing business and stressing the ins and neglecting the outs so as to maintain a stable social order. Businessmen in China were assigned a lower social status, without any political power. Yongle, the third emperor of the Ming Dynasty, once decreed Cheng Ho to make six maritime expeditions to the West[12]. Chinese giant ships sailed across the Indian Ocean and along the coasts of East Africa, which was an unprecedented sailing feat in human history. However, when the official maritime expeditions were carried out in full swing, folk maritime businessmen were still forbidden by government to take part in any oversea trade activities. After the official maritime expedition was halted abruptly in 1435, the policy of no maritime commerce imposed by Ming government on folk maritime businessmen was implemented more rigorously. Nearly all Chinese sea ships were forced to retreat from the Indian Ocean. Apart from Chinese official ships which appeared occasionally in the part of the Pacific to the east of the Malacca Strait to welcome or see off envoys, folk sea ships continued to do smaller-scale maritime trade privately till the limited opening in 1567 (the first year of Longqing reign).

---

12   The seventh expedition occurred in the reign of Ming Emperor Xuan De (1426-1435). Note by the author.

In light of normal ways of maritime trade (such as in the Song and Yuan Dynasties), Chinese sea ships could carry a large amount of porcelain, silk and tea, which could be mass produced in China[13] and were in great demand by the West, to the Indian Ocean and the Red Sea, and then carried to the Mediterranean by Arabs to supply Asian and European countries. If history could have run in this normal way, had China not forsaken oceans of the whole world to western ventures[14], world history after the 15th century might have been different.

2.3. Rise of the Western Europe

2.3.1. The Dormant Western Europe Began to Germinate

Western European countries[15] near the coasts of the Atlantic in the west end of the intercontinental road on the Eurasian continent, which had a great advantage in geographical position. The western expedition by the Mongols in the 13th century and the westward expansion by the Ottoman Empire in the 16th century both failed to go beyond 16 degrees east longitude. Countries in Western and Northern Europe far to the west of this "safety line" were never invaded. Technological advancement accumulated for centuries since the medieval period and the technological inventions and innovations received from the Eastern regions enabled the late medieval Western and Northern Europe to rehabilitate, multiply, and develop. Due to historical reasons, cultural exchange in Western and Northern Europe seemed to be in a state of "only-in-no-out", "more-in-less-out" or "take-ism" for several centuries. They "took" Chinese inventions and enjoyed silently the nutrition of eastern civilizations and wisdoms. Many advanced cultures and technologies from east represented by the three inventions were introduced without any reserve and even the early renaissance thoughts from Italy in Southern Europe were rapidly brought in with the sudden growth of printing industry in Western and Northern Europe, which played an important enlightening role. Countries in East Asia became increasingly secluded because of the confine from the closed-door policy and closed-mindedness, totally unaware of the burgeoning Northern Europe. Although the Ottoman Empire was near to Northern Europe geographically, the Turkish people blinded by their religious prejudices foolishly thought that Christians in Western and Northern Europe were as useless and worthless as those in the rest of Europe and thus had no interest to get to know them. Muslim scholars gained nothing out of their geographical proximity, completely ignorant of the epoch-making achievements in astronomy by prominent Christian scholars like

---

13   As early as the Song and Yuan dynasties, it seemed that China was capable of producing a large amount of porcelain so long as it could be shipped to and sold in overseas markets. Note by the author.
14   Stavrianos, L. S. *The World since 1500: A Global History*. Prentice Hall, 1999. Trans. Xiangying Wu and Chimin Liang. Vol. 2. Beijing: Peking University Press, 2006: 297.
15   Ancient historians considered countries north of the Pyrenees as Northern European nations, which are commonly referred to as Western European nations. Note by the author.

Copernicus, Kepler, and Galileo. The east and middle part on the intercontinental road had formed a "blood clot" in their knowledge of the extraordinary
changes in the west end. On the contrary, countries in Western and Northern
Europe had an increasing interest in China (and India) in the east end on the
intercontinental road. They felt dejected for the abrupt collapse of the non-
Muslim Mongolian Empire, taking it as a loss of a potential ally in their fight
against Muslims. They planned to get in direct touch with China in East Asia
but were impeded in the western end of Suez in the Red Sea, failing to reach
even the Black Sea, the Persian Gulf and the Indian Ocean.

After the Arabs had been squeezed out from the eastern Mediterranean and
had to retreated to the Red Sea and the Persian Gulf, and especially after Chinese
huge fleet of ships had withdrawn from the Indian Ocean in the 1430s, Arab
businessmen and Indian Muslim businessmen controlled again the sea route
across the Indian Ocean and the business road which connected the Persian
Gulf with the coastal East Africa. However, these Muslim businessmen conducted business on a small scale, lacked a sense of solidarity, and even could
not organize a relatively large fleet of hips so that they failed always to recover
a sizable maritime trade in the eastern Mediterranean and the Black Sea and obtain powerful support of their maritime trade from the three Muslim empires for
several centuries. The Ottoman Empire, the Safavid Empire (Persia), and the
Moghul Empire (India) were all land empires which turned their backs to the
sea and faced the land to Central Asia and Eastern Europe, having totally lost
the slight maritime tradition in the era of the Arab empire. They ignored world
maritime trade roughly to the same extent as the Ming and Qing dynasties in
East Asia of the same period. However, the Western European countries near
the sea stood out of the undeveloped area in Europe for 1,000 years (500-1500),
flourished, and were increasingly concerned with maritime trade. However, it
was not Western European countries that had marched eastward from the east
coast of the Atlantic in the 15th and 16th centuries but Portugal and Spain in the
Southwestern Europe. The Spanish firmly believed that the earth was round
which facilitated their eastward and westward explorations. To head east, the
Portuguese did not hesitate to sail southward round the Cape of Good Hope
in the southern end of African Continent for thousands of kilometers to the
Indian Ocean. At roughly the same time, the Ottoman Turks headed westward
by land. The Portuguese fleet of ships moved onward after rounding the Cape
of Good Hope while the Turkish horsemen were impeded by the city of Vienna.
The Turkish expansion was still the medieval enlargement of territories and
increase in tributes with hardly any commercial motives. The territories newly
expanded in Europe by the Ottoman Empire were the same as those broader
ones in Asia, which lacked economic foundations and were merely military and
administration alliances, not in essence unlike the ancient Cyrus Empire and
Alexandrian Empire. However, the Portuguese were obviously motivated by
commerce in the new era in their march into India.

2.3.2. The Rise of Portugal

The rising Portugal near the coast of the Atlantic was a small country with a maritime tradition in the 15ᵗʰ century. After the Portuguese entered the Indian Ocean at the turn of the 15ᵗʰ century, they established a commercial colonial empire. Portugal had a population of less than 1.5 million which was not even sufficient to be allocated in their emigration into Brazil in South America. In the beginning of the 16ᵗʰ century, it rounded for many times the Cape of Good Hope to enter the Indian Ocean. Aside from sale and purchase, they basically used forces to set up trading posts and monopolistic business system to force the purchase of spices. What the Portuguese businessmen brought to the east were the ridiculous and inferior European commodities, which were ignored and mocked at ports on the west coast of India, while what they purchased were the east spices, which had been out of stock for years or exorbitantly expensive because of the impediment of the land route and the blocking of the eastern Mediterranean by the Ottoman fleet of ships. Portuguese businessmen were ecstatic in such great business opportunities when they saw at Indian ports mountainous piles of various east spices, whose prices were less than 5 percent of those in the Mediterranean by Italians.

Aside from the new course around the Cape of Good Hope which had written records, the "new sea routes" discovered by Portugal in the end of the 15ᵗʰ century which stretched from the north of Mozambique along the seashore of East Africa and through seaports of the Red Sea to reach the Persian Gulf and cross the Indian Ocean were the traditional business sea routes run for thousands of years by the Arabs, Persians and Indians, among which the course over the Indian Ocean from the southwestern ports in India to those in East Africa was successfully opened up for the first time by Cheng Ho's fleet from China (1414)[16]. These newly arrived Portuguese in Europe were anxious to "control" Sofala in East Africa when they first arrived there. The words by a Portuguese captain articulated such a desire: "From the Cape of Good Hope onwards, we were unwilling to leave anything outside of our control; we were anxious to lay hands on everything....There was not a corner which we did not occupy or desire to have subject to ourselves"[17]. How did the Portuguese control the intercontinental road by sea? In terms of economic power, Portugal had never been strong, and their goods were despised by the Easterners. What they relied on was colonial violence.

Portuguese, in the first place, created new ships which were the most convenient to sail in the world, which enabled them to march on the ocean more smoothly than on the prairie, whose consecutive mileage could surpass

---

16   There are at least written records of the successful sailing of Cheng Ho's fleet. In view of archaeological discoveries along the coast of East Africa and the mastery of wind direction and ocean current by mariners in Song and Yuan China, boats of Song had successfully sailed across the Indian Ocean to reach the coast of East Africa. Note by the author.

17   Needham, Joseph. *Science and Civilization in China*. Vol. IV. Cambridge: Cambridge University Press, 1971: 534.

all previous transport vehicles: horses, camels, and even Cheng Ho's fleet. Portuguese advantage could partly account for the reasons why human beings could gradually decrease their use of prairies and deserts (as channels) not long after they had conquered the ocean so that the intercontinental road moved greatly southward. To meet the need of maritime explorations, Portugal under the sponsorship of Prince Henry developed caravels with two or three lateen triangular sails, which were easy to navigate and could sail against the wind even with an incline of 55 degrees. Portugal took the techniques to build caravels as a national secret. During the whole 15th century, Portuguese used caravels as their trump-card tool in maritime explorations, forestalled adventures into the unknown seashores and coasts, and gained rights of discovery. It was by means of these caravels that Bartolomeu Dias the Portuguese could round the Cape of Good Hope for the first time in 1488 and discovered the seashores of Brazil in 1500. Portuguese sea ships could not only sail against the wind but also had intense firepower on board. Chinese gunpowder improved by Europeans was applied in new cannons which could launch stones of 50 to 60 pounds, wreaking ships within the range of more than a hundred of yards away. In 1501, European ships achieved a crucial technological innovation: cannon windows were opened in the main deck (rather than the upper deck) of the actual ship, which greatly strengthened the firepower while maintaining the stability of the ship. When Vasco Da Gamma entered the Indian Ocean and near the seashores of Mozambique, he manifested his power by bombarding cities for three hours. Henceforth, when he reached every port in East Africa or India, he would also bombard, kidnap, or pillage recklessly not differently from pirates if the other party refused to do transactions in accordance with Portuguese devastating "business principles". In 1505, Francisco de Almeida led 22 ships and 2,500 navy soldiers entered the Indian Ocean for the third time. Because Sultan of Kilwa was not as submissive to Portuguese as Sheik of Mozambique, Almeida sent his troops to besiege the city and loot all the gold, silver and ambergris there. Sheik of Mombasa declined to acknowledge the suzerainty of Portugal, which led to the murder of 1513 and looting of 1,000 of his subjects. When the Portuguese left after the massacre, Sheik of Mombasa wrote to his counterpart of Malindi to inform him of this calamity:

56

May God protect you Sayyid Ali. I have to inform you that we have been visited by a mighty ruler who has brought fire and destruction amongst us. He raged in our town with such might and terror that no one, neither man nor woman, neither the old nor the young, nor even the children, however small, was spared to live. His wrath was to be escaped only by flight. The stench from the corpses is so overpowering that I dare not enter the town, and I cannot begin to give you an idea of the immense amount of booty which they took from the town. Pray hearken to the news of these sad events, that you may yourself be preserved.[18]

18 Strandes, Justus. *The Portuguese Period in East Africa*. Trans. Jean F. Wallwork. Ed. J. S. Kickman. Nairobi: East African Literature Bureau, 1968: 73.

Manuel of Portugal sent Almeida to the east in order to implement the plan of monopolizing all spice trade and controlling the east-west sea route in the Indian Ocean. The first step was to occupy the city-states in East Africa to establish posts (like Kilwa and Mombasa), control the sea route heading north to the Red Sea and the Indian Ocean; the second step was to occupy several ports on the western coast of India as colonial trading posts (like Calicut and Cochin), drive away Arab businessmen and control the sea route heading eastward through the Malacca Strait; the third step was to set up colonial trading posts at the mouth of the Red Sea (Socotra Archipelago and Aden) and in the Persian Gulf (the Strait of Hormuz) and prevent the transport of spices from the Red Sea to Egypt so as to cut off supplies of spices in Venice and manipulate spices' price in Europe. The Portuguese court ordained to monopolize trade of major commodities in Asia (passed the Indian Decree), including pepper, ginger, cinnamon, cloves, nutmeg, lac, silk and natural borax. Without the permission of the Portuguese court, Christians, Muslims, Indians or any other people were not allowed to have a part in the trade of these commodities. As to those who dared to encroach on the trade of these commodities, Portuguese king decreed to mount attack against them, cause as severe loss as possible, try very best to capture their merchant ships, extort goods and properties from the Moors (Muslims), bring pilots, captains, and major merchants to Portugal and release other captured under the condition of ransom. The second important decree issued by King Manuel was to mount destructive attack against the Egyptian Mamluks' fleets of merchant ships and its trade center in India, Calicut, so as to turn the Eurasian trading route in the Red Sea and the Persian Gulf around to the sea route round the Cape of Good Hope.

Da Gamma sailed in 1502 for the second time to Indian and encountered the passenger ship Merry with more than 400 pilgrimages on board back to Calicut. Da Gamma ordered to bombard the ship with cannons, which caused the death of all the passengers. In 1509, Almeida led the Portuguese fleet to fight fiercely with the combined fleet of India and Egypt at Diu. The Portuguese fleet inflicted heavy loss (with a casualty of 3,000 soldiers) on the Indian-Egyptian combined fleet by means of their intense gunfire. Henceforth, the supremacy in the Indian Ocean west of Ceylon was in the hands of the Portuguese. According to the lowest estimate, the commodities brought back to Portugal were worth 8 times those transported abroad calculated in Portuguese currency. The multi-functional and durable pepper became the best target of speculation in European market. By 1506, gold from West Africa and pepper and spices from Asia made up for more than one half of revenues of the Portuguese court. Portugal succeeded for the moment in increasing national wealth by means of its military power or colonial violence.

Portugal pressed onward into the Malacca Strait to control the sea route in the West Indian Ocean and the Pacific also by means of its colonial violence. Portuguese king appointed Afonso de Albuquerque as Eastern Governor to carry out this task. Albuquerque was very cruel in and flagitious of indiscriminate killing of citizens in occupied areas, killing off war prisoners and sacking properties. His conquest of Goa was a history of bloody violence that makes one's hair stand on end, which typically illustrated that commercial capital represented a system of robbery. Seen from the perspective of the eastern countries, their "buyers" of spices and pepper were not merchants but horrid naval power. Albuquerque employed extremely cruel means in the conquest of Goa (1510) and the Malacca Strait (1511) and controlled the sea route west of the Strait. Henceforth, Portugal reached out to China and then to Nagasaki of Japan in 1543.

Portugal's oriental empire straddled east to west over more than 140 degrees longitude (from Lisbon to Nagasaki). From Sofala on the coast of East Africa to Spice Islands of Dradi, Portugal established over 50 trading posts, forts, and settlements. Thus, Portugal set up three major intermediary markets: Malacca, Calicut, and Hormuz, plus a supplementary station in Aden. However, the number of persons stationed in the east had never surpassed 10, 000. Meanwhile, Portugal sailed westward over the Atlantic and established a colonial empire in Brazil of South America. There places were largely located south of the Tropic of Cancer and the Equator, which accounted for the historical reasons why countries classified in a geographical sense as "the South" were mostly underdeveloped.

Portuguese had never been able to cut off completely the east-west sea route controlled by the Arabs and the Indians effectively and suffered a severe loss of 300 ships in 8 years from 1522 to 1530. Although Portugal obtained enormous profits in their predatory business and increase the royal revenues, Portuguese commercial capital nevertheless declined. They had never succeeded in conquering Aden. Spices transported from the Red Sea to Alexandria in Egypt and then transferred to Europe in 1560 had reached the former level in 1488. In 1580, Portugal and Spain were united by marriage, the latter ruled the former. Spain's rivalry Holland seized the opportunity to round the Cape of Good Hope, entered the intercontinental route in the Indian Ocean and the Pacific, and drove Portuguese out of Ambon Island in 1605, out of Java of Jakarta in 1619, and out of Malacca in 1641. Portugal fell but its geographical expansion paved the way for the travel of European commercial capital over the whole world especially the Eurasian continent and dug the dun for "the rift between the North and the South".

2.3.3. Dutch Monopoly over Carrying Trade

Dutch commercial capital profited not only from the conflict between Habsburg Spain and European countries but also from trade in the New World without paying any great efforts in opening up the eastward or westward maritime commerce. Holland obtained many profits in carry trade, whose major profits lay not in the exportation of domestic products but the intermediary role in the exchange of productions among countries and regions backward both in commerce and economy. Although Holland had a strained political relation with Spain because of the "revolution", it had never broken up with Spain in terms of economy. Before it stretched to the East, it stretched to the West by way of Spain and set up carrying trade in American colonies across the Atlantic. Thus, the Dutch had virtually extended the west end of the intercontinental route to the other shore of the Atlantic.

The early activities of the Dutch after rounding the Cape of Good Hope in 1559 were to earn money both from trade and from capture of Portuguese ships. Dutch commercial capital carried the means of pillaging foreign merchant ships and their cargos to the acme. In the early 17th century (1622-1623), right after Dutch ships entered the Taiwan Strait they plundered flagrantly Chinese ships to and from the strait.[19]

Holland differed from Portugal in that the former was relatively developed in manufactured goods. Its agriculture (except grains) was on top of Europe in nursery, cows, and dye plantation. Its manual textile could compete with Britain. The most developed fishing (herring) industry contributed to the highly advanced shipbuilding industry. Low cost, high efficiency and mastery of the most advanced technologies were the reasons for Dutch dominance in world business in the 17th century. No countries possessed the mutual matching, closely connected and self-contained production system in agriculture and industry like that in Holland, which was made possible the chief production center in Western Europe. In 1670, it possessed a tonnage of sea ships three times that of Britain and over 500,000 tons of merchant fleet in 1700. Out of 20,000 ships in world maritime trade, Holland owned 15,000 to 16,000. The Dutch East India Company was established in 1602 not only to obtain more spices from East India than from Europe but also to avoid the inner strife between domestic companies and get united against foreign powers. The company was in great conflict with Portugal after it entered the Indian Ocean and the Pacific and decided to set up colonial rule by occupying all Spice Islands. Out of the same intention, the Dutch usurped Taiwan Island in 1624. Since the early 17th century, the Dutch successively occupied the islands and coastal areas held by Portuguese for over a century. In 1605, the Dutch drove the Portuguese from Ambon Island, and occupied Jakarta in 1641 and changed its name to Batavia, which became the east headquarter of the company. The commercial activities of the company were extended to India and Ceylon in South Asia, China and Japan in East Asia, and Persia and the Arabian Peninsula in West Asia. The east-west sea route in the 17th century was basically in the hands of the Dutch.

The Dutch manner of activities in the Indian Ocean and the Pacific (generally called as East India in the 17th century) was actually a repetition (or duplication) of that of Portugal with a larger scale and higher efficiency. The Dutch East India Company imposed cruel exploitations and physical (spices) tax on its occupied spice islands (now Maluku Islands of Indonesia). In 1696, the Dutch

19 Bontekoe, William Ysbrantsz. *Memorable Description of the East Indian Voyage: 1618-25*. London: Routledge, 1929. Trans. Nan Yao. Beijing: Zhonghua Book Company, 1982: 74-96.

introduced coffee from Yemen into Java and the company forced peasants to plant coffee, which was used to offset the tax or purchased by the company at a very low price. Peasants handed over 270 pounds of coffee with a pay less than the price for 14 pounds, inadequate to buy enough food to live on. In order to monopolize price, the company forced peasants to fall coffee trees whenever the price of coffee fell in European market (like that in the 1830s)[20] and to plant trees again when the price rose. The company purchased all cash crops at unified undercut prices, forbade peasants free sale, and did not hesitate to use violent means to oppose "contraband" trade. When the company found out peasants on the Banda Islands sold cardamom to merchants beyond the company, they killed almost all the inhabitants on the island. Peasants in many areas were in a dire condition so that they left the village where they had lived for generations and escaped into the high mountains and dense forests. Wherever Dutch metropolitan states went, the place would become desolate and sparse in population. There were still over 80,000 inhabitants in Banjuwangi province on Java Island in 1750 and only 8,000 in 1811. Accordingly, the profit of the Dutch East India Company rose from 100 percent to 200 to 300 percent from 1,600 to 1,600.

The Dutch was engaged in carrying trade by means of their advantage in fleets of ships composed of "freighters", second to none in world maritime trade of the time in their shipment, navigation capacity, and low cost of transport. In 1634, the transportation expense of Dutch ships was the lowest in Western Europe, only amounting to one third or half of that of Britain and France. In the first half of the 17th century, commodities from the East the Dutch East India Company imported mainly composed of such luxuries as spices, pepper, textiles (silk), with a respective proportion of 17.6 percent, 56.4 percent, and 16.1 percent in the total value of import from 1619 to 1621. By the end of the 17th century (1698-1700), the proportions of tea and coffee rose to 4.3 percent, textile to 54.7 percent, and other commodities (like porcelain) to 18.1 percent.[21] Spices and pepper were mostly condiments, which belonged to supplementary food materials, so that it was impossible for them to have a big increase. By the 17th century, European merchants had seized the major part of trade in Asian pepper and spices. The Dutch East India Company strived to control the sales volume of spices, 300,000 pounds of nutmeg, 300,000 pounds of cloves, and the extra would be destroyed, so as to monopolize the market and gain monopoly profits (generally at least 10 times the purchase price). The company frequently purchased spices from East India at a price of 30 cents a pound and sold at 4 Dutch guilders in Holland with a profit of 1,200 percent. However, pepper was different from spices, hard to be monopolized, and inclined to become a staple commodity, which was increasingly demanded by European market. In 1722, the Dutch East India Company imported 9,050

20   Furber, H. *Rival Empires of Trade in the Orient 1600-1800*. Minneapolis: University of Minnesota Press, 1976: 255.
21   Chen, Yong. *Commodity Economy and the Dutch Modernization*. Wuhan: Wuhan University Press, 1990: 112-119.

thousand pounds of pepper. Textile was more popular, Chinese raw silk and Bengal and Persian raw silk were carried by Dutch merchant ships to Europe, which European merchants vied to purchase. The gross profit from the raw silk carried from China was normally over 300 percent, and that of the low-end cotton fabric from India over 400 percent. From 1618 to 1621, the company imported 37,395 pieces of Asian cotton cloth with an annual average of 12,000 pieces. But the import was increased at a fast speed to reach an annual average of 224,000 pieces from 1684 to 1689 while the annual average import of raw silk was maintained around 150,000 pounds.[22] It is noteworthy that the goods carried by Dutch fleet of ships by the end of the 17th century were mainly no longer luxuries (spices decreased from 17.6 percent to 11.7 percent) but popular daily necessities: textile, condiments, and drink (tea and coffee), whose import value reached 72.5 percent. It was more noteworthy that, aside from spices which still occupied the position of monopolized good because its place of production was monopolized, other products especially textile with the greatest demand had become competitive commodities. The Dutch large cargo vessels carried goods from East India and West India (see below) rather than those produced in Holland to every destination. Industries, even the most prosperous shipbuilding industry, driven in Holland were only supplementary for maritime business and made very little contribution to national wealth. Holland was a typical "the ruling trading nation"[23]. The money earned by East India Company made a huge contribution to the increase in its national wealth. The biggest net income was obtained from colonies. Because of the enormous profit, the share value of East India Company rose successively five years after its establishment: up to 380 guilders 50 years later and 600 guilders in the 18th century. The average dividend was 21 percent in the 170 years of the company. The dividend per share paid by the company was no less than 107,665 guilders in 70 years. Each Dutch family could live a comfortable life if they possessed a few shares of stock worthy of 3,000 guilders for each share because if they sold one share, they normally could get 18,000 guilders.[24] Holland was the first northern country to gain enormous profit from "the South" (Asia).

2.3.4. Asia Shed Much Economic Light on Europe

British ships sailed around the Cape of Good Hope towards the Indian Ocean almost at the same time as Holland. Although, Britain had established East India Company (1600) two years earlier than Holland, the latter inherited Portuguese experience and had a stronger colonial power. Not as abundant in capital as Holland, British East India Company focused its business on Indian Subcontinent and mainly purchased Indian textile. In those fields

---

22   Chen, Yong. *Commodity Economy and the Dutch Modernization*. Wuhan: Wuhan University Press, 1990: 112-119.
23   Marx, Karl, and Fredrick Engels. *Collected Works*. Vol. 37. New York: International Publishers, 1998: 331.
24   Van Loon, Hendrik Willem. *The Fall of the Dutch Republic*. Houghton Mifflin Co., 1913. Trans. Ziyi Zhu. Beijing: Beijing Publishing House, 2001: 48.

not competitive with Holland, Britain resorted to state machine and stipulated in the 22nd article of Maritime Law in 1655: all foreign importing goods into Britain's domestic market shall be restricted. Nevertheless, Holland was much more powerful than Britain in carrying trade in the East.

By the 19th century, textile industry had become British trump-card industry after a long period. The seeds of British cotton-textile industry "were in fact brought to England in the ships of the East India Company"[25]. Before the 15th century, England mainly exported wool or semi-finished coarse wool cloth to Flanders across the channel (now the Belgian coast) for processing, cropping and dyeing. After the 15th century, Britain evolved from exporting wool to weaving coarse wool cloth. However, British wool cloth industry was run in the capitalist manner nearly since the beginning, increasing rather quickly in output and exporting 120,000 pieces in 1547[26]. But its sale in East market was not very large because Chinese people were accustomed to wear homespun cotton cloth or silk while India was a tropical country not fit for woolen clothes. Black slaves working in American plantations and mines had a great demand for coarse cotton cloth, especially Indian cotton cloth. Portugal, Holland and Britain all purchased a large quantity of cotton cloth from India. In 1698, Britain imported 180,000 pounds of various cotton cloth from Asia (mainly India), and Holland around 21,400 pounds. Exquisite cotton textiles were allowed to be imported into Britain before 1700, after which they were forbidden. Many other Indian industrial products shipped to Britain were mainly carried to Americas for sale. In the 17th century, Britain set up a dozen trading houses along the east and west coasts of India mainly for the purchase of local cotton cloth and other industrial products rather than the sale of British goods. Take British trade in Bengal as an example, Britain had an enormous demand for Bengal fine cotton cloth especially twist from Dacca, which became a textile town with a population of 150,000. Textile workers in Bengal increased up to a million. Not only Britain but also the whole Europe relied on Indian cotton textiles—muslin, calico, and grey cloth—for centuries and had to use American silver or spices carried from Southeast Asia to exchange them. Although Britain had a great demand for Asian products, Asia need hardly any European products, which caused British government to make rigid regulations that British products should account for one tenth of the total export value of East India Company. It was very hard for East India Company to achieve this goal. Even so, it was difficult to find a market for British export goods. Nine tenths of European export to Asia had to be precious metals (gold and silver).

In the 17th and 18th centuries, Europe and America by way of Europe had a huge demand for Asian commodities. The major commodities frequently exchanged on the intercontinental land route and sea route amounted to tens

25   Mantoux, Paul. *The Industrial Revolution in the Eighteenth Century: An Outline of the Beginning of the Modern Factory System in England*. Trans. Marjorie Vernon. New York: Routledge, 2005: 104..
26   Morton, A. L. *A People's History of England*. London: Lawrence and Wishart Ltd., 1951: 45.

or hundreds of kinds. Before Europe was qualified to take part in this prosperous market mentioned above, the market on the route had run for a dozen centuries. After the 7th century when the land route especially the sea route became unimpeded, exchanges among Asia regions and between Asia and the Mediterranean Africa and the Black Sea Europe were more frequent, the goods exchanged had a wider variety and larger quantity, and the nature of commodities had changed from mainly luxuries to daily necessities with a great demand. When Atlantic countries (Portugal, Spain, Britain, Holland, and France) entered this market with abundant American silver, they faced such a world market, from which they entered every native market—the native markets of China and India even more amazed Western Europeans. In 1669, a European (Domingo de Navarrete) said "that there are more Vessels in China than in all the rest of the known World. This will seem incredible to many Europeans"[27].

In the eighteenth century, a French Father (Father Du Halde), wrote that in China: "the particular riches of every province, and the ability of transporting merchandise by means of rivers and canals, have rendered the empire always very flourishing. The trade carried on within China is so great, that al of Europe is not to be compared therewith."[28]

In fact, Asian inland economy and transcontinental overland caravan trade were to maritime trade. Only by in-depth analysis of the entire trade could we have a glimpse of the grand panorama of Asian business market.

More and more Asian commodities in the 18th century, especially those from China and India, were transported through the intercontinental route to Western Europe and Americas. Europe used silver produced in Americas to pay Asia so as to make up for the large trade deficit. In the 18th century, there were roughly 26,000 tons of silver imported into Asia, which did not cause obvious inflation in Asia but stimulated production in circulation, expanded market, and multiplied population. European (mainly British, Dutch, and French) vessels transported and sold Porcelain and silk from China, cotton cloth from India, and raw silk from Persia among Asian countries, and shipped a large quantity of these traditional oriental commodities (plus tea) to Europe by rounding the Cape of Good Hope and the Red Sea, and carried a part to Americas. The output of these well-sold commodities in the 18th century China and India was stunning to Europeans. Chinese commodity grains circulated over a long distance was no less than 35 million dans (a unit of dry measure for grain, equivalent to 1 hectoliter), and 310 million pieces of cloth were sold in market (worth 95.44 million taels of silver)[29]. In Nanjing alone, the ceramic factories produced a million pieces of exquisite porcelain every year, not to mention places of larger

---

27   Ronan, Colin. *The Shorter Science and Civilization in China, An Abridgement of Joseph Needham's Original Text*. Vol. 3. Cambridge: Cambridge University Press, 1986: 89.
28   Qtd. in Frank, Andre Gunder. *ReOrient: Global Economy in the Asian Age*. Berkeley: University of California Press, 1998: 10.
29   Dai, Yi. *China and the World in the Eighteenth Century*. Introductory Volume. Shenyang: Liaohai Publishing House, 1999: 29.

production like Jingdezhen. A lot of the porcelain was specifically produced for Europe and Islamic countries (which could be detected from the European dynastic motifs and Muslim patterns). The seven major commodities from China were grains, cotton, cloth, silk, satin, tea, and salt, whose circulation value was 0.35 billion ounce of silver[30]. British East India Company purchased annually from China tea worthy of 4 million ounce of silver. China exported 6,000 load of raw silk each year. Kasimbazar, a medium-sized city in Bengal, turned out over 2 million pounds of silk a year while Gujarat in the west produced 3 million pieces of cotton cloth a year. By way of comparison, Leiden, the largest textile city in Holland, produced less than 100,000 pieces of cloth a year.[31] The South and the North in the 18th century were so widely different in their output value of industrial products.

In the 16th century, the gap of the demand for the other's commodities between Asia and Europe was increasingly widened. Europe needed a large quantity of Asian goods but could not produce goods demanded greatly by Asia. Taking China as an example, silk, homespun cloth and porcelain had been sold well. Since the 18th century, tea was added to the list of popular commodities. The surge in the population of British working class who had changed their dietary habit needed a large amount of Chinese black tea as supplementary drink for their meals so that East India Company had to import tea worthy of 4 million ounces of silver from China per year. The commodities which Britain could provide China were mainly woolens, metal (lead) and cotton resold from India, the total export value of which could not equal that of tea. In order to balance foreign trade, British merchants had to ship a large quantity of silver to China per year. Chang Lai, Governor of Fujian Province, reported to Emperor Yongzheng that "foreign vessels sailed with the wind and arrived in Guangdong in May or June with hardly any goods but foreign silver"[32]. In India, the British merchants who were engaged in carrying trade had to purchase Indian cotton with silver and transported to China for sale. Britain used silver to make up for trade deficit with India as well.

The world population in the year 1750 was about 731 to 749 million, among which about 500 million was in Asia, and 140 million in Europe. And, according to the estimates by Fernand Braudel (quote Paul Bairoch) in the year 1750, world's total GDP was 155 billion US dollars (calculated by currency value of US dollar in the year the 1960), of which 120 billion or 77 percent was in Asia and only 35 billion in Europe and Americas (including Russia and Japan). Whereas, Bairoch claimed that out of the total world GDP of 148 billion dollars, 112 billion or 76 percent was in "underdeveloped countries" in now South (including Latin America) and the remaining 35 billion or 24 percent was in now "developed countries". In 1750, Asia's share of world population was 66 percent while its total output was 80% (including Japan), which meant Asia

30   Xu, Dixin, and Chengming Wu. *Development History of Chinese Capitalism*. Vol. 1. Beijing: People's Publishing House, 1985: 284.
31   Park, Jeffrey. *The Times Illustrated History of the World*. New York, 1995: 206.
32   "Chang Lai's Memorial to the Throne". *Collection of Documents*. 17th Collection.

with two thirds of world population produced four fifths of world commodities.[33] By 1750, Asian average productivity was higher than that of European. Bairoch also discovered that life standard in Europe was lower than that in the rest of the world in 1750. He estimates that per capita GNP for China in 1800 was 228 dollars, higher than that he estimated for various years in Britain and France, which range from 150 to 200 dollars. In 1959, Ho Ping-ti suggests in Studies on the Population of China, 1368-1953 that the living standard in the 18th century in China was rising and peasant income was not lower than in France and certainly higher than in Prussia[34], which was in accordance with Adam Smith, who observed in 1776 in An Inquiry into the Nature and Causes of the Wealth of Nations that "China has been long one of the richest" countries in the world and now (in 1776) China is a much richer country than any part of Europe[35]. We consider these estimates to be near truth.

We can see, hence, it was Asian continent which could really provide a large amount of daily necessities (including food) by way of east-east Asian-European route or west-east European-Asian route. For centuries, Britain, Holland and France and previous Portugal and Spain used precious metals produced in America to exchange goods with Asia. It was for this reason that a (major) part of wealth flowing into Europe from Asia by way of the intercontinental route from the 16th to the 18th century was obtained not by trade but by plunder (including direct extortion) and then carried to Europe. Such primitive accumulation without payment of one shilling in advance was first carried out on a large scale in Africa and Americas.

2.4. A Brutal Dayspring of the North-South Relationship

2.4.1. Africa Became the Site of Commercial Hunting of the Blacks for Slavery

Between the Mediterranean North Africa and tropical Africa lies the vast Sahara Desert of 77.7 million square kilometers. There were only several camel business roads stretching over thousands of miles which connected the North and the South in economy, culture, religion, and politics. However, in the few centuries when the Mediterranean was scarcest in and thus most needed gold, bags of gold sands were carried from mines in the west of tropical Africa (West Sudan) by camel caravans to be supplied timely to gold markets in North Africa and Europe. Historians believe that it was the shining gold sand which was cast into gold coins in every Italian city-state: Genovino (in Genoa), Ducat

33   Frank, Andre Gunder. ReOrient: Global Economy in the Asian Age. Berkeley: University of California Press, 1998: 240.
34   Ho, Pong-ti. Studies on the Population of China, 1368-1953. Cambridge, Mass.: Harvard University Press, 1959: 213-263.
35   Smith, Adam. An Inquiry into the Nature and Causes of the Wealth of Nations. New York: Modern Library, 1964: 100. Trans. Dali Guo and Yanan Wang. Vol. 1. Beijing: The Commercial Press, 1983. 65.

(in Florence), and Florin (in Venice). In 1515, one of the motives for Portugal to sent troops to occupy Ceuta in North Africa (the first modern colony) was the attempt to control the business route in North Africa so as to block the northward transport of gold in West Africa (West Sudan). In 1518 under the scheme of Prince Henry, Portuguese fleet of merchant ships began to undertake southward expeditions along the northwest coast of Africa, which was obviously aimed to discover and occupy the sources of gold sands and ingots in West Africa. In their southward expedition which lasted for dozens of years, Portuguese did not discover any considerable gold deposits but found commercial opportunities in their numerous kidnapping of the blacks along the coast of West Africa: the blacks looted could be sold as slaves in Lisbon at a high price. This was the beginning of Portuguese sin in their trafficking of African black slaves. After 1455, the black slaves looted and shipped by Portugal were up to 927 per year. Since the trafficking of black slaves on a large scale, slave trade became an important form of colonialism practiced by Europe in Africa for four centuries. Black slaves were sold well in European market and became a hard-to-get commodity in Spain and Italy. Portuguese first used black slaves in sugarcane plantations on all Atlantic islands. Sugarcane introduced into Europe from the Southeast Asia by the Arabs failed to be planted on a large scale due to its high consumption of soil fertility and a lack of labor forces. When such Atlantic islands as Madeira (measuring 813 square kilometers), Azores (2,300 square kilometers) and Canary (7,273 square kilometers) were discovered, their fertile soil was fit to grow sugarcane and sugarcane industry developed well. But the lack of a large number of strong labor forces limited large-area plantation. Portugal used black slaves first on Madeira and Azores and succeeded in gaining high profits. The use of African black slaves in sugarcane plantation in the 15th century exerted a profound impact on modern world economy and the later formation of the North-South relationship. In order to obtain a large number of slaves, Portuguese began to purchase from African merchants slaves with "commercial means" and established a trading post in Arguin Island in 1455, which initiated the system of purchasing slaves on the spot.

John II of Portugal sent explorers after 1481 to go from Elmina Castle on the Gold Coast (now Ghana) deep into the inland and discovered rather large gold mines. Christopher Columbus, who was still working for the Portuguese Royal Family had once reached the Gold Coast. Because gold mining needed a lot of labor forces, John II sent vessels southward to look for new areas to kidnap slaves. In 1482, Portuguese arrived at the mouth of Congo River and the Angolan coast in 1484, and discovered an offshore black kingdom with a dense population. At the moment (in the 1480s), Portuguese had not set out to expand slave trade networks in Congo and Angola south of the Equator because the slaves provided by Africa north of the Equator were adequate to supply the demand for slaves by plantations in the Mediterranean and on the Atlantic islands. The fledgling capitalist plantation system grafted on slavery established on the east shore of the Atlantic by Portuguese was still in a poised stage.

Columbus who turned to serve Spanish King discovered the New World in 1492. He did not know at the time that what he discovered was the American new continent with an area of 42.17 million square kilometers, let alone that he had paved the way for the westward leapfrog extension of the intercontinental route on the Eurasian continent. However, he had made the history. The subsequent swarm of metropolitan states from Spain, Portugal, Holland, France and Britain finished their occupation (including the nominal "settlements" with stunning areas) of this vast continent from south to north in less than two centuries. The system of plantation and mines first established by Portuguese were taken over and "commercially" reformed by the French, the Dutch, and the British and flourished everywhere in the north and south of the American continent. American metropolitan states, including plantation owners, mine owners, and merchants, had a great demand for labor forces. It was again the Portuguese who first transported African slaves in Portugal to Brazil to meet the urgent demand. In 1537, slaves waiting to be transported in Lisbon slave market were up to over 10,000. But soon the supply of black slaves on the coast of the Gulf of Guinea fell short of the demand. Portuguese therefore occupied Angola. Congo and Anglo with dense populations gradually became the major supplying places of slaves. Portuguese manifested and maintained their monopoly for over a hundred years by means of contract system and issuing trading license (Asiento), selling 926,900 slaves[36]. The striking feature of Portuguese black slave trade was that Portugal used or employed people of mixed race (Portuguese-black) to capture slaves in the deep inland.

Employing the same strategies in the Atlantic as those in the Indian Ocean, the Dutch seized the opportunity of the union between the Portuguese royal family and that of Spain to recklessly snatch Portuguese slave purchasing stations in the Gulf of Guinea in West Africa in the name of attacking Spain, its rivalry, and loot 500 Spanish vessels and destroyed its sea supremacy in the Caribbean. Following the example of the Portuguese to hold on to slave trade as the most crucial strategy, the Dutch established permanent settlements on shore, set up over 40 factories, and deployed 368 soldiers. The Dutch sailed back and forth in the Atlantic to transport slaves by means of their colossal conveyance force which shared three fourths of the total world tonnage of merchant ships, which forced Spain who refused to recognize the "independence" of Holland to negotiate purchase of slaves with Dutch slave traders. The Dutch West India Company (set up in 1623) had become the major source of supplying Americas African slaves. In the latter half of the 17th century alone, it exported over 100,000 slaves from Africa. In the early 18th century, its value of slave trade was on the top of the world.

36   Carrera, Antonio. "Research on Slave Trade in Portugal." In *Slave Trade in Africa from 1500 to 1900*. UNSCO. Trans. Nian Li, et al. Beijing: China Translation and Publishing House, 1984: 254.

Britain, which started its slave trade in Africa much later than Portugal and Holland but surpassed the latter, rose to the first in the mid-18th century in the total volume of slave trade and became the largest trader in African black slaves. Britain stepped in slave trade with "Sunday Punches". It passed Navigation Acts (1650) and waged three wars with Holland (1652-1654, 1665-1667, and 1672-1674), which precluded the Dutch from having a hand in trade in British and French colonies and supplying slaves for British and French plantations in the Caribbean. For dozens of years, the British and French slave trade had been on a small scale, which could not meet the demand for slaves by in their plantations. Thus, Britain and France followed the example of Holland to establish large exclusive companies: Britain set up in 1660 Company of Royal Adventurers Trading to Africa, France set up in 1640 French West India Company, Britain set up a larger Royal African Company, fighting deadly with Holland in the supplying places of slaves in West Africa. The large Royal African Company shipped 116,000 slaves out of Africa from 1673 to 1711 and carried 90,768 slaves to the American coast with a death rate of 27.33 percent. In 1712, Britain extorted at the Peace of Utrecht from the Spaniards the privilege of carrying on the slave trade in Africa and Spanish Americas by the Asiento Treaty. The rate of profit was as high as 600 percent or even 1,000 percent. Private businesses rushed in, attempted to break the monopoly of large companies, and were more efficient in slave trade than monopolistic large companies. The ban existed in name only and slave trade undertaken by

private merchants ran rampant. In 1668, the British Parliament decided to officially open up slave trade to private merchants. Henceforth, the bloody trade in selling human flesh was confirmed as a justified privilege of the British. Slave trade of Britain had an unprecedented development. Thereafter, the British powerful fleet of slave ships sailed thousands of miles in the Atlantic, followed frequently by packs of sharks waiting for the dead bodies thrown into sea of slaves with a high death rate. From 1698 to 1707 after the opening up, there were 160,950 slaves shipped from Bristol alone with an average of 17, 883. In 1771, there were up to 190 slave ships which carried 47,000 slaves. It might be difficult to get to know the exact number of black slaves shipped away from Africa ports in the 4 centuries of Atlantic slave trade[37]. Two examples will suffice to for us see how much profit and income African black slaves provided to Britain: slave trade brought an annual income of 300,000 pounds to Liverpool in the 18th century. British Prime Minister Pitt the Younger estimated in 1798 that income from slave plantations run by the British in West India was 4 million pounds per year[38]. The economic significance of slave trade lay in "its methods of primitive accumulation"[39]. The chamber of commerce in Nantes, a slave trade city in France, admitted that African commerce as the source of

---

37 For detailed figures, see Zheng, Jiaxin. *The History of Colonialism: Africa*. Beijing: Peking University Press, 2000: 189.
38 Rose, J. H. *William Pitt and the Great War*. London: G. Bell and Sons, 1911: 370.
39 Marx, Karl, and Fredrick Engels. *Collected Works*. Vol. 35. New York: International Publishers, 1996: 705.

French national wealth was the most profitable for France. Thousands of Sub-Saharan (south of around 15 degrees north latitude) strong labor forces were shipped from Africa to America to work as slaves, the hunting and selling of which had caused eternal hatred and endless wars among tribes and exerted a negative influence and impact on African society, economy, politics, culture and psychology. "The South" was taken as tributes on alter of colonialism to the development of "Northern" capitalism and the Sub-Saharan Africa was the first sacrifice in the South.

2.4.2. Latin America: the Origin of the Unequal North-South Relationship

The practical meaning of Columbus's geographical exploration voyage and discovery in 1492 lies in that, his historical discovery connected the farthest west point (the east coast of Atlantic Ocean) of the intercontinental route in the Eurasian continent to the American Continent, which was later further extended likewise across the Pacific in 1512 by Ferdinand Magellan (Fernando de Magallanes) from the American Continent to the Philippines (just about 100 miles far from Taiwan of China across the Bashi Channel) which lies in the farthest east of the Eurasian Continent. Hereto, the final outcome of the potential the momentum accumulated by intercontinental route with endless branches for thousands of years in its continuous westward expansion was that it finally rounded the earth and came a full circle to East Asia in its continuous westward extension in the 16th century. Since 1565, Great Galleon Trade of Spain sailed off across the Pacific from Akapulco in Mexico to Manila in in the Philippines, which upgraded the intercontinental route on the Eurasian Continent to be a worldly global great channel and illustrated the integrity of world economic (system)[40].

The "discovery" of America in the end of the 15th century and the shaping of it into a subordinate economic entity was an extremely ominous beginning of the North-South relationship. America was vast in area and sparse in population, there was a scarcity of labor forces because the majority of native Indians had been exterminated, exhausted to death in mines, or killed by epidemics brought by Europeans in the early period of conquest by European metropolitan states and there were not yet many European immigrants. Aside from silver and gold, the New World could not provide few goods for the Old World and therefore was utilized to serve Europe in the very beginning. It helped Europe to solve the problem of serious imbalance in foreign trade with Asia because Europe needed Asian commodities could not exchange their own commodities but precious metals (silver and gold) with Asia. Europe itself was destitute of precious metals and thus needed America rich in mineral resources to produce adequate precious metals. Therefore, labor-consuming silver mining became the largest "industry" in America. The early "primitive industrialization" in Europe needed the New World to produce a large amount of raw materials like sugar,

---

40   A concept proposed by Andre Gunder Frank in *ReOrient: Global Economy in the Asian Age*. Note by the author.

cotton, tobacco, and coffee. Therefore, slavery plantations came into being all over the Americas and in the Caribbean, which provided the Old World many products. Such a production system subordinate to Europe kept Latin America despite its large area in underdevelopment and unequal economic relations with Europe, which was the origin of the unequal North-South relationship.

Spain (including Portuguese Brazil) occupied most America, which not only covered the whole South America but also stretched northward from Central America across the Mexican Gulf to North America at 48 degrees north latitude. Britain, France, and Holland mainly occupied the Caribbean the east coastal areas in North America. Potosi mine, a place of silver production in Peru, and silver mines in the north of Mexico were nearly all in Spanish colonies. The Portuguese used Indian serfs (mita system), black slaves and "free" labors for silver mining. The annual output of silver was 42,000 tons in the 17th century and 52,000 tons in the next century.

The Portuguese brought slaves from the Gulf of Guinea and Angola in Africa to Brazil, established sugar cane plantations around Pernambuco along the coasts of Brazil, and succeeded in producing sugar, which was expanded to include cocoa, tobacco and cotton. Slave labor was extended from plantation to the newly discovered gold mines and manufacturing industry in Brazil. Black slaves irrigated Brazil with sweat and blood, which turned the latter into the largest place of sugar production.

The Dutch and the British followed the Portuguese plantations in Brazil to use slaves to build up plantations: the use of organized slaves in labor-intensive production of sugar, cotton or tobacco on a large scale could greatly decrease the cost and gain huger profits than individual farmers, adequate to make up for the increased production cost due to the low efficiency of slave labor. Provided that the free labor was scarce (because of the vast field, free labor was easy to "evaporate" after landing the Continent) and new fertile field and slaves supplies were constantly obtained (Atlantic slave trade could provide sufficient slave "supplies", slavery would be full of vitality. Therefore, in the countless plantations on the West Indies, commercial capitalists of Britain, France, and Holland who produced for the world market ingeniously built their economy on the labor of black slaves and grafted their mode of production on slavery. To meet the demand of the world market, merchants first planted and produced sugar increasingly demanded by European market, and then cotton with a greater demand from British manufactories and textile factories. Black slavery plantations thus prevailed in the Caribbean (the West Indies) in the 18th century. From 1701 to 1810, there was an input of 1.4 million black slaves into British colonies, 1.34 million French colonies, and 0.46 million Dutch colonies. Intensive labor emerged on the narrow island. Spanish colonies in Cuba became for a time the major slave trading post, and over a million black slaves landed Cuba within a half century (1791-1840). The West Indies became the place of producing cash crops like sugar, cotton, coffee, and indigo demanded by Europe.

Thousands of black slaves shipped forcibly from the other shore of the Atlantic (West Africa) were involuntarily involved in the world market dominated by capitalist mode of production, which demanded all products from plantations to be exported to meet the great need. This led to an endless demand for the surplus labor of black slaves. Therefore, aside from the barbarous disaster of slavery, there was the civilized disaster of overwork. Commercial capitalist plantation owners were not concerned with the recovery of labor forces, i.e. did not have to guarantee the condition of labor force reproduction, which meant that the most effective economic way of running plantations was to extract labor to the utmost degree from chattel in the shortest possible time. The strong black slave shipped from Africa worked in the plantations and "us[ed] up... his life in 7 years"[41]. Thus, plantations on the West Indies devoured millions of Africans. To this, Marx pointed out with indignation that it was of necessity to have a look at the condition of slaves in plantations if we want to know how capitalists had transformed themselves and the slaves in their free-wheeling reform of the world in their own manners.

Many European traders travelled around the world, made great fortunes, and became tycoons through "triangle trade" between Europe, Africa and America, which was in turn connected with trade in India and East Asia. Slave traders of Europe (and later North America) shipped to Africa with full loads of shoddy goods produced in Europe and Indian coarse cotton cloth to exchange for a large number of black slaves in the Gulf of Guinea or Angola. They crammed slaves like livestock in the crowded cargo vessels, sailed across the Atlantic for ports on the West Indies, in Brazil and North America to exchange for white sugar, sugar, syrup, cotton, and tobacco, and then returned to Europe (or North America). A large amount of syrup brewed into rum in European mills and European industrial products were resold in America (to earn silver) and Africa (to obtain black slaves). The major part of silver earned by Britain, France, and Holland was shipped to India, Southeast Asia, and China to purchase spices, coarse cotton cloth, fine woven cloth, silk, porcelain, and tea, which were resold across Europe. The way Britain, France, and Holland obtained silver was relatively complicated. The Spanish Crown was the first owner of silver produce in Mexico and Potosi silver mine. Spain was underdeveloped in industry which could not meet the demand of colonies, and yet it strictly prohibited other countries from exporting industrial products into its colonies. Smuggling, pillage and war were the chief means adopted by Britain, France and Holland in their struggle with Spain.

First, smuggling was for a time prevalent. The legal total trade volume in 1624 was merely 1,446,346 pesos whole the total volume of smuggling trade was up to 7,597,559 pesos. Annals of Potosi recorded the bustling scene of smuggling goods from countries on the Eurasian intercontinental route were shipped to Potosi mine:

---

41 Marx, Karl, and Fredrick Engels. *Collected Works*. Vol. 35. New York: International Publishers, 1996: 244.

France supplied all kinds of textiles, white ribbons, galloon laces, serge, beaver hats, and linens; Flanders pictures of hanging brocade, engraving plates, valuable tables, Wales linens, laces, and some porcelains; Holland linen and clothes; Germany silver swords and table linens; Geneva paper.... Florence clothes and satin.... England brocade calicos, hats, and woolen textiles; Cyprus, Cartier, and African coasts white wax; Asia ivory products; East India clothes, crystal....and gemstones; Ceylon diamonds; Arab spices; Persia, Cairo, and Turkey carpets....China marvelous silk clothings.[42]

The smuggling trade volume of British commodities alone by 1761 had reached 60 million pesos, equivalent to the trade volume of Spain.

Secondly, pillage was another means to break the monopoly of Spain. Since the 16th century, pirate ships of Britain, France, and Holland had been waiting near the sea route of Spanish cargo vessels, pillaging all silver and gold on them, which lasted for 200 years. In 1628 alone, the Dutch pirated obtained 15 million Dutch guilders in their capture of Spanish silver vessels.

Thirdly, wars were waged frequently to seize Spanish colonies. In 1588, the British Fleet destroyed Spanish Armada, which laid the foundation for British economic advantage in Spanish American colonies. Historians had once described in the vivid image of "a funnel with double tubes" how Spanish wealth from American colonies, especially silver, flowed into Britain from "the other tube" of the funnel. In the words of Wallerstein, Spain played the role of a mere conveyor. A considerable part of the profits of American economy actually flowed in the direction of Britain. France and Holland also shared part of the profits. The details of how Europe opened up new markets in Asia by means of silver taken from the distant America were to be revealed, the rough outline of which was as follows: about 31,000 tons out of the total output of 42,000 tons of American silver were shipped to Europe in the 17th century, at least 40 percent of which or more than 12,000 tons were shipped to Asia by Europe. The Dutch East India Company and the British East India Company alone transported respectively 4,000 to 5,000 tons of silver to Asia. In addition, 6,000 tons were shipped to the Baltic Sea and 5,000 tons to Levant (now Lebanon and Palestine) in the East Mediterranean, which in turn shipped part of the silver to China and India in exchange for East and South Asian commodities. In the 18th century, the total output of silver in America was 52,000 tons, about 40 percent of which or 20,000 tons were shipped to Asia. Although statistics vary as to how many silvers were shipped to Asia from 1600 to 1800, some said 45,000 tons while others 68,000 tons, the major part was transported to China, around 60,000 tons (equivalent to around 1.92 billion taels).[43]

---

42 Madariaga, Salvador de. *The Rise of Spanish-American Empire*. London: Hollis & Carter, 1947: 65-66. Qtd. in *History of Latin American Countries* by Chunhui Li. Vol. 1. Beijing: The Commercial Press, 1973: 106.

43 Frank, Andre Gunder. *ReOrient: Global Economy in the Asian Age*. Berkeley: University of California Press, 1998: 202-210.

Before the middle of the 18th century, as mentioned above, due to the great geographical discovery, the intercontinental route on Eurasian continent extended westward to connect the Caribbean America; eastward to connect the ports on the west coast of Mexico by means of Spanish Galleons. America silver moved likewise on the intercontinental route: it was shipped eastward from the east coast of America to South and East Asia by way of Europe or westward from the west coast of America to China by way of the Philippines. Before the middle of the 18th century, it was basically an equal trade to exchange American silver for necessary commodities with the East, which was beneficial to the communication of the world market. However, as to the Sub-Saharan African blacks and American Indians weak in their power, such trade was not a question of equality or inequality but of the annihilation of millions of black bodies and Indian bodies, the murder of lives, and the destruction of former economic bases. The African blacks and Indians survived in the South were the first to be yoked with unequal economic relations, providing primary materials and commodity markets for Western European countries. Marx summarized in his letter to P.W. Annenkov in 1846 that if there was no slavery, there would be no cotton; if there was no cotton, there would be no modern industry. The direct slavery was the basis of modern industry just like machines and loans. American colonies led to world trade, which was the indispensable condition for machine industry[44]. The historical vision of Marx was so profound that it broke through the deep darkness like a searchlight in the night.

The economic development and goods produced in America made enormous contributions to world trade. However, after the middle of the 18th century, South and North America took utterly different roads. The factors of different colonial policies of metropolitan states were rooted in the depth of economic development.

2.4.3. Britain Conquered India by means of Colonial Violence

European industrial products failed to enter Indian and Chinese markets till the 18th century. The British East India Company tried all means to avoid offsetting trade deficit with silver. Yet it still had to spend 30 million pounds in the purchase of silver to pay the goods from India and China from 1733 to 1766. When the economic power of capitalism itself was inadequate, violence was often used as "an economic strength". Due to the disintegration of India, the central government of the Mughal Empire failed to issue its orders, which provided a stage for East India Company to resort to violence. The seven years of the war (1765-1763) between Britain and France in their rivalry for the Indian Subcontinent provided a golden opportunity for the British East India Company: it evolved from a commercial into a military and territorial power. Hereafter, it occupied Indian territories with the help of the British navy and army, which was actually a war of 200 years waged by the British government

44 Marx, Karl, and Fredrick Engels. *Selected Works*. Vol. 4. Beijing: People's Publishing House, 1972: 327.

against India in the name of the company. The British East India Company had won every battle against the French and the pro-French Indian Maharajas, which built up its troops and occupies large areas of Indian territories and forced the French power to retreat to five small coastal cities while British colonial power expanded viciously after the Battle of Plassey in 1757. In the subsequent 90 years, the British East India Company waged no less than 10 large-scale wars of conquest and countless small-scale wars to conquer the whole India. The British East India were not engaged itself in every battle against the Indian Subcontinent with a vast area of over three million and a large population of over 0.17 billion but, taking advantage of the fragmentation of the Indian Subcontinent with kingdoms and princely states went their own ways and the government of the Mughal Empire lacked co-operation in its departments, malignantly adopted the means of "Indians battling against Indians" and conquering India with the money of Indians, established the so-called Subsidiary System or Contract Subsidiary System, and reduced the rulers of numerous Indian kingdoms and princely states into vassals of the British East India Company. The concrete forms include: First, most contracts stipulated that Indian princes support or subsidize the East India Company troops stationed in their territories; second, some contracts imposed loans on princes with harsh terms that if they failed to fulfill the terms, their territories would be confiscated by the company. After the second Punjab war (1848-1849) ended in 1849, the British East India Company completed their conquest of India. The British used the Indian army supported by the Indian people to conquer, enslave, and rule India, which was a characteristic and important fact of the history of modern colonial conquest.

First, it was always under the impetus of colonial violence that the East-West relationship on the Eurasian Continent since ancient times (which was in accordance with the laws of cultural fusion for many centuries) evolved into the so-called North-South relationship. Britain first set up "direct political power"—gained sovereignty and then announced that the sovereignty of all conquered areas was owned by the British East India Company.

Second, the British East India Company's actual ownership of sovereignty had vital importance. This was because sovereignty in India meant the centralized ownership of land across the country. The state was both the owner of all land and the sovereign in opposition to direct producers with land rent and tax in one. After the conquest of Bengal by the British East India Company, the so-called land tax reformed was carried out, which demanded the former tax collectors zamindars to collect land tax in the name of landlords and submit ten eleventh of land tax collected to the treasury (East India Company). Subsequently, whenever East India Company conquered a place where "fixed" or "non-fixed" land tax was implemented, it basically followed the same way to take possession of most of the land rent or tax as the highest landlord in India. The British East India Company extorted land tax in India "with all the practised ingenuity of politicians, and all the monopolizing self-ishness of traders"[45]. Before the take-over of Bengal by the British East India Company, the actual amount of land tax in Bengal from 1764 to 1765 was 810,000 pounds, which soared to 1.47 million pounds in the first year of take-over (1765-1766) and 3 million pounds 26 years later (1792-1793), 2.5 times of the original amount. Henceforth, the British East India Company used more and more land tax extorted from India to purchase Indian commodities (mainly cotton cloth) to be shipped to England, Europe and America for sale, thus the East India Company, which was honored trade monopoly by the British queen, became so prosperous that, it no longer needed to rely on the American silver to narrow the trade deficit with China.

45   Marx, Karl, and Fredrick Engels. *Collected Works*. Vol. 12. New York: International Publishers, 1979: 126.

Chapter III

Colonial Expansion, Industrial Revolution and the North-South Relationship

3.1. Colonial Expansion and Its Abject Acts: New & Old

3.1.1. Arguments on the Impact of Colonialism from 16th to the mid-18th Century

Historians' arguments on the extent of colonial activities and their impact on the world history before the end of the 18th century (i.e. before the Industrial Revolution) are not quite the same. It is still subject to further scientific discussion whether the colonial acts in the 16-17-18th centuries have been one key factor, in enabling global interconnection. It also needs further study whether the number of colonies (regardless of the size) can be used to determine the high tide, low tide or descending tide of the colonial expansion. A specific analysis of different areas is the correct way to achieve a comprehensive understanding. But one thing is for sure from the 16th to the 18th century the colonial system contributed greatly to the development of shipping and trade and ensured the sales market for the emerging handicraft industry. Outside Europe (in America and Southeast Asia), the treasures, captured directly by the forced labor of the enslaved indigenous inhabitants and black Africans, corruption, looting and murder, and continuously floated back into the mother-country and turned into capital, became an important source of primitive accumulation. In this regard, the world economic development process paved the way for the Industrial Revolution.

From the 16th to the mid-18th century, due to the turning of tropical Africa into a warren for the commercial hunting of black-skins, the black population dropped sharply. In the plantations on the West Indies and some smaller islands in Southeast Asia, the population plundered became enslaved laborers. Tens of millions of American Indians were exterminated, enslaved or entombed in mines. These areas became the first places to be hit hard by colonialism.

But in the regions of ancient Asian civilizations, even in those which had been conquered by the colonialists with modern firearms, such as Bangladesh, Carnatic and Mysore in India, major disasters and even destruction by the savage interference and ravage of tax collectors and soldiers from Britain, Netherlands and France, just like other countless disasters in the history, had basically only touched the surface of some areas in the South, without causing structural concussion in local societies. Therefore, some historians say that, if the Europeans had completely withdrawn from their costal colonies in Asia before 1750, nothing important would have been left except few historical sites.

In the 18th century, China became increasingly involved in the trade with the world, especially with western European countries. The trade volume between China and the European countries increased dramatically. Because of the trade surplus, China's annual silver accumulation increased year by year. By the end of the 18th century, Britain was seeking for new means to offset its trade deficit with China. China remained a major power with the world's highest GDP and little colonialist invasions. China remained a large country with the world's highest GDP, which lacked vast colonies except a few little ones.

3.1.2. The Industrial Revolution forged "Heavy Artilleries" out of Cheap Commodities

In the western end of the east-west route from Asia to Europe, an industrial revolution was taking place quietly. In the 19th century, massive changes occurred, "the bourgeoisie, has created more massive and more colossal productive forces than have all preceding generations together". The occurrence of the Industrial Revolution in Britain was not solely relied on its own strength, which has become a received understanding for more and more people. The Industrial Revolution in Britain started from the cotton textile industry, which, as the most dynamic industry, emerged out of imitation of foreign industries. As mentioned previously, the seeds of British cotton textile industry "were in fact brought to England in the ships of the East India Company"[1]. Since the 16th century, Indian cotton textiles had already developed vast overseas

---

1   Mantoux, Paul. *The Industrial Revolution in the Eighteenth Century: An Outline of the Beginning of the Modern Factory System in England.* Trans. Marjorie Vernon. New York: Routledge, 2005. Trans. Renmo Yang. Beijing: The Commercial Press, 1983: 104.

markets in Americas, Europe and Asia, becoming one of the most-widely-used daily necessities of hundreds of millions of people. The cotton textile industry introduced from India was not constrained by any old conventions, and became an ideal test site open to various inventions and pioneering efforts in the mid-18th century. The first series of inventions of machines in the Industrial Revolution underwent smoothly in the roaring cotton textile factories. As the pioneer of European commercial capital, the British accumulated their strength in Americas, Africa and Asia, which created favorable conditions for the occurrence and success of the Industrial Revolution. According to Ernest Mandel, it is estimated that from 1500 to 1800 a total value of 1 billion pounds of gold was plundered by Europe from overseas colonies, of which, Britain alone had plundered 150 million pounds of gold from India between 1750 and 1800. Mandel believes that the inflow of capital at least promoted the investment in the Industrial Revolution, particularly in steam engines and textile technologies, if not to say it was the total capital of the British Industrial Revolution[2]. Eric Williams also believes that capital accumulated from the trade in the West Indies provided financial support for Watt and the steam engine. Industrial Revolution and its success had helped Britain take up finally a leading position in the locomotive of the world's economic train.

Since the technological basis of the Industrial Revolution was revolutionary, it had exerted a more profound influence on the European continent and the world outside of Europe than any other Euroepan political revolutions. With the roar of machines and the whistle of steam engines, the Industrial Revolution ushered in a new era of capitalist colonial system, which made major changes in both the content and form of colonial policies. The Industrial Revolution had first forged for western countries in Eurasia "heavy artilleries" out of cheap commodities. In 1785, the first steam engine in Britain was installed in Robinson Cotton Mill in Nottinghamshire. Since then, the whole country was rushing for installation. In 1826, there were 37,500 steam engines installed in Britain. In 1835, the number of steam-powered looms in Britain was over 10, 800 and reached nearly 250,000 in 1850. With its low price, British woven cotton cloth first sidelined the traditional cotton in mainland Europe, squeezed cotton goods from India out of the European market, and later with further growth advantage entered the market on the Indian subcontinent, "motherland of cotton goods". Previously, Britain had held dominion over India. It could order and allocate resources of the world market at will. First, it placed weavers working with spinning machines in Lancashire, Britain while weavers with traditional hand-looms in Bangladesh of India, and shipped massive cheap yarns produced by machines to India, so as to destroy India's hand looms and eliminate tens of thousands of textile workers in India. Second, Britain again used cheap cotton cloth to wipe out a large number of Indian weavers. During the 18 years from 1818 to 1836, the ratio of yarn exported from Britain to India was 1: 5200. In 1824, 1 million yards of British machine-woven cotton were exported

---

2   Williams, E. *Capitalism and Slavery*. New York: Capricorn Books, 1966: 102-103.

to Indian, and over 64 million yards 13 years later in 1837, with a high ratio of 1:64. A large number of Indian weavers were "destroyed" (starved). During this period, the population of the "cotton capital" Dhaka (now in Bangladesh) dropped from 150, 000 to less than 20, 000. Thus, many prosperous towns of India, once famous for the textile manufacturing, had declined or even disappeared. India, where high-quality Indian cotton and muslin were produced and sold to the whole world, was defeated by the Britain's "direct political and economic power".[3] The yarns from Lancashire and the cotton cloth from Manchester flooded the market of the Hindustan plain.

3.1.3. Alternate Use of Economic and Violent Means (Wars) as Two Levers

In the mid-19th century when the industrial revolution was advancing triumphantly, Western European capitalist countries, led by Britain, needed Asia to provide markets and sources of raw materials for their industrial goods. They needed to make significant adjustments to the colonial system, converting the colonies from sources of increasing economic wealth into places mainly for the extraction of surplus value of industrial capital. The rising industrial bourgeoisie feverishly sought to expand their capital. The colonies and the "informal empire" under the British control are the ideal places for Britain to obtain excess profits and expand capital. Asian colonies and semi-colonial countries were forced to make contributions: the lever of primitive accumulation of capital was turned into one of the main levers of capitalist accumulation.

The old colonial exploitation means in the period of primitive accumulation, such as the sale of black slaves, forced plantation system and the privileged monopoly stock companies, which could still bring considerable practical benefits to Western capitalism, continued to be used with slight alterations and lingered with a thick and long tail in the period of laisser-faire capitalism. But generally speaking, these means were after all outdated and difficult to adapt to the development of large-scale machine production after the Industrial Revolution. The emerging industrial capitalist groups witnessed that in Hindustan and the Indonesian archipelago under the monopolistic control of two East India Companies, the British and Dutch East India Company, public works in some areas, which were symbols of ancient civilization, had been destroyed as a result of vicious looting, large tracts of good farmlands degenerated into tropical forests and wilderness for tigers and leopards, and productivity was severely damaged. With the emerging trend to hire farm hands, the plantations in the West Indies went into a vicious circle: slaves were slack in work, the farmland fertility was used up, and production went down. Due to the war of hunting slaves in Africa for centuries, the population declined sharply, the residents escaped into the deep mountain forests to avoid the slave hunters, resulting in large tracts of desolate lands. By the end of the 18th century, the profit of a

---

3   Marx, Karl, and Fredrick Engels. *Collected Works*. Vol. 37. New York: International Publishers, 1998: 332.

shipload of slaves from Africa under the harsh environment was less than that produced by the production of a shipload of palm oil by the same number of local laborers.

The ruthless logic of historical dialectics showed that, with the development of Western capitalism, the basis of old colonial means characterized by ultra-economic force had been destroyed. As the commercial capital had been sidelined in Europe by industrial capital, and with the industrial bourgeoisie marching onto the central stage of history, the old colonial means had greatly lost their value and charm, which would definitely be gradually replaced by new colonial means.

An important new means of colonial exploitation in this period was to adopt the "free trade" policy. After the Congress of Vienna (1815) Britain had become a dominant power in the world. It controlled nearly all oceans. It had the most powerful industries. Its relative share of manufacturing in the world had risen from 4.3% in 1800 to 19.9% in 1860. Its share in the total world trade in 1850 had risen to 21%. All these had enabled Britain to declare the "free trade" policy. Britain demanded not only its colonies but also the whole world to open their markets for its products. It was considered more important by the British government to keeping the world's raw materials suppliers and markets open to British industrial products than obtaining special business interests in scattered colonies. Under the banner of free trade first raised by Britain, with the unequal treaties signed under duress as the locomotive, the heavy artilleries of cheap commodities were used to pry open the market everywhere and exploit and plunder the Southern colonies through apparently equal buying and selling. Industrial capitalists made money in the colonies under the cover of "free exchange" with industrial products at extremely low costs rather than plundering overtly without a shilling paid in advance in the period of primitive accumulation. This exchange was extremely profitable for industrial capitalists, because, first, their products were often sold in Southern colonial and semi-colonial countries at "favorable prices", much higher than those in the mother countries; second, their goods were sold as high-quality labor, while at home labor "ha[d] not been paid as being of a higher quality [wa]s sold as such"[4]. Meanwhile, raw materials were undersold from the colonies to metropolitan states, often not sufficient to cover the cost of production. This was also the secret why the industrial capitalists were flocking to the trading markets of the colonies and semi-colonies.

Nevertheless, looting with brutal violence was no longer the most important feature in this period of colonial aggression. But from the perspective of the world as a whole, it did not mean that the colonial forces in the South only conducted peaceful trade and no longer resorted to violence. In October 1860, British and French troops stormed into the Old Summer Palace[5] in the suburb

---

4   Ibid.: 264-265.
5   The Old Summer Palace, known in Chinese as 圓明園 Yuánmíngyuán (the Gardens of Perfect Brightness), and originally called the Imperial Gardens.

of Beijing. In this palace which contained the collection of China's art works and hundreds of millions of treasure for thousands of years, they looted for three days and nights. Their undisguised robbery with violence exceeded any violent lootings in human history. Victor Hugo (1802-1885), a French writer, disclosed the looting in November 1861 in a letter to Captain Butler: the looting of the Old Summer Palace by the British and the French surpassed the looting (1801-1803) of Greek Parthenon 60 years ago, when the British took home almost all priceless sculptures and treasures of the temple. What was done to the Parthenon was done to the Old Summer Palace, "more thoroughly and better, so that nothing of it should be left". In the [Old] Summer Palace contained rare treasures, antiques, gold and silver, paintings, porcelain, and silk.... "All the treasures of all our cathedrals put together could not equal this formidable and splendid museum of the Orient"[6]. According to a British clerk involved in the looting, "each person stuffed his pockets full and took them back to Britain".[7]

As mentioned above, different methods of primitive accumulation were based on the use of violence, and colonial means of liberal capitalism, almost without exception, used the power of the state, which was the very organized social violence. This was not only because the productive forces of liberal capitalism had not yet reached the level of discarding the boost of super-economic forces. As a matter of fact, the use of violence still had a great temptation for the bourgeoisie. Since the Industrial Revolution increasingly widened the gap of military power between the East and the West on the Eurasian Continent, which made it easier for Western colonial powers to launch large-scale colonial aggressions based on the comparative advantage of weapons and ships. When modern industries in Western countries were at the initial stage, their economy was not strong enough to open up the oriental market dominated by self-sufficient economy. In this case, although the trade between Western countries and Eastern countries was gradually expanding, it could meet the needs of the Western bourgeoisie, no matter in the volume or growth rate of the trade. After the Industrial Revolution, the Western colonial powers had mastered the two levers of economic means and violence (war). If they found that they could not fully reach their targets with economic means (including "free trade" of selling drugs like opium), they would not hesitate to use the lever of violence (war) to achieve economic goals. The two Opium Wars waged by Britain against China in the 19th century were typical examples.

---

6   Hugo, Victor. "Letter to Captain Butler". In *The Old Summer Palace in the Eyes of Westerners*. Beijing: University of International Business and Economics Press, 2000: 2-3.
7   *Reference Materials of Cultural Relics* 1(1953).

3.2. A Mutation of Laissez-faire: Opium Trade

3.2.1. Britain's Business Strategy of Widespread Planting of Opium Poppy in India

In ancient times, there was no farming of opium in India and China.[8] Between the 18th and the 19th century, opium was no longer used to relieve pain under strict control but as a drug inundated India and China. The main culprits were the British East India Company and British government behind it. In 1727, Britain first exported 200 boxes of opium to China. The Qing government of China prohibited the import of opium in 1729.

In the end of the 18th century, British government and the East India Company made business strategies for opium trade:

After the Battle of Plassey in 1757, the East India Company invaded Bengal, Bihar, and Orissa, and forced Indian farmers to expand the cultivation of poppy in fertile farmland. The company set up factories to refine high-quality opium (also called Patna Opium) in Benares and other places. Between 1817 and 1818, the company's army defeated Maratha alliance, and a large number of native states in western and central India became the company's vassal states. A large area of land around Malwa was suitable for planting poppy. And the opium produced there was better than that in Bengal. The area of good farmland for poppy cultivation in two areas kept rising and doubled soon. Up to the 1820s, about 8,000 boxes of Indian opium were exported to China, of which, less than 5,000 boxes came from Bengal and over 3,000 boxes from Malwa[9]. The British policy was very clear: India's opium was mainly exported to China. In view of the physical degeneration of Indian farmers addicted to opium, which affected the supply of labor, the first governor of the East India Company, C. W. Hastings, clearly stated in 1773 that opium was not a daily necessity but a harmful luxury, except for the foreign trade (with China), it was forbidden. A wise government should strictly limit[10] domestic consumption of opium. Opium factories of the company catered to Chinese opium-eaters in the process of steaming, drying and concocting of opium, and packed it with special boxes suitable for smuggling. They were amassed in Calcutta to be smuggled into China.

The East India Company had a monopoly over opium trade. Although the East India Company was flagrant due to corruption in India for two centuries and invited vehement criticism from British industrial bourgeoisie in Congress. In 1813, the company lost the business monopoly. But in order to promote the opium trade, the company still had the monopoly on the trade with China. The

---

8   *Britannica Concise Encyclopedia*. Vol. 8. Beijing: Encyclopedia of China Publishing House, 1986: 753.

9   See Lin, Chengjie. "Some Issues Concerning the British and Indian Opium Trade with China." *Peking University Historiography* 5(1998).

10   *Report of the Royal Commission on Opium* 7 (1894): 37. Qtd. in Ding, Mingnan et al. *History of Imperialist Invasion of China*. Vol. 1. Beijing: Science Publishing House, 1958: 10.

main concern of British Parliament was not the tea trade with China, but the interests of the opium trade with China. In 1833, the East India Company's privilege of trade in China was annulled. But the Company's opium's smuggling business in China had a history of nearly a hundred years. With a lot of experience and cunning tricks, the company was able to continue the business covertly. The company deliberately trained a large number of "country merchants"[11], which had become pioneers of smuggling opium. The company had strict rules which stipulated that these British and Indian merchants could smuggle the goods of the company into China only with the permission of the company. Because the Chinese government officially banned opium import several times while the East India Company and the British government hypocritically claimed that they were not engaged in the opium trade, all opium produced or purchased by the company was sold at auction in Calcutta to the country merchants, who in turn smuggled opium into China's coastal ports.

The profit rate of opium trade was very high, which generally could reach a staggering rate of more than 800%. The huge profits were shared by the British Indian government, the East India Company, the merchants and opium growers. The crucial role which the opium trade played in the finances of the British Indian government was unimaginable to an outsider. In 1871, a box of Bengal opium from the East India Company was sold at 1785 rupees in Calcutta with a cost of merely 222 rupees, which meant the price was more than eight times the cost. 3,552 boxes were sold this year with a profit of 5.51 million rupees. In addition, the British Indian government levied a tax of 2.37 million rupees on opium[12]. The country merchants smuggled and sold the opium into China at the price of 2,675 rupees (US $ 1300) a box, earning 893 rupees per box. The invading army in the Opium War acknowledged that this export business supplied huge profits for the interests of our Indian colony so that we could not give it up easily. An 1831 report produced by the British Parliament shamelessly said, in light of the current state of India's revenue and expenditure, it seemed to be inappropriate to abandon so important a tax, which was mainly imposed on foreign consumers [Chinese people]. On the whole, compared with any other tax which may replace it, it was much less likely to be opposed.[13]

3.2.2. Opium Exported to China Stayed at a High Level

As mentioned earlier, in the entire 18th century and the early 19th century, the British had a great demand for Chinese tea, silk and other goods while Britain failed to come up with any commodity for exchange. During the decade between 1781 and 1790, export tea from China alone amounted to 96.3 million silver dollars, while all the export commodities (including wool fabric, calico, cotton, and metal) from Britain to China amounted to only 16.9 million silver dollars,

---

11   Known for their use of "Kangkar boats". Note by the author.
12   Opium was taxed at a rate of 301.75 percent of the cost. Note by the author.
13   *British Parliamentary Papers, 1831-1832.* vol. 11. p. 10. Qtd. in Ding, Mingnan et al. *History of Imperialist Invasion of China.* Vol. 1. Beijing: Science Publishing House, 1958: 13.

accounting for merely one sixth of the volume of tea trade. China had been a trade surplus country. Britain exported drugs to overturn the trade deficit. The exports of opium into China increased year by year. The Sino-UK trade situation quickly reversed, when China turned from a trade surplus country into trade deficit country while the UK became a trade surplus country. For example, the total volume of Britain's trade with China in 1830 was 22.93 million silver dollars while the opium trade was up to 13.46 million silver dollars, which meant 6.73 million silver dollars flowed out of China this year.[14] Henceforth, a growing number of silver dollars flowed out of China in the following years.

The British merchants in India and some Indian wholesale merchants made a great fortune from the opium trade and had accumulated abundant capital, which was used to buy wholesale machine-made cotton textiles from Britain, and resold them to every corner on the Indian subcontinent, which prospered the British textile wholesale business in India. The whole Indian market was soon opened up, which inflicted catastrophic destruction upon tens of thousands of hand-loom weavers.

The British Indian government went into fiscal deficit year after year in the first half of the 19th century due to a huge amount of military expenditure of the perennial wars waged by the East India Company in India and the construction of disaster relief and resistance projects. Most of the expenditure was supplied by the income of opium trade. The British Indian Government acknowledged that the government would face finance crisis every year without the huge opium trade revenues. Against this historical background, it was easy to understand why the opium exports to China saw a constant increase, which is well illustrated by the figures given in the Table 3.1.

Table 3.1. Opium Exported to China 1795-1838 (Annual Average)[15]

Year	Boxes of opium into China
1795-1799	4, 124
1800-1804	3, 562
1805-1809	4, 281
1810-1814	4, 713
1815-1819	4, 424
1820-1824	7, 889
1825-1829	12, 576
1830-1834	20, 331
1835-1838	35, 445

Unit: box (each box weighing about 133 pounds)

14   Morse, H. B. *The International Relations of the Chinese Empire*. Vol. 1. Shanghai, 1910: 90-91.
15   Dai, Yi. *History of Qing Dynasty*. Vol. 2. Beijing: People's Publishing House, 1984: 541.

Opium inundated the land of China, where over 2 million people were addicted to opium. The Chinese nation was endangered. One described that the opium addicts were skeletons, deformed, lingering on with the last breath of life, unable to make a living outside or have a baby at home. The harm was not limited to the addicts but to the reproduction of descendants. The morality of the trade was described in China; Political, Commercial, and Social by Montgomery Martin, an Englishman, in the following terms:

Why, the "slave trade" was merciful compared with the "opium trade". We did not destroy the bodies of the Africans, for it was our immediate interest to keep them alive; we did not debase their natures, corrupt their minds, nor destroy their souls. But the opium seller slays the body after he has corrupted, degraded and annihilated the moral being of unhappy sinners, while, every hour is bringing new victims to a Moloch which knows no satiety, and where the English murderer and Chinese suicide vie with each other in offerings at his shrine.[16] What a tragic picture Martin painted!

Britain used the opium trade as a fuse to launch the first Opium War against China. William Ewart Gladstone, later British Prime Minister from the Liberal Party, had to admit the injustice of the war, denouncing it as "unjust and iniquitous" and criticized Lord Palmerston's willingness "to protect an infamous contraband traffic."[17] Between 1840 and 1949 colonialist and imperialist powers waged more than 10 aggressive wars against China. War reparations from China amounted to 710 million tales of silver. However, the annual treasury of Chinese government in the 19th century was less than 70 million taels. The extortion of huge sums of money after unjust wars against China was exhaustive exploitation and plundering. By means of wars, threat of force or diplomatic fraudulence, imperialist powers looted or "rented" some parts of China, coerced China into signing hundreds of unequal treaties, which granted them the right to garrison troops and consular jurisdiction in China, dominated China's customs, foreign trade, and transport by land, sea, air and inland rivers, and controlled all important trading ports in China. In many of these ports a part of the land was set aside as a concession under their direct rule to hold China in leash financially. Henceforth, the world's most populous country, which ranked first in terms of GDP for centuries, was reduced to a semi-colony as a member of the South.

3.2.3. Informal Empire: the Rise of Free Trade Empire

Colonial powers led by Britain reduced China, the largest country in Asia, into a semi-colonial country in less than 50 years. Likewise, the Ottoman Empire, the largest country in West Asia, was also gradually reduced into a semi-colony. In addition to the two biggest semi-colonial countries, a number

---

16   Marx, Karl, and Fredrick Engels. *Collected Works*. Vol. 16. New York: International Publishers, 1980: 14-15.
17   Willoughby, Westel *W. Foreign Rights and Interests in China*. Baltimore: Johns Hopkins Press, 1927.

of ex-colonies in Latin American, which gained "independence" in the early 19th century, became semi-colonial countries again. The British colonial planners included them in the "informal empire".

As described above, in addition to the "informal empire", Britain also needed to build a huge free-trade empire. The history of the past century proved that Britain did not hesitate to annex any place so long as it could guarantee the interest of the empire without resorting to force. From 1757 (roughly when the British industrialization began) to 1850 (roughly when the British industrialization was basically accomplished), Britain annexed more than 4.1 million square kilometers of territory on the Indian subcontinent, conquered Malaya and Burma in Southeast Asia, continued to expand territory in Canada of the North America, took over Australia and New Zealand in Oceania and occupied Cape, Natal and Basutoland colonies in Africa and some coastal colonies in West Africa. Between 1815 and 1865, an annual average of 259,000 square kilometers of land was expanded or occupied by Britain. More than 10 million square kilometers of land had been included in the "formal empire".

Countries included in the "informal empire" fell into the following categories: first, countries (like China [1840-1842] and Japan [1864]) which were coerced into signing unequal treaties as a result of the British gunboat policy and became Britain's merchandise sales markets and raw material suppliers; second, countries (in the Americas) which had to open their markets unconditionally to Britain due to its historical advantages in politics and economy and its disguise of free trade; third, some countries in West Asia were forced to open to Britain under the threat of British threat of force in addition to its diplomatic maneuvers, for example, the Anglo-Turkish Treaty signed in 1838 made the whole territory of the Ottoman Empire the target of British business expansion. So was the Persian Empire. Fourth, coastal regions in West Africa, East Africa, and some parts in South Africa were imposed paramountcy by Britain, although it did not send and garrison colonial officials and troops there, like Transvaal, Orange and Swaziland. In fact, Britain had paramountcy in nearly all regions of Africa where Europeans could reach the mid-19th century. Countries which were inflicted with these four types of colonial invasions almost without exception have become under-developed countries and been included in the category of the South.

Thus, we see the so-called informal empire was the broader regions which had not been officially incorporated into the British Empire but guaranteed stable interests for the empire so long as it could maintain its hegemony in the whole world.[18] Under the condition that Britain had the advantage in world economy and global colonization, the means of "informal empire", which did not require "a single soldier", was extremely beneficial for Britain to maintain its primary imperial interests.

---

18 Gallagher, J., and R. Robinson. "The Imperialism of Free Trade." *Economic History Review* 6.1 (1953): 3.

The fact was that in the mid-19th century colonial powers frequently used force against those powerful feudal empires and kingdoms in Asia (such as China, Japan, the Persian Empire, the Ottoman Empire, Myanmar and some princely states on the Indian subcontinent). The use of its warships and guns to make way for their cheap machine-made goods proved that they could not do without the use of violence no matter by means of "formal empire" or "informal empire".

3.3. The Fall of the Oriental World

3.3.1. Disintegration of the Social and Economic Structures of the Eastern Nations

The flooding of cheap goods into the eastern countries on the Eurasian continent, albeit with the smoke of artillery fire and even the odor of opium, but it is an objective historical process of the transformation of the history into the world history. It not only showed that the large-scale industry interconnected people around the world and integrated all small local markets into a world market, but also meant that it made it possible for all that happed in every civilized country to exert influence on the rest of the world (for example, the new machinery used in Britain deprived millions of people in India of jobs a year later), and even caused the change in the form of existence of these countries. Therefore, the colonial aggression during the period of liberal capitalism had a much more profound impact on the oriental society than in the previous period. It not only touched the surface of society but also began to change the economic foundation of the Asian society. Upon the impact of the rising tide of Western European colonization, the self-sufficient economy of Eastern nations began to break down.

Before capitalism, the mode of production in Eastern nations had its special structure and internal resilience, which was very hard for commercial capital to break down. In the period of primitive accumulation, the invasion of Western commercial capital was almost impossible to change it, because this mode of production was primarily based on the integration of individual farming and household handicrafts, and this direct combination would not only cause a high degree of economic self-sufficiency, but also huge savings and economy of time, which made it possible to resist not only foreign goods but also products of large industries. This was particularly obvious in India and China. The more seriously farmers suffered from colonial plundering, the lower their purchasing power became. They could not afford cheap muslin but wear home-made durable clothes. Till the 1860s, the integration of handicraft and agriculture was still dominant in China. India originally had village communes, a type of small-scale economic commune, based on public ownership of land. The self-sufficient agricultural economy based on village communes was more resilient (compared with Western Europe) and caused a greater obstacle to the commercial disintegration. Unlike China, cheap goods made by British steam machines in India were backed by the British "direct political power". Export cotton yarn from Britain to India increased by 5,199 times in 19 years, and export cotton cloth increased by 63 times in 14 years. However, without the support of "direct political power", the export of cotton yarn and cloth remained nearly the same over 30 years. Britain took two steps to annihilate the historically inalienable parts of the unity of handcraft and agriculture: first, the import of cotton yarn to India, second, the massive import of cotton fabric. This undermined the economic basis of village communes and also destroyed village communes. In Asia Minor, such as Persia and Ottoman Empires, the British cheap goods also played the same destructive role. But without the assistance of "direct political power", the disintegration process was slower. It is worth noting that, despite the existence of a large number of self-sufficient village communes in the Eastern rural areas, their presence did not make India, Persia and other countries (not to mention China) into countries exporting large quantities of various types of cotton goods (India) and carpets, tapestries (Persia).

For thousands of years, no matter how the superficial political situation of the Eastern nations changed and various internal and external rulers came to and fell out of power, the substrate economic basis of the self-sufficient agriculture and the village communes in India and Indonesia remained basically intact, just like the deep submarine world was not affected by the rough winds and surging waves. However, the invasion of cheap goods of liberal capitalism gave a devastating blow to the basis. As Karl Marx says, it "exerted here a revolutionising influence on the mode of production" of the backward capitalism in the Oriental countries[19]. This, of course, was a historical progress. As mentioned above, the backward pre-capitalist mode of production in the Eastern countries, due to its peculiar structure (like the village communes in India and Indonesia), the excessively strong remains of tribal societies (like tropical Africa), or the great resilience of agriculture-dominated economy (like that in China, Korea, and Japan) slowed down the economic development and impeded greatly the disintegration by commercial capital. An external invasion of Western capitalism promoted the development of commodity economy in urban and rural areas in the East, broke the firm bonds of agriculture and handicraft industry, loosened or disintegrated some outdated and backward production relations, and cracked the superstructure which had constrained the development of productive forces for a long time, so as to provide some objective conditions or possibilities for the development of the capitalist production in Eastern countries, where capitalist elements had burgeoned. This objectively played a beneficially stimulating role in the historical progress of Eastern countries. Although the conducts of Western colonial powers were entirely driven by the despicable interests and the way to seek these interests was very cruel and even bloody, which seriously damaged the sovereignty of those countries and brought many disasters to the East, it after all served as an unconscious tool of history.

19 Marx, Karl, and Fredrick Engels. *Collected Works*. Vol. 37. New York: International Publishers, 1998: 332.

3.3.2. The Two Objective Historical Roles of the Western Capitalism

The colonial expansion of the West and the penetration of the capitalist mode of production disintegrated the social and economic basis of the East. The decline of the Eastern world gave rise to the dependent relationship between the East and the West. Western capitalism, though very bloody and evil, unconsciously acted as a historical tool for the development of the Eastern world. Why could Western capitalism after the Industrial Revolution play such a positive role? It was because that it was based on the well-developed commodity-market economy, representing the advanced social productive forces. The market could reasonably allocate resources and achieve high economic efficiency. Compared with the feudal natural economy, it had obvious advantages. Marx attaches great importance to the decisive role of the development of productivity for social progress, and also to the significance of market economy in breaking the state of isolation and seclusion between different nations, which was replaced by the mutual exchanges and interdependence between countries. It was with this dialectic understanding of human history that Marx put forward the theory of "double role" of colonialism, which embodied the "destructive" role, as well as the "re-generating" role.[20] Thus colonialism was analyzed as the unconscious tool of history, for human beings to fulfill their mission of achieving an advanced society: socialism and communism.

However, the impact of Western capitalist invasion against Eastern countries was complex, which took place in the playing out of contradictions. The essence of Western colonial policies was to reduce Eastern countries into sales markets of merchandise and sources of raw materials, and to make the economy of the Orient dependent on the large industries of the West, which would not allow Eastern countries to develop capitalism independently. In a word, it must not allow Eastern countries to compete with the industries of Western mother countries in the development of industry. Therefore, in the liberal capitalism period the Western capitalism (in fact British capital alone at the time) only invested in and operated a few railways, transportation facilities, mines, plantations and a small number of initial processing industries rather than in any modern industries in the eastern countries. Till 1862, there was only one country, Britain, had invested 700 million abroad (mainly in North America). The colonial governments of various countries did everything possible to stifle the burgeoning capitalist industry in their colonies, hinder the normal independent development of the national capitalist economy in the colonies, and strive to deform the economy, which was reduced to a source of industrial raw materials needed by the West. The pre-capitalist production relations (especially feudal relations of production) preserved by Western colonial powers also impeded the burgeoning and development of the national capital in all aspects. As a result, the Eastern countries of this period not only failed to make

---

20   Marx, Karl, and Fredrick Engels. *Collected Works*. Vol. 12. New York: International Publishers, 1979: 217.

a swift and direct transition from the pre-capitalist mode of production to the capitalist mode of production but also lost the possibility of independent social and economic development, and eventually became subordinate to the West and joined the ranks of under-developed countries. The oriental countries could only stumble forward in pain. Western countries took only few decades to complete the industrial revolution, while the Eastern nations later spent more than 100 years to do that, and at an incomparably larger cost. The truth underneath it, just as Rosa Luxemburg revealed, was that capitalism was the first economic form with a power of spreading and a tendency to be universal. It was also the first economic form which could not exist alone but needed other economic forms to serve as conductor and breeding places[21]. Therefore, capitalism had a power of spreading, not to develop the global productivity to meet the needs of all humanity but to employ colonialism as a means and combine the backward feudal production relations and even the production relations of slavery, which served as the conductor of transmission to exploit the whole world. Through its disgraceful activities over centuries in the Eastern nations, colonialism had clearly revealed the real features and nature of Western capitalism.

3.4. On the North-South Relationship in Its Early Period[22]

3.4.1. Serious Challenges Faced by the Southern Nations

In addition to the flooding of cheap goods brought by the Western industrial revolution to the South, all kinds of military, political, economic and cultural means of oppression (such as a series of unequal treaties) were imposed on the Ottoman Empire, Persian Empire, China, as well as India and other Asian and African countries, where a large area of land had been or were being colonized, faced with not only the national crisis of becoming colonies or semi-colonies, but also the tremendous social turmoil and social crisis brought by the dumping of Western goods and the looting of land[23]. Under the economic and political penetration of Britain, France, the United States, 17 newly independent countries in Latin America, which just got rid of the colonial rule of Spain and Portugal, became increasingly dependent on European and American capitalism. The newly independent Mexico could not withstand the expansion and penetration of its powerful neighbor, the United States, and lost 940,000 square kilometers of land in the War (1846-1848). Argentina was completely dependent on Britain financially and fiscally and virtually became a British

---

21　Luxemburg, R. *The Accumulation of Capital.* London: Routledge, 1951. Trans. Zuoshun Peng and Jixian Wu. Shanghai: Shanghai Joint Publishing Corporation, 1959: 376.

22　In view of the increasing disparity between the economic development in the South and that in the North due to the colonialist-imperialist invasion after the industrial revolutions, the gap of economy, politics, culture, and military was widened and the contradiction in the North-South relationship became conspicuous, this chapter will use the new concept of the South in the place of Oriental Countries and Oriental Societies. Note by the author.

23　Peasants and herdsmen who were deprived of land were chiefly in Algeria and South Africa. Note by the author.

"commercial colony". European capitalist powers and the U.S. reduced the newly independent countries in Latin America into semi-colonial countries by manipulating the politics and economy of countries in Latin America with the help of the dictatorship of caudillos. All these were unprecedentedly new situations and challenges for the Southern nations. All social classes and social groups in the South stricken with the dual crises were forced to make their own response. As described above, the infiltration of western colonial powers and the reaction it caused were in essence the invasion of colonialism and the resistance and response of the South. But there was another side of the problem. As the history had increasingly become the history of the world, modern humanism, enlightenment, natural science and production technology rising Western Europe as well as various accomplishments of social, economic, political, military, cultural and religious reforms, that is, modernity had also spread into nations in the South with the colonial aggression and economic penetration and cultural impact of Western industrial nations, which gave rise to the clash and fusion of different civilizations in a broader sense. The Southern nations made different responses to these serious challenges based on their own conditions and the degree of the impact, presenting dual features: one was to fight against colonialism and aggression, or rebel against the feudal rule; the other was to learn from the West, absorbing achievements of modern industrial civilization, saving themselves, and implementing modernization reform of their nations.

3.4.2. Early Uprisings under the Cloak of Religion

There were a number of uprisings in Asia, including the Peasant Uprising of the Taiping Heavenly Kingdom in China, the National Uprising in India, the Babism (Babek Uprising in Iran (Persia) and other fights by Asian peoples, which formed a climax of Asian uprisings in the mid-19th century. The uprisings were basically the responses of the lower classes in Eastern countries to the colonial invasion and its consequences (In India and Indonesia, some feudal lords also joined the movement and assumed the leadership).

In Southern countries most of the people were farmers. Before the guidance of an advanced class, various religions and superstitions were not only an important part of the spiritual world of farmers but also their heavy spiritual burden. When they rebelled, farmers had to resort to religions for their revolutionary discourse and ideological weapons to initiate a revolutionary storm. Uprisings and national movements of this period in Asian countries were generally under the cloak of religion. If in the country there was no such a religion, one would borrow one from foreign countries. A typical example was the Taiping Kingdom. The choice of the cloak, be it orthodox, fundamentalist or heathen, depended on the targets in the movement, which generally fell into two categories:

First, when Western colonial powers conquered or ruled the Southern nations, the national conflicts between the people and the feudal rulers of the South and the colonial invaders escalated into a principal contradiction. In general, national insurrections or national self-defense was adopted in the direct and frontal confrontations against the colonial invaders. Different from domestic class struggle, the lower classes tended to lay their hopes on the feudal ruling class to defend and save the country. It was also easier for the latter to lift a national flag, represent national interests, and assume the leadership in the anti-colonial struggle. In general, "The ideas of the ruling class are in every epoch the ruling ideas... those who lack the means of mental production are on the whole subject to it"[24]. This was more so at the moment of intense national conflicts. Therefore, the orthodox religion originally advocated by the ruling class of Southern nations could serve as spiritual weapons against Western colonialists. Many Asian and African countries believe in Islam. Thus, the Islamic "jihad" had become the most common form of self-defense in modern oriental national uprisings and wars. Under the banner of "jihad", from the Dipo Negoro Anti-Holland Uprising of Java Island in South Pacific, the Abdullah Kardelj Anti-France War of Algeria in the coastal Mediterranean, to the Omar Anti-France War along the Senegal River of Inland West Africa, the majority of the people of Eastern Muslim countries launched wars against colonial invasion and oppression. Even in the National Uprising participated by Hindus in India, the last emperor of the Mughal Empire, Bahadur Shah, which had been grounded by the British for many years, was brought out and re-covered with the robe of "caliph".

Second, when the Western colonial aggression (especially the use "informal empire") caused the structural turmoil of society in the Southern countries, upgrading or aggravating the social class conflicts in these countries, people in the southern countries often took the form of civil wars, namely the uprising of the lower masses, as a response to the social crisis and the national crisis hidden behind it. Although Western colonial aggression was the ultimate reason of the uprising, however, as long as they were not the direct rulers, the uprising pointed more directly to the domestic reactionary rulers. Because of the sharp class struggle against the reactionary ruling classes, the uprising would not follow the doctrines of orthodox religions or ideologies advocated by the ruling class as its spiritual weapons. They needed to create a new religion or sect, use some religious form, or religions borrowed from abroad. In short, they deified a new god, which was dismissed as heretic, as a new orthodoxy and denounced the old orthodox god as heretical. They dethroned the old god from its altar to expel the holy halo around it which defended the old system so as to dethrone the reactionary rulers. The Uprising of Taiping Heavenly Kingdom in China has borrowed the Religion of Worshiping God. The Babism Uprising in Iran established new "Babis". And there were numerous Mahdi uprisings.

The cloak of religion played an important role in modern national movements in Southern nations. As a spiritual weapon, it has mobilized and called upon the majority of the people in the South. As a religious institution, it provided the organizational forms of struggle and the leader group for the lower masses who were economically isolated and culturally backward.

---

24 Marx, Karl, and Fredrick Engels. Collected Works. Vol. 5. New York: International Publishers, 1975.

Peasants in the Southern countries were scattered in different places. Most of them lived in villages on the basis of the natural economy. They focused all their attention to a small plot of land, they were naturally submissive, and they had little contact with each other, like a heap of loose sand. Although under the cruel exploitation and oppression, suffering from pain and humiliation, it was not easy for peasants to unite and fight against the rulers. Under the historical conditions of that time, it was the religious cloak over the movement or uprising that, to a great extent, congregated and organized these segregated and mostly illiterate peasants. It was the tint of religion that added a sacred halo around their economic, political and social demands. For the majority of peasants who were nearly numb under oppression and other craftsmen, this "sacred" halo amounted to giving them an ideological emancipation and baptism: they firmly believed their claims were supported by the strength of the mighty (God, Allah, Heavenly Father, Buddha…). Their devotion to the sacred cause aroused their enthusiasm and gave them great courage to break the blind obedience, submissiveness, intellectual inertia and other weaknesses which were formed under various spiritual shackles for thousands of years. Therefore, their inner defiant instinct was revived, and their potential energy was released, which formed an extremely powerful spiritual pillar to sustain their courageous fight against the previously dominant ruling classes.

The religious weapons had also caused a lot of weaknesses and limitations to uprisings. First, the religion of the rebellious peasants was narrow and exclusive of pagan peasants, which was not conducive to rallying all peasants. Meanwhile, intellectuals (like Confucianists) who did not believe in the religion look upon conversion to it as an objectionable pursuit. Second, the cloak of religion was only used as a banner and a cover to attack the old dynasty, or even just to "purify their faith", while the religion itself could do nothing to the social structure and the unfair land ownership system. Thus, the original economic conditions remained intact. Third, the rebellions often ended tragically because the rebellious leaders and followers were intoxicated with the fantasy of the "heavenly kingdom" and "paradise". After they achieved partial victory, they thought that they were approaching the "heavenly kingdom". Therefore, they were eager to realize their ideal of the "heavenly kingdom", ceased to make any progress, and resigned themselves to the siege and final annihilation (for example, the Babism Uprising in Iran was trapped in three strongholds while the Taiping Kingdom movement was defeated in Nanjing). Fourth, they often resisted or even destroyed modern industrial civilization and its achievements (like the destruction of railways and the removal of telegraph lines).

Uprisings and struggles of this period mostly ended up in failure. Despite the lack of the leadership of an advanced leading class, some of the uprisings had reached a very high level, different from the general unrest. During the strenuous uprisings, peoples in the South fought bravely and tenaciously, which demonstrated their spirit of resistance and unwillingness to succumb to colonialism and their lackeys and agents, which inspired their national morale and enhanced national self-confidence. However, the tragic failure of some large-scale uprisings often damaged the overall national strength and provided an opportunity for greater colonialist aggressions.

3.4.3.Self-Defensive Reforms by the Feudal Upper Classes in South

In some major countries in the South, the social structural turmoil and the precarious situation of the country and the nation caused by the Western colonial aggression, as well as the reactions of the lower masses mainly in the form of riots and uprisings, awakened some insightful people of the feudal ruling class. They began to feel that the spreading of Western Learning was quite different the invasion by the old nomadic tribes or neighboring countries. Relying on their advantage in the machinery, superb technologies, and advanced economy, politics, military and culture, the West challenged the traditional society and traditional culture in the south, which gave rise to unprecedented changes. The reaction of the upper ruling classes in the South to the serious challenges could be basically divided into two different levels: the first was a shallow level, namely, to make a direct response to the military threat from the Western ships and armaments, follow the West to strengthen the army, and implement military reform so as to empower the army, consolidate the national defense, and stabilize the rule. This level mostly occurred in the early period. The second was an in-depth level, namely, to switch gradually from the reaction to the Western invasion to the history (traditional culture) of their own country, which meant to divert gradually the reforms to their own country. Such social reforms could be further divided into two categories based on the depth of the reform. One was the study of the superficial modern industrial civilization, which basically did not the touch the social and economic foundation (like the reform of the administrative system); the other was the introduction of some systems of modern industrial civilization, which somehow touched the socio-economic foundation (like the reform of the feudal land system).

95

The reforms started by the upper ruling classes in the South in the mid-19th century were considerably prevalent: Muhammad Ali in Egypt initiated a reform w from 1820s to 1830s, which reached its peak in 1841; Mirza Taji Khan in Iran also carried out reforms from 1848 to 1851; a series of reforms in the Ottoman Empire which reached a climax with the Supreme Edict of the Rose House in 1839; Myanmar and Thailand (Siam) also carried out some upper reforms; Ethiopia, Madagascar, Tunisia and other countries also carried out reforms. China started the self-improvement movement. Japan also carried out reforms by the end of Tokugawa Shogunate.

These reforms of the feudal upper ruling classes presented some common characteristics: First, the Western colonial aggression and its profound impact had threatened the stability of feudal governing so that the upper ruling class could not maintain their ruling. Therfore, the reformists of the ruling class or a new ruling group surpassed the obstinate feudal ruling bloc to become reformers. Second, no matter how these reforms were different in the scale, content and depth, they were essentially the self-help (or self-improvment) movements of the upper classes in the Southern countries, which were dedicated to building a prosperous country with a powerful army. Regions and countries in the south which had not been relegated to colonies by the mid-19th century basically, except for a small number of early compradors, had not yet paved the soil for the widespread propagation of the ideology of modern Western bourgeois. Therefore, it was hard for these self-protection movements to break away from the scope of feudalism in terms of the leadership, guiding ideology and the system to implement reforms. Third, some new elements of modern Western industrial civilization were absorbed in the process of self-rescue, which provided things completely new to the oriental history. Reformists in the Eastern countries reached a consensus, that is, to learn skills from the enemy to fight against it. Their interest of reform focused on the Western "skills" which they thought would have immediate effects. These "skills" were nothing more than "sophisticated battleships" and "advanced machines". In fact, they introduced advanced Western science and technology and advanced productive forces of capitalism. But the reformists in countries such as China, Japan and Korea had still set several bottom lines as "adopting Western culture that should serve the fundamental Chinese culture" and "combining the Japanese spirit with Western talent".

Although these advanced productive forces from the West were transplanted to backward relations of production in many regions in the South, or the Western advanced technology was simply used to fix cracks on the building of the old system or even just to paint some colors, the logic of historical dialectics still let first reformists (including some colonial governments, such as the East India Company government in India) act as the unconscious tool of history. Since the advanced Western machines and productivity (even military plants) were introduced, these new productivity (like machines and railways) would truly become pioneers of modern industry. The introduction of advanced western science and technology also needed to cultivate talents who could master these advanced technology; and to train these types of talents, it was essential to run all kinds of schools or send young students to study abroad to inform them with the outside world and acquaint them with the capitalist production relations and the various aspects of the superstructure (like political systems, legal thoughts, humanities). The bourgeois intellectuals in the Southern countries, who had been influenced by modern industrial civilization and had a new outlook on the world, were growing up this way before the formation of national bourgeoisie. Furthermore, since the introduction of material achievements of the industrial revolution opened the Pandora's Box, it was bound to accelerate the disintegration and collapse of all ossified pre-capitalist social frameworks. All these had provided some essential prerequisites and foundation for the development of capitalism in the South. Therefore, we can say that although the reforms of the upper classes of the Southern nations in the mid-19th century could not be called "modern movements", they should be regarded as the earliest attempts of modernization activities in the South in the 19th century. It was undoubtedly a loud echo of the irresistible world modernization among the feudal upper class and intellectuals in the South. Its significance was self-evident. As what Marx and Engels pointed out, these were self-rescue movements of the insightful people in the South in a very serious situation, when the Western bourgeoisie "compels all nations, on pain of extinction, to adopt the bourgeois mode of production".[25] Under the extremely severe circumstances, people of vision in the South launched self-help movements[26].

---

25   Marx, Karl, and Fredrick Engels. Collected Works. Vol. 6. New York: International Publishers, 1976: 488.
26   See He, Fangchuan. "Upper Reforms in the East in the mid-19th Century." *Study of History* 4(1981).

Chapter IV

Expansion and Contraction of Colonial Empires

4.1. The Contention for the South in the Period of Monopoly Capitalism

4.1.1. Expansionism by Handful of Colonial States

The period wherein monopoly capitalism was formed in modern history was roughly from 1870 to the early 20th century. This was the period of imperialism, wherein capitalist productive forces had advanced rapidly, world market was finally established, and laissez-faire capitalism had completed the transition into monopoly capitalism. Following England and France, the US, Germany, Italy, Russia, and Japan completed their industrial revolution successively. The industrial productivity of the US and Germany overtook and surpassed that of England. Within 30 years, world industrial production had increased fourfold. World capitalist production relations expanded and deepened. The economic power and industrialization level of all major countries in the world also underwent great changes. Relative share of world manufacturing output, industrialization level per capita, and major industrialized countries in the order of importance are listed as follows:[1]

1   Kennedy, Paul. *The Rise and Fall of the Great Powers: Economic Change and Military Conflict from 1500 to 2000*. New York: Vintage Books, 1987: 181-182.

Stavrianos, L. S. *Global Rift: The Third World Comes of Age*. New York: William Morrow & Co, 1981. trans. Chi Yue, et al. Beijing: The Commercial Press, 1993: 265.

Table 4.1. Relative Share of World Manufacturing Output (%) (1830-1938)

	1830	1860	1880	1900	1913	1928	1938
UK	9.5	19.9	22.9	18.5	13.6	9.9	10.7
US	2.4	7.2	14.7	23.6	32	39.3	31.4
Germany	3.5	4.9	8.5	13.2	14.8	11.6	12.7
France	5.2	7.9	7.8	6.8	6.1	6.0	4.4
Italy	2.3	2.5	2.5	2.5	2.4	2.7	2.8
Russia	5.6	7.0	7.6	8.8	8.2	5.3	9.0
Japan	2.8	2.6	2.4	2.4			
China	29.8	19.7	12.5	6.2			
India/Pakistan	17.6	8.6	2.8	1.7			

Table 4.2. Industrialization Level Per Capita from 1830 to 1938 (taking the Great Britain in 1900 as 100)

	1830	1860	1880	1900	1913	1928	1938
UK	25	64	87	100	115	122	157
US	14	21	38	69	126	182	167
Germany	9	15	25	52	85	128	144
France	12	20	28	39	59	82	73
Italy	8	10	12	17	26	44	61
Russia	7	8	10	15	20	20	38
Japan	7	7	9	12	20	30	51
China	6	4	4	3			
India/Pakistan	6	3	2	1			

Table 4.3. Major Industrialized Countries in the Order of Importance

	1860	1870	1880	1900
1	UK	UK	US	US
2	US	US	UK	Germany
3	France	France	Germany	UK
4	Germany	Germany	France	France

It can been seen from the above three tables that due to the unbalanced development of capitalist economy the balance of economic power of the major countries in the world had undergone great changes. From 1870 to 1913, industry in UK and France had increased by 1.3 times and 1.9 times respectively while in Germany 4.6 times and in US 8.1 times. Around the same time (1815-1913), export commodities from Germany increased by 3 times, those from US nearly 4 times while from UK only 1.2 times and from France 0.8 times[2]. The order of the international status of major industrialized countries had changed abruptly: UK ranked first, US the third and Germany the fourth in 1860 while

---

2   Beaud, Michel. *History of Capitalism: 1500-1980*. New York: Monthly Review Press, 1983. Trans. Aimei Wu, et al. Beijing: Oriental Press, 1987: 177.

US ranked first, Germany the second and UK fell to the third in 1900, which bespoke that conflicts among capitalist countries would be intensified.

The development of world capitalism since modern times had been closely associated with colonialism, which took colonial rule as a super-economic means to plunder and exploit underdeveloped countries, accumulate capital, and strengthen power. For more than one hundred years, capitalist economic power of European countries was roughly in direct proportion to their occupied American colonies. The collapse of Spanish American colonial empire was the very manifestation and inevitable outcome of the flagging capitalist force of Spain for a long time. In 1876, among the six powerful European and American countries (UK, US, France, Germany, Italy, and Russia), exclusive of the "domestic colonies" of Russia, only UK and France owned 23.4 million square kilometers of colonies, 22.5 million of which was in the hands of UK, while US, Germany, and Italy were all devoid of any colonies. There was a great disparity in the possession of colonies and economic power of every country, behind which lurked sharp conflicts.

An unprecedentedly severe economic crisis arose in capitalist countries in 1873, which caused a depression which lasted till the middle of 1880s and aggravated the already sharp capitalist conflicts. World capitalist economy had almost reached a point of being unsustainable. It was in this period that the gradual transition of laissez-faire capitalism to monopoly capitalism began. After the 1870s, capitalism of laissez fair competition had obviously declined. Finance capital gradually became dominant in the place of industrial capital, and financial syndicates penetrating into governments, parliaments, and social groups began to increasingly influence policy-making of government and dominate the media to a certain extent.

With their desire of colonial plunder intensified, monopoly capitalists tried to seize as many colonies as possible and connect colonies with metropolitan states to form colonial empires. The internal impetus for this desire was extremely strong, which was manifested in a hunger to grab monopoly profits. The law of the decline of profit which worked in the stage of free competition continued to play an important role in the stage of monopoly. The decline of profit led to the surplus of capital, which aggravated capital competition. In every country, the obstruction of investment and reduction of additional investment by monopoly capital led to a large amount of surplus capital. It was necessary for monopoly capitalists to export the surplus capital to foreign countries, especially the underdeveloped ones where capital was scarce, land low-priced, wages low, and raw materials cheap, to gain high monopoly profits. Although there existed higher risks to build railways, obtain land, build ports, set up and run mines in foreign countries than in pure merchandise trade, the establishment of local legal relationship and institutions also lagged far behind. Therefore, finance capital always resorted to violence to surmount economic obstacles. Thus, capital exporting countries demanded to implement colonial rule in the underdeveloped areas[3]. The internal pressure of grabbing monopoly profits to transfer domestic capital was always combined with the fierce competition in the world market. After the complete formation of the world market, it was of a greater necessity for emergent industrial countries to seize and expand market than old colonial countries to maintain and expand market because any increase and expansion of capitalist production needed matching market and materials. Monopoly capitalism not only needed merchandise market and the sources of raw materials but also capital market so that it had a particularly strong intention to expand market to consolidate its competitive position in the world market. Before the middle of the 19th century, capital export was nearly monopolized by UK—no country was able to compete with it, which ensured the absolute dominance of UK on the world market. It was a golden age of nearly a century when UK was not worried about the competition of other countries in industry or finance. "Laissez faire" and "market freedom" were resounding slogans in UK, whose advantage in colonies prompted other countries like France, Holland, and Russia to strive to maintain and expand their rule in seized territories and control over their spheres of influence. All these motives boiled down to the seizure of colonies. As what Lenin said, "[t]o the numerous "old" motives of colonial policy, finance capital has added the struggle for the sources of raw materials, for the export of capital, for spheres of influence, i.e. for spheres for profitable deals, concessions, monopoly profits and so on, economic territory in general"[4] (Lenin, Imperialism the Highest

Stage of Capitalism).

The advancement of scientific and technological revolution also made it more likely for monopoly capital to seize more remote colonies in its outward expansion. First of all, the technological revolution in transportation industry also made epoch-making advances in this aspect. The opening of the Suez Canal (1869) and the Panama Canal (1914) greatly shortened the distance of world ocean transportation: the voyage distance from London to Bombay in India was shortened 41%, to Hongkong 26%, from Liverpool to San Francisco 42%. Steamships driven by steam engine propellers of great horsepower taking the place of most sailing ships were greatly advanced in speed and volume of freight. The one-way voyage from London to Calcutta was shortened from 3 months to 18 days. The freight volume of each ship was uplifted from an average of 184 tons in the 1840s to 5,000 tons in the early 20th century. The cost of transportation was reduced over a half. Railways were built everywhere and within a short period of time railway lines over land increased in leaps and bounds. Aside from Europe and North America, the total length of railways had reached over 170,000 kilometers. The transcontinental railway lines had been built successively. After the railway from Europe to Constantinople (Istanbul) in Turkey was opened in 1888, the railway to Baghdad and Basra were planned. In

3   Hilferding, Rudolf. "The Inevitability of History and the Inevitable Policy". in *The Second International Revisionists' Fallacy on Imperialism*, 1976: 218.
4   Lenin, Vladimir. *Imperialism, the Highest Stage of Capitalism*. New York: International Publishers, 1939, 1974: 113.

1904, the first "Eurasian Bridge Railway" through Siberia was successfully established. Railways and steamships paved ways for the creation of the so-called macro-economic regions, which became the most important means of opening overseas markets. Regional markets took this opportunity to develop rapidly into the world market. When submarine cables in the Mediterranean, the Atlantic, and the Indian Ocean were laid, world communication network came into being. In 1901, wireless radio wave crossed the Atlantic, which made all continents more closely connected. Posted rates of banks in London and financial information could be transferred to Calcutta, Cape Town, and Hongkong via submarine cables and posted on the local market lists. A real world market linking five continents had finally been set up. Goods, labor, capital, and non-governmental contacts stopped to take hardly any account of national barriers. Commodity prices across the world were nearly identical because merchants could know prices and financial news all over the world by means of cables and submarine cables to adjust prices accordingly. World economy had been closely linked to form an interdependent single entity. Countries in the East were incorporated into the system of world economy. The more convenient and speedy transportations and communications greatly reduced the costs of goods transportation, which created more convenient conditions for European and American developed countries to acquire profits when they dumped commodities to remote and lesser developed countries, obtained raw materials, and exported capital. The opposing gap in the North-South relationship became deeper.

World capitalist economy in dozens years around the formation of monopoly capitalism was enervated and even on the verge of a dead end due to the extreme intensification of all kinds of conflicts. Taking the road of capitalism successively UK, France, Germany, Italy, Russia, Belgium, US, and Japan expected to solve the dilemma by imperialist policies and monopoly policies. However, monopoly arising out of free competition could not eliminate competition but coexisted with the latter, which gave rise to many intense and acute conflicts, frictions, and clashes. Lenin contended that the very combination of the mutually contradictory principles of competition and monopoly was the essence of imperialism. The attempt of major capitalist countries to solves these conflicts by means of "protective tariffs" and setting up colonies was tantamount to drinking poison to quench their thirst, which intensified the conflicts and came to a deadlock on the question of colonies to be solved (in fact mitigated) in the end by resorting to war.

Western great powers waged a fierce war in "protective tariffs" to protect and expanded markets respectively occupied. Intolerable with the excessive share of commodities from UK in "their own markets", Germany set up new tariffs in 1878 and 1903, the US issued McKinley Tariff in 1890 and Dingley Tariff Act in 1897, France made new tariffs in 1892 for the French to monopolize import and export trade in French colonies, into which all goods from France were free of tariff while those from other countries were imposed a high tariffs. One third of export commodities from Britain were shipped to British colonies but colonies of other countries in the past were the markets for British commodities. The economic crisis in 1873 had a very late and small impact on UK, which was closely related to the vastest colonial market possessed by the country. Britain was the first to export capital to build projects like factories, railways, and ports, which in turn supplied Britain with a large number of orders for goods. Britain obtained many profits from capital export, which became a highly effective instrument of encouraging commodity export and had a perpetual drive for the expansion of markets. From 1890 to 1915, Britain and Germany invested 4 billion dollars in Argentina, Brazil, and Uruguay and controlled 46 percent of total business in these three countries. Therefore, Curzon, the British Viceroy of India, exclaimed that "the loss of a market is a retrograde step that cannot be recovered; the gain of a market is a positive addition to the national strength."[5]

Driven by the new motives of plundering colonies, the capitalist great powers all took the road of seizing new colonies and carved out "spheres of influence". Since the middle of the 1870s, the great powers fastened the pace in their contention for colonies and partition of the world, which was completed within 30 years. Britain and France grabbed most colonies among old colonial countries. New imperialist countries, Germany, Italy, Japan, America, and Belgium, which had not obtained any colonies in the period of laissez-faire capitalism, were actively engaged in the struggle for colonies. From 1876 to 1914, the capitalist great powers gained 34.9 million square kilometers of colonies, and carved up 14.6 million square kilometers of "spheres of influence" (semi-colonies). The total area of colonies in the world reached 74.9 million square kilometers. In the history of colonization, the contention for colonies had lasted for a long time, which reached the peak point in 1921 with 168 colonies.

4.1.2. Causes behind the Changes in the Colonial Policies of Western Powers

Some western historians like Fieldhouse, Ronald Robinson, and John Gallagher who denied that imperialism was a stage of capitalism in their study of the history of colonial expansion (in fact mainly the history of British colonial expansion). They argued that the continuous expansion of Britain in the 19th century laid more stress on setting up "an informal empire" under the policy of laissez-faire rather than "a formal empire". The expansion after 1870 was merely a continuation of that in the first half of the century. Since these Cambridge scholars adopted the interpretation method of "taking a step back" (admitting the expansion of Britain) in their study of the foreign expansion of Britain and seemed to lay the stress on critiquing Hobson's masterpiece Imperialism: A Study, they were in fact opposed to Lenin's thesis of imperialism as a stage of capitalism. They even criticized J. Strachey, a Labor Party theorist, who saw in The End of Empire "'imperialism' as the external

---

5 Curzon, George Nathaniel. *Persia and the Persian Question.* Vol.2. London, 1892: 604.

expression of the surplus capital"[6]. It was because these arguments had aroused people's attention to the causes for the emergence of imperialism. Robinson and Gallagher considered imperialism had a political function even before the 1870s of incorporating some countries (like colonies) into the international economy, which they thought was not driven by the so-called competitive accumulation of capital. In the first half of the 19th century of "Laissez-faire imperialism" mentioned above, the Great Britain had never completely followed "Laissez-faire" but adopted the means of indirect interference (informal empire) and outright annexation only if necessary, such as the annexation of Natal in South Africa in 1842. They argued that the Great Britain maintained their old policies after 1870 rather than adopted new policies of annexation. Even if politicians like Salisbury, Rosebery, and Chamberlain who were called "representatives of new imperialism" did not implement indiscriminate annexation policies in Egypt, Sudan, and South Africa only if necessary. This situation was the same as that in the first half of the 19th century when the Great Britain for the sake of national interest insisted on "informal empire if possible, formal only if necessary". Therefore, in the entire 19th century, the Great Britain did not forsake its old colonies while continuously adding new ones.[7]

Fieldhouse, likewise, did not agree to separate imperialist expansion from the development of "early imperialism"[8]. He contended that if the need of economic interests in the early 19th century did not rest with political background, the relationship between economy and politics by the end of the 19th century was reversed: economic considerations were subordinate to political considerations while national security, military power, and national authority were the top priorities. He argued that "it is clear that imperialism cannot be explained in simple terms of economic theory and the nature of finance capitalism"[9]. He attributed the phenomenon of imperialism to "the rise of this imperialist ideology, [a] belief that colonies were an essential attribute of any great nation"[10], which he thought "can properly be understood only in terms of the same social hysteria"[11]. Likewise, Robinson and Gallagher ascribed colonies which were "permanent gains for western civilisation" to "the expansive energies of Europe"[12]. However, the crucial question is how this ideology and social mentality or "energies" arose.

6   Fieldhouse, D.K. "'Imperialism': A Historiographical Revision". *The Economic History Review* 14.2 (1961): 194.
7   Gallagher, J., and R. Robinson. "The Imperialism of Free Trade." *Economic History Review* 6.1 (1953): 1-15.
8   Fieldhouse, D.K. "'Imperialism': A Historiographical Revision". *The Economic History Review* 14.2(1961): 187-208.
9   Ibid.: 209.
10   Ibid.: 207.
11   Ibid.: 209.
12   Robinson, R.E., and J. Gallagher. "The Partition of Africa." *Material Progress and World-Wide Progress: 1870-1898*. Ed. F. H. Hinsley. *The New Cambridge Modern History*. Vol. 11. Cambridge: Cambridge University Press, 1962: 639.

The new theories of Robinson and Fieldhouse were praised and criticized at the same time by some western scholars like D.C. M. Platt, A.G. Hopkins, P. J. Cain and V. Wehler, who published papers on these theories. This book aims not to repeat these criticisms but point out we need to probe into the research of Robinson, Gallagher, and Fieldhouse on imperialist economy and their theoretical frameworks. However, if we disparage like Fieldhouse any accounts for imperialism from the perspective of economy as "simple terms of economic theory"[13], we practically take ideology and social mentality as the main reasons, which might cause us to fall into a narrower trap and arrive at the conclusion that "that imperialism owed its popular appeal not to the sinister influence of the capitalists, but to its inherent attractions for the masses"[14]. In fact, before 1807, the account of Basil Davidson in Africa in Modern History of the attitude of British bourgeoisie was most vivid and pertinent: "For a long time Africa was 'opened up' by persons of small standing in their home countries, and, the missionaries apart, often of dubious reputation. Much of the initial drive for conquest and enclosure came from those segments of middle-class European society that stood outside the ring of real economic power. Received with contempt in bankers' parlors, they had to be careful to knock twice and wipe their feet. Those who went in as of right were the men and interests concerned with India and the 'white colonies' in Britain's case, or with Indo-China if they were French. For long they toiled in vain."[15]

The apparent changes in overseas colonial policies of major industrial countries after 1870 (or 1876) were brought about by several interactive elements, among which economic facts still played a decisive role.

The Great Britain had an advantage in the 19th century market, possessed most colonies, and was the earliest and only country to export capital in the first half of the 19th century, which led to different characteristics of its economic changes in the end of the 19th century from those of any other western countries: first, when nearly all industrial countries like Germany, France, America, Italy, and Russia practiced high tariff protectionism, Britain did not jump into the fray (because the fray was mainly against the dump of British commodities) and announced to give up laissez-faire till 1932. Second, British monopoly progressed at a slower pace than that of other countries so that most industrial enterprises by 1887 were still family businesses with fewer monopoly institutions and lesser degrees. However, the concentration of British enterprises also resulted in monopoly, which was only slightly later and in different forms. Third, as the world financial center, bank monopoly capital in Britain developed at a fast speed. In 1913, there were 27 banks whose capital surpassed one million pounds, representing 85.7% of all bank deposits, among

13   Fieldhouse, D. K. "'Imperialism': A Historiographical Revision." *The Economic History Review* 14.2(1961): 209.
14   Ibid.: 209.
15   Davidson, Basil. *Africa in Modern History*. Harmondsworth, Middlesex: Penguin Books, 1978. Trans. Zhan Shu, et al. Beijing: China Social Sciences Press, 1989: 73-74.

which the largest five banks shared 39.7%. British banks did not mainly rely on their credit relations with native industrial enterprises but their investment of the substantial deposits taken at home in foreign trade, colonies, and other countries to gain excess profits. Therefore, bank capital was most concerned with foreign trade, colonial enterprise, and colonial expansion while ignored relatively the expansion of native industry, which mainly depended on the accumulation (gaining profits in foreign trade) of enterprises themselves. Fourth, due to the colonial advantage in nearly a century, Britain had monopoly over raw material production in colonies, for instance, De Beers Diamond Mining in South Africa and South Africa Gold Mining Company were all international monopoly companies, and Managing Agency which controlled investment in Indian industry, mining, and plantation were also a monopoly institution in a special form.

Britain, as mentioned above, was engaged in overseas colonial expansion in the entire 19th century and because of its advantage gained monopoly over its vast colonies for a long time. Therefore, after 1876, British expansion was naturally continued to maintain its advantage and military hegemony was strengthened in business and capital expansion in the name of "securing the lifeline of the British empire". In 1882, Britain occupied the Suez Canal, many new colonies (Egypt, Sudan, British Somali) in the following several years in the name of protecting the new sea route, and all ports and military vital areas on the west coast of the Indian Ocean in South Africa and many strategic vital areas along the coast of the Indian Ocean in East Africa in the 1880s and 1890s. Britain not only deepened and strengthened its military and economic control over new and old colonies but also spared no efforts in expanding colonial areas. From 1876 to 1914, Britain seized 11 million square kilometers of new colonies with a colonial population of 0.1416 billion, ranking first among western countries, so that it subsumed one fourth of world land area under the Union Jack flag of the British empire. It can be seen that these facts were of a nature different from that of the mere "continuation of policies" in the first half of the 19th century asserted by Robinson and Gallagher and of the rhetoric the end of old history not the beginning of new history uttered by Fieldhouse. British colonial expansion was truly a manifestation of storm and stress in the new stage[16]. Even the forthright apologist for the British Empire L.C.A. Knowles also claimed in The Economic Development of the British Overseas Empire that this period (after 1870) was the really important period of development of the new British Empire.

With the rise in colonial values, British commercial bank scrambled to provide loans and export capital to foreign trade and colonies. The convenient transportation over sea and land greatly enhanced the use value of formerly remote and vast colonies as sources of raw materials and food suppliers for the empire. The invention of Bessemerizing made it possible to substitute cheap and durable steel rails for iron rails, which enabled railways to be stretched into

16 Fieldhouse, D.K. *The Colonial Empires*. Ithaca: Cornell University Press, 1973: 460-461.

the vast inland of remote colonies so that long-distance transportation of raw materials and commodities could also obtain substantial profits. The improvement of health care greatly enhanced the survival rate of Europeans in tropical Africa. Europeans in business, missionary, and Garrison barracks could go safely and quickly into the inland and live for a long time there, which bestowed new values to tropical African colonies considered as "European tombs" in the past. There were two important technological inventions on ocean steamers: compound steam engine and surface condenser (fresh water could be used repeatedly) which transformed ocean transportation. The extension of voyage greatly cutting off the shipping rate, the use of cold store[17] and the shortening of the voyage on the Suez Canal by one third led to on the one hand 70 million pounds of shipping income which consolidated British sea power and on the other hand great impacts on the development of colonies in every aspect. In 1900, New Zealand alone shipped four million frozen sheep to British market. When British farmers in colonies could ship and gain substantial profits from cream, cheese, beef, mutton, vegetables, and fruits to British market for sale by cold-storage equipment, "further immigration" became an appealing policy in Britain. In 1895, when Cecil Rhodes returned to Britain from South Africa, he broadly expressed his views on imperialism and the new impacts of the increased colonies on Britain: "I was in the East End of London (a working-class quarter) yesterday and attended a meeting of the unemployed. I listened to the wild speeches, which were just a cry for 'bread! bread!' and on my way

home I pondered over the scene and I became more than ever convinced of the importance of imperialism.... My cherished idea is a solution for the social problem, i.e. in order to save the 40,000,000 inhabitants of the United Kingdom from a bloody civil war, we colonial statesmen must acquire new lands to settle the surplus population, to provide new markets for the goods produced in the factories and mines. The Empire, as I have always said, is a bread and butter question. If you want to avoid civil war, you must become imperialists"[18].

It can be concluded from the words uttered by Rhodes, a member of British cabinet and imperialist politician tremendously influential in foreign policy making that colonial expansion had gained a new significance in British foreign policy.

The major reasons and driving forces behind British colonial expansion in the end of the 19th century and the 20th century could be seen clearly in South Africa Incident and a series of other incidents and the Anglo-Boer War. It is of necessity to clarify a concept here: the favorite trick played by British government was to separate completely British colonial government in South Africa from British imperialist government in terms of policy and instrument. But in

17 Vessels of New Zealand equipped with cold store in 1882 carried to England a large amount of muttons, which were made as valuable as sheep pelts. Queensland of New Zealand developed large farms to raise livestock. Note by the author.
18 Lenin, Vladimir. *Imperialism, the Highest Stage of Capitalism*. New York: International Publishers, 1939. Beijing: People's Publishing House, 1974: 71.

fact the former was merely the executor of the latter's decisions and could not exceed its authority. Just as it is not right to shuffle off decision-making responsibility for the Opium War with China in 1840 from Downing Street onto the British East India Company government in Calcutta[19], where was the source of "the driving force for imperialism".

First, annex all regions which British government considered as vital to the empire. In the 1870s, Britain annexed by force or guile the largest Kimberley Diamond Mine into Cape Colony[20]. In 1886, Rand Gold Mine much more valuable than Kimberley Diamond Mine was discovered and mined in Transvaal Republic of South Africa. British capitalists controlled the mine and coveted to annex it into British Empire. Twelve years later (1898), the annual output of Rand Gold Mine soared to 117 tons, representing 27.5 percent of world gold output. Gold ingots produced in Rand were shipped steadily to the underground vaults of the Bank of England in London. The abundant gold reserve would save the disaster caused by gold standard monetary policies in the 1890s and henceforth laid the economic basis for Britain to implement gold standard system and London to be the center of world finance. "City of London" became capital of the financial kingdom much broader than British Empire. Transvaal gold mine was the keystone to maintain such an important position. No matter by direct or indirect control, formal or informal, British government must annex it into the empire.

Secondly, the long-term overseas investment by Britain from 1870 to 1900 rose from one billion pounds to 2.5 billion pounds, ranking first in the world. Although British formal foreign trade deficit rose steadily with an annual average deficit of 65 million of pounds, it could still maintain an income of 23 million pounds due to its income of 50 million pounds from overseas investment and a shipping income of 18 million pounds each year plus incomes from insurance and commission trade. Thus it can be seen that the income from overseas investment played an important role in maintaining a balanced international income. After the 1870s, British overseas investment rose so rapidly that the volume of (long-term) investment within 30 years was 1.5 time than that in the past half century. However, due to the default in British usurious debts of Egypt, the Ottoman Empire and Central and South American countries, British investors suffered losses since the 1870s so that they needed new outlets for investment and demanded British government expand its imperialist spheres of influence. Thereafter, British spheres of investment were enlarged continuously. Most British capital was exported to provide necessary materials for railway construction and railway equipment. British enterprises and investment capital

---

19   See remarks made by Sir George Campbell in the House of Commons: "If the Chinese are to be poisoned by opium, I would rather they were poisoned for the benefit of our Indian subjects [!] than for the benefit of any other Exchequer." Qtd. in Morton, A. L. *A People's History of England.* London: Lawrence and Wishart Ltd., 1951: 462
20   For details see Zheng, Jiaxin. *The History of Colonialism: Africa.* Beijing: Peking University Press, 2000: 385.

not only firmly connected colonies as well as many non-colonial countries (including so called informal empire) but also created conditions for British further investment in Africa, Asia, South America, North America, and Oceania, especially for opening up mineral resources and agrarian resources. The pursuit for profits allured private capital to every British colony, and tea plantations and rubber plantations in colonies like Ceylon and Malaya developed rapidly. To the large-scale investment in Indian railways, British government adopted the preferential measure of guaranteeing British investors an annual interest rate of 5%. Such a guaranteed bonus aroused great passion of British investor for investment in India.

Thirdly, British export trade and transit trade was violently impacted by "protective tariffs" of other western countries. The inquiry in 1886 by British Royal Commission of Inquiry revealed that Britain was confronted with powerful opponents in international trade, among which Germany and America were the toughest. They adopted the latest technologies and processing methods in production and sale of new products, and strictly protected their native markets by issuing tariff acts. American and Germany salesmen with great energy, wisdom, and adaptability travelled around the world and with the flexible credit system snatched many markets formerly dominated by Britain. Among all British colonies, only the tariff system developed by Indian colonial government was most beneficial in protecting British manufacturers. The assertion of "the gain of a market is a positive addition to the national strength" by Curzon, the British Viceroy of India, was fervently acclaimed by British manufacturers. Industrialists of cotton textile in Lancashire highly applauded the exercise in colonies of "direct political power" of colonial governments by viceroys like Curzon to effectively protect suzerain business markets. India imposed a revenue tax on import cotton textiles from Britain while British colonial government in India imposed a commodity tax of the same rate on Indian cotton textile factory owners, which prevented textile factories in Lancashire from suffering any loss in the interest of export to India. British manufacturers and overseas investors concluded from the practical interests gained from such non-immigrant colonies like India that Britain needed such ideal colonies like India. Queen Victoria, also Empress of India, was an active advocator and supporter of the imperialist expansion of British Empire. Likewise, French colonies brought about benefits to French Empire but on a smaller scale.

In addition to all of the above, seeing that colonies and spheres of influence were greatly beneficial to the future development of world economy and politics from the great benefits for suzerain economic development brought about by the vast colonies possessed by Britain and France, all emergent industrial countries followed their examples. The struggle of Britain, France, Russia, Austria to partition the Ottoman Empire, the contention of Britain and France in Egypt, and the partition of semi-colony China by numerous foreign powers drew the attention of colonial powers to the Middle East, Africa, and Fast East. Colonial expansion was increased several times in scale and intensity than that before the middle of the 19th century and taken as the pattern of great powers by more colonial countries. British supremacy in Africa (there were still territories of over 90 percent not incorporated into the spheres of influence of any country) was lost and the leading positions of Britain and France in co-lonial expansion were undermined, which indicated that the balance of power among European countries maintained since the Congress of Vienna in 1815 was under change. Germany rose in power and gained material advantages, which made it possible for Germany to play an indispensable role of check and balance in the world pattern of colonialism and begin to link its European interests with overseas interests. All these elements undermined British posi-tion and repeatedly provoked Britain to preempt several economic territories and strategic vital areas. In 1882, Britain occupied Egypt and the Suez Canal, in 1895 launched Jameson Raid in South Africa, in 1898 occupied the entire Kowloon Peninsula in the name of lease, and British expeditionary forces oc-cupied Sudan and repelled French expeditionary forces at Fashoda village in the south of Sudan, all of which were not contingent incidents but the necessary steps taken by Britain in the end of the 19th century in colonial expansion.

Lastly, there were still some important British politicians who thought Britain had sated territorially in 1870. However, in the following 30 years, Benjamin Disraeli and Joseph Chamberlain uncharacteristically urged impe-rialist expansion[21]. In 1852, Disraeli proposed the famous thesis in a letter to Lord Malmesbury that these wretched colonies were a millstone round our necks and insisted on saying in his letter to Prime Minister Lord Derby in 1866 that Britain could succeed only if it gives up all colonies except India and the Mediterranean territory (Gibraltar). However, in 1872, Disraeli proposed the idea of consolidating British Empire and claimed that he was an adherent of "the idea of empire" and advocator of expansion of British Empire. In 1874 when he first presided over the cabinet (1874-1880), he further put forward the colonial expansion policy of "consolidating and expanding" (British Empire). Chamberlain was even "against imperialism" in the early 1880s but became a frantic imperialist advocating aggression and expansion several years later. The rapidly changing world situation prompted prominent figures of British ruling class to become "fashionable" imperialist. Although Queen Victorian was not outstanding, she was increasingly keen to be the symbol of British Empire in her late years, which was not only because that she was proclaimed as Empress of India but she had great passion for British colonial expansion. She welcomed any territorial annexation of Britain and disapproved of any renouncement of colonial posts in Africa or Asia. When Britain was defeated in the early period of the Anglo-Boer War, the message that the queen was not frustrated inspired British people across the country. On 22 January 1901, her last words before death were if there were any new messages from General Kitchener, which il-lustrated well the imperialist sentiments prevalent in British society.

---

21   Hinsley, F. H., ed. *Material Progress and World-Wide Progress: 1870-1898. The New Cambridge Modern History*. Vol. 11. Cambridge: Cambridge University Press, 1962: 531.

The economy of Germany developed rapidly in the latter half of the 19th century and the early 20th century. Its industrial production doubled from 1895 to 1913, overtook and surpassed the most advanced country in economy, France. Germany became not only an important industrial country but an important element in the world economy, occupying a leading position among capitalist countries. After 1871, the explosive development of German industry also demanded overseas markets and sources of raw materials while other capitalist great powers had already occupied the most advantageous regions of world resources. German capitalist exclaimed that they also needed territories under the sky. Certainly when this later comer arrived at the banquet, there was not much ambrosia left. In order to compete for an advantageous position in world market, Germany first had to spare no efforts in making protective tariffs and implementing dumping policies, which needed to exclude or even eliminate free competition within the country and practice monopoly to maintain high prices so as to compensate for losses in overseas dumping. Therefore, monopoly developed more violently and swiftly in Germany than in any other European countries. German capital took advantage of young chemical industry, precision instruments and optical industry to achieve a dominant position in the world. In 1913, German export shared 12.6% of the total volume of international trade, second only to Britain (17.3%). The achievement of the advantageous position in export trade not only contributed to the rapid development of industry but also increased capital accumulation of Germany. Because native agriculture could not yield high profits, companies like Siemens urged to expand in overseas investment. Capital export of Germany soared and surpassed quickly Britain and France. Its overseas investment reached 12.5 billion gold francs in 1902 and 44 billion gold francs (around 24 billion marks) in 1914.

The Pan-German Society took the lead in Germany to make extensive propaganda that Germany lacked enough space and territory: if Germany could have more space, all dire poverty would disappear. It also preached social Darwinism, propagandizing that East Europe, Africa, and Asia were inhabited by inferior races that could not live by themselves but need the rule of "the ruling race". German colonialism was established on such a theoretical basis, which was developed further by Emperor William II of Germany into the ideal of Großdeutschland (Greater Germany) that "the world has to rely on Germany alone for survival". Such an ideology of racial superiority agitated Germany to implement the policy of colonial expansion, whose primary targets were West Asia, East Asia and Africa. However, these regions were mostly British and French spheres of influence so that fierce confrontation arose when Germany coveted these areas, which further intensified conflicts among the capitalist great powers.

The flow of German capital into South Africa and West Asia typically illustrated how the colonial expansion in the periphery countries aggravated the conflicts among the imperialist countries in the core regions. The most aggressive organization of German capital in South Africa was the Pan-German League, whose chief objective was to set up "a new South African Greater Germany", namely, a German South African colonial empire, covering vast areas which include Republic of Transvaal, Republic of Van Die Oranje Vrijstaat, German Southwest Africa (now Namibia), and Portuguese colonies from the coast of the Atlantic to that of the Indian Ocean. The construction of the railway from Johannesburg to Delagoa Bay was mainly funded by German capital. When the railway was opened in 1895, Germany dispatched two battleships to the northeast coast of South Africa for "celebration". Adolph von Hansemann (1826-1903), head of Direction der Disconto-Gesellschaft, planned to build a central line from German Southwest Africa to German East Africa (Tanganyika), which was fully supported by the Pan-German League. Georg von Siemens, the executive of the Deutsche Bank advocated implementing an urgent expansion policy in Transvaal to compete with Britain but shifted its focus to compete for the construction of "three B railway" from Constantinople to Basra of the Persian Gulf in the Ottoman Empire when it found out that Britain had laid a solid economic basis in South Africa and the plan of the Pan-German League was not realistic. German Emperor William II was immensely interested in the investment in and strategic interests of this railway with an overall length of 5,000 kilometers. Because Turkish government received German credit capital, its finance was increasingly monitored by German finance capitalists, which made it possible for Germany to exert decisive impacts on domestic and foreign policies of the Ottoman Empire. In such a situation, Germany decided to forsake its unrealistic plan of annexing Transvaal and exchanged its "concession" in South Africa for British compensation for Germany in other parts of the world.

France had always had a colonial tradition. Its contention with Britain for the Indian Subcontinent had once reached the climax in the latter half of the 18th century and only restrained for dozens of years after the defeat in Napoleonic Wars in Europe. However, the defeat in the Franco-Prussian War provoked France into raving overseas expansion to make up for the dire losses inflicted by Germans spiritually and otherwise. Its calculating attitude in the contention for colonial territories and spirit of Gallic rooster made it possible for France to establish a vase colonial empire, second only Britain. French banks had a far higher degree of capital concentration than that of industry concentration. Particularly, the advanced export of credit capital not only obtained high-rate profits in Russia but successfully signed the Franco-Russian Alliance Treaty awed by Germany. Although France was inferior to Britain in economic strength, it managed by means of the antennae of its credit capital to draw in the contention for Egypt with Britain and gained an advantage in the contention for Tunisia, Morocco, and Madagascar.

Although Italy was dubbed as the "impoverished capitalism" so that Bismarck ridiculed that it had a great appetite but there were caveats in its teeth. Although Italy had insufficient domestic capital and foreign capital was dominant in Italian industry, it had sensed an irresistible desire to promote its interests…and lay a foundation for its overseas expansion. In 1885, Italian Premier P.S. Mancini claimed that Italy would not hold its troops in leash while other great powers waged wars to democratize Africa. In the end of the 19th century, it took advantage of the confrontation between Britain and France in Horn of Africa to grab Somalia and fought against Turkish troops to seize Tripoli (now part of Libya) from the Ottoman Empire in the early 20th century.

If Italy squeezed money out of its impecunious national treasury to pay for war expenditure, King Leopold II of Belgium relied almost entirely on international finance capital to seize Congo with an area of 2.34 million square kilometers. When European powers attending Berlin Conference deadlocked on Congo, the rare trophy in Africa Continent, they decided to invest jointly their finance capital into Congo Free State, which did not belong to any country. This was a rare and significant co-operation of international monopoly capital, which was reflected in the later on co-funded joint mining company.

It can be seen, thus, driven by the new motives of pillaging colonies the imperialist great powers had all taken the road of contending for new colonies and dividing "spheres of influence". Since the middle of 1870s, the great powers pressed on with their contention for colonies and partition of the world, which was completed within 30 years. Old colonial countries, namely Britain and France, seized most colonies. Young imperialist countries like Germany, Italy, Japan, America and Belgium which did not have any colonies in the period of laissez-faire capitalism were all actively engaged in the contention for colonies. From 1876 to 1914, the imperialist great powers seized 25 million square kilometers of colonies and partitioned 14 million square kilometers of "spheres of influence" (semi-colonies). The number of colonies rose from 106 to 162. Roughly from this time onward, the boundary of the South was basically demarcated and scenes of the North-South relationship were successively produced on the world stage with the progress of history.

4.1.3. Scrambling for Colonies in Africa

Because Africa was the largest continent in the South, it became the primary target of colonial expansion. Therefore, in the latter half of the 19th century, colonial countries culminated in the contention for colonies and partition of Africa. Since the 1960s, some western historians have been enthusiastic about who or which country on earth took the initiative in the contention for colonies so as to set up a new surge in the partition of Africa and the unoccupied territories in the world? Influenced by the historical materials in their hands or their positions or even dominated by their "theoretical systems", the arguers tended to take a certain event or a certain figure as the initiator of this surge so that they had different arguments and arrived at different conclusions. In fact, some arguments stressed contingent events, some "the strong role" of historical figures, and others even attributed it to the general social psychology and social consciousness generated out of the desire of some countries and nations to become "powerful countries". Although this chapter has made an analysis on the elements and causes for the changes in the policies of every country, it still emphasizes that economic conditions have an ultimately decisive significance.

Within the 30 years from the end of the 19th century to the early 20th century of the contention for colonies and partition of the world, we can still clearly see that economic conditions are the red thread running through the entire process, which was hided, glared, and covered due to such elements as strategic considerations, election needs, balance of power, diplomatic maneuvers, and narcissistic racial superiority so that it took on the variegated and hazy appearance. In the latter half of the 19th century, drastic changes occurred to world capitalism, especially the productivity called out by the second industrial revolution, which made it possible for the rapid increase in the output of goods produced by western countries. The soar of the accumulated capital caused by monopoly that had taken its early shape had a dire need to open up more and larger outlets for goods, sources of raw materials, and capital investment markets. The invigoration of such an immense vitality made industrialized countries more active in their colonial enterprises. First, expedition activities increased dramatically, especially those into the unknown south continent—Africa shot up (see table 4.4). Subsidized by companies, enterprises, and media, dozens of expedition teams crossed over every corner of African continent, the alluring vista of which was given vivid descriptions in the discovery reports by the explorers. They even made a ridiculous prescription of opening up African continent as the panacea for the most severe capitalist economic crisis in the 1870s. In 1872 when British American Henry Morton Stanley returned from Africa, he published the well-known How I Found Livingstone: Travels, Adventures, and Discoveries in Central Africa. He proclaimed there were no difficulties in the colonization of Equatorial East Africa, the expenditure for which would be quickly made up from the development of natural resources, which was so alluring to some colonial pioneers from European countries that they were eager to rush for Africa.

Table 4.4. Number of Military Expeditions to Africa[22]

Year	Number of Expedition Teams
1841-1850	6
1851-1860	27
1861-1870	29
1871-1880	47
1881-1890	84

22 D.A. Olderogge and I.I Potemkin. *Peoples in Africa*. Shanghai: Shanghai Social Sciences Press, 1960: 22.

The economic crisis which broke out in the 1870s swept over Germany, America, France, and Britain, the prolongation of which made the already fierce contention for the world market reach a perfervid state. The new situation which appeared in the world economy was that the further intensified trade protectionism made imperialist thinkers in all countries realize the irreplaceable importance of colonies as outlets for goods, capital investment markets and sources of raw materials. The British finance capitalist and politician Rhodes spoke for all colonialist politicians: In order to avoid cruel civil war among forty million British civilians, we the colonialist politicians should occupy new territories to settle the surplus population and find new outlets for goods. In the struggle for new colonies, Europeans powers looked around and saw the whole world as the battlefield but most of their attention was turned to Africa, vast territories of which as "the last continent" was not yet occupied by Europeans countries. Till 1876, only 10.8% of the vast continent was occupied by European countries, namely, there were still more than 25 million square kilometers of territories unoccupied by any Western power. Since the 1870s, the decision-makers in departments of foreign affairs in every European country were engaged in studying Africa maps in order to gain an advantageous position in the contention for the last vast land in the world.

Belgium spearheaded in the international partition of Africa by European powers since the 1870s. Formerly a part of Netherlands, Belgium was a small country, which had been jealous of its sister nation—Holland in possession of such a vast colony as Indonesia (East Indies). However, Belgium was small in its territory, weak in its power, and narrow in its domestic market. Since the rapid development of industrialization since the 1840s, its industrial output came to the fore in the world, which demanded overseas markets for a large amount of goods. King Leopold II of Belgium was the cousin of Queen Victoria of Great Britain, who had already possessed the vastest colonies in the world when he took the throne in 1865. Leopold was determined to develop Belgium into a powerful country, strengthen national defense, and set up a strong army. As one representative of Belgian finance capitalist, he thought it was essential for Belgium to rank among colonial powers in order to solve its economic poverty and uplift its economic and political position in Europe. However, after several defeats in Mozambique and Transvaal, Leopold, the "financier and profiteer" dubbed by Lenin, realized a country with weak military power could not gain profits from the imperialist contention among colonial countries under the national banner of Belgium. Instead, it was necessary for Belgium to uphold "an international banner" to obtain concessions and compromises from competitors in the name of "participation of interests" and reassure the great powers in the name of "neutralization".

When a dozen European explorers returned from African inland forests to Europe from 1875 to 1876, Leopold procured information from them at great costs and generously subsidized explorers in dire poverty, which gained him a reputation rapidly. In September 1876, Leopold held Brussels Geographic

Conference in the high-sounding name of "sponsorship for great scientific research". Representatives from the participating countries—Germany, Austria-Hungary, Britain, France, Italy, and Russia had their own intentions in their discussions upon the British proposal of setting up posts in the name of "science stations" along the east coast and west coast of tropical Africa. Germany, France, and Russian were firmly against the setting up of shore bases near Bagamoyo on the east coast for fear that Britain with the strongest navy would control these posts and only agreed to establish International Association on Inquiry into and Development of Central Africa (known as International African Association) and set up branches in every country. Brussels Geographic Conference passed the second proposal and delimited the scope of activities of the association to be north from Sudan, south to the Zambezi River, east to the Indian Ocean and west to the Atlantic. The "academic" conference had revealed all European great powers would not give up the fertile African continent. Leopold disclosed his attitude in a letter on 17 November 1877 to Baron Salvans "I do not wish to reveal my dissatisfaction to the British nor miss the good opportunity to have a share of the delicious African cake"[23].

After the end of the Brussels conference, all countries were busy setting up their branches. Belgium was the first to found Belgian African Association on 6 November 1876, France founded French African Association in 1877, and Germany founded its African Association in 1879. Once the Belgian association was established, its capitalists across the country quickly raised a fund of 0.5 million francs to form the first inquiry team, whose members were provided by the army. At that time, the international geographers were not aware of a route which stretched from the west coast upward along the Congo River to the inland. In October 1877, the first Belgian inquiry team set off from Europe, reached the inland by way of the east coast of Africa in the early 1878, and approached Lake Tanganyika in August 1879. After they were joined by the second inquiry team in Carema in November 1879, the team failed to move westward no matter how hard they tried. At the same time, expedition teams from France and Germany were eager to march into the inland of Africa. On 9 August 1877, British-American explorer Stanley spent 1,001 days in trekking from the east coast to the Great Lakes and downward along the tributaries of the Congo River, turned westward in the Congo River, and reached the coast of the Atlantic. After he returned to Europe, Stanley proposed "the grand plan" of entering the Congo River from the west side (the coast of the Atlantic) to develop the fertile and vast inland of Africa. Stanley depicted the life in the 3.96 million square kilometers of fertile and abundant land along the Congo River, with his brilliant narration. He spent three months to gather material and write out his masterpiece "Through the Dark Continent", his second bestseller which caused great sensation in Europe. He gave talks in industrial cities like Manchester and Liverpool, preaching that if the half-naked Congolese started to wear clothes, Britain could sell 26 million pounds of cloth in Congo per year.

---

23   Qtd. in Lewin, Pierre Joye et Rosine. *Les trusts au Congo*. Bruxelles, 1961: 13.

He advised European business community invest in building railways near the mouth of the Congo River, over rapids and waterfalls and along the river to develop the tropical resource in Congo. The tremendously appealing propaganda and his grand plan of developing the largest future colony surely invigorated the battered and frustrated European capitalists mired in the economic crisis, arousing their vitality and greed.

Leopold II frustrated by the futile expedition team in the east was the first to send his men to talk with Stanley that he was willing to bid a high price for Stanley's special knowledge about Congo. In July 1978, the two parties signed a contract, in which Stanley pledged that he would work five years in any place assigned in Africa and would not announce any information and hold any conference without the permission of the king during the period. On 25 November of the same year, Leopold convened a plenary session of International African Conference, where European capitalists made inquiries to Stanley about what tropical commodities could be exchanged with Congo and how much freight volume could be guaranteed by the railway in plan from the mouth of the river. Seeing that the passion of European finance capitalists for investment had been fired up, Leopold seized the moment to take the lead in investment, which reached 0.5 million plus the capital from several private banks, and set up the Upper Congo Commission of Inquiry. In January 1879, the commission ordered Stanley to lead an expedition team to Africa with a budget. The order stipulated that Stanley would lead an expeditionary force under the banner of the International African Association to blaze a trail over 300 kilometers along the waterfalls and torrents which separated the mouth of the Congo River from Malebo Pool to reach the navigable part of river in Congo so as to approach the inland of the Congo River Basin. Stanley planned to set up bases to develop the lower Congo, and "persuade" the local tribal chiefs to sign treaties which acknowledged the "protection" from the international commission and provide Belgian capitalists right of lease, privileges, and other rights. In August 1879, Stanley led the expeditionary army set off from the estuary on the west coast to the inland along the Congo River.

Leopold had thought his preempted plan of seizing Congo would be infallible. However, not long since the implementation of the plan, intense conflicts with France and Portugal arose. Before the establishment of French African Association, France had already devised their plan in 1875 to expand southward from the inland of Gabon to the lower reaches of the Congo River. After 1877, France implemented its plan of expansion in the name of French African Association. Almost at the same time, Pierre Savorgnan de Brazza the Italian head of the French expeditionary army marched in the end of 1879 upstream from Ogooué River he had been around for two years and was the first to enter Congo. On 10 September 1880 he became the first to sign a contract with King Makoko of the Batekes that he acknowledged that his kingdom ranging from the Congo River to the west coast of Malebo Pool was under the protection of the French flag. Eight months later when Stanley hastened to the left bank of

Malebo Pool on 27 July 1881 and saw the French tricolor flag flying on the right bank, he was furious that Brazza with "tattered uniform and deformed hat" had gained an edge over him. He was so exasperated to announce that the Brazza treaty was as invalid as "waste paper". On 7 November, he induced King Makoko to sign another treaty with him to allow the international association to camp on the left bank. On 3 December, the expeditionary army of Stanley camped on the left bank, confronting in the name of the International African Association with France. In order to strengthen the position of Brazza, French National Assembly issued a decree on 30 November 1882 to acknowledge that the territory seized by Brazza all belonged to France and allocated 100,000 francs as the fund for further "exploration". After the loss of the priority over the mouth of the river, Leopold instructed Stanley to speed up their march into the inland. In April 1883, Stanley summoned all African tribal chiefs in the lower reaches of the Congo River to convene in Leopoldville and sign protection treaties with the International African Association by force or guile to transfer the possession of large tracts of territories to the association. By 1884, Leopold and his assistants had established over 40 colonial posts in the vast Congo River region and signed 450 protection treaties with tribal chiefs everywhere so as to take in most territories of the inland along the Congo River.

When the International Association of Leopold was engaged in fierce contention with France along the Congo River, the contention for North Africa was also being carried out in full swing. French capital had long penetrated into Tunisia contiguous to Algeria and obtained many important rights of lease from the Bey[24]. France and Britain controlled the government of Tunisia financially. After 1878, French pressed on their plan to occupy Tunisia for the following reasons: First, to join Algeria with Tunisia so as to uplift the position of France in the Mediterranean African and strengthen its power to contend with Britain for Egypt from the flank; second, preempt Italy already in possession of Sicily from taking further actions: control the narrowest part of the Mediterranean on the northern bank of Tunisia so as to cut off possibly French connection with Near East (West Asia) and pose threat to France in its contention for hegemony over the East Mediterranean; third, practice the rule of violence was also an economic power: to enforce the position of France in Tunisian capital by means of military occupation. After gaining the forgiveness of Britain and Germany, Britain sent troops to occupy Tunisia abruptly in April 1881, forcing the Bey to agree to the terms of Treaty of Bardo, which officially made Tunisia a French Protectorate in 1883.

The same situation occurred to Egypt where Britain gained a slight edge over France in their economic penetration into Egypt over years. Britain was waiting for the most appropriate occasion to occupy Egypt which had become a national policy of Britain. Britain needed not only the cotton fields in the Nile Delta of Egypt as the source of sufficient raw materials for cotton textile industry in Manchester (which was extremely essential when the supply of American cotton was cut off during the American civil war) but also the occupation of

---

24   An appellation for the ruler of Tunisia.

the Suez Canal to ensure the absolute security of "the lifeline of the empire". In 1875, British government allocated a huge amount of money to purchase 44 percent share of the canal, which implied Britain had controlled the equity as well as the canal economically. In July 1882, taking advantage of the occasion when France was in anarchy due to the cabinet re-shuffle, Britain set aside France and took independent action in occupying quickly the Canal and Cairo in Egypt and the entire Egypt in a short time. France had important economic and political interests in Egypt so that British independent occupation of Egypt intensified the conflicts between these two countries in their contention for Egypt. Meanwhile, the move by Britain set an example for other European great powers to occupy other territories in Africa in the same military way.

The complex conflicts between France and Belgium, Britain and France, France and Italy enabled wavering Germany to occupy an extremely advantageous position. German Chancellor Bismarck, who had been unwilling to expose his position on the question of colonies, made full use of the situation. In reply to an advocate of German colonialism, Bismarck said, "Here is Russia and here is France and here we are in the middle. That is my map of Africa"[25]. However, the abrupt change in domestic and foreign situation forced Bismarck to modify his attitude. In 1882, Germany founded the Colonial Association, in which the commercial capitalists and ship-owners of the Hanseatic League played the leading role. In 1884, when Stanley was occupying territories in the Congo basin, Germany took abrupt actions in Southwest Africa (now Namibia), and announced that the territories from Angola to the Buchan Bay and the adjacent coastal areas were under the protection of Germany, which the first challenge of Germany against "the legal right" of British supremacy. Henceforth, Germany gained a spring-board to enter the inland of South Africa. In May 1884, Germany sent a warship to the Gulf of Guinea, intent upon seizing the slave coastal areas (now the coastal areas of Togo). In June of the same year, Germany forced the tribal chief of the Lome district to sign a treaty of protection. In July, German national flag rose from the coastal areas of Togo. The rapid annexation of Germany led to its conflicts with France in West Africa. After its occupation of Togo, German warships rushed southward to Cameroon in the same month and gained the right of protection over it in the same way, running up German eagle flag. This prompt move by Germany restrained the southeast expansion of Britain in the Nile Delta. Within the time of less than half a year, Germany rose up from a country without any territory in Africa to taking possession of three colonies with an area over a million square kilometers, ranking among the top European colonial countries. The swift occupation of African colonies by Germany and the frantic annexation of the Congo River Basin by Stanley and Brazza made a great impact on Europe. The participation of the three new comers, Germany, Italy, and Belgium, in the scramble for Africa among colonial countries aggravated and complicated the contention in partition.

25   Kissinger, Henry. *Diplomacy*. New York: Simon & Schuster, 1994: 146. Trans. Shuxin Gu and Tiangui Lin. Haikou: Hainan Publishing House, 1997: 126.

The contention for Congo in 1884 had not been settled before a new struggle broke out among the colonial countries. In May, French National Assembly denied the legitimacy of the Stanley treaty, and the government of Portugal also announced that it had an indisputable "historical right" over the mouth of the Congo River. Seeing that the Congo River Basin was profitable, Britain became actively involved and signed a treaty with Portugal in February 1884, backing Portugal's sovereign rights on both sides at the mouth of the Congo River and the Atlantic coastal areas between 5.12 degrees and 8 degrees south latitude in exchange for Portuguese permission for Britain to enjoy the same right of business and shipping in the area. France made a prompt protest against the treaty between Portugal and Britain, which aggravated the discord between it and France caused by their contention for Egypt. Germany, which had been attempting consistently to alienate Britain and France and anticipating the conflicts between them became even worse, took the occasion to stir up trouble by voicing its support for the protest of France. Drawing on its high-speed development and world-expanding commerce, America also poked its nose into Africa. It would rather that the Congo River Basin was in the hands of the relatively weak Belgian association to share equal profits so that it firmly advocated that the legal force of treaties signed by the International African Association be acknowledged and claimed that the flag of the association was "the flag of a friendly nation" with sovereignty. The statement by America created a favorable atmosphere for Belgium. Seeing that the major colonial opponent Britain quickly gained power in Congo after its occupation of Egypt, France felt greatly uneasy. Of two evils choose the less, France would rather make some compromise and concession to the Belgian association so as to partially solve or mitigate its dispute with Belgium and to get united in their fight against strong enemies, France, Germany, and America tended to support the Congo Free State advocated by the Belgian association. The basically unanimous position of the three countries isolated Britain, which made it fear that it would encounter the united opposition of France and Germany in the lower reaches of the Nile where it had greater profits and that if the Belgian association failed to control the mouth of the Congo River the inland economy would be stifled, which instead would strengthen French power in Gabon, adverse for Britain to carry out its foreign policy of equilibrium. Weighing the advantages and disadvantages, Britain announced to give up its treaty with Portugal on 26 June 1884 and suggested together with Portugal to submit the issue of Congo to an international conference.

The competition among many countries over Africa generated a temporary balance of power and the possibility of reaching a sort of compromise. The alert Bismarck grabbed the opportunity to express the willingness of Germany to contribute its efforts to hold an international conference over the conflicts in Africa and suggest that the conference be located in Berlin. The high-sounding reason the expert in diplomacy proposed was that European countries should negotiate to prevent wars in Africa. In fact, what he insinuated was that western countries had better divide the vast tropical Africa and follow the rule of sharing equal interests than fighting against each other in Africa. Out of its diplomatic considerations, France was the first to support the proposal of Bismarck. When all European colonial countries agreed to hold the Berlin Conference, many of them launched the campaign of signing treaties of lease along the coastal areas of Africa on an unprecedented scale. For a short while, Africa became the center of international diplomatic focus.

On 15 November 1884, the Berlin conference was held under the auspices of Bismarck. Participants in the conference included Germany, Portugal, Belgium, Spain, Britain, France, America, Italy, Russia, Switzerland, Denmark, Austria-Hungary, and Turkey. The conference was devoted to African affairs yet there were no African countries in the conference, which set an extremely vile precedent of the strong bullying the weak in international conferences. The Berlin Conference aimed to mitigate the contradictions and conflicts among colonial countries and define principles of occupying and dividing colonies by the colonial powers. The Conference lasted for 104 days and discussed mainly about the following issues:

The first issue was relating to Congo. Leopold used free trade as the bait to gain through bilateral talks the recognition of participant countries for the sovereign rights of the Belgian Association in the vast territories of the Congo River Basin. Under the pressure of the identical diplomatic notes from France, Germany, and Britain, Portugal was forced to give up its sovereign rights in the territory on the north bank at the mouth of the Congo River, maintaining only the enclave of Cabinda. The Belgian Association obtained a territory with a width of 36 kilometers on the north bank at the mouth of the Congo River. The conference agreed to set up the Congo Free State with Leopold as its head. Thus, the great powers in Berlin far away from Africa demarcated on map for the first time their respective geographical boundaries of interest in West Tropical Africa.

The second issue was about "effective occupation". The participants believed that it was necessary to make regulations on "the peaceful partition" of Africa to prevent wars and mutual destructions. France and Germany strived to curb the further expansion of Britain, which had already possessed the vastest territories of "informal empires" and repeatedly claimed its supremacy, so that they jointly proposed that the principle of "effective occupation" be followed in the fresh act of taking possession of territories in Africa, that is, the occupation of any regions in Africa by any countries must obtain recognition of participant countries while "effective occupation" must be realized in controversial regions to obtain "legal transfer". Britain had the status of mere "supremacy" instead of "effective occupation" in nearly all African "protectorates" so that the new regulations proposed by France and Germany would deny its status in "protectorates" and made it difficult for the policy of "informal empire" to be carried out. After bitter bargaining and debate, a rather ambiguous General Act was passed[26], the sixth article of which put forward two conditions as to the

26 "The General Act of African Conference". in *Selections of Modern World History Materials*. Vol. 2. Beijing: The Commercial Press, 1964: 212-213.

recognition of the annexation by every country of African territories: first, participants must notify other signatory powers when they annex further coastal territories in Africa (the mention of only "coastal" rather than inland was the favor given by Germany to France); second, signatory powers "shall exercise sovereign rights to maintain present interests in the occupied coastal areas in African"[27]. In fact, the latter principle required metropolitan states sent armies and administrative officials to the claimed protectorate, which was an effective check of the nearly boundless "informal empire" implemented by Britain for many years and a double-edged sword to sponsor countries as well (France and Germany), especially when France was sparing no efforts in establishing a vast colonial empire in West Africa. Because the General Act did oblige the signatory powers to state the boundaries of their occupied territories, these two conditions would lose some of its efficacy in practical implementation.

The third issue was about free trade and sea traffic. Free trade and sea traffic in colonies and spheres of influence were in conflict with the imperialist monopoly and exclusion. To share equal benefits, the signatory powers delimited the territories of the Belgian Association, French Congo, and the north of Portuguese Angola in the Congo River Basin as the free trade zone and practiced free sea traffic in the Congo River and the Niger River. However, both Britain and France forbade "free sea transport" in the Niger in respective occupied areas supervised by "the International Commission". As a result, they only reached a treaty to implement the principle only in the Congo River Basin because every signatory power refused to open up its occupied territories and spheres of influence.

123

The fourth issue was related with the high-sounding announcement of forbidding the slave trade.

The Berlin Conference was a significant event in the history of colonialist and imperialist partition of Africa: it marked the beginning of the frantic partition of Africa and sent capitalist great powers the signal of setting off an upsurge of building respective colonial empires. The entire process of the conference demonstrated the balance of power among the colonial countries in their scramble for Africa therefore they made mutual compromises and concessions yet unanimously took Africa as their prey. For this goal, the conference fixed "the plan for scramble" and the conditions of annexation. Thus, the conference gave a green light to the bullying of the weak by the strong not only in Africa but also in the whole world.

After the Berlin Conference, great powers reached a climax in the partition of Africa and occupied 65% of the total African territories in less than 15 years. British Foreign Secretary Salisbury said: When I returned to the Foreign Office in 1885, European countries were querulous for the African territories they could obtain. Right after the Berlin Conference, the colonial explore Carl Peters sneaked back to Berlin from East Africa and submitted to Bismarck

---

27   Ibid.: 212-213.

the twelve treaties over the territory of Ijsagara he signed with tribal chiefs in East Africa on behalf of Germany. On 5 March 1885, Bismarck was the first to notify other signatory powers in light of the 36th article of the General Act that Germany had obtained "effectively occupation" of Ijsagara, Nguru, and other regions in East Africa. One month later, Germany took possession of Wituland. In November 1885, the Germany fleet sailed into the waters in East Africa. By virtue of its accomplished experience in colonization, Britain responded immediately by announcing that it had gained "effective occupation" of several vital areas (Taveta being included) at the foot of Mount Kilimanjaro in East Africa, which crisscrossed with the occupied territories of Germany so as to forestall the contiguity. In 1886, Britain, Germany and France achieved a temporary compromise, delimiting the coastal area 16 kilometers wide and 1,600 kilometers from Kipini in the north to the Ruvuma River in the south as part of the territory of Zanzibar Sultan under the control of Britain. The territory between the Ruvuma River and the Tana River were delimited as the spheres of influence of Britain and Germany. The northern part belonged to Britain while the southern Germany, the boundary between which is that between the present day Tanzania and Kenya. Britain and Germany recognized the freedom of action of France in Madagascar.

The swift and violent actions of Britain, Germany, and France in their partition of East Africa opened the floodgates, the elevator of which was sufficiently lubricated in the Berlin Conference. In the unprecedented fierce partition for Africa, Britain, France, Germany, Portugal, Belgium, and Italy were all ambitious to break through the linking areas of their colonies in al directions in Africa so as to build a contiguous enormous empire. Instigated by the actions of finance capitalist Rhodes, Britain drew up a plan of linking Cape with Cairo, building railways, and building a colonial empire across the south and north of African continent. France also drew up Cape Verde-Red Sea plan of expanding northeastward from Senegal across the east and west of African continent to the Red Sea along the coastal area of Somalia[28]. Germany likewise planed to link German East Africa with Southwest Africa, forming an oblique fault in Africa. Portugal strived to exercise its "historical rights" across the vast area between Angola on the west coast to Mozambique on the east coast. The Belgian Association of Leopold vigorously expanded to the vast Congo River Basin and its tributaries. After missing the opportunity of taking over Tunisia, Italy actively carried out its plan of building a Red Sea-Indian Ocean colonial empire in Northeast Africa. Striving to maintain the remaining colonial empire in Cuba in the Caribbean and in Philippines in the Pacific, Spain was incapable to take part in the scramble for Africa, adopting a defensive strategy in small colonies like Spain Sahara. The diplomatic and military machines of European colonial great powers began to run wildly, all striving to carry out their plans of colonial expansion in Africa, which were crisscrossed, overlapped, and bound

---

28   Some historians termed the plan of Britain as 2 C Enterprise while that of France as 2 S Enterprise. Note by the author.

to cause severe conflicts of interests. The hottest areas of the scramble were the following three:

The upper reaches valley of the Nile. The temporary compromises achieved by the treaty between Britain and Germany in 1886 could not meet the demand of these two countries for territories in East Africa. Germany was unwilling to allow the access from its inland colonies in East Africa to the Indian Ocean to be intercepted by the coastal territory of Zanzibar under the control of Britain while the latter was not satisfied that German Witu was embedded in its spheres of influence. The colonial companies of both countries were eager to advance into the unclassified regions. Germany led by Peters expanded to Uganda so as to break through the access to the upper reaches valley of the Nile while Britain occupied the region west to Lake Victoria to intercept the access of Germany to the Nile valley. In 1890, in order to contend with the entente group of France and Russia in Europe, Germany had to make concessions to Britain in territories in East Africa, transferring some important territories like Witu and part of Uganda on the access to the Nile valley and consenting that the business center of East Africa, Zanzibar, was officially under the protection of Britain. In return, Britain transferred Helgolandin in Europe to Germany. In July, they signed the Anglo-German Agreement: Germany obtained the coastal area in East Africa including Mafia Island, the western boundary of which was extended to Lake Victoria and even the eastern border of the Congo Free State. And Germany promised that it would not cross northward Lake Victoria to expand to Uganda and the Nile Basin. In 1894, Britain declared Uganda to be its protectorate.

The seizure of Uganda, however, did not completely settle the issue of British control over the upper reaches of the Nile valley, which was not only out of the need to link its territories in North and South Africa but also to control the water of the Nile so as to command Egypt. France was approaching secretly the upper reaches valley of the Nile from the east and west sides. The east access of France was to go through Ethiopia so that it instigated Emperor Menelik II to expand westward its boundary to the banks of the Nile. The west access of France extended eastward from French Congo to the sough of Sudan in the upper reaches valley of the Congo River. In order to forestall France more expansive than Germany from entering the Nile from the east access, Britain upheld Italy to penetrate into Ethiopia as the bunker against France. The plan of checking France on the east access was carried out rather successfully in the early period but suffered a complete failure when Italy was vanquished by the troops of Menelik II in Adwa. On the west access, in November 1893, Britain endorsed Germany to expand its territory of Cameroon to the south bank of Lake Chad, which might result in the grapple between the two European adversaries near the lake, so as to forestall France from opening the access to the Nile in the west. However, Germany did not fall into this trap. It allowed France to enjoy the freedom of action in the east part of Cameroon in March 1894. Britain was forced to change its plan and urged the Congo Free State under the control of Belgium to forestall France from expanding eastward. In the name of Egypt, Britain upheld Leopold to expand to the left bank of the Nile. In exchange, in May 1894 Belgium "leased" the long strip 25 kilometers wide from the south bank of Lake Edward to the northern tip of Lake Tanganyika to Britain as the subgrade land of the future railway from Cape-Cairo to the Nile. It seemed that only Cape-to-Cairo scheme could be fully implemented hopefully. On hearing the news, France and Germany made severe protests against the Anglo-Congo Treaty. Belgium retreated under pressure and was even forced to give up its sovereign rights over the left bank of the Nile in the Franco-Belgian Agreement in August 1894. Therefore, France again gained momentum, and the west access to the Nile was no longer impeded. In 1896, France sent Major Jean-Baptiste Marchand to command an expeditionary force to march into the left bank of the Nile from French Congo. After two years of trek, the Marchand expedition entered and garrisoned in Fashoda village on the left bank of the Nile and forced the tribal chief of the Shilluks to accept the treaty of protection. The French announced triumphantly that they had obtained "effective occupation" of the upper reaches valley of the Nile. The abrupt change in situation was rather favorable for France to carry out its Senegal-Somalia Plan of traversing Africa. However, without a sign of weakness, Britain claimed that if necessary they would build a formal empire. As early as 1896, the British Parliament agreed to provide financial allocation to reconquer Sudan. General Horatio Herbert Kitchener commanded the southward army to march while

pave the way and defeated the forces of Mahdi at the battle of Omdurman on 2 September 1898. On 19 September, the southward British troops (in fact the Anglo-Egyptian gunboats forces led by British officers) went up the Nile to arrive at and garrison in Fashoda village, at a stalemate with the French forces. Kitchener announced in the name of the Egyptian Sirdar (Commander-in-Chief of the Egyptian army) that the regime in the Fashoda area belonged to the Egyptian Khedive. Leaving part of the force to monitor the French army, the main force of Kitchener continued to march southward along the White Nile and reached Tawfīqīyah at the intersection with the Sobat River to block the French army from fleeing southward to Uganda. The Marchand expedition with less than 150 men was besieged by the British army, which consisted of 20,000 well equipped expeditionary soldiers with reliable traffic lines and logistic support. At that time, the British navy more powerful than the sum of the forces of the Russian, French, and German was capable to have a lion's share in the partition of Africa. In view of the strategy of the colonial empire, whether Britain was able to link its territories in the south and north of African continent through building the Cape-Cairo railway mainly depended on the final outcome of the battle to seize the upper reaches valley of the Nile. British Ambassador to Paris said, the Marchand expedition "will cut off our traffic line between North Africa and South Africa while it is the goal of our policy to build this traffic line." In light of its severe confrontation with Germany on the issue of Europe, the French government took the occasion to degrade the issue of Fashoda to that of "a colonial issue" despite the clamor of the French military to fight for Fashoda and bargained with Britain, demanding another area on the left bank of the upper reaches of the Nile. Britain agreed to hold "negotiations on demarcation". On 3 November 1898, the French government ordered the Marchand expedition to retreat from Fashoda on the ground that the local sanitation was not fit for garrison. The British scramble for the upper reaches valley of the Nile had achieved a complete success. In March 1899, Britain and France reached an agreement to divide the African territories in Sudan, Britain allowed France to possess a large area in the west of Darfur in Sudan (middle Sudan) which enabled France to link its colonies in West, Middle and North Africa to form an enormous French African colonial empire with an area of nearly 10 million square kilometers.

South Africa. With the rapid development of German monopoly capitalism and the growing colonial expansion, the contention between Britain and Germany after 1893 for African continent became intensified, which was mainly manifested in South Africa. In 1886, by virtue of German geologist Carl Mauch who had been exploring mines for many years, Transvaal Republic discovered a gold mine with the largest reserves in the world. Rhodes Financial Group established South African Gold Mining Company, gaining control rights of most gold mines in the area of Rand. However, with the surge in the output of gold mines, gold mine capitalists led by Rhodes fell in severe economic and political clash with the big Boer landlords in Transvaal Republic. The discovery of the tremendous gold mines and the conspicuous output and huge profits urged Britain to step up its plan of annexing two republics of the Boers (the other one was Orange Free State) to set up Union of South Africa. To realize this plan would lead to three outcomes: Frist, it would guarantee South African gold with the largest output in the world kept flowing into the underground gold treasuries of Bank of England so as to ensure gold standard system; second, it would sustain the absolute advantage of British colonial rule in South Africa; third, it would also keep the south part of Cape-to-Cairo scheme from being threatened by Germany with increasing powerful colonial strength.

In 1884, after the seizure of Southwest Africa, Germany made a deep thrust into the inland, marching into the residential area of the Botswanians along Caprivi Strip in the north and Molopo River in the south, approaching quickly the west border of Transvaal Republic and drawing Dutch Boers to their side in the name of Teutonic descendent. German capital kept flowing into the area. For fear that German colonies in Southwest Africa would be linked with Boer republics to cause a sweeping situation in the north of South Africa, Britain announced in 1885 Bechuanaland (now Botswana) to the north of Molopo River was its protectorate and incorporated it into the map of British formal empire so as to intercept the link between Transvaal Republic and German Southwest Africa in the northwest. The British also occupied the territories of Zulus in the east, which blocked Germany from "leasing" the Bay of Santa Lucia near the Indian Ocean to enter Transvaal in the east. Thereafter, the Boer republics besieged by British Cape colony had only one way to the outside world while Germany also had one access to penetrate into the Boer republics, that is, Port Lourenco-Marques in Portuguese Mozambique. In 1893, German capital won the bid for building the railway from Pretoria (capital of Transvaal) to Lourenco-Marques. In January 1895, to protect its interest in the region, Germany sent warships to the final harbor—Delagoa Bay (now Maputo Bay). The investment of Germany into Transvaal soared to 0.5 billion marks mainly from Deutsche Bank and Berlin Trading Company. The export from Germany to Transvaal rose from 300,000 pounds in 1886 to 12 million pounds in 1896 and German immigrants rose rapidly to 15,000. Germany upheld the Boers openly in several incidents which led to the white-hot conflicts between Britain and the Boers. Britain made repeated protests against Germany (in February and October 1895) and German paid no attention. German media rattled that Germany was "the loyalist friend" and "independence defender" of the Boer republics. In 1896, Britain plotted the James Attacking Incident, intending to overturn the Boer regime of Transvaal Republic by means of the armed forces of Rhodes' South African company and replace it with that of outlanders (mainly British immigrants). The attack was a fiasco. Emperor William II of Germany aggressively wired his congratulations to the Boer republics, insinuatingly stressing that the Boers relied on their own forces rather than support from other friendly nations to defeat the armed bandit gang"[29]. These words stated openly that the Boers would be supported by friendly nations if necessary. Germany took the occasion to unite France to exert pressure on Britain so that it had to make greater concessions to Germany on the issue of colonies. Faced with the aggressive Germany, Britain was even more apprehensive that the former was going to set up a protectorate in the heartland of British colonies in Africa. With the Anglo-Boer War cloud hovering, Britain made the following suggestion to Germany in exchange for its neutrality on the issue of South Africa: Portuguese African colonies would be divided between Britain and Germany under the condition that the latter ceased to support the Boer republics. In September 1898, Britain and Germany signed a secret treaty which stipulated that if Portugal needed "financial support", they would jointly offered loans secured by Portuguese colonies in Africa: Britain would obtain the south of Mozambique and the middle of Angola while Germany the north of Mozambique and the south and north of Angola. The secret treaty making promises only for the future was the reward of the betrayal of the Boers by the cunning British and Germans. In October 1899, Britain signed a treaty with Portugal to guarantee the integrity of the above mentioned Portuguese African colonies as a reward for Portuguese prohibition on the shipment of weapons to Transvaal by way of Delagoa Bay. Britain assisted Portugal in regulating finances which made it unnecessary for the latter to demand for any "financial support". The transaction between Britain and Germany practically came to nothing.

29   "Die Grosse Politik der Europaischen Kabinnette". B. XI. No. 2610. S. 31-32. In Потёмкин, В. П. *History of World Diplomacy*. Vol.3. Trans. Dake. Beijing: The 50's Press, 1950: 122-123.

While German strictly observed neutrality, Britain waged a war with the Boers for two years and eight months (1899-1902) and ended in the Treaty of Vereeniging which entailed that the Transvaal and the Republic of the Orange Free State gave up their independence. Thus, Britain realized its long-dream scheme of exercising sole sovereignty over South Africa, gained a complete control of the largest gold mine in the world—Rand Gold Mine, and cleared away the obstacles in the south end to carrying out Cape-to-Cairo Scheme, which implied that the British blueprint of establishing a "formal empire" with an area of over 9 million square kilometers on African continent had been virtually realized.

Morocco. France strived to make up for its failure in the Fashoda Conflict in Morocco in North Africa. Due to the increasingly deteriorating Anglo-German relationship, Germany was considered as the most dangerous opponent by Britain. In April 1904, Britain signed the Entente Cordial with France, reaching a package deal of dividing North Africa (contained in the secret treaty): Britain acknowledged that Morocco was under the sovereignty of France. Thus, Britain had forsaken its non-aligned position in Europe and became one member of the Allied. However, when Germany decided to make drastic reactions to French attempt to annex Morocco, it was not because its commercial interests in Morocco could suffer losses although Germany indeed had considerable commercial interests there nor because France had violated the treaty of ensuring the independence of Morocco but because Germany attempted to test how effective the Entente Cordial reached between Britain and Germany in 1904 would be. Meanwhile, French finance capital expanded speedily to Morocco, offering a loan of 83 million francs to Morocco from 1903 to 1904. In 1905, France proposed the plan of "reform" to the government of Morocco, attempting to Tunisianize Morocco (protectorized). In order to buy off Sultan of Morocco, Germany made protests against France. In March 1905, Emperor of Germany "visited" Morocco by yacht and declared that Germany was determined to defend the independence of Morocco when landing Tangier, which was virtually an admonition that Britain and France not bargain over Morocco and a blunt challenge of these two countries: Germany demanded a port on the west seashore of Morocco. However, British government had sensed that the threat of Germany to British colonial interests was going to be global in that Germany was commanding the alliance of the entire Europe in their opposition to British Empire. This was unbearable to Britain so that it expressed its firm support for France. In January 1906, all parties agreed to hold Algeciras Conference to discuss the issue of Morocco. Britain expressed resolve that it must not allow Germany to occupy the west bank of Morocco. Germany was forced to restrain for it discovered that the flurry of diplomatic efforts made itself isolated while consolidated the Entente Cordial between Britain and France. After the first Morocco crisis, Germany was deliberating what price it would ask if France attempted to obtain freedom of action in Morocco: either the cession of a territory in Morocco or other French colonies to Germany. In

1911, the second Morocco crisis broke out. On 1 July, the German gunboat Leopard sailed into Agadir and the light cruiser Berlin also sailed into the territorial waters of Morocco. In the diplomatic negotiations between Germany and France on 9 July, Germany demanded an exorbitant price that France should transfer French Congo to Germany in exchange for the transference of carte blanche of Morocco to France. On 21 July, Britain declared solemnly that Britain was ready to make tremendous sacrifices to maintain peace even if at the cost of giving up the supremacy obtained by means of heroism and triumphs in several centuries. British navy was on a war footing. Germany retreated and signed an agreement with France in November which stipulated that Germany unconditionally acknowledged the "protectorate" of France over Morocco while France transferred a territory of 275,000 square kilometers (mostly swamps) in French Congo to Germany as a "compensation", which linked German Cameroon with the Congo River. France declared officially that Morocco was its protectorate in 1912.

After its debacle at Adwa when invading Ethiopia in 1896, Italy strove to obtain territories in North Africa. As early as December 1900, Italy gained the permission from France to occupy Tripoli in exchange for French occupation of Morocco. Taking the occasion of the second Morocco crisis, Italy sent troops to land on Tripoli on the south shore of the Mediterranean in September 1911, attempting to occupy Libya of the Ottoman Empire. Choosing the option that delivered least harm, Britain opposed Germany while tolerated the relatively weak Italy as the neighbor in the east of its Egyptian colony. Turkey had a garrison of 7,000 in Libya and its reinforcement reach there quickly because the Italian fleet of warships controlled the Mediterranean Sea while Britain did not allow Turkish troops to pass through Egypt. In November, Italy declared its annexation of Tripoli and Cyrenaica and Libya henceforth became a colony of Italy.

From 1876 when the international conference on the issue of Congo was held to 1912 when France declared Morocco to be its protectorate, the partition of Africa by European colonial great powers was basically a stage of "peaceful" division of the world. With the period of 36 years, the great powers occupied and divided African territories of around 25 million square kilometers in addition to the colonies before 1876, which implied nearly all African countries and regions were reduced to colonies or protectorates except Ethiopia and Libya which remained to be independent semi-colonies in name only. The entire African continent of 30.2 million square kilometers entered the scope of the South. Thus, the North-South relationship in the entire African continent was embodied in the subordinate relation between metropolitan states and colonies and semi-colonies.

Table 4.5. The Political Map of the Partition of Africa by Colonial Great Powers in 1914

Country Name	Area of Occupied African Colonies	Proportion in the total area of Africa	Population of colonies
Britain	9,020,920	30%	51,660,000
France	10,387,521	35%	38,500,000
Germany	2,447,018	8%	11,527,000
Italy	2,397,260	7.9%	1,368,000
Belgium	2,345,809	7.9%	15,007,000
Portugal	2,061,720	6.9%	8,352,000
Spain	330,000	1%	Unknown

British colonies from Cape to Cairo were almost linked to be one piece from the south to the north (there was only a loophole in German Tanganyika). The region from South Africa to Rhodesia was the richest mining area with the highest economic and strategic values, the region from Egypt to Kenya had the burgeoning plantations, and the Suez Canal British Somalia held the estuaries of the Mediterranean and the Red Sea, and the Strait of Gibraltar as the west estuary of the Mediterranean was also in the hands of Britain, which therefore implied that the main access from Europe to Asia was controlled by Britain. The four colonies in British West Africa (Gambia, Sierra Leone, the Gold Coast, and Nigeria) were the most prosperous regions. The vast contiguous colonies in French Northwest Africa controlled most pats along the coast of the Mediterranean in North Africa, the economic and strategic values of which were only second to those of British colonies. Madagascar as the largest island (with an area of 627,000 square kilometers) in Africa was also in the hands of France. Belgian Congo located in the center of African continent was contiguous and had high economic values. African colonies possessed by Portugal, Italy, and Germany were all scattered and far away from each other in some cases, the economic and strategic values of which were not significant at the time. German East Africa had a relatively dense population. Although Italian Africa was larger in area (a part of Sahara), it had a sparse population and lower economic values because it was mostly in the desert. Portuguese Africa was the most backward in terms of economy but it had the potential for growth. Spanish colonies were the smallest, separated, and mostly in the desert, the economic and strategic values of which were not high. The trend of dividing African continent emerging in the 1880s was the most important part of the second climax in building colonial empires in the history of colonialism, which was an important manifestation of the transition from laissez-faire capitalism to monopoly capitalism. Three of the seven major crises in the international policies of the great powers caused by the colonist partition of the world from 1871 to 1914 happened in Africa: the Fashoda Incident when the conflicts between Britain and France were the most severe; the two Morocco crises when a European war almost broke out between Germany, France, and Britain; and the conflicts arisen out of the demand of Germany to re-divide Africa finally contributed partially to the World War I in 1914. Thus, it can be seen it is significant in the history of world colonialism to classify African continent into the South.

4.1.4. The Rise of New Colonial Empires and the New Rivalry

The trend of dividing African continent was not an isolated phenomenon but synchronous with the colonial partition of the rest of the world when old and new imperialist countries fought over colonies and spheres of influence. And the new colonist imperialist countries displayed powerful strength, challenging against old colonial empires and demanding to re-delineate new colonial maps. The fiercely contended colonies included:

Islands in the Pacific[30]. The South Sea Islands (Oceania) spread over one third of the surface area on the earth, which were basically the remote and wild areas of British informal empire before the mid-19th century. With the exception of France on certain islands, no country could compete with Britain. The supremacy possessed by Britain over all islands had no grounds of law or treaty only the annual patrol of warships sent by British Admiralty around all islands to demonstrate "the power of Britain". After the 1870s, new capitalist great powers like Germany and America began to be keenly interested in the South Sea Islands. These isolated islands in the Pacific were developed by western capital to produce cotton, sugar cane, copra, struvite, and phosphate rocks while the labor forces were recruited from India, China, and Southeast Asia. After the annexation of New Zealand by Britain in 1840, British metropolitan states in Oceania instigated and urged British government to occupy all islands in Oceania to forestall the occupation of France, Germany, America, and Holland. In 1874, Britain annexed Fiji Islands and established Higher Commissioners for the Western Pacific. In 1877, Britain exercised right of protection over Tokelau Islands. In 1884, Germany followed the example of Britain to annex a part of New Guinea including Bismarck Archipelago in the northeast. In the same year, Britain declared the southeast of New Guinea (later called Papua) to be under its protection. In 1885, Holland delimited the boundary in the west of New Guinea whole established rule over the east (Irian Barat). In the same year, Germany annexed Marshall Islands but failed to annex Caroline Islands due to the opposition of Spain. In 1887, Britain and France set up the allied naval committee to jointly control New Hebrides. In the same year, Britain officially annexed Pitcairn Islands while France annexed Wallis Islands. In the following year, the sphere of protection was extended to Futuna Islands, Germany annexed Nauru Island, and Britain announced that Cook Islands were under its protection. In 1889, German, Britain, and American jointly controlled Samoan Islands.

---

30 Several geographical regions named "-nesia", located between the Tropics of Cancer and Capricorn in the Pacific and all including islands, are from west to east Indonesia, Micronesia, Melanesia, and Polynesia, among which only Indonesia has become a united great country. Note by the author.

The domino effect caused by the contention for Pacific Islands gave rise to the installment of submarine cables, coaling stations, and naval bases, which in turn brought about the occupation of new islands. In the 1880s and 1890s, Britain and America respectively seized Phoenix Islands, Line Islands, Guam, and American Samoa. In 1892, Britain exercised rights of protection over Gilbert Islands and Ellice Islands. In 1898, after it annexed Hawaii, an important Pacific island, with an area of 16,635 square kilometers, America became even more ambitious and attempted to annex the entire Samoa Islands so as to establish a second naval base in the South Pacific, which was in conflict with the attempt of Germany to build a naval base in Samoa for its fleet of warships. Britain also opposed the attempt of Germany, which repeated the old trick to provoke a dispute over succession to the throne in the royal family of Samoa. American and British fleets of warships sailed into sea waters of Samoa, bombarded its capital, and destroyed German consulate. Germany took the occasion to make a scene, proposing only the partition of the islands could settle the disputes. Britain would have disagreed on the proposal of Germany to divide Samoa yet because the war between Britain and the Boers in South Africa was imminent and in order for Germany to give up its protection over the Boers, it had to make concessions and used the South Sea Islands as bargain chips in exchange for the "co-operation" of Germany in South Africa. On 14 November 1899, an agreement was signed which stipulated that Germany had possession of two of the Samoa Islands (Upolu and Savaii), America another two islands (Tutuila and Aunu'u) while Britain ceded all rights over Samoa Islands so as to obtain Tonga Islands and part of German Solomon Islands. Henceforth, South Solomon Islands belonged to Britain while North Solomon Islands Germany, which further purchased Mariana Islands and Caroline Islands from Spain. Britain also picked up its pace, declaring in 1900 Oceania to be its protected area and occupying Niue Island. In 1906, Britain and France in agreement exercised joint control over New Hebrides island group.

Table 4.6. The Partition of Islands of Oceania by the Great Powers (by 1914)[31]

Island Name	Suzerain	Year of Occupation	Area (Square Kilometers)	Population	Notions
Papua (Southeast New Guinea)	Britain	1884	46.2	1.05 million (the entire island in 1500)	In the east of Irian
Fiji	Britain	1874	18, 200	110	
British Solomon Islands	Britain	1899	28, 300 (covering the entire islands)		The total area of Solomon Islands was 40,000 Square Kilometers
New Hebrides	Britain	1906	12,1		Now Vanuatu
Gilbert Islands	Britain	1892	260		Now part of Kiribati
Ellis Islands	Britain	1892	27	50,000 (including Niue and Tokelau in 1900)	Now part of Tuvalu
Ocean Island	Britain	1892			
Cook Islands	Britain	1888	240	80,000 (in 1900)	
Niue	Britain	1900			
Tonga	Britain	1900	747	200,000 (in 1900)	
Tokelau Islands	Britain	1877	10		
Pitcairn Islands	Britain	1887	47		
New Zealand	Britain	1840	270	Around 100,000	
Australia	Britain	1788	7.692 million	Around 250,000	
The West of Samoa	Germany	1899	2934	400,000 (the entire islands in 1900)	Also known as West Samoa, including Upolu and Sawaii
Nauru	Germany	1888	21		
Marshall Islands	Germany	1886	181	720	Now Micronesia
Caroline Islands	Germany	1899	458		Now Palau, including Babeldaob
Mariana Islands	Germany	1899	457		Except Guam. Now known as Northern Mariana Islands
The northeast of New Guinea	Germany	1884			
Bismarck Islands	Germany	1884	49,7		
The north of Solomon Islands	Germany	1885	28,000 (including the entire islands)		Including Buka and Bougainville
New Caledonia Islands	France	1853	18,5		

31   For population in the table see Mcevedy, C. and R. Jones. *Atlas of World Population History.* New York: Facts on File, 1979: 385-409.

French Polynesian Islands	France	1842	4167	300,000 (in 1900)	
Wallis Islands	France	1887	60		
Futuna Islands	France	1888	64		
Guam	America	1898	549	Around 100,000 (in 1500 including the entire Micronesia)	
Hawaii Islands	America	1898	16,3	200,000 (in 1775)	
American Samoa	America	1899	199		Also known as East Samoa, including Tutuila and Aunuu
West New Guinea	Holland	1885	410	1.05 million (including the entire New Guinea)	Also known as West Irian delimited in 1885, the west of which possessed by Holland

It took over a hundred years (1776-1890) for America to transform from thirteen colonies in North America to a country of colonial expansion, the early form of which stressed more on commerce and annexation of neighboring territories. The substantive rifts between the northern states and the southern states restricted and even contained the outward expansion of America. The triumph of industrial revolution, the development of finance capitalism, and the apparent victory of the northern states in the Civil War all invigorated the outward expansion of America. In 1867, America purchased Alaska with an area of 1.518 million square kilometers from the fatuous Tsar of Russia, which provided a finger pointing at Asia because Alaska Peninsula and Aleutian Islands stuck eastward into the Pacific for over 3,460 kilometers. The islands in the Pacific with the highest strategic values and development values were Hawaii with an area of 16,635 square kilometers and Guam with an area of 532 square kilometers, which were the best stopovers on the route to Asia. At that time, Guam was in the hands of Spain while Hawaii was the object of the covetous Britain, France and America. America occupied Midway Island (with an area of only 4.7 square kilometers), a small island which was the nearest to the northwest of Hawaii as a base to penetrate into Hawaii. In 1875, America signed a treaty of trade reciprocity with Hawaiian Kingdom, which was practically reduced to be a protectorate of America. In 1878, America was entitled to establish a naval base on Tutuila Island of Samoa. In 1887, America was entitled to set up a coaling station and a naval base at Pearl Harbor of Hawaii Islands. Meanwhile, American plantation owners controlled the lifeblood of economy on the islands.

The investment of 33 million dollars in sugar industry was mostly American capital. The domestic media of America made propaganda for the annexation of Hawaii. The newly enthroned queen was against the annexation and strove to weaken the influence of America. In 1883, Pacific Fleet of America sailed into Pearl Harbor. Under the support of the navy, American plantation owners and merchants launched a coup, established an interim government, dethroned the queen, and forced Hawaii to sign the treaty of annexation. In 1898, Hawaii Islands officially joined the United States of America, which took Hawaii as the stopover to open up a navigation channel across the Pacific. In the last several years of the 19th century, the rapid development of American economy (ranking first over Britain and Germany), fast growth of finance capital, and the increasing advocacy of A.T. Mahan's theory of sea supremacy by many social interest groups all urged America to speed up its overseas expansion and compete with other colonialist great powers. The American-Spanish War provoked by America in 1898 was the logical outcome of the development of all these factors. Spain in possession of colonial heritages was vanquished in this imperialist war. In December 1898, a treaty was signed which stipulated that Spain cede Puerto Rico, Guam, and the Philippines to the United States, which became colonies of the latter. The Philippines had an area of nearly 300,000 square kilometers, a population of 8 million, and high economic and strategic values, which henceforth became the largest colony of the United States and the long-dreamed stepping stone to China. The words uttered by the US senator Henry Lodge after the colonization of Philippines by America in the 19th century revealed the future ambitions of the US for the world hegemony: Our economy was very powerful and we were moving forward to strengthen our position.... You can not check the activity of economic power neither the move forward of the U.S. American people and the economic power as the basis of everything will propel us to the position of world economic hegemony. At the turn of the century, colonialism around the Pacific islands—the imperialist contention for the area—ended with the relative triumph of the United States and Germany.

Central Asia was mainly the stage of contention between Russia and Britain. In the 1840s, momentum of Russia's rise in Central Asia was temporarily weakened in the Crimean War (1853-1856), which interrupted the military action of outflanking and conquering Central Asia. After the end of the Crimean War, Russia waged several battles from 1857 to 1864 to complete its control over Caucasus and commanded the triumphant troops to march eastward in the conquest of Central Asia. In October 1860, the Anglo-French Allied Forces invaded Tianjin, Tongxian County and the suburban areas of Beijing in China in the Second Opium War. Russia took the occasion to intermediate and forced the Qing Government to sign the Convention of Peking between China and Russia, which dictated the alignment of the western boundary line between China and Russia and designated the permanent Karuns (Chinese checkpoints) near the cities and towns within China as the border marks and Lake Dsai-Sang and Lake Issy-Kul as the boundary lakes. Before the negotiation in 1862, Russian troops seized passes and key posts in China, heaped stones and set up border marks, presenting a fait accompli. In the negotiation, Russia forced Qing Government to accept the demarcation formation that territories beyond Chinese checkpoints (which were far within the borderlines of China) to be incorporated into Russia and sent troops many times to pose threats to China. Under the military intimidation, Qing Government signed the Convention of Peking between China and Russia in 1860 and Protocol of Chuguchak in 1864, in which Russia forced Chinese government to cede a territory in Xinjiang of over 440,000 square kilometers to Russia and built a series of bunkers within the borderlines of China.

The contention between Russia and Britain for Central Asia was intensified. Britain set up consulates in Central Asian cities like Astarabad (now Gorgon). Russian expansionists believed Britain would henceforth obtain the key to Central Asia, which was the only remaining territory for Russia to undertake commercial and industrial activities because Russian industry was too weak to compete successfully with other countries. It was a time when cotton was in short supply in Russia due to the Civil War in the U.S. in 1863 so that Central Asia rich in cotton was increasingly enticing in the eyes of Russia. Because the supply of American cotton was suspended, the price of cotton in Central Asia grew six-fold from 1660 to 1662.

Different from Britain, America, and Germany whose colonial expansion was undertaken mainly with gunboats, Russia ordered ground troops to perform military actions in Central Asia, marching forward on the basis of "bunker policy". In the 1820s and 1830s, Russia had already occupied part of Kazakhstan. In 1853, Russian bunkers brazenly extended into Verniy (now Almaty) within borders of China. In the summer of 1864, Russian troops advanced southward in Central Asia from the east and the west under the banner of "civilization", attacked and occupied Shymkent, linked the line of bunkers in Syr Darya with that in Verniy (still within the borders of China before 1860), which cut off the connection between the Kazakh grasslands and three khanates in the south of Central Asia. Henceforth, taking advantage of the conflicts among the three khanates, Russia adopted the strategy of defeating and annexing them one after another. On 17 June 1865, Russia attacked and occupied Tashkent, the largest city in Central Asia. In 1866, Russian army worked out the plan of occupying the entire Khanate of Kokand and attacked it. In 1867, Russia set up the Turkestan Governorate, exercising colonial rule in occupied territories in Central Asia. In June 1868, Russian troops defeated Khanate of Bukhara, the main force occupied Samarkand, and reduced Khanate of Bukhara to be its protectorate. In November 1869, Russian troops set off from Caucasus to occupy the Red Water Bay on the east shore of Caspian Sea, surrounding the Khanate of Khiva and Turkmenistan on three sides from Bukhara in the east, Orenburg in the north, and the Red Water Bay in the west. In March 1871, Russia had planned to occupy the Khanate of Khiva but postponed the military action because it sent troops to occupy Ili of China in June 1871. In February 1873, Russian army branching out into four columns advanced to the Khanate

137

of Khiva and took it in May, and forced Khan of Khiva to acknowledge the protection of the Khanate of Khiva by Russia. From 1873 to 1877, Russian troops attacked tribes in Turkmenistan but encountered considerable resistance and suffered great losses. In 1880, Russian troops attacked Turkmenistan with heavy artilleries. However, it took four years for Russia to reach Tejen Oasis because Turkmenistan was mainly in the desert and its tribes attacked Russian troops. In 1884, Russian army approached Persia and Serhetabat River Valley near the border of Afghanistan and was ready to advance southward to Hirat District to peek over the Arab shore of the India Ocean. The heady southward advance of Russian troops posed threat to British colonies in India and its sphere of influence in Afghanistan. If Russia continued to advance southward, it would reach the door of India. The military actions of Russia sharply aggravated the colonial contention for West and South Asia between Russia and Britain, which was implementing Forward Policy from the 1870s to 1880s, attempting to expand British India and invade Afghanistan, and therefore sensitive to the closure of Russian forces in Central Asia. In March 1885, Britain instigated Afghan troops to clash with Russian forces in Serhetabat River Valley in the north. Meanwhile, Britain strove to destroy the Russian base of attacking Turkmenistan in Caucasus, which failed because of the drag effect of Three Emperor's League among Russia, Germany, and Austria. By 1885, Russia had basically finished its colonial conquest over Central Asian countries, which wreaked havoc on the intercontinental Silk Road meandering on the Eurasia continent for over 2,000 years.

138

The total area of Kazakhstan, Central Asian countries, and Turkmenistan occupied by Russia was 3.9 million square kilometers, which was equivalent to that of India (3.91 million square kilometers) but with a smaller population of 11 million. The colonial rule in Central Asia by Russia was different from that of Britain and European colonial powers, which had three characteristics: first, taking advantage of the geopolitical feature that Russian territories was adjacent to the lands of Central Asian countries, Russia first of all ceded the most fertile territories in the khanates to Russia to set up the so-called Samarqand Province and Transcaspian Province for cotton plantation. Second, Russia disdained to set up informal empires similar to those of Britain but was determined to set up a unified enormous empire. However, in order to decrease resistance, it took two political steps to rule these annexed countries, which were allowed "to exist for a time under separate, but entirely dependent leaders"[32] and then removed nearly all local feudal headmen from the lower ruling institutions to be replaced by Russian officers or government officials. Just as what Markov had described in Russia in Central Asia: "There are not only forts but also many barracks with glistening bayonets and cannons at the door in Tashkent. In addition, most officials are former servicemen, most institutions are military, gatherings were for servicemen, clubs, libraries, and schools are military, and even the churches here are military.... Wherever you go, you will seldom see any

32   Marx, Karl, and Fredrick Engels. *Collected Works*. Vol. 17. New York: International Publishers, 1981: 142.

people except soldiers, officers, generals, and their wives, children, and relatives. Non-military men will be involuntarily overwhelmed by the majority of the army-men"[33]. Third, after the military situation was stabilized, an increasingly larger number of Russian peasants who had lost their lands because of Serfdom Reform migrated to Central Asia: there 50,000 in 1904, which rose to 216,000 in 1906, 577,000 in 1907, around 2 million in 1911, accounting for 40 percent of the total population in Central Asia[34]. The establishment of colonies by Russia through military immigration into Central Asia surpassed those by France and Germany in tropical Africa so that Lenin once listed Turkestan with India and Egypt as "the purest colonies".

East Asia and Northeast Asia. After the Meiji Restoration, Japan rose rapidly to become a colonist-imperialist country in East Asia just as Germany grew up to be an emergent imperialist great power on European continent. However, after a period of semi-colonization by western great powers after 1853, Japan had been still trampled upon and restrained by some unequal treaties although it grew stronger in the process of modernization since the Meiji Restoration of 1868. This gave rise to special characteristics of Japanese government: sheepishly subordinate to western countries rather than arousing the people to abrogate unequal treaties while whimsically desirous of the east to make up for the loss in the west, attempting to bully the weak by invading and looting economically and politically China and Korea for compensation so as to uplift the international position of Japan. In 1872, Japan announced to have the so-called sovereignty rights over the Ryukyu Islands. In 1873, the Meiji government once decided to conquer Korea (but had to postpone the decision later). In the same year, the Bonin Islands (with an area of 104 square kilometers) around a thousand kilometers away from Japan's main island were taken over by Japan. In 1874, Japan waged a war to invade Taiwan Island of China and would not leave there unless forced months later. In 1875, Japan seized the entire Kuril Islands in a transaction with Russia and invaded Ganghwado of Korea. In 1876, following the Gunboat Policy of western countries, Japan forced Korea to sign the unequal Treaty of Ganghwa, obtaining unilateral extraterritoriality and consular jurisdiction. In 1879, ignoring China's protest, Japan annexed the Ryukyu Islands and arbitrarily turned it into a prefecture (part of Okinawa Prefecture, with an area of over 2000 square kilometers). In the 1890s, the capitalist economy of Japan had been greatly developed but its inherent weakness also seriously impeded the progress of modernization in Japan. The semi-feudal economic system of Japan itself led to intense domestic conflicts. For instance, the decadence of parasitic landlord system and the improvisation of peasants gave rise to the extremely narrow domestic market while the privileges stipulated by the unequal treaties not yet abrogated brought

---

33   Qtd. in Покровский, М.Н. *Collected Essays on Russian Diplomacy and Wars in the 19th Century*. Trans. Zhangheng Bei. Beijing: The Commercial Press, 1994: 337.
34   Qtd. in History of Tsar Russian Invasion and Expansion, by Writing Group of History of Tsar Russian Invasion and Expansion, History Department, Peking University. Vol. 2. Beijing: People's Publishing House, 1980: 122.

about the dumping of western commodities, which infringed the narrow market of Japan. All these unfavorable factors imposed great restrictions on the increase in the primitive accumulation of capital in the domestic market of Japan. The serious imbalance in economy aggravated domestic class conflicts. In the 1880s, the Meiji Government adopted the policy of strengthening the army as the basis of national prosperity to solve the problem, increasingly feverish to invade neighboring countries. Feudal warlords and Japanese Corps (Imperial Army General Staff Office) even unscrupulously transgressed the authority of the government to take aggressive actions. In 1882, taking the occasion of Imo Incident in Korea, Japan outrageously sent troops to the Korean Peninsula and forced Korea to sign the Inchon Treaty, from which Japan not only obtained indemnity but also the privilege of stationing troops in Seoul. In 1884, after it provoked the Jiashen Coup, Japan was even more ambition to invade the Korean Peninsula. Japanese Government and Corps attempted to get out of plight, promote the international position of Japan, and prompt the solution to the problem of unequal treaties through triumphant foreign wars. Therefore, after the 1880s, frantically expanding arms and preparing wars, Japan awaited an opportunity to launch the Sino-Japanese War so as to solve the problem of the Korean Peninsula and domestic difficulties of insufficient capital and resources. The drastic changes in the international situation in Far East in the middle of the 1890s were in favor of Japan. Having finished its occupation of Central Asia, Russia concentrated on the expansion in Far East and announced it would build the Trans-Siberian Railway, which posed serious threats to the colonial advantage of Britain in Northeast China and the Korean Peninsula. Britain attempted to avail of Japan as the outpost of resisting the southward expansion of Russia and the vanguard of further invading China so that it had to improve relations with Japan. Britain signed a commercial treaty with Japan on 16 July 1894, giving up some unilateral privileges. The commercial treaty relieved the anxiety of Japan for the interference with the Sino-Japanese War by western great powers. Nine days later, Japan provoked the undeclared Sino-Japanese War, whose fleet struck the Chinese fleet on the sea near Toshima on 25 July. Japan defeated China in the first Sino-Japanese War of 1894-1895 and forced Qing Government to cede Taiwan Island (with an area of 36,000 square kilometers) and the Pescadore Islands (with an area of 64 square kilometers) to Japan, which became the first colonies of Japan. In the late 1890s, Japan made transactions with Russian over Northeast China and Korea became practically a protectorate of Japan. After the Russo-Japanese war in 1905, Japan officially annexed Korea (with an area of 222,000 square kilometers). Hereto, Japan had a possession of colonies with an area of around 260,000 square kilometers, equivalent to 76 percent of the area of Japan proper. Henceforth, Japan changed from a semi-colony country to one of colonial great powers by means of invading neighboring countries, which was a special case in the history of modern colonialism (while the US was an example of ranking among colonial great powers from a colonized country). Japan entered the scope of the South in the 1860s but ranked among countries in the North through invading and looting

China and Korea, and modernization, which was unique in the world history before the 21st century.

After the Treaty of Nerchinsk, Russia did not stand still for long but availed itself of the debility of Qing Government to expand vehemently towards Northeast Asia, sending troops to invade the north shore of the upper and middle reaches and both shores of the lower reaches of the Heilongjiang River, setting up posts, and establishing villages. In March 1858, when the Anglo-French Allied Force stormed the forts of Dagu and invaded the suburb of Tianjin, Russian warships under the command of Nikolay Muravyov-Amursky, the General Governor of Eastern Siberia, sailed to Aihui (formerly known as Aigun) of Heilongjiang. Muravyov-Amursky put forward the draft treaty to Yishan, the Heilongjiang General of Qing Government, and alleged that the border between Russia and China should be demarcated around Heilongjiang. Otherwise, Russia with Britain would wage a war against China. Russian warships fired shots and cannons to intimidate Qing Government by force. On 28 May, Yishan, the incompetent Heilongjiang General, was forced to sign the Treaty of Aigun, which stipulated that a Chinese territory of over 600,000 square kilometers to the north of Heilongjiang and the south of Stanovoy Range jointly governed by China and Russia while Russian ships were allowed to sail in China's inland rivers, the Heilongjiang River, and the Wusuli River. This treaty seriously damaged the integrity of territory and sovereignty of China. Qing Government did not approve the Treaty of Aigun and imposed punishment on local officials like Yishan. On 13 June, taking the occasion of intermediating between China and the Anglo-French Allied Force, Russia coerced China into signing the Tianjin Treaty. In order to seize Chinese territories in accordance with the Treaty of Aigun, Russian negotiators insisted Article IX should state that both countries will name delegates to examine the "parts of the border between China and Russia which are not yet determined", attempting to override the demarcation of the border between China and Russia in the Treaty of Nerchinsk in 1689. After intermediating between China and the allied force for the second time when Beijing was under the siege of the Anglo-French Allied Force on 14 November 1860, Russia again coerced Qing Government into signing the Convention of Peking between China and Russia, which ceded a Chinese territory of 400,000 square kilometers to the east of the Wusuli River to Russia. And Qing Government was forced to virtually acknowledge the Treaty of Aigun denied by Qing Government in 1858, which implied another Chinese territory of 600,000 square kilometers to the north of Heilongjiang was ceded to Russia. In the west of China, after the conquest of the Khanate of Kokand and the Khanate of Bokhara, Russia approached Ili of China and occupied it in July 1871. Bullying the weak, Russia coerced Qing Government into signing the Ili Treaty between China and Russia, seizing a Chinese territory of over 70,000 square kilometers. Russia repeated the same trick and unscrupulously occupied the vast Pamir to the west of Sarykol Range of China. Tannu Uriankhai was China's territory at the time with an area of 170,000 square kilometers. Treaty of Kyakhta between China and Russia signed in 1727 stipulated clearly that Sayan Mountains were the boundary between the two countries while Tannu Uriankhai was to the south of Sayan Mountains. Chinese Government stationed 46 assistant commandants in the region. In the late 19th century, Russia penetrated into the region, and a large number of Russians sneaked there and dug gold dust, which reached 12,000 people in 1911. In June 1914, Russian Government sent troops to occupy Tannu Uriankhai. Russia had been covetous of Outer Mongolia (with an area of around 1.56 million square kilometers) for a long time and sent Cossacks to enter and garrison in Kulun in 1900. In 1911, taking the occasion of the 1911 Revolution in China, Russia provoked Outer Mongolia to declare "independence", increased troops in Kulun, drove away ministers of Qing Government from there, and signed a treaty with the puppet government of Outer Mongolia, which granted Russia a series of privileges and reduced Outer Mongolia practically to be a Russian colony. Tsarist Russia was one of the most aggressive colonialist countries. Because of geographical relations, its conquered and occupied colonies were adjacent with the territory of Russia, which did not have overseas colonies. Taking advantage of this geographical characteristic, Tsarist Government divided the seized colonies or foreign territories into provinces or autonomous prefectures of Russia in order to gloss over its colonial imperialism. The history of Tsarist Russia was a history of plundering territories of other countries and nations. In the 370 years of expansion, Russia changed from Grand Duchy of Moscow situated in the corner of East Europe to an enormous colonial empire across Asia and Europe with an area of 22.8 million square kilometers, which was unique in the world history of colonialism. Tsarist Russia with Britain and France of the same period was the source of colonialist oppression, whose neighboring countries had all been bullied and taken away large territories.

Southeast Asia. In the late 19th century, the struggle between Britain, France, Russia, America, and Spain arising out of colonial expansion and scramble for rights of control was increasingly intensified. With the opening of the Suez Canal in 1869 and the advent of the second industrial revolution in Europe, Southeast Asia was even more marginalized. After suppressing Indian Rebellion (1857-1858), Britain consolidated its rule over India and used it as a base for further expansion in Asia, especially Myanmar. After three Anglo-Burmese wars, especially the military action of 1886, Britain overturned Burmese dynasty and colonized the entire country (with an area of 676,000 square kilometers). Since the establishment of colonial rule over Straits Settlements (Singapore), Britain effectively controlled the sailing through the Malacca Strait. Britain had not annexed the princely states on the Malay Peninsula for a long time, maintaining paramountcy over the area with informal means (informal empire). After the 1870s, German warships flooded to the Malay Peninsula and America began to encroach upon the area. Britain changed its policy and took military actions before other countries. In 1873, British Lieutenant-General Sir Andrew Clarke was sent to serve as the governor of the Straits Settlements and implemented new policy of expansion in the Malay Peninsula, gradually imposing protection upon five princely states in the north and four princely states in the south of Siam. In 1894, the colonization of the Malay Peninsula was completed. Kalimantan Island (formerly known as Borneo) was the third largest island in the world with an area of 734,000 square kilometers, which had been contented by Holland and Britain. Sultan of Brunei in the north of the island upheld by Holland inserted a wedge in the north of the Kalimantan Island. In 1846, British adventurer James Brooke took Brunei and coerced Sultan into signing a treaty, which stipulated that Labuan be ceded to Britain as a colony and separated Sarawak from Brunei. Holland and Britain respectively had an advantage in the south and the north. Henceforth, British colonial power based on the Kalimantan Island expanded to the Sulug Island in the corner of the Philippines, which alerted Spanish metropolitan states. Spain picked up the pace in its infiltration into the unoccupied islands of the Philippines while turned from the defensive to the offensive, making territorial claims to Sandakan of the Kalimantan Island. In 1885, an agreement was reached between Britain and Spain, in which Britain acknowledged the possession of the Sulug Island by Spain while the latter gave up its claim to the territory in the north of the Kalimantan Island. Hereto, Britain decided to officially turn Brunei to be its protectorate, imposed rule over the entire North Kalimantan Island (with an area of around 200,000 square kilometers) while acknowledge that South Kalimantan Island (with an area of around 530,000 square kilometers) as a colony of Holland.

Losing the Cape Colony in South Africa after the end of the Napoleonic Wars, Holland concentrated its forces to operate East Indian Colony (Indonesia), especially the colonization of Java Island and the north of Sumatra Island. In the late 19th century, western colonist great powers stretched into the unoccupied islands in the Thousand Island Region of Indonesia. Holland picked up its pace to occupy the entire East Indies with a population of around 6,000. In 1869, the opening of the Suez Canal changed the shipping route from the Atlantic to the Indian Ocean. The shipping route round the Cape of Good Hope was replaced by the Suez Canal and the shipping route of through the Sunda Strait was replaced by that of the Malacca Strait. The strategic position of Aceh Kingdom on the northern tip of Sumatra Island was increasingly important in that it controlled the vantage point of the Malacca Strait. However, it had not been ruled by the Dutch metropolitan states. In 1871, the U.S. signed the Draft Commercial Treaty with Aceh Kingdom and sent a fleet of warships to sail into Port of Aceh, which forced Holland to be determined in putting an end to the independence of Aceh Kingdom. Britain was not willing to allow the U.S. which had become increasingly powerful after the Civil War to occupy Aceh and control the sailing route through the Malacca Strait while preferred the relatively weak opponent Holland to complete its occupation of Sumatra Island. Holland also made it clear to Britain that it was willing to pay for the "kindness" of Britain with a prosperous stronghold (Elmina) on the Gold Coast. In March 1873, backed up with a fleet of four warships, the Dutch special envoy declared war against Aceh Kingdom, which lasted for many years and ended till the early 20th century when the entire island was conquered by Holland. Meanwhile, Holland tightened its control over the princely states like Bali Island, South Sulawesi, Maluku

Islands, and Lesser Sunda Islands by force or guile. Holland proper with an area of merely 41,000 square kilometers and a population of several million had to find the fulcrum and managed with great efforts to fully conquer and directly rule the Thousand Island Country consisting of over 13,000 small or large islands with an area of 1.91 million square kilometers till the eve of World War I.

It took comparatively shorter time for France to conquer the entire Indochina Peninsula. France was the most powerful colonial countries on European continent before 1814, rich in colonial experiences, and strove to recover its position of a colonial great power after the Congress of Vienna. Seeing that Indian Subcontinent had irreversibly become the colony of the British Empire, the French metropolitan states in Asia chose to conquer the Indochina Peninsula with an area of two million square kilometers. However, the spearhead of British colonial conquest did not stand still after it had reached Naga Hills and Arakan Yoma, mountain range in western Myanmar. In the late 19th century when imperialist great powers competed for the spheres of influence in mainland China, Britain attempted to enter the southwest and Tibet of China by way of Myanmar so that to link the southwest with its sphere of influence in the Changjiang River basin. After it had gained a firm foothold in Cochin-China since the mid-19th century, France strove to enter Guangxi and Yunnan of China by way of Vietnam and Laos. In 1871, French colonial adventurers sneaked into the inland of China and Vietnam and illegally opened an access to Yunnan of China by way of the Red River, which sped up the French plan of invading Tonkin of Vietnam by force. Confronted with the threatening France, Nguyen Dynasty of Vietnam appointed Liu Yongfu, head of the Black Banner Army of China, as the defense governor. On 21 December 1873, the Black Banner Army ambushed under Paper Bridge in Hanoi, defeated the French army, and killed Francis Garnier, head of the French army, and his aide, which forced the French army to retreat from Hanoi and occupied provincial capital. It was when France was defeated in the Franco-Prussian War so that it was impossible for France to send more troops to the Indochina Peninsula. The defeat in the Paper Bridge Battle forced France to postpone its plan of invading the north of Vietnam for ten years. In the early 1880s, the cabinet of Jules Ferry came into power. Engels once pointed out that Jules Ferry was one of the most consummate representatives of colonialists who only wanted to "bleed…its colonies white"[35]. Once Ferry came into power, he aggressively pursued the policy of colonialist expansion, occupied and annexed Tunisia in 1882, and waged the first war of conquering Madagascar from 1883 to 1885. In 1882, Ferry Cabinet launched attacks against Tonkin of Vietnam for the second time. In May 1883, the French column was defeated in the Second Battle of Paper Bridge and its chief commander Henri Laurent Rivière was killed on the battlefield. French Government sent more troops to Vietnam and dispatched a fleet of warships to the east, and expanded the invansion of Vietnam, the purpose of which was to delimit Yunnan, Guangxi, and Guangdong of China into its spheres of influence. In August, the reinforced French army coerced the Nguyen

---

35   Marx, Karl, and Fredrick Engels. *Collected Works*. Vol. 27. New York: International Publishers, 1990: 417.

Dynasty of Vietnam into signing the humiliating Treaty of Hué or Protectorate Treaty. In December, the Frenched army launched attacks against the Chinese army, the Sino-French War broke out. In the Treaty of Tientsin which concluded the Sino-French War in June 1885, the incompetent Qing Government ended the Sino-Vietnam suzerain-vassal state relationship and officially recognized France's right of colonial protection over Vietnam. Meanwhile, availing itself of the overwhelming deterrence of colonial wars, France coerced Cambodia into signing the second French-Cambodian Treaty, which reduced Cambodia to a protectorate. The situation was complicated in Laos, which was a vassal state of Siam (Thai). Britain was reluctant to allow the power of French to be expanded to Siam. The two countries had deadlocked over the colonial interests in Indochina Peninsula. Finally, they agreed that Siam be the boundary between them: France would not encroach upon the sovereignty of British and Burmese authorities over Kengtung while Britain would not interfere into actions taken by France against Laos. In 1893, France attacked Laos, clashed with garrison troops of Siam, approached Bangkok, and coerced Siam into ceding Laotian territory on the east shore of the Mekong to France. In 1899, France annexed Laos into French Indochina. Thus, the entire Southeast Asia was classified into the South.

The contention for Asia and the Pacific by colonial great powers did had not end before the World War I, but continued in a more intensified form—a general war—in 1914.

Table 4.6. The number of colonies established and revoked by metropolitan states of Europe, US and Japan and the annually accumulated colonies

Year	Established	Revoked	Annual accumulated net number	Year	Established	Revoked	Annual accumulated net number
1877	2	1	107	1897	1	0	141
1878	2	2	107	1898	5	4	142
1879	1	1	107	1899	2	1	143
1880	1	0	108	1900	5	1	147
1881	1	0	109	1901	5	5	147
1882	3	1	111	1902	4	0	151
1883	1	0	112	1903	1	0	152
1884	6	0	118	1904	2	0	154
1885	5	0	123	1905	1	0	155
1886	4	0	127	1906	2	1	156
1887	3	0	130	1907	3	0	159
1888	2	0	132	1910	1	3	157
1890	1	2	131	1912	5	0	162
1891	1	0	132	1913	1	1	162
1892	1	0	133	1914	3	5	160
1893	2	0	135	1915	0	1	159
1894	2	0	137	1916	4	1	162
1895	3	1	139	1917	1	1	162
1896	2	1	140	1918	0	1	161

4.1.5. The Southernization of Semi-Colonies as the "Intermediate" Form of Transition

Semi-colonies as the "intermediate" transitional form should not be ignored in the study of the evolution of colonialism, which can be linked with the concept of "informal empire" implemented by Britain since the middle of the 19th century. Seeing from the perspective of the subjects in colonial invasions, informal means gave rise to "the informal empire" while from the perspective of the invaded informal means gave rise to a form of "semi-colonies", which was the most common transitional form in nature and society. Such political entities exhibited salient features:

Its formation was that colonial great powers could exert political, economic, and military control over these countries or regions. In the early and middle 19th century, Britain practiced a policy of laissez faire, its economic strength ranked first in the world, and its navy controlled the major seas in the world. Therefore, it was possible for Britain to possess dominance over territories not officially occupied or not openly under its rule. Under this main premise, while maintaining the form of independent countries, the politics and economies of these countries or regions were under the strict control of Britain, and became its sales markets, sources of raw materials, outlets for investment, or strategic regions. These countries or regions were different from colonies deprived of sovereignties in that they could still maintain political (semi-)independence and formal governments, like China after the Opium Wars, Egypt before 1882, Zanzibar Sultanate in East Africa, Ethiopia, and the Ottoman Empire. By the late 19th century, capitalism was dominated by finance capital, which could play a decisive role in all economic relations and international relations by controlling politically independent countries with financial means (like conditional huge loans). Therefore, when imperialist great powers were deadlocked in their contention for an independent country or region, they might adopt the form of semi-colonies, mitigating conflicts by delimiting spheres of influence, equal shares of interests, and balance of power. For instance, imperialist great powers adopted this form in declining countries like China and the Ottoman Empire.

Semi-colony was the form of intermediate transition, which was a politically independent country not entirely under the control of imperialist countries. In the stage of (private) monopoly capitalism, it was most "convenient" and beneficial for imperialists that these semi-colony countries were deprived of political independence. But in certain historical periods or when imperialist countries were deadlocked, it was possible for the semi-colonies to have a certain degree political independence. If there occurred changes in the balance of power among the interest-seeking imperialist countries, that would certainly effect certain regions in the South, and some imperialists would strive to deprive semi-colony countries from their political independence. For instance, after the September 18th Incident in 1931, Japan attempted to colonize Northeast China , and North China and even more than half of China after the Marco

Polo Bridge Incident in 1937, Therefore, semi-colony status was a transitional form (an indispensable form of transition in certain stages), which might turn into colony status due to the local contention among imperialist great powers, thus changes in the balance of power—in certain cases—has led to invasions or strengthened the rule over semi-colony countries by imperialists during the great war periods.

If, generally speaking, fewer imperialist great powers took part in the partition of spheres of influence in semi-colony countries, the deepening semi-colonization would be an inexorable trend. For instance, Britain and Russian reached an agreement between them in 1907 which entitled them to divide Persia into the south and north spheres of influence between them, which reduced Persia into "already almost completely a colony"[36]. Therefore, fewer countries took part in partition, more clearly the balance of power would be displayed, easier to reach compromises and make concessions and achieve, regain balance of power and readjust conflicts. However, in most cases, it was not easy for those semi-colony countries—which are divided into spheres of influence—to expand their activity space and maintain their political independence by taking advantage of the conflicts among the imperialist countries.

It might possible for semi-colonies as a form of transition to regain complete independence when the international situation had undergone great changes, domestic anti-imperialist forces were reinforced, and national liberation movement surged ahead. In the struggle of defending national sovereignty, protecting domestic resources, developing national economy, and regaining complete political independence, if the balance of power among all class and in society of semi-colony countries underwent favorable changes, not only nationalist bourgeoisie would devoted themselves to the move of defending national sovereignty and regaining complete political independence but also some agents and intermediaries would shift their ground to the side of patriotic movement.

It must be pointed out that there were no differences in quality or even quantity between semi-colonies and colonies in terms of classification into the South, marginalization, subordinate areas of agricultural production and sources of raw materials in the coercive international division of labor. Because semi-colony countries were generally deprived of rights of imposing tariffs, coerced into granting the great powers unilateral most-favored-nation status, consular jurisdiction, right of internal navigation, and right to stationed army, their national sovereignty were inflicted great damages so that they were economically undeveloped countries and the victim of oppression in the unreasonable international economic order, not different from colonies. Therefore, they were economically controlled and exploited by the North in the North-South relationship, which could be illustrated in the fact that dozens of independent countries transformed from colonies were still economically exploited, plundered, and controlled by countries in the North.

---

36 Lenin, Vladimir. *Imperialism, the Highest Stage of Capitalism*. New York: International Publishers, 1939. Beijing: People's Publishing House, 1974: 72.

At the turn of the 20th century, the contention among imperialist countries for spheres of influence in semi-colony countries reached its climax, which was most intensive in China, the Ottoman Empire, and Persia. During 1895, in China, including the rising Russia, France, and Germany, each for the sake of its own aggressive interest, jointly intervened and forced Japan to return Liaodong Peninsula to them; and after this event by the signing of Sino-Russian Secret Treaty in 1896, Russia began to exert a greater influence on Qing Government.[37] Entitled to the highest interests in China granted by unequal treaties since the Opium War, Britain was dissatisfied with the new situation and was worried that with the rise of Russian power in China and its expansion in Manchuria, it would occupy the entire Manchuria, which would necessarily diminish and damage British interests in the region. The conflict between Britain and Russia in China had once risen to be the most serious. Taking the occasion, German fleet sailed into the sea waters near Shangdong and rented the Jiaozhou Bay as the military harbor on the pretexts that a German missionary was killed in Caozhou. Russia made a deal with Germany, sent its fleet of warships into Lushun Harbor on the Liaodong Peninsula in the Bohai Sea, and asked Qing Government for a loan with harsh conditions. British fleet also sailed into Lushun Harborr, moored besides the Russian fleet, and exerted pressure on Qing Government to prevent Germany from getting the loan. However, the real purpose of Britain was to negotiate with Russia on the filthy lucre. Russia held negotiations with Britain in Petersburg in 1898, when Britain was

on a tight rope with France at Fashoda in the Nile River Basin and split with Germany due to the contention for the Republics of the Boers between them so that it could not afford to be isolated in confrontation with three countries simultaneously. Britain was more concerned that German capital would expand to the Changjiang River Basin to be invested in building railways. Therefore, it bargained with Russia over the northeast of China, reached a compromise, and agreed that the north of China belonged to Russia's spheres of influence. However, Britain insisted to follow the principle of laissez faire in the spheres of in Russia's spheres of influence, that is, it strove to maintain its advantageous position in economy and trade. Although Russia recognized the Changjiang River Basin as Britain's spheres of influence, it would not allow other countries to compete in its spheres of influence (northeast and north of China). It was difficult from Britain and Russia to reach reconciliation in the interest of aggression. Meanwhile, Russia and Germany came to an understanding after secret negotiations, and agreed to offer each other mutual support for actions in China: Russia recognized Shandong as Germany's spheres of influence while Germany acknowledged the north of China as Russia's spheres of influence.

---

37 Russia, France, and Germany, each for the sake of its own aggressive interest, jointly intervened in demanding Japan to return Liaodong Peninsula ceded according to Treaty of Maguan. Under the pressure from the three countries, Japan had to agree to retreat from Liaodong Peninsula within three months after it had received 30 million taels of silver from the Qing Government. In fact, Japan extorted 0.23 billion taels of silver from China in the Sino-Japanese War of 1894-1895. Note by the author.

Germany, under the situation, coerced Qing Government into signing Convention Respecting the Lease of Jiaozhou, which stipulated that Qing Government ceded to Germany on lease of Jiaozhou Bay and all islands within it (with a total area of over 550 square kilometers) for ninety-nine years, left the exercise of sovereignty rights in the ceded territory to Germany, Germany was entitled to make regulations on ships of all nations including China in and out of the bay. Germany set a bad precedent of occupying forcibly harbors of China as colonies in the name of "lease". The convention also stipulated that a 100-mile zone within Chaoping in the Jiaozhou Bay was delimited as "a neutral zone", German fleet had the freedom to sail through while Qing Government had to negotiate with Germany before it garrisoned troops in the region with an area of 6,500 square kilometers, which practically became a condominium of both countries. These stipulations illustrated that Germany did not consider Jiaozhou Bay as a territory of China but a colony of Germany, which was not different from German African colonies. Germany unscrupulously set up Jiaozhou Governor's Hall, issued 188 decrees, exercised tight control over military, economy, culture, and even everyday lives like weddings and funerals, and imposed numerous taxes in the capacity of governor. Jiaozou Bay became an important base of German East Asian Squadron. Therefore, it is clear that semi-colonies were hardly different from colonies under the imperialist yoke. They might be reduced to colonies at any moment and fall into the scope of the South.

In December 1897, Russian fleet sailed into Lushun Harbor, pretending that it would help Qing Government to withdraw German fleet. After the conflict between China and Germany was almost settled, Russian fleet broke its promise, refused to retreat, demanded to lease Lushun, Dalian and build a branch line of Chinese Eastern Railway, and coerced Qing Government into signing the treaty within a definite time. In March 1898, Convention for the Lease of Lushun and Dalian, which stipulated that Lushun, Dalian and nearby waters be leased to Russia for ninety-nine years, a vacant space was demarcated to the north of the leased territory, which Chinese troops were allowed to enter only with the permission of Russia, and Qing Government must not transfer the vacant space, ports, and rights of railways and mines to other countries. When Russia, France, and Germany interfered into the return of Liaodong Peninsula in 1895, Qing Government paid 30 million taels (a unit of weight used in east Asia approximately equal to 1.3 ounces) of silver to retrieve from Japan Liaodong Peninsula, which fell into the hands of Germany less than three years later. After Russia was defeated in the Russo-Japanese War, the leased Liaodong Peninsula was possessed by Japan against the objection of China and renamed as Guangdongzhou.

Russia took Lushun and Dalian in 1897 and controlled the Bohai Sea of China, which provoked Britain into pressing on with occupation of Weihaiwei, which was still under the occupation of Japanese troops (since the First Sino-Japanese War). Japanese army threatened it would not retreat unless Qing Government paid the reparation of 100 million taels of silver to Japan, which forced the latter to get a loan of 100 million taels of silver (equivalent to 16 million pounds) at an annual interest of 4.8 Li discounted at 17% from HSBC (Hong Kong and Shanghai Banking Corporation) of Britain, guaranteed with customs revenues, likin (a form of internal tariff in the Chinese Empire and Republic) upon goods salt and at the huge cost of recognition of the Changjiang River Basin as the Britain's spheres of influence. Japanese army did not retreat from Weihaiwei until it gained the reparation in May 1898. In July of the same year, China and Britain signed the Convention for the Lease of Weihaiwei, which stipulated that Weihaiwei, nearby waters, and Liugong Island being included with an area of 16 square kilometers was leased to Britain for 25 years. Weihaiwei and Lushun across the sea, which were two portals of guarding Beijing as capital of China, fell respectively into the hands of Britain and Russia (and was transferred to Japan in 1905) and became their important military bases in Far East. The leased territories of China had actually turned from semi-colonies to colonies.

Following closely Germany and Russia, France also demanded to set up coal depots in the Leizhou Peninsula in the south of China. Russia voiced support for its ally. On 13 March 1898, France put forward four requirements towards China: first, China promised not to transfer provinces like Yunnan, Guangxi, and Guangdong to other countries; second, Head of China's General Post Office should be held by the French; third, France was in charge of building the railway from Vietnam to Kunming of Yunnan; fourth, France set up landing pontoons along the south seashore of China. On April 9, France gave Qing Government the ultimatum, claiming that the draft treaty be not altered one word and responded to at least tomorrow. Qing Government was coerced into accepting the requirements and agreed to lease the Guangzhou Bay (Leizhou Peninsula) to France for 99 years. France immediately sent a fleet of warships to land on the Guangzhou Bay, occupied artillery batteries, and strenuously expanded its spheres. In 1899, it was stipulated that France was entitled to construct artillery batteries and garrison troops in the leased territory (the Guangzhou Bay and nearby waters), and imposed inward port charges on inward ships and vessels, which implied one more leased territory in the south of China was reduced to colonies.

The successive scramble for China by colonialist great powers was turned into simultaneous and unscrupulous plunder of China from 1897 to 1898. Britain claimed it would extend the boundary of Hongkong on the excuse of preventing French power from advancing into Guangdong. The former boundary of Hongkong (with an area of 75.6 square kilometers) under the control of Britain was only equivalent to that of a minor part of Kowloon Peninsula (to the south of Boundary Street with an area of 11.1 square kilometers) with a total area of 86.7 square kilometers. In June 1898, Qing Government was coerced into signing the Convention for the Extension of Hongkong, which stipulated that Kowloon Peninsula (including Dapeng Bay and Shenzhen Bay) and more than 200 nearby islands (altogether known as the New Territories) were leased to Britain for 99 years. The area of the New Territories was 975.1

square kilometers, 12 times that of the total area of Hongkong Island and South Kowloon Peninsula already occupied by Britain.

Germany, Russia, Britain, and France respectively occupied by force important ports in the coastal areas of China from 1897 to 1899, the period of the frantic partition of the world by imperialist great powers, which set up administration bureaus, garrison troops, establish independent management system, imposed colonial rules in the coastal areas completely separated from China's administration system, and further expanded power in China on the bases of leased territories.

Another striking feature of the expansion of power in China by imperialist great powers was the wanton expansion of concessions at trading ports and cities of China, which as a particular phenomenon in semi-colony countries epitomized the colonized nature of semi-colony countries. Concessions lasted for nearly a hundred years in China, which were the permanent or long-term living areas at some trading ports and in some cities of China in the name of residence and business in accordance with the unequal treaties signed by Qing Government with imperialist great powers. Due to the continuous extension of consular jurisprudence in concessions, imperialist countries set up police stations, law courts, municipal administrative institutions, and tax authorities while foreigners opened shops, constructed depots, wharves, and factories, which were not restrained by Chinese laws. Smuggling, drug dealing, kidnapping, and human trafficking often occurred so that concessions became "countries within the country" and important strongholds of invading China by colonialist great powers. Before the First Sino-Japanese War, concessions were mostly public. After the war, concessions of Japan, mostly exclusive, sprang up across six large cities. It was followed by Germany, Russia, and France which established and expanded exclusive concessions. By the end of Qing Government, concessions at 16 trading ports scattering across riverside and seaside areas of China reached up to 43, among which 5 were public, 38 were exclusive, and 11 of which were under the control of Britain. China's rights of sovereignty were inflicted grave damages. The presence of leased territories and concessions as an anomalous phenomenon illustrated forcibly the transitional nature of semi-colonies, which was an effective handy tool to turn semi-colony China into colonized in due time by imperialist great powers. For instance, after Japan took the leased territory of Liaodong Peninsula from Russia in 1905, it arbitrarily set up Guangdong Governor's Hall (later reorganized as Guandong Office) and Guandong Army, consisting of a division of regular troops, railway garrison, Lushun brigade with heavy artilleries, and military police, which was basically the same as the authorized size of the Governor's Hall established in the colony of Korea. After the September 18th Incident, Japan sent Guandong Army to occupy the northeast of China. Later, the headquarters of Guangdong Army moved from the leased territory of Lushun to Changchun, exercising immediate rule over the colony of the northeast (Manchuria) by officers of Guangdong Army.

The Ottoman Empire was ruled by the Turks with Islam as the official religion, consisting of the Turks (relatively few), Arabs, Slavs, and Armenians, stretching across Europe, Asia, and Africa, with an area of 6 million square kilometers in its heyday. There were many reasons for the fall of the Ottoman Empire but its disintegration was mainly the outcome of semi-colonization. The Ottoman Empire, with vast territories in East Europe, West Asia, and North Africa, rich resources, and key strategic positions, had long been the coveted target of colonial countries like France, Britain, Germany, Russia, and Italy. However, the Ottoman Empire was like a colossus which could not be devoured by any single colonial country although France, Britain, Russia, and Germany sought to control the internal and foreign affairs of the Sultan and the Empire. Due to the mutual intense contention among the great powers, no European great power could unilaterally maintain its control over the Sultan and the entire empire for a long time. Meanwhile, the great powers strenuously forestall power vacuum in the Ottoman Empire from being exploited by any single country, the complexity of which was not different from that in China. Before the end of the 19th century, territories on the edge of the Ottoman Empire kept shrinking due to the encroachment of Russia, Austro-Hungarian Empire, France, and Britain. However, the entire empire maintained nominal control over its vast territories due to the "support" of the great powers out of private interests. Although the Ottoman Empire had unwisely offered consular jurisprudence to Christian countries like France and Britain out of cultural and religious considerations before the 19th century, most unequal treaties were signed after the middle of the 19th century. For instance, the Anglo-Turkish Commercial Treaty (1838), which deprived the Ottoman Empire of rights of setting tariffs, stipulated that the Ottoman government could only impose a tariff of 5 percent on imported foreign commodities, forbade the exercise of sales monopoly system on any goods and materials in the empire, and foreigners were entitled to trade in any areas (including Egypt) in the empire. After the Crimean War (1856), financial forces of European great powers infiltrated further into the Ottoman Empire and controlled some important economic sectors. Domestic laws made under the manipulation of foreign powers from 1856 to 1870 were increasingly favorable for foreign capital to encroach upon the Ottoman Empire, like granting foreigners privilege of possessing lands, allowing foreign capital to enter agricultural sectors while enjoy extraterritorial jurisdictions and be free of tax. Therefore, foreigners could not only refuse the administration and supervision of Ottoman governments at all levels but also utilize their privileges to lower operations costs than those of the Turks, which gave rise to unequal competition in Ottoman markets favorable only to foreigners. The Ottoman Empire was deprived of tariff autonomy, import tariff throughout the country was set at 5 percent while export at 12 percent, much lower that those in European countries. The outcome was that it was reduced to be an outlet of commodity dumping by European industrial countries, which inflicted serious damages on the infant national industry in Turkey. The corrupt Sultan and imperial government constantly borrowed large sums of money with high interest rates, which and was mainly for military spending to maintain the rule of the royal family. The foreign debt reached up to 2.5 billion francs by 1870 and soared again from 1870 to 1874 when the Ottoman Empire borrowed 3 billion francs with high interest so that the total foreign debt was 5.5 billion francs and the return of the interest would take up a large part of annual national budget. The Ottoman Empire had to declare partial fiscal debacle in 1875 and complete fiscal debacle in 1879, and set up Ottoman Public Debt Administration, which became "a state within a state" and was controlled by the committee consisting of representatives from creditor countries like Britain, France, Germany, Austria-Hungary, and Italy. Taking advantage of the financial subordination of the Ottoman Empire to them, imperialist great powers seized rights of lease which could enable them to obtain huge profits and dominant positions. For instance, the right of building railways (Germany seized the right of building the Three B railway from Berlin to Basra via Istanbul) which had strategic significance and made it possible for them control the economic lifeline of the Ottoman Empire, mining concessions, and right to start banks and land companies. All great powers sent consultants under all sorts of names to the army, navy, military police, and administrative institutions of the Ottoman Empire. The German Officer Corps trained and controlled the few combat-worthy brigades of Turkish troops. The semi-colony Ottoman Empire was also included in the South and became the subordinate areas of agricultural production, sources of raw materials, and outlets for investment. Because the Ottoman Empire was located in the joint of Europe, Asia, and Africa with convenient for shipping and advanced in transportation, European countries invested more capital into the empire and its dependent territories, which reached up to over 63 million pounds in 1914 in Turkey and 100 million in Egypt (not including investment into the Suez Canal). These investments were mainly spent on railways construction, irrigation projects, opening of small canals, and plantations, among which Aswan Dam in Egypt and the Hindiya Barrage in Iraq were the famous projects. The former dependent territories of the Ottoman Empire began to export agricultural raw materials on a large scale: a large amount of wine from Algeria and silk from Lebanon. Egypt became an important base of high-quality cotton with an increasing export volume: 213,000 kantars[38] in 1835 with an export value of 1.06 million pounds and 7.5 million kantars with an export value of 26.71 million pounds in 1912.

The boundary of the Ottoman Empire kept shrinking till its disintegration, which fell into two categories: first, the increasing demand for political and religious independence by people of several nationalities within the empire gave rise to the separation or transference of large territories from the Ottoman Empire or to other countries (like Russia and Austro-Hungarian Empire), for instance, Greece became independent after the Greek War of Independence in 1821, Slavic nations broke away from the Ottoman Empire in the first Balkan War (1912), and Bessarabia was annexed by Russia; second, dozens of dependent territories of the Ottoman Empire became colonies or dependent countries of Britain, France and Italy during the expansion into North Africa and West Asia (Middle East) by European colonial great powers, which gave rise to the complete disintegration of the Ottoman Empire during and in the few years after the World War I. The major parts of former Ottoman Empire fell into the scope of the South.

---

38   "Kantar" is the official Egyptian weight unit for measuring cotton roughly equal to 99 pounds.

Table 4.7. The disintegration of the Ottoman Empire and the partition of its former dependent territories

Name of the territory	Area (square kilometers)	Relationship with the Ottoman Empire	Year of independence, partition, annexation or occupation	Country affiliated	remarks
Aden		Dependent territory	1839	Colony of Britain	
Albania	28	province	1812	Independent principality	
Algeria	238	Autonomous province	1830-1847	Colony of France	
Bahrain	622	Independent Emirate of the Khalifa Family	Under the protection of Britain in 1820, became a protectorate of Britain in 1892	Protectorate of Britain	
Bessarabia		province	1812	Russia	United with Romania in 1918
Bosna and Hercegovina	51	Dependent territory	1878, 1908	Governed by Austria, annexed by Austria	United with Yugoslavia in 1918
Bulgaria	111	Autonomous province	1908	Independent kingdom	Merged with Eastern Rumelia
Crete	8260	province	1898	autonomous	United with Greece in 1908
Eastern Rumelia		Autonomous territory	1908	independence	Merged with independent Bulgaria in 1885
Egypt	100	Province (ruled by local kingdom)	1882	Occupied by Britain	
Greece	13	dependent territory	1821	independence	Crete Island in 1908 and Macedonia in 1913 being included
Hasa		province	1913	Occupied by Saudi Arabians	United with the Kingdom of Saudi Arabia in 1932
Hejaz		dependent territory	1916-1924	Ruled solely by Sharif	United with the Kingdom of Saudi Arabia in 1932
Iraq	438	province	1921	Ruled by Britain	Trust territory of Britain after being occupied
Kars and Ardahan		province	1878	Occupied by Russia	Retrieved by Turkey in 1920
Kuwait	16	Autonomous emirate under jurisdiction of the Ottoman Empire	1899	"protected" by Britain	Controversial (Germany, France, and Russia were against the "protection" of Britain and supported the sovereignty of the Turks)

Lebanon	10	Special district	1918	Occupied by France	Later became trust territory
Libya	1,750,000	Ruled directly by the Ottoman Empire	1911	Colonized by Italy	Ruled by local governors before 1835
Macedonia		province	1903	Specific jurisprudence under the control of European powers	Parts of it united with Greece and with Bulgaria in 1913
Mingrelia		principality	In the early 19th century	Russia	
Montenegro		Autonomous district	1878	independent	United with Yugoslavia in 1918
Nejd		Controlled by Egypt, a dependent territory of the Ottoman Empire	1891	Protected by Britain	United with the Kingdom of Saudi Arabia in 1932
Palestine	27	Dependent territory	1917	Occupied territory	Later became trust territory
Qatar	11	emirate	1916	Protected by Britain	
Romania	23	province	1878	independent	Moldavia and Wallachia united
Serbia		Autonomous district	1878	independent	
Cyprus	9251	Dependent territory	1878	Crown colony of Britain	
Sudan	2,500,000	Ruled by Egypt	1821	Governed by Mahdi from 1881 to 1898, co-supervised by Britain and Egypt	
Syria	185	province	1820	Occupied by France	
Trans-Jordan		Part of Damascus Province of the Ottoman Empire	1920	Occupied by France	
Tunisia	164	Autonomous province	1881	Colonized by France	
Turkey	780	Central part of the Ottoman Empire	1922	Changed into a republic	
Yemen	190	Ruled by local governors under jurisprudence of the Ottoman Empire	1918	independent	

After Qajar Dynasty was established in Persia in 1794, Persia (Iran) had been the target of contention between Russia and Britain. Britain had vital economic interest in the south near the Persian Gulf while Russia infiltrated into the north and controlled the royal family, the garrison force of which was composed of a Cossack brigade commanded by Russian officers. The situation in the Middle East changed rapidly in in the late 19th century: German naval force was strengthened, Baghdad Railway was built near the Persian Gulf, and British Government on a wide range of considerations decided to ameliorate conflicts with Russia in the Middle East and sought to reach compromise with Russia on clash of interest in Persia so as to approximate an alliance with France in opposition to Germany. In 1903, British official Lord Ellenborough alleged in the House of Lords: I would rather see Russians in Constantinople than German naval arsenals on the shore of the Persian Gulf, which revealed the possible shifts in British policies. After long-term negotiations between Britain and Russia, the Anglo-Russian Agreement was reached on 31 August 1907, according to which Britain offered a much large sphere of influence than what the media had formerly surmised to Russia. Persia was divided into three parts: first, Russian sphere of influence which took Qasr-e-Shirin, Isfahan, and Zabol as the southern boundary with an area of 790,000 square kilometers and a dense population in the north; second, British sphere of influence which stretched from the border between Persia and Afghanistan to Kerman, Bandar Abbas, and Jask near the Persian Gulf with an area of 355,000 square kilometers and a small population; third, the neutral zone between Russian and British spheres of influence (with an area of around 500,000 square kilometers), into which both countries were forbidden to expand. The British territory formed a blockade which cut off the access taken by Russia to Afghanistan and Baluchi in India. The agreement mitigated temporarily the contention for Persia in West Afghanistan (districts like Heart) between Russia and Britain. In addition, Russia consented that Afghanistan was not within its sphere of interest while Britain promised not to undertake any annexations in Afghanistan. Thus, Britain and Russia were deadlocked in their intensified contention for Afghanistan, which maintained independence of sovereignty in the form of semi-colony. The Anglo-Russian Agreement was also related to Tibet of China. After contention and scramble for many years in addition to the resistance from China, neither Britain nor Russia could take Tibet alone. They had to admit hat Tibet was a territory of China and promised to respect territorial integrity of Tibet, not to interfere into the internal affairs of Tibet, and only to make connections with Tibet with the approval of the Chinese Government. Covering Persia, Afghanistan, and Tibet of China with a total area of nearly 3.5 million square kilometers, the Anglo-Russian Agreement was the first important bilateral agreement concerning the division of spheres of influence in semi-colonies in the history of colonialism so that it was of geopolitical significance. Henceforth, Turkey (the central region of the Ottoman Empire, namely Anotolia), Persia, and Afghanistan constituted a corridor of semi-colony countries from 26 degrees to 74 degrees east longitude, adjacent to Xinjiang and Tibet of China, the largest semi-colony country in East Asia, which formed a geopolitical "semi-colony peninsula" surrounded by many colonized countries in Middle and Central Asia. For the British Empire, the "peninsula" intercepted the access from Russia in its expansion to the Indian Ocean, maintained a temporary balance of power in the Middle East on the eve of the World War I, and enhanced and consolidated the formation of the Entente Countries. For Russia, the compromise with Britain was significant both to the consolidation of its colonies in Central Asia (turned them into domestic colonies) and the coordination of its alliance with France. For semi-colony China, the linkup in the west with the "semi-colony peninsula" in adjacency to Afghanistan by sharing a borderline of 92 kilometers, which formed an indirect protective screen for Xinjiang and Tibet of China.

With the development of geological exploration, the region was proved to be the richest in petroleum and natural gas in human territories with an increasingly higher availability of natural resources as time passed. However, no colonial great power had exercised an absolute monopoly control over the "semi-colony peninsula", which was bound to be a region of continuous contention among great powers and turmoil of nearly a hundred years.

4.2. Capital Export, Cultural Infiltration and the Awakening of the Bourgeoisie in the South

4.2.1. Capital Export

In the period of monopoly capitalism, capital export became the dominant feature of world economy and the overriding form of colonial exploitation. In the half century period between 1855-1913, British overseas investment increased 6.5 times and France 11 times, the rate of increase was higher for the late-comer Germany.

Table 4.8. Overseas investments by

major imperialist powers (1914) (unit: a million of dollars)

Country	Total investment	Investment in Asia, Africa, and Latin America	Proportion in the total investment
Britain	19,935	7,812	39
France	9,280	3,628	39
Germany	5,650	2,167	38
Holland	4,100	——	40*
America	3,510	1,855	52
Belgium	900	——	28*
Russia	500	——	

*Note: * as the percentage in 1939.*

The investment into Asia, Africa, and Latin America by Britain, France, the US, and Germany reached up to 15.4 billion US dollars, which mainly included export of bank capital and industrial capital. Bank capital export mainly refers to the purchase of government bonds issued by the governments of the colonies (such as the British Indian Government) by the speculative capitalists of the suzerain countries and those loans with servile terms to the governments or banks in the colonies and semi-colonies which were under the imperialist yoke of major great powers, for instance, British Indian Government guaranteed an interest of 5% out of investment into Indian railways. The economic recession in western countries in the 1870s and 1880s resulted in the decrease in interest rate, which prompted finance capitalists to advocate for capital export into Asia, Africa, and Latin America. Production capital export referred mainly to the investment of private capital or government capital from great powers into indirect fields of production in the form of enterprises, like railways, harbors, shipping, banks, insurance, public utility, trading companies, plantations, mines, and factories.

Capital export in the period of monopoly capitalism was a central colonial policy, which exerted a wide and profound influence on the historical development process of capitalism in the world. The colonial plunder of capital in the whole world enhanced the further expansion of capitalist large enterprises (multinational companies later were one of the forms) and provided favorable conditions for the continuous development of social productivity. Before World War I, so to speak, imperialist colonial expansion was one of the important factors in the advancement of world capitalist productivity aside from the development of science and technology. The worldwide colonial plunder in the latter half of the 19th century and the early 20th century mitigated temporarily the economic contradictions within the suzerains. Just as what a French Historian said overseas expansion could become an extraordinary means to achieve domestic stability and peace. Indeed, overseas expansion could put off the outbreak of social revolutions in some countries.

Imperialist colonial policies, especially capital export, contributed to the dual trend in the economy of semi-colony semi-colony countries: on the one hand, because the basic objective of imperialist colonial policies was to maintain the subordinate position of semi-colonies as backward agricultural countries and sources of raw materials so as to prevent their national industries from developing into competitors, these policies were biased and repressive of social development in the South, which resulted in the slow economic development or even stagnation in the South due to the serious distortion of the original social and economic forms by foreign commodities and capital before it was able to break away from colonist rules. On the other hand was the trend of the irrepressible independent development of national capitalist economy, which was the inexorable outcome of the export of capital into countries in the South. Lenin pointed out, "The export of capital influences and greatly accelerates the development of capitalism in those countries to which it is exported"[39]. This trend was independent of the will of any group. The export of capital from imperialist countries into the South would necessarily speed up the development of national capitalism in the South. The adversarial dual trend was the objective reflection of the dual functions of imperialism on national capitalism in

39   Lenin, Vladimir. *Selected Works*. Vol. 2. Beijing: People's Publishing House, 1972: 785.

semi-colonies, which was also the concrete embodiment of the "dual mission" of colonialism. The development of national capitalism in semi-colonies was undoubtedly a progress not only to countries and regions in the South but also for the whole world.

During the period of free capitalism when the further destruction of natural economies of the South provided commodity markets and labor markets for capitalism, national capitalism had been bourgeoning or developing. By means of capital export from western colonial countries, capitalist mode of production was transplanted to the South at a faster speed. It was of great historical significance for the rise of capitalist mode of production and advanced productivity in the multi-componential economy in semi-colony countries in the South. It was a sign of the emergence of new productivity in the South, which contributed to new factors in the economic structure of countries in the South. This new capitalist economic factor exerted an increasing influence on the economy in the South. At the turn of the 20th century, with the rise of national capitalist modern industries, national bourgeoisie came into being in the South. Before that, the direct management of enterprises by western countries gave rise to the working class in the South. The class of intellectuals in the South arose before national bourgeoisie. Thus, important and profound changes occurred to structure of social classes and balance of class power in the South.

Different from the bottom-up development of capitalism in western countries, capitalism in the South usually was transplanted from top to bottom (although there were differences in the rise of capitalism and the maturity of economic bases favorable for the development of capitalism in countries in the South). The up-bottom transplantation of capitalism would exert a profound impact on the class structure, character, power, and position in social conflicts of the bourgeoisie in the South. It is undeniable that there were some capitalists in the bourgeoisie who were closely related to foreign capital in the business profit and became comprador bourgeoisie and prone to betray national interests. Most capitalists (commonly known as national capitalists) of the bourgeoisie in the South were repressed, marginalized, and damaged by foreign monopoly capital no matter in accumulation of capital, domestic market, development of their productivity, investment, and finance. Meanwhile, domestic semi-feudal forces (or semi-feudal governments) upheld by and colluded with colonial forces imposed oppressions and restrictions on national capital. All of these resulted in the tortuous and slow development of national bourgeoisie in the South under extremely difficult conditions. There existed deep contradictions between colonialism-imperialism and national bourgeoisie in the South, who was pressed for the liberation from oppression of colonialism-imperialism and bondage of feudalism for the sake of their own economic development and political interests.

4.2.2. Cultural Infiltration

The transplantation of ideological and cultural factors of capitalism was basically synchronous with or even ahead of the transplantation of the economic factor of capitalism. Therefore, changes in the superstructure (like culture and ideology) were earlier and faster than those in economic basis so that there were some precocious capitalist ideologies in the South. In the constitution of bourgeoisie in the South, bourgeoisie intellectuals tended to be the pioneers of their class. In India, the Great Britain advocated English education in the 19th century and Indian students went to study abroad, which gave rise to a large number of Indian bourgeoisie intellectuals in the 1820s. With the increase in capital export into India from Britain, Indian bourgeoisie came into being in the 1860s, which was different from the situation in the West where capitalist mode of production preceded capitalist ideology. This was due to the exchange of culture and fusion of civilization. Feudal economy in the South under the impact of western commodities was on the verge of disintegration (almost synchronous with the impact on traditional ideology in the East by that of Western bourgeoisie), which could have provided favorable conditions for the formation and development of national capital. Western countries made colonial policies to strenuously repress capital export, which inadvertently gave rise to the development of national capital in the South. However, in terms of cultural export, western countries made every effort to advocate and encourage wholesale westernization of ideology. Because colonialist-imperialist countries needed to cultivate or produce new intellectuals to serve them well, who were distinct from traditional intellectuals and had to be cultivated in a great number in their pursuit of study in primary schools, middle schools, and universities in suzerains.

During the period of primitive accumulation and laissez faire capitalism, the infiltration of western culture mainly propelled by the Christian Church was tinged with a strong religious color, which, however, had a limited impact on the South because of different levels of resistance from Islam, Buddhism, Hinduism, and Confucianism. By the period of early imperialism, the governments and enterprises of western countries[40] directly pushed and subsidized the implantation of western culture in the South to cultivate intelligentsia to serve the West. Thus, a prevalent phenomenon occurred in the South: western capitalist culture exerted strong impacts on Eastern cultures, blended into the surface layer of national cultures in the South, and had profound influences on education, ideology, and politics in the South. Capitalist spiritual civilization began to be promulgated in the South widely. It should be mentioned that western bourgeoisie spiritual civilization was a part of western modern industrial civilization, the dissemination of which was an important factor

---

40 "Western countries" here actually refer to "Northern countries", "the North" in the North-South relationship. Likewise, "the South" actually includes "the East" used by the scholars in the past. Note by the author.

in the enhancement of modernization in the South. However, there was, in fact, a cultural imperialism. Because western modern industrial civilization was an expansive dominant culture, it had a feature of expanding vehemently from the center to the periphery. Meanwhile, wholesale westernization entertained an obviously malicious scheme of spiritual enslavement and check on peripheral development, which was embodied in the early forced conversion to Christianity to the coercive instillation of western ideology through global mass media. Therefore, the fusion between strong civilizations and weak civilizations and between strong civilizations and strong civilizations (like Western civilization and Chinese civilization, Islamic civilization, and Indian civilization) was extremely complicated. Although the encounter of different civilization was particularly tortuous in that it experienced victories or defeats in violent clashes, conflicts, and colonial invasions, civilizations in the South as the counterpart of dominant civilizations had always preserved its independence in culture, which was illustrated by extant major world civilizations like Chinese civilization and Indian civilization.

4.2.3. The Awakening of the Bourgeoisie in the South

The first high tide of revolution in the South occurred at the critical moment of national peril when imperialist great powers divided the South. The lower working masses, who were not yet influenced by capitalist spiritual civilization in the South and were still sustained by historical inertia in a subjective world bestowed by the traditional society, devoted to the campaigning of saving their nations from peril after the feudal ruling classes fled successively from the battlefield of anti-colonialism. Carrying forward patriotism of people in the South and revolution tradition not subordinate to foreign oppression, they rose in resistance to powerful imperialist armies equipped with modern military arms, which included the Boxer Uprising in China (1900), Jiawu Farmers War in the Korean Peninsula (1894-1895), the Sudanese revolt under the leadership of Mahdi (1906), Bambata Uprising in South Africa (1911), Mexican revolution led by Pancho Villa and Emiliano Zapata (1911). The tragic ending of these rebellions of lower people illustrated that it was impossible for spontaneous peasant uprisings and resistance to succeed in that they could not meet the needs of the age. In the East, the center of historical stage was no longer occupied by peasant movements. The intelligentsia of the emergent bourgeoisie in the South was first called upon to take central stage.

The early activities of the bourgeoisie intelligentsia in the South were focused on ideology and culture: running newspapers, developing education, launching publicity, and establishing their own political organizations or parties. In the early political activities from the 1870s to 1890s, the majority of the bourgeoisie in Asia demanded for a series of reforms, the dominant of which was political constitution. Reforms in China and Turkey even practiced constitutional regime for a while, namely, Hundred Days' Reform and Constitutional Reform under the leadership of Ahmed Şefik Midhat Pasha.

The early bourgeoisie politicians in the South (like Kang Youwei of China, Midhat Pasha of Turkey, Jose Rizai of Philippines, and Ahmad Arabi of Egypt) were true patriots. Faced with the invasion and partition of imperialist great powers and greatly concerned with the fate of their countries and nations, they advocated for reforms, the chief objective of which was to liberate and strengthen their countries. Although the early bourgeoisie activists had no or little touch with the lower masses, they fought bravely patriotic wars. However, compared to the struggle undertaken by the lower masses, the early political activities of bourgeoisie in the South assumed some new features. Their political vision overcame the limitation of pre-capitalist natural economy and understood the serious situation of the outside world from the general trend of global imperialist partition. Their ideal of saving their nation was no longer to pray to saviors like Mahdi for the millennium or to uphold an intact feudal kingdom. Their objective of saving the nation from peril was to transform it into a power country like western capitalist ones or Japan after Meiji Restoration. Therefore, their patriotism could be included in the category of modern bourgeoisie nationalism. Their activities proper marked the beginning of the formation of modern nations in the South. The other important new feature of the early political activities of the bourgeoisie in the South was the demand for the reform of absolute monarchy. They were devoted to the movement of political constitution, demanding to implement gradually the representative system like that in western bourgeoisie countries, which hit upon the core issue of social reform in these countries, namely, bourgeoisie democracy. Although their demand for democracy was still puerile and feeble, they reached a modern ideological and political height matchless to any traditional peasant struggles in the South.

With the development of capitalist economic, political, and cultural factors and the further enhancement in the strength of the bourgeoisie in the South in the early 20th century, the early puerile and feeble and somewhat reformist bourgeoisie political activities were gradually replaced by bourgeoisie revolutions or revolutionary movements. Bourgeoisie revolutionaries took central political stage, in whose hands was converged the driving forces of history. Bourgeoisie revolutionaries proposed clear principles and revolutionary ideals of nationalism and democracy and set up revolutionary organizations to mobilize, call upon, and organize the masses, who, including even the emergent proletariat, followed the bourgeoisie. Bourgeoisie revolution broke out in Iran (Persia) from 1905 to 1911 as well as in Turkey from 1908 to 1909. Xinhai Revolution broke out in China from 1911 to 1912, bourgeoisie democratic revolution in Mexico from 1910 to 1917, and national revolutionary movements in India from 1905 to 1908 as well as in Indonesia from 1908 to 1913. Lenin described the hide tide of a series of bourgeoisie revolutions and revolutionary movements in Asia in the early 20th century as "the awakening of Asia", and believed that it marked a new era in the world history[41]. Bourgeoisie revolution

41   Lenin, Vladimir. *Selected Works*. Vol. 2. Beijing: People's Publishing House, 1972: 447-448.

also broke out in Mexico of Latin America from 1910 to 1917. The high tide of revolution marked by "the awakening of Asia" could be dubbed as the first revolutionary high tide in the South.

The South, henceforth, entered a new historical stage. If the Meiji Restoration of Japan was the only exception in Asia which added a new page to world bourgeoisie nationalist revolutions, the series of bourgeoisie revolutions and revolutionary movements in the South marked by "the awakening of Asia" became an important part of world bourgeoisie revolutions because of the awakening of "the down trodden and benighted…from medieval stagnation"[42], the greatest number of people involved, the most tremendous struggles, and high tides arising repeatedly. The South in the modern era became the vastest battlefield of anti-colonialist and anti-feudalist struggles and rose significantly in world history.

Although the series of bourgeoisie revolutions which occurred in the South in the early 20th century, however, made certain achievements in setting up constitutional government systems (like in Turkey and Iran) and establishing republics (like in China) and launched attacks on the invasive imperialist forces in the South, they did not win a complete victory but suffered defeats in most cases. In terms of internal factors, the collusion of three reactionary forces, which included imperialist forces in the South, xenocentrist local feudal forces and comprador bourgeoisie, hindered the revolutionary forces in the South. Due to their inborn weakness, national bourgeoisie acting as revolutionary leading forces were not powerful enough to cope with this strong reactionary force. The weakness of bourgeoisie in the South had deep economic roots. Because capitalism in the South was transplanted from up to bottom, many national capitalists were transformed from landlords making investment into enterprises. Meanwhile, not a little national capital competing with foreign monopoly capital under unfavorable conditions was reinvested into purchasing lands to engage in semi-feudal land rent exploitation so that national bourgeoisie could not purify their own class but have an affinity with semi-feudal rent system. Such capitalized landlords or businessmen-landlords had a personal stake in the preservation and extension of remnants of feudalism in land system, which was the deep economic root for the ambiguous and wavering position of national bourgeoisie in the South in their struggle against feudal land system. Moreover, national bourgeoisie in the South maintained a closely reliant and dependent economic relation with foreign monopoly capital since the beginning of the transplantation of capitalist mode of production. While the worship for the West inculcated in the instillation of wholesale westernization and education of enslavement made it impossible for national bourgeoisie in the South, particularly some of its strata, to distinguish the assimilation of western modern industrial civilization from anti-imperialism, which greatly frustrated their struggle against imperialism. Therefore, all bourgeoisie revolutionaries in the South in the early 20th century revolution had not been able to mobilize millions

163

---

42   Ibid.: 447.

of peasants to fight against feudalism so that no great changes occurred in the countryside in the South. This was a fatal weakness. The unrealistic fancies entertained by national bourgeoisie in the process of revolution were all shattered by ruthless reality while the revolutions under their leadership (like those in China and Mexico) were all shadowed by the armed intervention of imperialist great powers. In the end, most revolutions and revolutionary movements were strangled by the armed intervention of imperialist great powers (like those in Iran, Philippines, Korea, and Egypt).

The failure of bourgeois revolutions in the South were also due to profound international reasons. History to a greater extent became history of the world, which meant western colonial forces could be united by means of steamers and telecommunications in their intervention in revolutions in the South. In the early 20th century, world capitalism had become a world system of colonial oppression and financial containment on most residents in the South by a few advanced countries. Hereto, imperialist colonial system had been fully formed. The primary interest (first and foremost that of Britain) of imperialist great powers in the South was to maintain strenuously the balance of power after the partition of the world and sustain vested interests provided by unequal treaties. For example, great powers took pains to restrain Xinhai Revolution which aimed to change the semi-colony and semi-feudal status of China meant only a reconstruction of the extant order, so that they unanimously upheld and monitored Yuan Shikai to seize the fruits of the revolution. They also spared no efforts to moderate the revolutions in Turkey so that they become a state coup from above which could not mobilize the masses and then manipulated the leading party to degenerate into a tool of imperialism. After the agreement reached between Britain and Russia in 1907 on the division of spheres of influence in Iran and the adjustment of their policies, these two countries sent troops to intervene in and strangle the revolution in Iran and restored the autocracy of Qajar Dynasty.

Although the series of bourgeois revolution and revolutionary movements in the South all failed due to great disparities in strength at the first stage, every struggle of people in the South added fractures and cracks to the castle of colonial order constructed by imperialist countries in the South. The inherent political, economic and cultural contradictions in the fledgling imperialist colonial system began to loom large. The crisis in the colonial system was the necessary outcome of the growing contradictions. The era of colonies and semi-colonies in the South as the solid rear of world capitalism for centuries had begun to recede.

4.3. Global Colonialism, Two World Wars and the End of Colonialism

European countries waged many wars in their overseas colonial contentions in modern history, like the War of the Spanish Succession (1701-1714), the Seven Years' War (1756-1763), the two Sino-British Opium Wars (1840-1842, 1856-1860), which was described by Marx in Capital as "the commercial war of the European nations, with the globe for a theatre"[43]. At the turn of the 20th century, European countries contended vehemently in their partition of Africa. In fact, there were at least two incidents (the Fashoda Incident and the second Morocco crisis) in the contention when Britain, France, and Germany were on the verge of war with one another were it not for the vast African continent with an area of over 30 million square kilometers, where there were still territories not yet ceded by any party in the contention. In 1898, expeditionary forces of Britain and France were at a stalemate and nearly fell into direct military confrontations in Fashoda Village in the south of Sudan in their scramble for the upper reaches of the Nile River Basin. The French military threatened that their soldiers had done up the last button of their leggings. However, France retreated at the last moment because Germany as its strong neighbor had occupied Alsace-Lorraine and was ready to weaken France to strengthen its hegemony in Europe while France was indeed unable to wage a war of attrition without sufficient supplies with Britain in the distant tropical Africa. During the second Morocco crisis in 1911, a rising broke out in the ancient city of Fès in the north of Morocco. France took the occasion to occupy Fès while Germany gunboat Leopard sailed into Agadir to extort "whether France was willing to…exchange its colony with our retreat from these ports as proper compensations"[44], and the light cruiser Berlin also sailed into the territorial waters of Morocco. Britain claimed it would not allow Germany to keep a foothold in the area near the Strait of Gibraltar (the west bank of Morocco). British cabinet authorized David Lloyd George to make a speech, declaring that Britain would make great sacrifice to maintain peace. British navy was ready for combat. After a long period of negotiation, an agreement was reached between France and Germany in November 1911: Germany unconditionally recognized that Morocco was under the protection of France while France would transfer a "swamp" with an area of nearly 270,000 square kilometers in French Congo in West Africa to Germany, which was incorporated into German Cameroon. Russia once cautioned France as an ally that its military reform was still under way. Although it doubted whether it was to its advantage to take military actions, it would fight side by side with France if the war between France and Germany broke out. "Agadir Crisis" was thus over. The scramble for Africa did not become the blasting fuse. The outbreak of the World War I was postponed from three years.

165

The colonial history of nearly five hundred years has already proved that concomitant with colonialism were numerous wars of all levels, which embodied two rules of colonial history: First, there occurred relatively more colonial wars in the periods, for example, in the 17th and 18th century, when several colonial great powers contended for colonial hegemony and carried out policies of monopoly trade; there occurred relatively fewer colonial wars mostly against the oppressed nations in the periods when one colonial great power established colonial hegemony and implemented so called laissez-faire policy,

Marx, Karl. *Capital*. Vol.1. Beijing: China Social Sciences Press, 1983: 812-813.
44 V.M. Rostov. *History of Diplomacy*. Vol. 2. Shanghai: Shanghai Joint Publishing Press, 1979: 963.

for example, in the period from 1814 to 1816 when Britain established world colonial hegemony. Second, what followed from the local colonial wars in the colonial history no matter which country won was that one or two colonial countries became even more powerful (for instance, Britain had once seized the colonies of Holland or Portugal), which was only the change in the balance of power among colonial forces, while no change occurred in the favor of anti-colonial forces in the balance of power between the colonial forces and the anti-colonial forces. By the time when the conflicts among imperialist great powers gave rise to world wars, the outcome of which not only weakened the overall colonial forces but also the most powerful colonial countries and changes began to occur in the favor of anti-colonial forces in the balance of power between colonialism and anti-colonialism.

Why did such changes happen? It was because the development of colonialism in the world promoted market exchange and mass production. Market exchange gave rise to internationalized economic relations and capital while the large scale of mass production enabled monopoly to take the place of free competition. Colonialist great powers divided all the colonies and spheres of influence in the world at the turn of the century, which resulted in 24 million square kilometers of colonies and semi-colonies in 1914. Finally, colonialism-imperialism had to resort to war to settle their contention for hegemony, which thoroughly exposed the subordinate, dependent, and extremely unequal North-South relationship shaped by them. Imperialist great powers not only employed their domestic forces for the warring purposes but also utilized the human and material resources in colonies and semi-colony countries, from which all imperialist great powers have benefited. Certainly, the greatest imperial powers (Britain and France) obtained the maximum benefit and won final victories with the help of these resources grabbed from the South.

Things, however, grew independent of human's will. Since colonialist countries had to fully mobilize and utilize human and material resources in colonies and semi-colonies and for this purpose had to ease some historically restrictive policies, the exploitation and utilization of resources had its own laws: in this period there appeared an accelerated development of wartime national capitalism in colonies and semi-colony countries which not only enhanced the economic strength of them but also empowered their national bourgeoisie and the working class, which spurred changes in the social and economic structure in the South which would be more favorable to the further development of their capitalist economy. Colonial imperialism paved the way for its own destruction, which was the dialectical principle of historical development.

The World War I was basically the continuation of colonialist policies which had been carried out by western great powers for many years. The war was the outcome of colonialist policies, so to speak. For dozens of years, European great powers implemented predatory colonial policies, accumulating tens of millions of square kilometers of colonies in the hands of several European countries. When the world had yet not been completely divided, colonial conflicts could still be assuaged with the "compensation" of another territory. However, when the last territory had been divided, the expansion of colonial territories by means of (re-)division had to resort to the plundering of colonies occupied by other countries. With the increase in the pressure of colonialist expansion in the form of re-division, it was more likely for the outbreak of great wars among colonialist great powers. In the end, the settlement of the issue of colonial territories had to resort to force. The war between colonial predators was thus inevitable. Britain, Germany, France, Russia, and Italy all possessed hundreds of millions of capital in addition to colonies in Africa, Asia, the Pacific, and Americas so that the war among them became world-wide.

The World War I (1914-1918) was unprecedented in human history, which was a catastrophe for human beings brought about by colonialism. The war lasted for four years and three months, which involved 33 countries and 1.5 billion people, mobilized over 67 million people on both sides, over 29 million among which directly entered the war, caused a casualty of 8.4 million people, injured 21 million people, ravaged 1.3 billion people, cost 208.4 billion dollars, and caused an economic loss of 270 billion dollars. The unprecedented expenditure of the World War I generally weakened European colonial great powers, which was a turning point of the fall of European colonialism-imperialism under severe impact.

Britain, first and foremost, as the greatest colonial power was impaired. The war was at a great expense of the British Empire. British economic power was whittled, lost its position of the strongest country in the international financial system, the solid position of pound was undermined, and the traditional gold standard policy virtually came to an end. 70 percent of British merchant ships were destroyed in the war, and the navy was greatly impaired in the naval battles and for this reason lost the strength of the most powerful navy. The two trumps were formerly the most important guarantees for the British Empire to maintain its global colonial system. Although Britain as a victor not only preserved the integrity of its empire but also expanded some of its colonies by seizing German colonies, it was only an apparent phenomenon. The revolutionary tides all over the post-war colonies exerted great impacts on the colonialist banks of the British Empire, which forced Britain to reinforce repressive measures while adopting new ruling strategies to adapt to the new situation after the war. Second, the situation of France as the second largest colonial empire was similar to that of Britain in that it expanded the total area of colonies by annexing German colonies and was faced with the rising revolutionary movements in the colonies at the same time. Germany surrendered all of its colonies (including Tanganyika, Togo, Cameroon, Southwest Africa, Rwanda, Burundi, and islands in the Pacific) and dropped out of the colonial countries. Third, the United States and Japan with a possession of relatively few colonies were strengthened in the war. Japan became the most aggressive and covetous colonial great power in East Asia.

4.3.2. Colonies Face Massive Loss of Resources during the WWI

Because of the subordinate, dependent, and extremely unequal North-South relationship, people in the South were forcibly involved in the war and suffered great losses of human and material resources. Colonialism first utilized colonies as the war rear and reserve forces on a world-wide scale from 1914 to 1918, making use of all of their resources. The role of colonies as the bases of human and material resources for suzerains became visible during wartime. Fighting in the central area, European colonial suzerains formed two types of relations with peripheral colonies and semi-colonies according to their distance from the battlefield and their different strategic positions:

The first type was colonies and semi-colonies which were relatively near to the main battlefields and the auxiliary battlefields, for instance, Lebanon, Syria, and Egypt of the Ottoman Empire became strategic vital areas which were contended by both parties in the war while Tanganyika in East Africa and Togo and Cameroon in West Africa became the auxiliary battlefields of military confrontations. All the areas were greatly affected by the war. Egypt provided 2.5 million civilian workers to build fortifications and lay the tracks of railways in West Asia, the Peninsula of Turkey, and France. 12,000 Egyptian soldiers were mobilized to assist British army to defend the Suez Canal in the Canal Zone. In Southwest Africa, 60,000 South African soldiers in British Dominion launched attack against German troops in East Africa, which lasted for nearly one year till the surrender of German troops. The formerly German Southwest Africa was incorporated into the sphere of the British Empire. In Cameroon, the British and French joined forces attacked German forces, which lasted for one year and a half till German troops were forced to surrender. Britain and France divided Cameroon equally between them. In the battlefield of Tanganyika territories, around 100,000 soldiers of the Allied Forces were engaged in intensified fighting. The British forces were defeated at the first stage. However, both sides of the war were still involved in arduous fighting in East Africa fourteen months after the storm of Dar es Salaam in September in 1916. The first faction of German troops entered Northern Rhodesia and surrendered to the Allies till the conclusion of the Armistice Agreement in November 1918. The war history in African battlefields revealed that the human and material resources of African colonies were important to suzerains at war. France not only deployed African soldiers in West African battlefields but also mobilized thousands of Senegalese black infantrymen to European battleground. Britain also mobilized African soldiers in European battleground. The persistence of Germany in East African battleground for four years depended on the development and management of its East African colonies for nearly 30 years. Germany paid much attention to infrastructure construction in colonies (a railway of 1250 kilometers was built across Tanganyika from east to west in 1914) and implemented maneuvering policies to win over the upper class of the native people, which enabled Germany to mobilize 12,000 native soldiers properly furnished and well trained. This army was not inferior in any respect in fighting with British troops and South African white soldiers and inflicted severe losses on the Allied forces. In addition, colonies in North Africa like Egypt as the nearest rear provided indispensable strategic and rear support, like the supply of munitions, food, cotton, oil, cocoa, corn and meat, to the Allied forces, which played a key part in the final victory of the Allies. The value of colonies as bases of human, material and strategic materials was greatly highlighted by suzerains. The food of Egypt was requisitioned to supply the frontline British troops while Egyptians were starved; the grains of British-Egyptian Sudan was requisitioned, the export of which increased 26 times from 2.08 million tons to 54.94 million tons; 12 million war-time Egyptian civilians were assigned to transport teams.

The second type was the "peripheral" colonies and semi-colonies distant from the battleground, like India and China. They played more complicated and various roles in the war. On the one hand, they provided soldiers, human resources, and all kinds of material resources. After declaring war with Germany, Beiyang Government of China successively sent hundreds of thousands of civilians to Europe to replenish factories and farms extremely short of labor forces in the front line and rear and served as civilian workers to trench for the Allies. The role of India as the rear and base was even more conspicuous. The upper class in India, especially princes of Native States favored by British Government, strenuously demonstrated their adamantine allegiance and vowed solemnly to provide unflinching support for British Government[45]. In wartime, India sent altogether 600,000 combatants and 474,000 non-combatants to European battleground with a casualty of 53,000 people. India supplied the Allies over 3 million tons of wheat, 2.5 million edible oil, 8 million pounds worth of rawhides, and 12 million pounds worth of dressed cowhides to make army boots for British soldiers. Indian cotton and linen factories produced 42 million pieces of uniforms and army quilts. Indian steel factory supplied 300,000 tons of steel for laying rails in the Near East battleground, outputting altogether 1,800 miles of steel rails and 6,000 sets of rolling stocks. In addition, India provided the Allies with 2 million tons of manganese ores. India contributed 0.145 billion pounds to British Treasury. British-Indian Government spent another 0.203 billion pounds of Indian in the name of other members of the British Commonwealth of Nations. British-Indian Government made maximum use of the human and material resources of wartime India because it adopted national monopoly capitalism. Lord Curzon was full of praise for India: the contribution made by India was inexpressible by words.

4.3.3. The Growth of Anti-Colonial Forces and the Second Revolutionary High Tide in the South

While contributing all types of resources, the second type of colonies and semi-colonies (including Egypt which was near to the battleground) took the occasion when colonial great powers were engaged in fighting in European

45   Marriott, J. A. R. *Modern England 1885-1945*. London, 1948.

battleground and relaxed the economic restraint on the South to develop their own national capitalist economy on an unprecedented scale. With the growth of the national capitalist force, the intelligentsia was augmented, social and economic structure underwent profound transformations, and the configuration of class power was modified.

The development of wartime industry in India was due to not only such factors as the decrease in the import of Indian industrial products because of the war in Europe and the relaxation of control by Britain but also the stimulation of the development of Indian industry by means of state monopoly capitalism adopted by Department of Military Supplies Administration. The registered stock companies increased 9% from 2552 to 2789 with an increase of 47% in capital sum from 0.721 billion rupees to 1.066 billion rupees. The output of cloth in India soared from 1.176 yards (1914-1915) to 1.616 yards (1917-1918). The share of cloth produced in national capital factories in the total consumption of cloth in India rose from 23.8% (1911-1912) to 35.4% (1916-1917) while that of import cloth decreased to 48.3%. National capital invested in cotton textile industry rose from 0.065 billion rupees to 0.125 rupees, dividend increased four times from 10.5% to 53% accordingly. Indian nationalist bourgeoisie made a great fortune and consolidated their status. For example, Tata Group built three more hydro power generation plants by use of accumulated enormous capital. The total number of workers in Indian factories reached 1,367,000 in 1919. Indian bourgeoisie growing substantially were rather intoxicated with the wartime prosperity, claiming that if they were given the policy of protective tariff India had all the qualifications for industrialization.

National industry in China also had the chance to develop during the war, which was most conspicuously embodied in cotton textile industry: the number of factories run by Chinese in 1915 was 22 with 544,000 spindles, 2,200 weaving machines, which were nearly all doubled to 64, 1.593 million, and 7,800 respectively in 1922. Silk reeling, silk weaving, and knitting had grown significantly. The number of flour mills increased from over 40 to over 120. National capital also developed in such light industries like match, cement, cigarettes, oil manufacture, paper making, sugar manufacture, soap making, and candle making. The import volume of China in 1915 was 0.454 billion taels, 0.11 billion taels less than that before the war, while the export volume remained the same, the annual import surplus decreased from 0.026 billion to 0.083 billion taels (while that before the war was 0.1 billion to 0.2 billion tales each year), which was the best period of import and export trade for dozens of years.

National capital in wartime Egypt also developed in light industry, establishing quickly a batch of cotton mills, flax mills, woolen mills, and silk weaving mills. The largest Egyptian national textile company had a possession of 20,000 spinning machines, 560 weaving machines, and 800 workers in 1917 with an annual output of cotton yarns worth 3.5 million pounds and 8 million to 9 million yards of cotton cloth, which implied an increase of 15% to 20% than that before the war. Foreign trade export volume increased 70% from 0.024

billion pounds in 1914 to 0.041 billion pounds in 1917. The number of workers increased 39% from 457,451 in 1907 to 639,929 in 1917.

The good time, however, did not last long. After the end of the war, colonialist economic forces came back, which almost immediately interrupted the progressive momentum of national industry in India, China, and Egypt. It fully proved that the invasive and oppressive western colonialism was the fundamental factor of impeding the development of national capital in the South. The contradiction between colonialism-imperialism and colonies and semi-colonies was deepened and intensified.

The World War I weakened European colonialist forces and brought about temporary growth of national capitalist economy in the South, which paved the way for the postwar revolutionary movements. Between the two world wars, the South became the center of global revolutionary movements, and national democratic movements spread over Asia, Africa, and Latin America. The great anti-imperialist May Fourth Movement broke out in China in 1919. In March and April 1919, anti-Japanese uprising happened on the Korean Peninsula. From 1918 to 1921, an anti-imperialist movement flamed up. In 1919, the Afghans waged an anti-imperialist war, which forced Britain to recognize the independence of Afghanistan. From 1919 to 1937, the anti-British struggle kept surging and developed into the Wafd Movement. Kemal's Revolution and the subsequent reform movement happened in Turkey from 1919 to 1922. The anti-American guerilla war under the leadership of Nicaraguan Sandinistas began in 1926. Mohandas Karamchand Gandhi led Nonviolent and Noncooperation Movements in India between the wars. From 1924 to 1936, the First and the Second Revolutionary Civil War broke out in China. The revolutionary movements in the South were spectacular and vigorous.

Capitalism had awakened the South as early as the turn of the century. The First Word War from 1914 to 1918 and the October Revolution of Russia completely roused up the South. Nationalist movements in the South entered quickly from the first stage to the mature stage, which was facilitated by several important stimulating factors: first, the barbarous fighting among colonialist great powers for the contention for colonies exposed the true nature of the so-called superior races and outstanding nationalities, which made it possible for nations in the South humiliated by white metropolitan states to be emancipated ideologically. Second, nationalism in the South was not different from anti-colonialism since its appearance. The colonialist-imperialist nature of the World War I reinforced the concept of anti-colonialism among the intelligentsia in the South, and ideological trend of nationalism gained great support. Nationalism as a part of anti-colonialist theories provided systematic theoretical instructions for national independence movement. Russian revolution supplied countries in the South (like China) with Marxism and Leninism so that many countries in the South founded communist parties. Third, the development of national capitalist economy reinforced the bourgeoisie and proletariat in the South. Great changes occurred in social structure and power configuration in the South. The anti-colonialist struggle in China and Vietnam was under the leadership of the working class parties while that in most countries was led by bourgeoisie. The general objective of national movements led by national bourgeoisie was self-government and independence, which were separated from social revolution in that their guiding principles did not cover the elimination of the (economic) subordinate relationship to suzerains. Only in China did the Communist Party include the thorough attack on imperialism and the elimination of feudal land relationship in the main guiding principles of anti-imperialism and anti-feudalism.

Although the second wave of revolution after the World War I spread extensively, lasted long, and launched severe attacks on colonialist forces, this revolutionary movement neither basically narrowed the sphere of colonial rule nor fundamentally undermined colonial rule. The 2.5 million square kilometers of formerly German colonies were allocated among Britain, France, Belgium and South Africa in the form of "mandatory administration" by the League of Nations after the war, which did not change the nature of the colonies despite the change in name. Britain and France exerted rule on Lebanon, Syria, and Palestine, formerly provinces of the Ottoman Empire. Therefore, colonial great powers as victorious nations not only preserved the integrity of their own empires but also expanded their colonies, which was mainly because the total balance of international power between the two wars was still not favorable for anti-colonialist forces. A striking example was the "transference" of all of the colonial interests of Shandong in China (one of the victorious nations) from the defeated Germany to Japan, another rising colonial great power, by colonialist great powers in Paris Peace Conference in 1919. The unscrupulous division of the spoils among colonist powers gave rise to the May Fourth Movement in China. Another reason for the postwar power configuration was that revolutionary storms did not occur in the North. There was still room for the development of productivity when capitalism entered the stage of monopoly capitalism. Although Russia became the center of revolution after the October Revolution, it was still not powerful, unable to give substantial support to revolutionary movements in colonies and semi-colonies in the South. Meanwhile, the emergent revolution in the South could still not launch fatal attacks on world colonialism. It was during the "time lag", world colonialism got through the first stage of Crisis after the World War I.

The great damages to semi-colonial countries caused by the world economic crisis from 1929 to 1933 proved that the unequal international division of labor imposed on countries in the South by colonialist countries through super-economic coercions would inflicted painful catastrophes on countries in the South during world-wide economic crises. Agricultural products produced under the system of single cropping suffered slump in price in world market, which inflicted catastrophic blows on colonial governments which relied on one or two cash crops to maintain national finance, and peasants and farmers who relied on the plantation of a sing cash crop to survive. The import volume in four British colonies in West Africa dropped dramatically from 56 million pounds in 1929 to 29 million in 1931, with a decrease of 48.2%, in Six British colonies in East Africa from 40 million pounds to 21 million pounds, with a decrease of 47.5%, and in twelve French colonies in West Africa and Equatorial Africa from 30 million pounds to 18 million pounds, with a decrease of 40%. Financial revenues of all colonial governments and the income of peasants dropped rapidly, economy was in great trouble, the rate of unemployment soared, social life was chaotic, and people were desperate in their lives. Just as a researcher on Africa said, economic crisis (also known as depression) "destroyed the economy and society of the entire Africa"[46]. Every place from Sierra Leone to Egypt assumed an extremely "horrible" appearance of the complete collapse of economy. Colonies and semi-colonies in Asia like China and India were under the similar situation. The price of major export agricultural products from China decreased two to three times while that from India decreased 50%. Foreign trade export volume of China dropped from 0.704 billion dollars in 1928 to 0.116 billion dollars in 1932, with a decrease of six times. Foreign trade volume of India also dropped rapidly. The decrease in favorable balance of trade had to be made up by the export of a large amount of gold (2.04 billion rupees). The year from 1931 to 1932 was considered as an unprecedented year of economic catastrophe in economic history.

The role of colonies as the targets of crisis export from suzerains became conspicuous in the situation of general catastrophe. Colonies fully manifested its "value of existence" in the system of capitalism in helping suzerains to get through economic crises. First, under the control of suzerains, the decrease in the prices of industrial products imported from suzerains into colonies was much less than the decrease in the prices of agricultural products exported from colonies so that the extremely unreasonable "price scissors" were largely widened, which imposed unprecedentedly heavy oppression on colonies. Second, suzerains restrained the production of colonies to force up the prices or forced colonies to make way for exports from suzerains, for instance, Britain imposed coercive limit on the export quota of sugar from British East Africa to force up the price of sugar so that the export volume of sugar from Uganda was decreased two thirds in 1938. These coercive practices caused the level of production in many colonies to regress to that before the 1920s. Britain overtly restrained the development of coal production in Tanganyika, a former Germany colony, under its mandatory administration. In 1930, Ernest Bevin, later British Foreign Secretary, exclaimed, when seeing that the export of coal from Britain was influenced by that from Tanganyika, that it was necessary to exert proper control on the development of coal mining in Tanganyika. For colonialists, if colonies could not sacrifice themselves for the sake of suzerains at critical moments, what the colonies were for! Third, during the economic crisis from 1929 to 1933, monopoly capitalist enterprises of suzerains, particularly of the

---

46 Qtd. in Davidson, Basil. *Africa in Modern History*. Harmondsworth, Middlesex: Penguin Books, 1978: 142.

Great Britain, completed the monopolistic control of trade and investment in their colonies. Economic crisis prompted Britain to follow France and Portugal to take two measures to raise the economic value of colonies for suzerains. One was Imperial Preferences implemented in 1932, which stipulated that the trade of the suzerain and that of the colonies were mainly conducted within the imperial system so as to increase the trade volume of the entire empire. Henceforth, Britain followed the example of its opponents to set up tariff and quota barriers around its territories. Within the empire, Britain forced colonies (like India) to reduce competition with the suzerain in export through extra-economic means. The implementation of these protective measures prompted the investment in colonies by Britain to rise rapidly. British investment in India rose rapidly from 0.583 billion pounds in 1930 to 1 billion in 1931. Second, Britain deeply troubled by economic depression and the issue of unemployment strived to recuperate its economy and solve the issue of unemployment by developing and utilizing resources of colonies. Britain realized the premise for this was to develop colonies and improve their social productivity so that colonies would be reinforced in purchasing power for British products to solve the issue of unemployment in Britain. In 1929, the Colonial Development Act was issued, which stipulated Britain would provide one million pounds of fund (raised by means of high-interest government bonds) for the development of industry and agriculture in colonies so as to promote British industry and commerce. Giving overt priority to British interests, this act was not quite effective in that the colonial societies did not respond to it enthusiastically. However, it became the guiding ideology for the subsequent British plans of developing colonies and postwar policies. Its significance in the history of colonialism was that the glaring flash of light it emitted before the set of the colonial sun near dark reignited the extravagant hopes of the British for the colonial empire. British government and people and media paid more attention to the role of colonial resources in revitalization of economy in the suzerain during the crises. In fact, the Colonial Development Act was based on the experience of the Gezira scheme in Sudan. In 1925, the Sennar Dam on the Blue Nile was established in 1925, which increased the cotton planting area in Sudan from 60,000 feddans (a unit of area equal to 1.308 acre) to 300,000 feddans within five years, and export volume of raw cotton from 8,300 tons to 30,400 tons, which turned the upper and middle Nile River Basin into another important source of raw materials for British cotton textile industry. The enforcement of the Colonial Development Act of 1929 and subsequent Development Acts on a larger scale further consolidated the British colonial system in the South, the structure of which was even more closely bounded with British economy. British colonies increasingly became economic and social extensions of the suzerain. In this sense, the economic crisis from 1929 to 1933 demarcated a new era in the history of colonialist economic plunder. On the one hand, it disclosed that during monopoly capitalist stage capitalism was more dependent on colonialism because the colonialist extra-economic power (including colonial administrative violence) was still the chief means in coercing colonies and semi-colonies into accepting unequal international division of labor. It was the reliance on the "help" of colonies and semi-colonies that capitalism in suzerains got through crises and was revitalized during the twenty years from the World War I to the economic crisis (1929-1933). On the other hand, however, when it turned the formerly prevalent undisguised plunder (like tax) and primitive extorting polices into investment in infrastructure (like power plants, dams, and railways) and modern extorting policies based on investment funds, the new part played by national monopoly capitalism in colonies revealed its importance for the first time. British policy makers considered their position in colonies unassailable. Some historians were beguiled by such phenomena and predicted that British government had started to consider carrying out systematic de-colonization in the South before the World War II[47]. The antedating of historical changes, which occurred due to dramatic changes in the international situation a dozen years after the war, to the prewar period was far from the historical truth. In fact, it was a new elevation of the North-South relationship by modern monopoly capitalism to maintain its own existence.

4.3.4. The World War II and Changes in the Balance of Power between Colonial and Anti-Colonial Forces

The World War II was an unprecedented bloody war in human history. As to the invaded nations, the war meant national liberation movements in the form of anti-fascist struggles (colonial countries like Japan and Italy overtly invaded semi-colony China and Ethiopia) since the beginning. Therefore, the World War II, with a strong anti-fascist character, was different in nature from the World War I which was purely imperialist. However, because both sides of the war (both the Allies and the Axis) included several traditional colonialist countries, they conspired to insist on colonialist interests when setting goals of war (which only referred to the Aix), making strategies of alliance, the outcome of the war and making postwar arrangements. Therefore, the turbid of colonialism surged from time to time despite the major trends of anti-fascism and national independence and liberation during the World War II. For instance, the U.S. President Theodore Roosevelt and British Prime Minister Winston Churchill signed the Atlantic Charter on 14 August 1941, in the third article of which the two countries solemnly declared "they respect the right of all peoples to choose the form of government under which they will live; and they wish to see sovereign rights and self government restored to those who have been forcibly deprived of them"[48]. This declaration had once stimulated people of colonies to participate in the anti-fascist war. However, there were different interpretations for "all peoples" mentioned in the charter: Roosevelt referred it to all nations in the world including those of colonies while Churchill insisted it only stand for European nations under the occupation of Germany, not including all nations

47   Flint, J. "Planned Decolonization and Its Failure in British Africa," in *Colonialism and Nationalism in Africa*. Vol. 3. Ed. G. Maddox and T. K. Welliver. New York, 1933. 13-26.
48   World Affairs Press, ed. *Collections of International Treaties*. Beijing: World Affairs Press, 1961: 337-338.

of colonies. The purpose for the interpretation of Britain was to maintain colonial rule and preserve the British Empire. 26 days later, that is, on September 9, Churchill even alleged in the House of Commons that this article (the third article) had nothing to do with British colonies. In December 1942, he declared openly that "I have not become the King's First Minister in order to preside over the liquidation of the British Empire"[49], obstinately insisting that postwar Britain should maintain its colonies. Second, when mapping out joint strategies while the Anti-Fascist League was under the most severe situation, Britain, out of selfish motives, insisted to counterattack the European continent from North Africa, the Mediterranean, and Italy. At the end of 1941, Britain was once opposed to the joint operations of the allied forces in China and Burma so as to preserve British colonial interests in Burma and India. Third, one of the goals of the war waged by Germany, Japan, and Italy, the Fascist Axis Powers, was to establish the Third Reich, the Atlantic Empire, and the Roman Empire respectively. Their ambition was to realize their long-dreamed and unscrupulous plan of establishing colonial empires. Fourth, the outcome of the war and postwar arrangement. Before the end of the World War II, British army, which had run away from Hongkong, planned to train the so-called guerilla forces in the peripheral areas of Hongkong, so as to take over Hongkong again after the defeat of Japan. During the period when Japanese troops occupied Hongkong, the guerilla force in Dongjiang River under the leadership of Chinese Communist Party had besieged Hongkong. On every occasion like international conferences and bilateral talks, Britain was strongly against the entitlement of China to the position of a great power. These contemptible and sordid motives and practices revealed that Britain attempted to maintain forever colonies of Hongkong and Kowloon in the territory of China.

The impact of the World War II on colonies and semi-colonies, wider and more profound than that of the World War I, played an incomparably great part in the historical fate of colonialism. The World War II as a general war was fought with the total sum of economic forces and human resources of warring countries and colonies and semi-colonies. The U.S., Britain, and the former Soviet Union as the allied nations were the three largest industrial countries in the world; Britain and France had a possession of over ten million square kilometers of colonies with a population of nearly one hundred million respectively; semi-colony China and colonized India with the largest populations, broadest areas and richest natural resources aligned themselves firmly with the Allies. Therefore, the human and material resources of the Allies were insurmountable by the Axis. The Axis of Germany, Japan, and Italy were limited in local resources and had a possession of colonies less than 5 million square kilometers at best (including the French colony in Petain and the Manchurian colony of Japan). As early as 1931 and 1935, Japan and Italy waged wars against, occupied and annexed the three provinces in the northeast of China and Ethiopia respectively, which provoked general protests in the world. In

---

49   *The Times* 11 November 1942.

1939, Germany suddenly attacked Czechoslovakia and waged an invasive war against Poland, which was against the general will of the people.

The mobilization and utilization of all kinds of resources in the colonies by the suzerains in the World War II well surpassed those in the World War I. Britain made full use of resources in colonies and dominions. Canada made a large number of warships, merchant ships, planes, tanks, trucks, and weapons for Britain. The arsenals of Australia also produced a large amount of weapons. Indian factories manufactured locomotives, carriages, small vessels and weapons for Britain. It took India 2.8 billion pounds of war funding.

The abundant material resources in Africa played a great part in the persistence of Britain in the war for 6 years. When the access to imported mineral ores from Europe to Britain was cut off by Germany troops, more than one half of the industrial raw materials needed by Britain from 1944 to 1955 was supplied by Africa: 78.4% of iron ores, 96.8% of manganese ores, 94% of chromium, 72.7% of copper, 54.5% of tin, and 90.8% of aluminum[50]. Agricultural raw materials from Africa became the main source of British food industry. 100% of palm kernels, 90.7% of coffee, 98% of cocoa, 48.4% of peanuts, 40% of cotton, and a large supply of sisal, rubber, timber, and wool, all depended on Africa. Without the supply of all kinds of material resources from African colonies, a considerable part of dozens of food and daily necessities rationed by coupons in wartime Britain would not have been able to be distributed while the production of some military supplies would have been suspended and run out of stock. When a major part of European continent was occupied by the Axis, the British Isles were destitute of food, and British residents looked eagerly forward to merchant ships which had sailed from African ports and protected by convoys. No wonder Viscount Cranborne said in a speech delivered in June 1945 that, only if the African colonial empire exists, will[51]. These words revealed the truth and the essence of the North-South relationship during the World War II.

The Axis relied on resources in Africa as well. After Germany occupied France and Belgium, a large stock of raw materials in French and Belgian African colonies fell into the hands of Germany. Raw materials shipped to Germany in 1941 alone reached 3.5 million tons, including important and rare cobalt. Agricultural products shipped to Germany included 200,000 tons of wheat, 100,000 tons of barley, 1.25 million tons of fruits and countless wines.

Colonies and dominions of European suzerains also provided the most precious sources of soldiers and abundant labor sources. Canada as a British dominion provided 750,000 soldiers in 1943 and trained 86,000 pilots. Australia recruited 800,000 men into the army, the soldiers from which increased to 1.18 million. The smaller army of New Zealand was expanded to 189,000 soldiers.

---

50   A.Y. Shpirt. *Africa in the World War II*. Trans. Xin He. Beijing: World Affairs Press, 1960: 16-17.
51   Holborn, Louise W. *War and Peace, Aims of the United Nations 1943-1945*. Vol. 12. Boston: World Peace Foundation, 1948: 577.

South Africa set up an army of 200,000 soldiers with their own equipment. Colonies recruited more soldiers, military men in India alone increased to 2.25 million. African armies not only recruited many soldiers but also committed many to the battlefields. In 1940, Germany and Italy controlled Mediterranean North Africa, attempting to intercept the Suez Canal, lifeline of the British Empire, which greatly threatened British African colonies and forced Britain to launch an all-out counterattack, mobilizing and equipping a large number of soldiers in colonies. In 1941, tank corps led by Rommel entered North Africa, posing threats again to the Suez Canal and its surrounding area, which forced the British army for the second time to deploy many troops to counterattack. In 1942, both sides deployed hundreds of thousands of soldiers in the Battle of El Alamein. Both sides recruited nearly a million African armed forces and unarmed personnel to take part in the battle, Britain alone recruited 400,000 Africans to serve for the battle. In North Africa, Britain and France altogether made use of nearly a million soldiers and civilian workers in a dozen African colonies including Egypt, Libya, Algeria, Morocco, Gabon, British West Africa, and British East Africa.

Africans were also recruited to serve the armies of the Axis countries. In 1940, 150,000 among 250,000 soldiers of Italian troops garrisoned in Northeast Africa were Africans. Vichy France garrisoned 373,000 soldiers in North Africa, 206,000 among which were Africans, which had become a formidable opponent of the Allies within two years. After British and U.S. troops landed on North Africa in November 1942, 800,000 African soldiers surrendered to the Allied forces successively, which gave rise to changes in the balance of power unfavorable to the Aix and laid the foundation for the victory of the Allied forces in North Africa. After 1941, Japanese army invaded and occupied Southeast Asia, South Asia, and British, French, and Dutch peninsula and island colonies in the Pacific, and took the place of Britain, France, and Holland to become the owner of these new colonies. Japan also made use of the abundant resources in these tropical colonies, particularly rubber, oil, and rare minerals. The main island of Japan decreed clearly the major economic policy of Japan was to obtain resources. Japan denuded 86,524,000 barrels of oil from Indonesia from 1942 to 1943, and 517,000 tons of coal and 3.55 million tons of rice from Indochina from 1940 t0 1944. 300,000 laborers were recruited from Java Island for overseas service and 75,000 laborers from Malaysia to construct Burma-Thailand Railway.

The core of the Free French Forces under De Gaulle was comprised of Africans from French colonies, which played an important part in inducing African soldiers from Vichy France to surrender to the Free France. In 1942, Fighting France (renamed from Free France in 1942) set up the 19th Corps, which was merged with surrendered soldiers from Vichy France a year later to form French Expeditionary Forces. This African force sailed across the Mediterranean in 1943 to take part in the Italian Campaign, and had once broke through the Gustav Line of Italian troops, playing an important part in the campaign. In August 1944, the newly formed First Corp mainly comprised of Africans took part in the campaign of counterattacking the north of France, therefrom turned northwest to Alsace, joined with the Allied forces of the Western Front, and attacked Germany, experiencing many hardships, fighting bravely, and achieving great triumphs. The 11th and 12th Division of East African soldiers suffered severe losses in fighting with Japanese troops in Burma. In 1945, the African Division and Indian Division of Britain and the main force of Chinese troops drove Japanese troops out of Burma.

In the battlefield of China and the Pacific, semi-colony China made great efforts in the anti-fascist war. After the outbreak of the Pacific War, Chinese troops were resisting half of overseas Japanese troops. In August 1945, there were 1.283 million Japanese soldiers in China, which accounted for 50% of the total 2.746 million overseas Japanese soldiers (except the Japanese army in the northeast of China). Before the former Soviet Union declared war against Japan on 8 August 1945, there were 677,000 Japanese soldiers garrisoned in the northeast of China, which were restrained and attacked by Chinese armies, especially those under the leadership of Chinese Communist Party[52].

Some scholars believe that the World War II could be looked upon as a war of contending for, controlling, and utilizing strategic resources in the world, which was in a sense reasonable. From this point of view, there existed insurmountable conflicts between the Axis which, with few colonies, desired to realize the strategic aim of world hegemony (including establishing the three colonial empires mentioned above) and the limited material, financial and human resources they possessed. The broad colonies of Britain, France, Belgium, and Holland possessed far more abundant human and material resources than the Axis. In addition, because of the anti-fascist nature and the generous promise of the Atlantic Charter, these resources were comparatively fully mobilized and utilized. Stavrianos in Global Rift made the following thought-provoking remarks, "the independent variable that decisively affected the fortunes of all the colonies was the availability of human and natural resources that could be exploited by the metropolitan centers"[53]. This sentence can also be understood in the way (taking Britain as an example) that, in the World War II, the successful development of colonial resources saved Britain. At the critical moment of survival or extinction, Britain had a deeper understanding of the extreme importance of colonies in economy, politics, and military and the significance of properly handling the relation between the metropolitan state and the colonies. The World War II forced Britain to realize that colonies were indispensable to preserve the position of postwar Britain as a world power (far from the position of world hegemony). Therefore, Britain spared no pains in consolidating its position in colonies during and after the World War II. The same was France:

---

52   "The World War II." *Encyclopedia of China: Foreign History*. Beijing: Encyclopedia of China Publishing House, 1990: 235.

53   Stavrianos, L. S. *Global Rift: The Third World Comes of Age*. New York: William Morrow & Co, 1981: 98.

without the vast French African colonies, France would have had no retreat after Metropolitan French fell into the hands of enemies, not to mention setting up the base of counterattack.

It can be properly understood, from this point of view, why Britain put forward colonial development plans and reform schemes in the difficult period during and after the World War II. So did France to a certain extent. During the war, some officials of the British Colonial Office noticed the political crises in colonies. In 1942, the Under-Secretary of State for the colonies Daub suggested that Britain should figure out a way to make the colonies continue to be on the side of the Great Britain. Otherwise, the British Empire would lose another continent in the 20th century[54]. Under the premise of preserving its colonial rule, in order to draw over British colonies to continue to support Britain in the war, British Government set out to make reform schemes in colonies in 1943 and issued the Colonial Development and Welfare Act in 1940. The latter was the continuation of the Colonial Development Act (1929), which stipulated that 5 million pounds should be allocated to develop colonies in the following 10 years so as to appease the dissatisfaction in the colonies and mobilize more actively resources in the colonies to support the war. However, in the implementation of the act, the actual allocation was only one sixth of the fund formerly stipulated. The reform scheme was called Williams Scheme, which stipulated the five stages of constitutional development in West Africa.

In light of the scheme, only in the fifth stage was West Africa allowed to enter the autonomous stage with any concrete content while the previous four stage were too long (after many generations) so that these empty stipulations were in fact on paper only, exerting no substantial influences[55]. In one word, wartime British Government obstinately carried out the inflexible policy of Churchill that Britain must preserve its colonies. The view that Britain began to implement "planned decolonization" since the war at the latest proposed by some western historians was based on no historical grounds.

The colonial policies of wartime France was more inflexible than those of Britain. In 1944, Conference in African Brazaville once clearly stated that "any possibility of establishing autonomous regimes in French colonies, even in the far distant future, must be denied"[56].

Colonialism as the derivative of capitalism had accompanied the latter for over 400 years. In the World War II, the huge support it made for the metropolitan states in human and material resources proved that they were indispensable for the metropolitan states. In addition, the availability of colonial resources was unusually raised in the situation of war, which gave rise to the illusion

---

54 Qtd. in Li, Anshan. "The Collapse of the British Empire." *Study of History* 1(1995): 169-186.
55 Flint, J. "Planned Decolonization and Its Failure in British Africa," in *Colonialism and Nationalism in Africa*. Vol. 3. Ed. G. Maddox and T. K. Welliver. New York, 1933. 13-36.
56 "La Conference Africaine Brazaville." Qtd. in CKOPOB, Г. E. *French Imperialism in West Africa*. Trans. Ren Lu. Beijing: World Affairs Press, 1958: 153.

that they would be utilized by the metropolitan states to the same extent in the peaceful postwar circumstance. It was based on such estimation that the Great Britain, which was depressed in economy and destitute of material resources in the early period after the war, prolonged in 1945 the Colonial Development and Welfare Act for another ten years and increased the annual allocation to 12 million pounds. By means of this plan, Britain hoped, on the one hand, to demonstrate to colonial people and the U.S. its competence and confidence in colonial administration and, on the other hand, to enhance the productivity and living standards in colonies, which could appease the colonies and form a huge market for Britain. The chain of three development schemes played a role in the development of resources in British colonies, especially those in tropical Africa, which at least prolonged the British rule over British tropical African colonies for another 12 to 22 years.

4.3.5. The Development of and Changes in Capitalism and the Decline of Colonialism after the World War II

The half century after the end of the World War II was the period when social productivity was raised fastest and economy developed most rapidly in human history. The annual increase of world economy approximated 4%, the improvement of social labor productivity was also stunning, and the GDP per capita in developed countries, like the U.S., increased from 1,350 dollars in 1945 to 30,000 dollars by the end of the century. The total volume of international trade, as the bond linking the economy of every country in the world, which was merely 20 billion dollars in the early 20th century, 60.1 billion dollars in 1950, five years after the end of the World War II, henceforth rapidly increased 7.2 times from 1950 to 1980 and reached 6 trillion dollars in 1995. International direct investment, merely 51 billion dollars in the early years after the war, increased to 580 billion dollars in 1965 and reached 3 trillion dollars in the 1990s. All the achievements made by world economy were closely related to the rapid advancement of science and technology. After the war, the world entered the third revolution of science and technology when science and technology developed at an unprecedentedly fast speed. The scale and speed of development of the third revolution of science and technology far surpassed those of the previous two revolutions. The increase in Gross National Product (GNP) of developed countries was largely relied on the application of new sciences and technologies. Oil became the dominant source of energy in the world, petro-chemical technologies made rapid progress, nuclear power generation was generally used, synthetic raw materials were widely developed, electronic industrial technologies achieved unprecedented developments, space navigation industry, laser industry, automatic control industry, and biological engineering were established, and information technology gave rise to tremendous changes, the establishment and expansion of these emergent production sectors gave a totally new outlook to production technologies in the world and increasingly internationalized the productive process. All these were achieved when science and technology were constantly innovated. Science and technology are the primary productive forces, productivity was the most active and revolutionary determinant factor in the production of human society, the unprecedentedly rapid development of human social productivity inevitably gave rise to correspondingly profound transformation in relations of production, which made huge changes in modern capitalism. The fast development of economy in modern capitalist system revealed that contemporary capitalism had quite strong ability to adjust itself and great capacity for the development of modern productivity. Since capitalism had not yet run out of its vitality, it had the ability of and necessity to adjust its relation with colonies under violent impact of national independent movements, which directly or indirectly influenced the fate of colonialism always concomitant with capitalism. The new development of modern capitalism and the mutually associated relation with the fate of colonialism and the new changes in the North-South relationship it presaged were manifested in the following four aspects:

Firstly, modern capitalism developed from general (private) monopoly capitalism to state monopoly capitalism. In developed capitalist countries, with the exponential growth of GNP, the disposable wealth of the government increased constantly. The nationalization of capital production turned the state into a collective capitalist, which possessed huge amounts of assets, not only the owner of enormous means of production and means of consumption but also the decisive big investor, a big producer, and a big consumer. The immense strength of capitalism and that of the state converged into a super strength matchless by any single capital group. Utilizing this deterrent strength, in all ways and by all means, the state could make overall intervention into and adjustment of, directly or indirectly, the domestic economic life and foreign economic relation, and exerted an immense influence on domestic and even world economy, particularly powerful in the latter case. For instance, the US and Britain imposed control and domination over colonies and semi-colonies especially over those with economic difficulties by means of financial aid and the Colonial Development and Welfare Act respectively. In many cases, the support of the state for the overseas economic expansion of private monopoly capital was more effective than that given by colonialism for the overseas expansion of private monopoly capital, surpassing the effect of the gunboat policy implemented since the 19th century, because this kind of support was not only backed with military and political power but also increasingly depended mainly on the immense economic strength of the state. Converged into a gigantic force closely with private monopoly capital, the state was even more effective and positive in overseas economic infiltration and expansion than colonialism, which mainly relied on super-economic power, like the economic expansion of the U.S. in economically backward countries (later known as developing countries).

Second, monopoly capitalism gained enormous development in its overseas economic expansion, and a large number of multinational companies came into being and developed rather rapidly, which constituted an effective form of overseas export of capital by developed countries. From the war time to the 1960s, developed countries owned 7,276 multinational companies, and 27,300 overseas branch companies and subsidiary companies. Nearly one trillion dollars of direct investment have been exported through multinational companies, which have rigorous plans of production, marketing and investment and advanced management system, can transmit and process information instantaneously, and make prompt responses to changes in world economic situation and market. Through monopolizing the production and sales market of certain products and even a certain production sector, multinational corporations can not only obtain high monopoly profit but also dominate and control the economy of other countries and even the world market. Therefore, multinational corporations as an economic form have been increasingly favored by the monopoly groups in developed countries (in the North). After colonialism began to collapse, multinational corporations rushed to establish production and sales systems in developing countries. By 1977, the number of multinational corporations increased to 10,373 with 104,000 overseas branch corporations and subsidiary corporations. Why have the position and role of multinational corporations in the modern capitalist system received so much attention? First, it seems that developed countries have found an effective institution to replace colonialism in the collapse of colonialism. They are capable of plundering and expanding overseas, and raking in maximum profit. For instance, one of the most powerful functions of colonialism was to annex territories while that of multinational corporations is to merge other corporations, which is one of its main forms of overseas expansion embodied in the power of capital export, making it possible to move into the new turf of overseas market without having to spend time and efforts in setting up new corporations. Overseas capital export from developed countries increased 30 times within a generation, most of which was through overseas investment of multinational corporations, accounting for nearly 75% of capital export volume. Its scope of activity was much broader that the boundaries of colonial empires. Just like what Spenser, former chairman of the First National City Bank of New York, once said, the political boundary of a nation-state is too narrow for the free roaming of modern enterprises. Multinational corporations must take the world as a market, looking for new technologies, talents, new production process, raw materials, new visions, and capital. Second, multinational corporations are quite idealistic as monopolists of technology trade. When the great part played by science and technology in promoting productivity has been recognized, the monopoly of the latest advanced, sophisticated, and high-precision technology has become one of the most important measures taken by developed countries (mostly former colonialist countries) to prolong the vitality of capitalism and seize monopoly profit. Economic statistics suggest that no more than 400 largest multinational corporations in developed countries are capable of taking part in the economic partition of the world but they possess and control 90% of production technologies and 75% of technology trade in these countries. The monopoly of advanced technologies by multinational corporations is the Incantation of the Golden Hoop for developing countries. Therefore, some scholars describe modern capitalism as technology monopoly capitalism. The monopoly of advanced technologies (including advanced equipment and high-performance computers) is one of the largest sources for monopoly capital to obtain enormous monopoly profit, manipulate and arrange the international division of labor.

Third, modern capitalism adjusts international division of labor through organized activities of its multinational corporations. Compared to colonialism which relied on super economic powers and spontaneous international division of labor in the stage of primitive accumulation and laissez-faire capitalism, it is featured with more powerful and organized capitalist international division of labor so that it has become a dominant factor in international division of labor. Making use of the advantages, multinational corporations choose and organize some developing countries for specialized productions, closely associated with their domestic production activities, which has become a component of the overall production process of multinational corporations in the world. Such economic controls and integration, unprecedented in allocation of resources in the world, have surpassed previous controls of colonies in any colonial periods in history.

The third revolution in science and technology gave rise to further division of labor in regard to new technology, production of components in different countries and production process. Developed countries have not only transferred domestic low-tech and labor-intensive industries, pollution-intensive industries, and secondary components production or process to developing countries (mostly colonies and former colonies). In addition, because the advancement of science and technology has promoted highly mechanized and modernized agriculture, some developed countries have also shifted the production of some agricultural products and primary products from formerly colonized developing countries to their own countries, greatly improving the self-sufficiency degree of agricultural products (food). The development of plastic industry, synthetic fiber industry, and synthetic rubber industry which have emerged after the World War II raised the self-sufficiency degree of agricultural products and raw materials in industrialized developed countries so that some developed countries have supplied a major part of food, wool, flowers, and diary products, and a half of edible oil and cotton in world market, which have reduced their reliance on agricultural raw materials of former colonies.

The direct investment of international capital has also changed in the distribution of regions and industrial sectors. Previously, the direct investment of international capital was mainly distributed to colonies and semi-colonies, which accounted for 62.8% in the total volume of direct investment, and rose to 65.7% by 1938. After 1945, the direct investment of developed countries has been distributed to developed countries, which accounted for 67.3% of the total volume of direct investment while to colonies and developing countries accounted for 32.3%, and continued to decrease to 27.8% in the 1970s. The change in allocation of resources mentioned above have inevitably influenced the nearly fixed role of colonies as sources of agricultural products and raw materials and position in international division of labor for several centuries. Such a change has not changed the international capitalist relation of production: developed countries are still original and primary industrial sites while developing countries are "derivative" and "secondary" industrial sites[57]; the international division of labor between countries in the core and those in the periphery remain basically the same. This is the fundamental factor of the persistence of the old international economic order, which is fully embodied in the North-South relationship.

Fourth, the old international economic order was a world economic system formed in the colonialist period of several centuries in the control and exploitation of colonies and semi-colonies, which fully illustrated the worldly exploitative relationship of international capitalist economic system. Such a world economic system was absolutely favorable to countries in the core, developed countries, in any periods. Although world economy has undergone great changes, the old international economic order still attempts to maintain this unequal and unreasonable relationship. Historically, the maintenance of the old international economic order was one of the chief economic functions of colonialism, which not only relied on the economic power of colonialism but also more on the political power of colonialism. However, it was increasingly less possible for colonial regimes under severe impacts of national liberation movements to assert super economic powers. Modern capitalism begins to rely more on the internal mechanism of international relation of production so as to raise the original and primary relation of production in developed countries over the derivative and secondary relation of production and turn the original and derivative capital relation of production into a fixed economic structure accordingly: industrialized metropolitan states and agricultural colonies, and manufacturing metropolitan states and raw material colonies were all embodied in the North-South relationship. Because modern capitalism has virtually monopolized the most advanced science and technology and possessed strong economic power, it draws on its strong economic power, employs the old economic structure and world pattern of labor division, and makes use of the dire inertial force evolved and prolonged in history to maintain strenuously: a) the old international division of labor division international production system; b) the unequal exchange in the international trade; c) the relation between the exploiter and the exploited in the international flow of capital; d) the relation of the dominant and the subordinate in international monetary system; e) the unequal relations in the international finance system; f) the weak status of developing countries in the international economic organizations and monetary funds

---

57   Marx, and Engels. Collected Works. Vol. 28. New York: International Publishers, 1986: 47.

(IMF, WTO etc.). The maintenance of the old international economic order was based on the control and maintenance of the economic relationship of developing countries in the former colonial period. In particular, former metropolitan states can sign preferential trade agreements with former colonies, maintain the old monetary blocs (the sterling bloc and the French franc bloc); control and uphold the ruling class of former colonies to maintain special influence on former colonies so as to forestall social revolution from affecting the interest of metropolitan states; and influence and control the direction of economic development in former colonies so as to exert most impacts on the policy-making of their governments concerning allocation of resources, which result in a higher degree of dependence on the monetary markets of former metropolitan states. All these were political and economic controls over colonies and semi-colonies that colonialism strived to and had once realized by means of super economic powers for centuries. However, with great changes in the international situation, if colonialism still mainly relied on political power (or colonial violence) to maintain and realize the old order in the economic field, the negative effects would become increasingly obtrusive and even threaten monopoly capitalism, primarily the economic, political and military interests of the U.S. in the world.

The political and economic effects of colonialism would face severe challenges (only the cultural effects did not meet severe challenges, yet), and the political effect, in particular, suffered heavy blows from national liberation movements and was hard to continue. Since modern colonialism came into being, political rule was closely related to economic plunder, and super economic powers were the bonding agent of this political-economic combination. The adhesion and combination between them was very secure, Marx wrote in his analysis of the relation between colonialism and violence in the first volume of Marx's *Capital*: colonial system "depends in part on brutal force" and that force "is itself an economic power."[58] During different stages of the development of capitalism, colonialism assumed different forms and modes. However, one thing in common in different stages was that colonialism depended on direct political rule or control or super economic coercions, in a word, "on brute force". Therefore, the premise of the existence of colonies was direct political rule[59]. If any colony has achieved independent sovereignty, it is no longer a colony but a sovereign state, although it depends economically on former metropolitan states in various degrees. The author does not agree on the proposal of colonialism without colonies because in the previous stages in the development of capitalism, colonialism had always exploited resources of colonies for

---

58 Marx- Engels. *Collected Works*. Vol. 35. New York: International Publishers, 1996: 739.
59 When analyzing the history of the U.S., Marx once employed the idea of "economic colonies" in the sense of political economy. Likewise, Engels pointed out that the economic development of the U.S. was the outcome of British big industry till the U.S. became the second industrial nation in the world by 1890. But its colonial nature had not been completely rinsed. Our understanding is that before the accomplishment of agricultural reforms, the international division of labor, historically formed and correspondent to machine production center, has a deep-rooted historical inertia. Note by the author.

the service of capitalism by imposing direct political rule and extra-economic coercions on vast colonies. After capitalism has reached the stage of state monopoly capitalism, tremendous changes have occurred in international situation, colonialism can no longer sustain political rule over colonies, while the immense development of science, technology and productivity has provided a new and rather effective form and new North-South relationship for monopoly capital to plunder world resources, exploit and control developing countries. In this situation, the end of colonialism was put on the agenda. However, it seems that we might agree on the view of colonialism without colonies since imperialism is a stage of capitalist development although the arrival of imperialist stage had once resulted in the widespread partition of colonies. But as a stage of capitalism, its relation with colonies is not the same as that of colonialism with colonies, which had to depend on colonies as the targets for extra-economic coercions and political rules. When monopoly capitalism persists and dominates in most areas of the world, imperialism and hegemony[60], which have taken the place of colonialism, can still make use of the world production system based on unequal international labor division, the world financial system based on monopoly capital, and the old international economic order to exploit, plunder and even control developing countries. Socialist countries, coexistent with monopoly capitalist countries, pick up the pace of economic development to lay a solid foundation for highly advanced social productivity, and they fight calmly and prudently against the "peaceful evolution" strategy of major capitalist powers and against their hegemonic practices.

187

The North-South relationship has been developing under such circumstances and conditions after the World War II.

---

60   In the multipolar world configuration, imperialism often assumes the appearance of hegemony. Note by the author.

Chapter V

The Third World Embracing Political Independence

5.1.0 The Global Situation after World War II

5.1.1. World War II and the Collapse of the Colonial System

World War II was a heavy blow to long-established imperialist countries like Britain and France as well as the late-comers such as the Germany, Japan, Italy, undermining their political rule and economic control over colonies and semi-colonies after the war. And with the development of capitalism and prevalence of the idea of "sovereignty and self-decision", countries and regions in Asia, Africa and Latin America who remained to be colonies and semi-colonies when the war was first ended started to seek national independence. But far from forfeiting the colonies after taking the heavy blow of World War II, the colonizers in the West even dreamed about taking them as the foundation for revitalization. They left no stones unturned to restore their colonial administration as before the war, consequently engaging in fierce conflicts with the activities for independence of the people in colonies. As the nationalist movements in the colonies was set against the backdrop of the Cold War, some western scholars believed: "the exigencies of Cold War led to the curious East-West competition in courting colonial and ex-colonial peoples. The latter quickly exploited this situation to extract maximum assistance from Moscow and Peking as well as from Washington, London, and Paris"[1]. The United States and the Soviet Union, the great powers emerged during the war, participated in colony affairs, despite their different purposes, to some extent accelerated the collapse of the old colonial system of the West.

World War II speeded up the falling apart of the colonial system being established in about three to four hundred years in many ways.

First, the war significantly weakened colonial metropolitan states in the West. Germany, Japan and Italy defeated and other western European countries undermined decided that they could not afford the consumption of long-term colonial wars and their people's aversion to wars. The victor and affluent US wished to claim the position of Britain and France, but was forced to place the priority on containing the expansion of the Soviet Union on both sides of the Eurasia and on the rejuvenation and stability of Europe. Feeling insufficient in interfering in the affairs of Asia and Africa, it mainly imposed its impacts through the United Nations.

Second, the expansion of socialist forces inspired and supported the fight for liberation in the Third World countries and diverted the forces of the West. World War II not only strengthened the Soviet Union, but also enabled socialism to go beyond one country and become a world system. Under the support of the Red Army of the Soviet Union, East Europe witnessed the establishment of a number of people's democratic governments; in the Orient, socialist systems were erected in China, North Korea and North Vietnam, confronting the capitalist camp of the West. Not only did they distract some forces of Western countries, but also served as a great inspiration and support to national liberation activities all over the world. The support derived from both the international proletariats and the dependence of the consolidation of socialism on the triumph of national liberation movements. "Without the destruction of colonialist system and the construction of dozens of newly independent nations, socialism will not come into being"[2]. It was testified by the fact that many newly-independent countries claiming to be socialist nations after the war.

Third, World War II greatly enhanced the revolutionary consciousness for national liberation of the people in colonies and semi-colonies and the political awareness of the people around the world. During the war, tens of thousands of colony people broke away from the isolated lifestyle and conservative thoughts and traditions after joining the anti-fascist war at home or in the battlefields in Europe, Asia or Africa away from home. Through their extensive contacts with other nations, they gained a deeper understanding of the misery and misfortunate of their own nations, thus intensifying their dissatisfaction with the colonial rule. Through their participation in the war and the recognition that it

1   Stavrianos, L. S. *The World since 1500: A Global History*. Prentice Hall, 1999: 597.
2   S.A. Tyushkevich. *History of the World War II, 1939-1945*. Part II. Vol.12. Shanghai: Shanghai Translation Publishing House, 1989: 193.

was easy for the Axis to defeat the metropolitan states, they gained a further understanding that they had huge potentials while the metropolitan states were feeble, thus boosting their courage and confidence in the fight against colonialism. After the war, world progressive opinions gave more compassion and support to national liberation activities. It was considered against the spirit of the time to suppress the will of the enslaved nations to struggle for freedom and self-decision and to vigorously defend colonial rule. Within the metropolitan states, the middle- and lower-level people more strongly opposed colonial policies and supported national liberation activities.

Last but not least, the war facilitated the development of national economies and the emergence of nationalist parties for colonies and semi-colonies, preparing important conditions for national democratic movements in the post-war period. The metropolitan states, to meet the demand of the troops during the war, increased military orders from and economic investment in the colonies. Coupling with the sharp decline of industrial product export of the metropolitan states, the national economies of the colonies achieved tremendous progress. As a result, National bourgeoisie and the proletariat grew from strength to strength. Under the influence of western nationalist, democratic or socialist ideology, a series of nationalist parties came into being. For example, by 1961, in Africa there were 146 parties and organizations, only 8 of which were founded before the War. In many countries, the proletariat, the bourgeoisie or other political organizations, by taking advantage of the War, developed their own capacity, deepened their impact on their compatriots and enhanced the leadership and organization of national liberation movements.

191

It is beyond doubt that World War II severely shook the old colonial system and prepared the oppressed nations politically, ideologically and organizationally for the fight over national liberation, thus providing greater guarantee for victory. Being blessed with these favorable conditions, after the War, people in Asia, Africa and Latin America started the ever-going fight to win and safeguard national independence, delivering a great situation in terms of nationalist movements worldwide. Asian colonies and semi-colonies gained independence one after another through struggles. Meanwhile, fights against capitalism and colonialism in Africa were surging and national democratic movements in Latin America became increasingly active.

However, long-established colonizers who were severely undermined during the War reneged on their commitments made in the War and disregarded the demand for independence of the people in colonies and semi-colonies. They took colonies as the foundation to rejuvenate their economies and to return as world powers, wishing to restore the old colonial order. To achieve this goal, initially they played two-side schemes. On the one hand, they endeavored to create illusory prospects by means of some reforms; on the other hand, when the former failed to work, they resorted to violence to suppress nationalist movements. But facts proved that neither could contain the robust nationalist movements in Asia, Africa or Latin America.

5.1.2. The Struggle for Hegemony between the United States and the Soviet Union and the Collapse of the Colonial System

After the War, in order to rule the world and struggle with the Soviet Union, the United States went all out to infiltrate into Asia, Africa and Latin America. It planned to squeeze in the territory of long-established colonizers, to contain the Soviet Union's influence and to suppress nationalist movements in some countries and regions as well. The three tasks sometimes went parallel, but intertwined other times. With the slogans of "Communist Threat" and "counter-colonialism", the US frequently disguised itself as a sympathizer and supporter for nationalist movements in Asia, Africa and Latin America, thus promoted its infiltration and expansion in these regions. The US also exploited foreign aid as a tool of expansion. Although the newly independent countries who suffered from colonial rule and exploitation for a long time won political sovereignty, they remained reliant on colonizers economically. To develop national economies, they had no choice but to import a great amount of capital and technology. Taking advantage of this situation, the US provided them with various economic and military assistances, reinforcing its economic control and political influence over assistance-receivers as a result. On January 20, 1949, the US president Harry S. Truman in his speech brought up Point Four Program3 which intended to aid underdeveloped countries. The US also signed all kinds of treaties and agreements with countries in Asia, Africa and Latin America to include them in its military group for control. It was estimated that, from 1946 to 1955, the US entered into treaties and agreements for political and military alliance with over 30 countries in the three continents, including Inter-American Treaty of Reciprocal Assistance and Southeast Asia Collective Defense Treaty. In addition, it instigated a series of mutinies in local areas to prop up pro-US regimes. With two super powers standing firmly against each other after the War, a great number of newly independent Third-World countries stayed away from the US policies out of the necessity of safeguarding their national interests. However, to impose its control over them, the United States frequently supported military coups to suppress oppositions and promoted the establishment of pro-US governments. This policy was often applied in Latin America.

When World War II ended, the Soviet Union was the only power strong enough to contend with the United States, forming around it an international system distinct from that of the West. But after sacrificing a great deal during the War, it focused on revitalizing its national economy in the post-war period

---

3   "[W]e must embark on a bold new program for making the benefits of our scientific advances and industrial progress available for the improvement and growth of underdeveloped areas.... I state these differences, not to draw issues of belief as such, but because the actions resulting from the Communist philosophy are a threat to the efforts of free nations to bring about world recovery and lasting peace." See webpage of US Embassy in China: http://www.usembassy-china.org.cn/infousa/living-doc/GB/pointfour. htm

and helping newly-founded socialist nations in Eastern Europe and East Asia to consolidate people's democratic governments and to develop their economies. The Soviet Union founded Communist Information Bureau in Europe In September 1947 and The Council for Mutual Economic Assistance with Eastern European countries in April, 1949. It acted actively in international affairs to preserve world peace by revealing in various platforms the colonial and invasive policies held by Western powers and supporting nationalist movements around the world. But these actions were mainly conducted within the United Nations, "since the foundation of the United Nations, the Soviet Union has been dedicated to maintaining the rights of national independence of every nation"[4]. The Soviet Union acted separately from other powers in the United Nations, which boosted the confidence of people in backward countries and regions to win in nationalist movements.

5.2. Victories for National Independence in Southeast and South Asia

The collapse of the colonial system started in the Southeast Asia. In modern times since the 19th century, this region had fought against colonial rule for a long time, laying a great foundation for its people in terms of ideas, organization, leadership and armed struggles. This region was under the colonial rule of Britain, France, Netherland, the US and other colonizers before being occupied by Japanese fascists during World War II. In order to consolidate its rule, under the pretext of "Asia for Asians", Japan tried to win over local nationalists and allowed their independence at the end of its occupation. Tokyo granted nominal independence to Burma and Philippines in 1943, to Indochina in March 1945, and to Indonesia in August 1945 before the surrender. The surprisingly sudden end of the Pacific War created favorable conditions for people in Southeast Asia to struggle for independence. They swiftly seized a large number of weapons from Japanese occupiers and took the transient opportunity of the collapse of Japanese colonial rule, thus forming their own preliminary regime and armed forces. "But no metropolitan power was prepared to accept this, nor did the nationalists feel themselves strong enough to resist outright the return of colonial rule. While insisting on real independence within a short space of time, initially they preferred negotiations"[5]. Through a series of tough negotiations, protests and even armed struggles, Southeast Asia witnessed the rising of independent sovereign states one after another. And in South Asian Subcontinent, due to the timely change of policies by British colonizers, India and Pakistan gained political independence quite smoothly.

193

---

4   A.A. Gromyko & B.N. Ponomarev, eds. *History of the Soviet Union's Foreign Policies*. Vol. 2. Trans. Zhengwen Han, et al. Beijing: China Remin University Press, 1989: 15-16.
5   Tarling, Nicholas. *The Cambridge History of Southeast Asia*. Vol. 2. New York: Cambridge University Press, 1999: 588.

5.2.1. The Independence of the Dutch Indonesia

Known as "Thousand Island Country", Indonesia was colonized by the Netherlands in 1596. In March, 1942, after forcing surrender out of Netherlands colonial authorities, Japan started fascist rule in Indonesia. After Japan declared its surrender on August 17, 1945, Bung Sukarno, a national bourgeoisie leader in Indonesia, released the Declaration of Independence in Djakarta. On August 18, the Preparatory Committee for Indonesian Independence founded before Japan surrendered, the Communist Party of Indonesia, youth groups under its leadership and other political representatives held a conference, in which the Constitution of the Republic of Indonesia was passed and the Indonesian government was founded with Bung Sukarno as President and Mohammad Hatta as Vice President. August 29 saw the official establishment of Komite Nasional Indonesia Pusat (Indonesian Central National Committee) exercising the congressional power. On November 4, the first cabinet was formed with the Prime Minister being Sutan Syahrir, a right-wing socialist. Meanwhile, local political power was set up all over Indonesia and regular armed forces—People's Security Corps.

The founding of the Republic of Indonesia and the further development of the nationalist movement caused damage to the established strategic and economic interests of Britain, the Netherlands, US and other metropolitan states. To guarantee their vested benefits, they schemed to return at every possible opportunity. On 25 September 1945, the British force, under the name of accepting Japan's surrender, landed on Java Island and occupied big cities like Djakarta, Bandung and Semarang afterwards. Its steps were followed by the Dutch colonial government in exile in Australia. The British force released and rearmed Dutch Indonesia soldiers kept in concentration camps by the Japanese army so that they could violently take over and occupy big cities and strategic strongholds in Indonesia. On November 10 of the same year, Britain and Netherlands sent army, navy and air forces to attack Surabaya, a vital military spot, intriguing the 21-day heavy battle with Indonesian troops and civilians. The British and Dutch troops had to pay a heavy price before barely seized the city area[6]. And public opinions around the world forced the British force to withdraw from Indonesia later. But the colonizer Netherlands still refused to recognize Indonesia's independence and performed a double strategy of negotiation and war. On the one hand, it actively prepared for a new colonial war; and on the other hand, it negotiated with Indonesia. On November 15, 1946, the Syahrir Government signed with the Netherlands the Linggadjati Agreement, in which the Netherlands recognize the Republic as the de facto authority over Java, Madura, and Sumatra. Both parties agreed to the formation of the United States of Indonesia, a semi-autonomous federal state with the monarch of the Netherlands at its head. The agreement also required Indonesia to restore and compensate foreign assets, which was rejected by its people and caused the step down of the Syahrir Government.

194

---

6 November 10 was later stipulated as Indonesian Martyrs' Day. Note by the author.

In July 1947, the Dutch launched a major military offensive against the Republic of Indonesia with a troop of 120,000 soldiers, starting the first colonial war between the Dutch and Indonesia. Though it fought forcefully, the newly founded government failed to thwart the offensive due to limited strength and internal conflict. With the US's mediation, the Hatta government signed the Renville Agreement with the Dutch in January 1948. Areas of affluence and great strategic significance, i.e. two thirds of Java, Madura, and Sumatra were transferred to the control of Dutch colonizers, thus the Republic of Indonesia shrinking a lot.

In this situation, the Communist Party of Indonesia decided to formulate new guidelines, roadmaps and policies to lead Indonesians to fight for the abolishment of the Linggadjati Agreement and the Renville Agreement. In August 1948, the Central Committee of the Indonesian Communist Party (PKI) passed the Resolution entitled as the New Path of the Republic of Indonesia, which re-ignited ithe national movement. Under the pretext of fight against the threat of "Red Terror", the US and Netherlands schemed with the Hatta government and plotted the terrifying Madiun Affair in September 1948. The Hatta government claimed that the Communists in Madiun were behind political events of the so-called "seizing power" and "establishing Indonesian Soviet Republic". Using it as an excuse, the authorities, after surprise attacks, arrested and slaughtered the Communists. This affair saw the arrest of about 36,000 people and the death of over 10,000. The Communist Party's armed forces and its leading core were devastated.

In December 1948, the Dutch started the second colonial war intending to end the Republic of Indonesia. The Dutch colonial army conquered the city of Yogyakarta—the location of the temporary Republican capital and captured Bung Sukarno and Mohammad Hatta. Once again, international opinion of the Dutch military campaigns was one of outrage. With intervention from the United States, Indonesia and Netherlands on November 2, 1949 signed the Round Table Conference Agreements, which stipulated that the "United States of Indonesia" consisted of the Republic of Indonesia and 15 pro-Dutch puppet states recognizing the Dutch queen as the national leader and Indonesia and the Netherlands should remain cooperation in national defense, diplomacy, finance and culture.

This agreement once again encountered opposition from the Indonesians. The year 1950 saw in Indonesia the movement with the aim to abolish the puppet states supported by the Dutch and to form a unified republic. Without direct obstruction from the Netherlands, this movement went smoothly. By August 15, 1950, Bung Sukarno declared the abolishment of the federal system and the establishment of a unified Indonesian Republic. After diplomatic negotiations, in August 1954, Indonesia and the Netherlands agreed to end the Dutch-Indonesia Alliance and to cancel agreements concerning diplomatic, military and cultural cooperation. In April 1956, Bung Sukarno abrogated the Round Table Conference Agreements. Indonesia started to perform in the international arena as an independent sovereign state.

5.2.2. The Independence of the American Philippines

In 1898, after the Spanish-American War, the Philippines became the colony of the United States. Since it encountered revolt from the Filipinos, the US conducted a Pilipino constitutional reform to buy over and win the upper circles. In 1916, the US Congress passed the Jones Law, which provided for the establishment of House of Representatives (the Philippine Assembly) and the Senate (the Philippine Commission) and that ministers(except the minister of education) in the government should be Filipinos. Still, the real power was in the grasp of the Governor General of the Philippines and the US President. 1935 saw the pass of the Tydings–McDuffie Act (officially the Philippines Independence), which provided for self-government of the Philippines and for Filipino independence from the United States after a period of ten years. .The US army returned to fight the Philippines Campaign in October 1944, with the Philippine Commonwealth troops, pushed the Japanese troops out of the country in February, 1945. The United States, the country claimed to support nationalist movements in the Third World countries after the War, did not honor its pre-war commitment but intended to re-control the Philippines. This kind of practice led to a large-scale demonstration participated by 60,000 people demanding independence on September 23, 1945 in Manila. Meanwhile, the Anti-Japanese Army, the Communist forces grew during the War of Resistance against Japan, has been actively expanding in rural areas to lead the struggle for independence. Facing great pressure, the United States agreed to grant the Philippines independence. In July 1946, Manuel Roxas supported by the US became the first president of the independent Republic of the Philippines. The new government, on the one hand, conducted all-out attacks against the Communist party and its armed forces; on the other hand, signed with the United States the US-Philippines General Relations Treaty, the US-Philippine Trade Pact (June 1946, the US-RP Military Basing Agreement March 1947, the US-RP Military Assistance agreement, US-RP Mutual Military Defense Treaty (1951), which guaranteed that the United States could impose actual control over the Philippines in politics, economy, military and other crucial fields.

The features of the independent Philippines was determined by America's Filipino and Americano policies for a long time. "While the US was controlling the Philippines, it promoted the inclusion of people from the upper class and intellectuals in government departments and established a legitimate pro-US political party, the US promoted the the upper class nationalists to give up the armed struggle and follow a peaceful parliamentary path.... As a result, the independent Philippines kept many colonial heritage and traces by the effect of the United States."[7]

---

7   Liang, Zhiming, ed. *A History of Colonialism in Southeast Asia*. Beijing: Peking University Press, 1999: 471-472.

5.2.3. The Independence of the British Malaysia and Burma

The British Malaysia and Myanmar won independence in 1948 and 1957 respectively. After the Japanese surrender, Britain restored its colonial rule in Malaysia. Regardless of the Malaysians' aspirations, it adopted the policy of "divide and rule". In February 1948, it created the Federation of Malaysia, separating Singapore form the Federation as its Crown Colony. June of the same year saw Britain's issuance of Emergency Ordinance, which outlawed the Malaysian Communist Party and other progressive parties and suppressed the Malaysians' requirement for independence. In February 1949, the Malaysian Communist Party founded Malayan People's Liberation Army to fight against British colonial rule. To ease the conflict between the Malaysians, Britain in 1955 granted Malaysia "some autonomy". On August 31, 1957, Malaysia declared independence as Britain granted the independence for the Federation within the commonwealth and handed the power to a pro-Britain group. It was followed up by Britain and Malaysia signing The Anglo-Malayan Defence Agreement (1957), which provided for the continued stationing of British troops in Malaysia and its economic lifeline being held by British capitals.

British Burma went through another journey than Malaysia. Burma people had a long history of fighting against British colonial rule. After it established a colonial empire in India, Britain had to wage three Britain-Burma wars (1824-1826, 1852, 1885) before it included Burma as a province of Britain India. In 1937, the British separated Burma from India to cut contacts between Burmese and Indian nationalists. During World War II, to fight against Japanese invaders, several Burmese nationalist political groups co-formed Anti-Fascist People's Freedom League with Aung San as the leader for armed struggles and supporting the allies in anti-Japanese war. In March 1945, the League recaptured the capital Rangoon and established grassroots authorities in many places after nationwide uprisings. However, the British troops returned Burma with the aim of re-establishing its colonial rule. The League decided to fight for independence through negotiation since it had conducted some cooperation with the British force before. The British government rejected the demand from the League of starting an autonomous government. On May 1945, the British Labor government issued a white paper on Burma, declaring that after three-year administration by the British governor in the post-war period, Burma would be granted with the Dominion status. In September, the British colonial authorities signed with the Freedom League another agreement on anti-Japanese army, taking in and reorganizing the troops led by the League. December 1945 saw the forming of an executive committee excluding the People's Freedom League, which provoked resistance form the Burmese. In January 1946, the League held the first National Convention, in which the demand of establishing constitutional convention, organizing national government and realizing complete independence was presented. In August and September, the Burmese Communist Party led the largest-scale national strike after the War. Since the strikes paralyzed the administration and economic activities of the Executive Committee, Britain was forced to sign the

Aung San-Attlee Agreement on January 27, 1947. It consented in April 1947, to hold an election for the Constitutional convention, which was responsible for drawing up the constitution. But the constitution must be approved by the British Parliament. The British would accept any decision concerning the future status of Burma made by the Convention. On October 17, 1947, Burma and Britain signed in London Treaty on Burmese Independence and Related Issues, stipulating that Britain officially acknowledges Burma Federal State as an independent country within the British Commonwealth. On 4 April 1948, Burma separated from the Commonwealth and became officially independent.

5.2.4 The Independence of the French Colonies

The unconditional surrender of Japan was followed by the ensuing of August Revolution, which was led by the Indochina Communist Party with Ho Chi Minh as the commander and obtained nationwide victory before long. On September 2, 1945, the Democratic Republic of Vietnam was officially founded. The provisional government renounced its French colony position, abolished every previous treaty signed between Vietnam and France and denied all privileges enjoyed by the French in Vietnam. October saw the declaration of independence by Laos, culminating national liberation movements in Indochina. However, its previous colonizer-France took colonies as the cornerstone of its world power position and managed to return Indochina with its troops under the support of Britain and the US. On September 23, 1945, the French troops seized Saigon and France restored its colonial administration. On March 18, 1946, the troops took hold of Hanoi and were stationed in Northern Vietnam as well as Laos and Cambodia. December 19, 1946 saw the ensuing of a full-scale colonial war in Vietnam by the French. The Vietnamese people, under the leadership of the Indochina Communist Party, went on the 9-year Anti-French Resistance War.

The success of Chinese Revolution provided the most favorable conditions for the Vietnamese people who carried on the Resistance War. In early 1950, Ho Chi Minh secretly visited China and tried to gain its assistance. President Mao Zedong provided all-rounded aid for Vietnam by sending there Chen Geng as the representative of the Central Committee of the CPC, accompanied by a military advisory group led by Wei Guoqing and a political advisory team headed by Luo Guibo. January 18, 1950 saw the establishment of diplomatic ties between China and the Democratic Republic of Vietnam. With China's support and assistance, Vietnam People's Army, by waging the Border Battle, liberated Lao Cai, Cao Bang, Lang Son and other places along Sino-Vietnam border, consolidating and expanding Northern Liberated Area in Vietnam and connecting it with Chinese territory. The Liberated Area was backed with a strong supporter, China, which offered stable assistance.

In March 1951, Vietnam, Laos and Cambodia held a meeting to further consolidate the Anti-French United Front. In March 1954, the Vietnamese blew the French troops heavily at the notable Battle of Dien Bien Phu, killing over 16,000 enemies, capturing the French commander and liberating Dien Bien Phu.

Suffering from the hard blow hit by Indochina people, France fell into plight. One fourth of its military forces were stuck in Indochina battlefield, its large bill of military expenses severely hampered its economic re-construction after the War and there occurred large scale anti-war movements at home. During the period between 1946 to 1953 France saw 17 successive government changes, which were frustrated mainly by the Indochina War. As a result, the French was compelled to sit down for negotiations, which greatly contributed to the concessions made by France at Geneva Conference and the signing of the Geneva Agreement, which respects the sovereignty, independence, unification and territorial integrity of the above three countries in Indochina.

5.2.5. The Independence and Partition of India

Indian independence was one of the most significant events at that time. During World War II, with the reinforcement of the Indian bourgeoisie, its national liberation movement under the leadership of the Indian National Congress and the Muslim League realized rapid development. After the war, with the struggles being dominated by strikes demanding for better economic situation and protests against trials on Indian National Army soldiers and against using Indian troops to suppress independence movements in Southeast Asia, the popular enthusiasm for political fight in India reached an unprecedented climax. From November 5 to 11, 1945, many places in India witnessed the protests of Indian National Army Week, with the largest one in Calcutta which was participated by about 300,000 people, the gatherings included Javāharlāl Nehru and other leading figures as addressors. On February 18, 1946 saw the breaking out of Royal Indian Mutiny (also Bombay Mutiny) in and around Bombay with the slogans of "Down with British Imperialism" and "Long Live the Independent India". On February 20, 200,000 workers in Bombay went on massive strikes and demonstrations to support the mutiny. By February 21, all Indian Navy soldiers participated in the fight. In June of the same year, Hyderabad saw the breaking out of the Telangana Rebellion. It was estimated that there were 1,629 strikes participated by 1.96million workers in 1946 and 5 large-scale peasant uprisings from the second half of 1946 to the first half of 1947. "It indicates that the fight of the Indians has been conducted at every front, with anti-colonial struggles being intertwined with the fight against feudalism and riots and mutinies taking place simultaneously.... The Labor Government was compelled to make the ultimate resolution of accepting India's demand for independence and handing over the political power. It realized that once the fight went beyond the control of the Indian National Congress, the British would not only lose the political power but even the economic interests."[8] In the fear of the armed struggles leading to social revolutions, the Indian National Congress and the Muslim League persuaded against and disintegrated armed struggles.

---

8   Lin, Chengjie. *History of India under Colonial Rule*. Beijing: Peking University Press, 2004: 462.

The following key issue was how Britain should hand over the political power to India through constitutionalism. The Indian National Congress and the Muslim League agreed on a peaceful manner of handing over, but the Muslim League insisted on the founding of Pakistan, which received strong opposition from the Indian National Congress, thus an agreement on the handing over could not be reached. The British-Indian authorities, the usual instigator, this time acted as the mediator, even the arbitrator. With every effort failed, the only option left was separated independence. On June 3, 1947, after negotiation Viscount Louis Mountbatten, the new British Governor-General of India announced Indian Independence Act (also Mountbatten Plan), with the most important provisions being: a. division of British India into the two new and fully sovereign dominions of India and Pakistan, with the former dominated by Hindus and the latter by Muslims; b. recognition of the right of states to accede to either or neither dominion, maintaining the former relationship with Britain without the right of autonomy; c. the division of Pakistan into East Pakistan and West Pakistan, with the under direct administration of India join the Dominion; d. establishment of government, constitutional conventions and the office of Governor-General in each of the two new countries, and both Dominions will be members of the British Commonwealth. Though the plan encountered oppositions among the public and in the Indian National Congress and the Muslim League as well, the two parties accepted it for their narrow national and religious interests. On January 26, 1950, the Republic of India was officially proclaimed and the Islamic Republic of Pakistan was founded on June 23, 1956.

It was irresponsible of the British to divide India into two countries on the basis of religious beliefs. Although being partly influenced by internal religious sect struggles in India, it was the unfortunate consequence originated from the long-term instigation and connivance of British colonial authorities during its rule. The Partition of India destroyed the existing foundation for Indian reunification, created large-scale migrations and a large number of refugees, resulted in numerous religious killing and even the death of the Mahatma Gandhi, and gave rise to the long-standing Kashmir issue between India and Pakistan.

5.3. Chinese Revolution and its Influence on the North-South Relationship

As early as in World War II, the United States placed China in a vital position in its post-war global strategy. It took China with the largest population as a country of great strategic significance in containing the Communist Party and the Soviet Union, stabilizing Asia-Pacific region after the war and providing a large market. The new Far-East strategy should focus on China. Before the conclusion of the war, Cordell Hull, the then Secretary of State said: "It was obvious to me that Japan would disappear as a great Oriental power for a long time to come. Therefore, the only major strictly Oriental power would be China.... Consequently, if there was ever to be stability in the Far East, it could only be assured with China being at the center of any arrangement that was made."[9] In order to make China of real assistance to it in the Far East and in world politics after the war, the US during the war insisted in including China among the major world powers. It even took the liberty to trade part of China's sovereignty (Lushun, Dalian, China Changchun railway and Outer Mongolia) to take the agreement and support of the Soviet Union in the Yalta Agreement, thus in Yalta the US drew China into its sphere of influence. The Soviet Union was also in favor of Chiang Kai-Shek taking the lead in unifying China and signed with the Kuomintang government the Sino-Soviet Treaty of Friendship and Alliance on August 14, 1945. To better achieve its objective, the US interfered in China's internal affairs and vigorously fostered the Chiang Kai-Shek government in gradually carrying out the policy of containing and combating the Communist Party of China. In 1944 during the Resistance War against Japan, the US replaced Joseph Warren Stilwell, the Chief of Staff to China Theater and the Commander of the China Burma India Theater, and Clarence Edward Gauss, the Ambassador to China for their friendly attitude towards the CPC and due to their dissatisfaction with Chiang Kai-Shek.

After the war, in order to satisfy the public demand, the KMT and the CPC signed the October 10 Agreement after a 43-day negotiation in Chongqing from August 28, 1945 to October 10, 1945. However, Chiang Kai-Shek had received a large amount of military aid from the United States, who trained 150,000 military personnel, equipped 45 army divisions and airlifted 540,000 servicemen to go on battles against the CPC forces across the country by the end of June in 1946. A US Marine Corps was also sent to assist the KMT in seizing Shanghai, Qingdao, Beijing, Tianjin, Qinhuangdao and other crucial cities. Considering victory guaranteed, Chiang Kai-Shek started the all-out civil war, attempting to wipe out the CPC, unify the country and establish the reactionary administration by the KMT. But till July 1947, one year after the war started, the CPC forces, far from being eliminated, went from defense to offenses. Facing with the rapid development of Chinese Revolution, knowing the corruption, incompetence and unpopularity of the KMT government, but to keep its position in China, the US Congress passed the China Aid Act of 1948 to provide a total of 463 million US dollars on April 2, 1948. But the nationwide victory of the Chinese Revolution would not have been obstructed by even more aid. On April 2, 1948, the People's Liberation Army of China crossed the Yangtze River, liberated the KMT's capital, Nanjing, and continued to chase the remaining KMT forces like great wind sweeping off fallen leaves in autumn. The unexpected failure of the KMT caused a serious stir in the US, especially in its China Relief Group in and outside of the US Congress, who condemned the Truman government for its flaws in aiding the Chiang Kai-Shek government and consequently "losing China". To shirk the responsibility, President Truman took the advice of the Secretary of State, Dean Gooderham Acheson, and on August 5, 1949, issued a "white paper" titled "Sino-US

---

9   Hull, Cordell. *The Memoirs of Cordell Hull*. Vol. 2. New York: Macmillan Co., 1948: 1587.

Relationship: Focusing on 1944-1949" trying to point out that the failure of the KMT in the civil war resulted from its own corruption and incompetence, not from the lack of aid from the United States. But against his will, the right-wing forces in the US vigorously promoted the fight against the "Red Terror", and propogated the existence of pro-communists in the government, Congress and various social circles. The prevailing McCarthyism was also extended to international relations, the US government advocated the theory of ideological collisions, refused to recognize the People's Republic of China, contained it through economic blockade, political isolation and military besiegement, obstructed China in resuming its legitimate seat in the United Nations and interfered in the Taiwan Question.

However, the victory of Chinese people's revolution was already settled. From September 21 to 30, 1949, the First Plenary Session of the Chinese People's Political Consultative Conference being held in Beiping (now Beijing) was participated by the Communist Party of China, democratic parties and democrat figures from various circles. The conference passed Common Program of the Chinese People's Political Consultative Conference and the Central People's Government of the People's Republic of China and founded the Central People's government with Mao Zedong as President and Zhou Enlai as Prime Minister and Foreign Minister.

In conducting foreign relations, the CPC initiated three guiding principles: "making a fresh start", "inviting guests after cleaning the house", and "leaning to one side". The first principle means that "rather than acknowledging the diplomatic relationships established by the KMT government with other countries, the new government will forge new diplomatic ties on a new basis"[10]; the second one indicates that it will demy privileges and eliminate impacts of imperialists to prevent the infiltrating of hostile forces and their meddling in China's own affairs[11]; the last policy means that considering the opposition of two strong camps formed after the WW II, the People's Republic of China will stand firmly on the side of the socialist camp. The presentation of the three guidelines effectively prevented military interventions by imperialists in China. The People's Republic of China, as an independent nation, gained a firm stand in the jungle of world countries.

The success of Chinese Revolution had made a significant influence on the North-South relationship. It was another victory not only of the revolution of the world proletariat, but also for the liberation movements of suppressed

10   Chinese Foreign Ministry and Party Literature Research Center of CPC Central Committee, eds. *Zhou Enlai on Diplomacy*. Beijing: Central Party Literature Press, 1990: 48.
11   In early February 1949, Mao Zedong said in his conversation with Mikoyan that "Our country, if compared to a family, is in a mess.... After the liberation, it is essential for us to clean our house.... After it has been cleaned, ordered, and furnished, we will invite guests. Our true friends can visit us earlier to help us in the cleaning. But other guests have to wait for a while." (Shi, Zhe. *Memoire of Shi Zhe: Besides the Giant*. Beijing: Central Party Literature Press, 1991: 379.

nations. It ushered in a new epoch in China's history and exerted vital and positive influence on the course of world history. First, the triumph of Chinese Revolution reshaped the pattern of international political power. China, the largest semi-colony in the world, breaking loose from the colonial system, significantly undermined the power of imperialist countries and greatly enhanced the revolutionary forces of people around the world, thus bringing in favorable changes for national libration movements in the Third World Countries. Secondly, it served as a glorious example for people around the world, especially those in Asia, Africa and Latin America to fight against imperialism and colonialism and provided many valuable experiences, in turn driving national liberation movements in the post-war period to move forward. Lastly, the success of Chinese Revolution immensely hampered the US strategy of seeking hegemony in the Far East, forcing it to adjust its diplomatic policy in the Asia-Pacific region. In response to the victory, the United States formed a military alliance with Japan, South Korea and countries in Southeast Asia attempting to besiege China and invaded North Korea and Vietnam to contain China.

The newly-founded People's Republic of China thus assumed the triple identity of a socialist nation, a world power and a developing country, putting it in a special and significant position in the complicated North-South relationship after World War II.

5.4. National Liberation Movements in Middle East

The Middle East, with no definite boundaries, roughly encompasses the area from the west bank of the Mediterranean in the west to the Persian Gulf in the east, including Egypt, Palestine, Lebanon, Jordan, Israel, Arabian Peninsula countries, Turkey, Iran and other countries. Lying at the juncture of Eurasia and Africa, it boasts 60% of the oil reserve in the capitalist world, thus assuming a critical strategic location. This region, previously being largely in the control of the Ottoman Empire, was seized by British and French colonizers since the modern times, particularly after World War I. After World War II, through robust national liberation activities, countries in the Middle East achieved independence one after another. While Britain and France strived to maintain their influences in this region, the US, out of the necessity of seeking global strategic interests, gradually infiltrated to it and attempted to squeeze out the two long-established colonial empires. The most distinct conflict of the two sides was found in the Arab-Israeli conflict.

Before World War II, among the Middle East nations, only Iran, Iraq, Turkey and Saudi Arabia maintained their formal independence or semi-independence. During the war, since the Middle East people offered active support to British and French troops to drive out the fascists, the post-war national liberation activities in the region concentrated on opposing the occupation force of Britain and France, demanding the abolishment of unequal treaties and taking back the sovereignty over the oil. In the course of their common fight, the Arabian countries moved gradually towards coalition. In September 1944, under Egypt's initiative, foreign ministers in the Arab world gathered in Alexandria to hold a conference, on which the Alexander Protocol was drawn up and the resolution was made to establish the League of Arab States. On March 22, 1945, the representatives of seven Arab countries, i.e. Egypt, Syria, Iraq, Lebanon, Saudi Arabia, Yemen and Jordan, held a meeting in the capital of Egypt, Cairo, drafting and passing the Charter of the Arab League and declaring the formal founding of the League of Arab States[12]. The League's main goal is to draw closer the relations between member States and co-ordinate collaboration between them, to safeguard their independence and sovereignty, and to consider in a general way the affairs and interests of the Arab countries. Its establishment for the first time delivered the Arabian nationalists a common tool to fight against Western powers and Zionists in Palestine. Cem burda kaldık

5.4.1. The Course of National Liberation Movements in the Middle East

The independence of Syria and Lebanon was the prelude to the national liberation movements in the Middle East. During World War II, the French and British troops entered Syria and Lebanon. In order to win the support of the local people, Charles de Gaulle declared the conclusion of mandate administration since World War and the independence of the two countries. Shortly after this, national governments were founded in both states. However, when the war ended, rather than withdrawing their troops, Britain and France deployed reinforcements, attempting to extinguish the people's fight for independence. This kind of action provoked even fiercer response in the people of both nations, who organized guerilla forces to conduct armed struggles. In May 1945, after French occupation troops performed armed oppression on demonstrations in some cities and bombed Damascus and other cities with heavy weapons, Syria and Lebanon cut diplomatic relations with France. "The Arab League promptly demanded the evacuation of all French forces, and was supported by Churchill, who was anxious to avoid a confrontation with Arab nationalists while the war was still in progress".[13] Pressed by Britain, the French withdrew its troops. In January 1946, Syria and Lebanon presented a referendum to Britain and France, demanding the withdrawal of all their troops. And in February of the same year, the two countries filed charges against Britain and France to the Security Council of the United Nations. Forced by the United States, the Soviet Union and public opinions around the world, the Security Council made a resolution that required foreign troops to withdraw from Syria and Lebanon immediately. The last French and Britain forces withdrew in August 1946.

---

12   There are currently 22 members: Algeria, Bahrain, Comoros, Djibouti, Egypt, Iraq, Jordan, Kuwait, Lebanon, Libya, Mauritania, Morocco, Oman, Pakistan, Qatar, Saudi Arabia, Somalia, Sudan, Syria, Tunisia, United Arab Emirates, and Yemen.
13   Stavrianos, L. S. *Global Rift: The Third World Comes of Age*. New York: William Morrow & Co, 1981: 692.

After the war, Iraq joined in the fight against British colonial rule. Although it was declared in 1932 by the League of Nations that Iraq would no longer be a League of Nations mandate under British control, Iraq remained a satellite of Britain under the terms of the Anglo-Iraqi Treaty of 1930. When the war first ended, Iraqi people conducted national struggles to abolish the treaty and drive out British troops. Pressed by Iraqi people's anti-Britain campaigns, the British reduced the troops deployed but still attempted to fool the Iraqi people with a new treaty to hold its control over Iraq. On January 15, 1948, the United Kingdom and the Iraqi government signed the Portsmouth Treaty of 1948 which would last 20 years. The treaty stipulated that the U.K. agreed to retreat its army except in special periods when Britain was allowed to send troops to Iraq and establish Anglo-Iraqi Joint Committee of Defense, responsible for making joint strategies and training troops.[14] After the treaty, many cities witnessed the outbreak of demonstrations and armed uprisings. The great pressure forced the Prime Minister Gabre, the one who signed the treaty, to resign and the Parliament to reject the treaty. The struggles of the Iraqi people foiled the British conspiracy of keep enslaving them and safeguarded national independence.

Iran, the oil-rich country, witnessed the fight for national independence and oil nationalization, as Iran's oil industry was basically seized by the British at that time. Influenced by the campaign for independence in Syria and Lebanon, from 1950 to early 1951, Iraq saw the breaking out of large-scale movements for the abolishment of unequal concession treaties and oil nationalization. The Iranian people set up the Liberation Association of Iran and the National Association against the Anglo-Iranian Oil Company. On March 15, 1952, the Iranian Congress passed the oil nationalization plan. It was denied by the British government, who sent warships into the Persian Gulf for intimidation. The Anglo-Iranian Oil Company made the decision to pay 30% less of subsidies to Iranian oil workers. As a consequence, the end of March saw a great strike by the oil workers. On April 29, 1951, Mohammad Mosaddegh, the leader of the National Front of Iran, assumed the position of the Prime Minister, speeding up the pace of oil nationalization. In June, the Mosaddegh government took over the Anglo-Iranian Oil Company and renamed it the National Iranian Oil Company. Britain kept imposing military pressure on Iran on the one hand and economic blockade against it on the other, embargoing oil products from Iran, freezing Iranian deposits in British banks and forcing bankruptcy out of Iran's oil industry. It also pressed a charge against the Iranian government to the United Nations. All these pressures being coupled with some errors of the Mosaddegh government, as a result, on August 19, 1953, the government was toppled in a coup d'état by some pro-West groups with vested interests under the support of Britain and the US. The new Zahedi government resumed the diplomatic relationship with the United Kingdom and sold oil resources to oil companies of Britain, US and Netherlands. By then, the robust oil nationalization activities in Iran were set back. Through twists and turns, the victory of oil nationalization in Iran was achieved in 1973.

---

14 Longrigg, S. H. *Iraq: 1900-1950*, 1977: 742-743.

5.4.2. The Intricate Israeli-Palestine Issues

In this period, the most significant event in the Middle East was the question of Palestine, from which derived the birth of Israel and the first Middle East War between Israel and Palestine. Palestine is a geographic region in Western Asia between the Mediterranean Sea and the Jordan River, covering about 27,000 km^2. This region encompasses complicated ethnic groups and religious elements with it being the birthplace and junction of Judaism, Christianity and Islam and the Holy City-Jerusalem being the hot spot for fight among the three religions. Jews were the first residents here, but fled their home and started to drift around in Europe in the mid 2nd century BC after encountering fierce suppressions from the Romans for their fight against the Roman rule. During the past 1800 years, a number of ethnic groups inhabited in this region with the Arabians being the creator of history and culture in the most recent hundreds of years. The Jews in their long exile encountered discrimination and persecution in their inhabited countries due to differences in religion, nationality, economy and politics. All major European countries witnessed cruel anti-Semitism movements. The most recent and also the largest-scale one was the so-called Endlösung (Holocaust) by the German Nazi, killing over 6million Jews in Europe. At the end of the 19th century, the rise of Zionism, the national movement of the Jewish people started in Europe seeking to recreate a Jewish state in Palestine. In 1896 Theodor Herzl, a Hungarian playwright published Der Judenstaat (The Jewish State), in which he asserted that the solution to growing antisemitism in Europe (the so-called Jewish Question) was to establish a Jewish state in the Palestine region. In 1897, under his leadership in Basel, Switzerland, the Zionist Organisation was founded and the First Zionist Congress proclaimed its aim "to establish a home for the Jewish people in Palestine secured under public law."[15] Since then, the Zionism grew from a scattered local thought to an organized international political movement of nationalism. But this movement ever since the beginning was over-dependent on the British government, who offered its support during World War to acquire economic assistance from the Jewish people and to consolidate itself in Palestine. On November 2, 1917, Arthur James Balfour, the then British Foreign Minister wrote to a leader of the Zionist movement a public letter, which stated that the British government viewed with favor the establishment in Palestine of a national home for the Jewish people, and would try the utmost for its realization[16]. The letter later became known as the noted Balfour Declaration, which gained approval of other Western nations. In 1922, the US Congress passed the resolution of establishing a national home for the Jewish people.

In 1922, after being awarded a mandate over Palestine, it acted on its commitment. Supported by the British colonial authorities, Jewish people migrated from very corner of the World to settle down in this region and the number reached 445,000 by the year 1939. The large-scale settlement of Jews invoked

---

15   International Relations Institute, ed. *Referential Materials on the Issue of Palestine.*
Beijing: World Affairs Press, 1960: 1.
16   Ibid.: 5.

conflicts with the local Arabians. Considering this situation, the British government in May 1939 issued the White Paper of 1939, which stated the limitation of Jewish migration and the promise of granting autonomy to Palestine. However, attempting to replace Britain, the United States vigorously supported Zionism and imposed pressure on the United Kingdom. After the war, fully aware the trickiness of the question of Palestine, the United Kingdom requested that it be handled by the United Nations in April 1947. After long-time discussion, on November 29, 1947, the United Nations, voting 33 to 13 in favor with 10 abstentions adopted Resolution 181(II)-the Partition Plan, recommended a partition with Economic Union of Mandatory Palestine to follow the termination of the British Mandate and the withdrawal of the armed forces of the mandatory Power not later than 1 August 1948. The plan was to partition Palestine into Independent Arab state alongside a Jewish States, and the Special International Regime for the City of Jerusalem, with the first state taking up about 11,000 km2, the second about 14,000 km^2 and the City of Jerusalem and its suburb area with an area 176 km^2 being governed by the United Nations.

The Partition Plan appropriated 57% of the land to the Jewish people who only accounted for less than one third of the Palestinian residents, but left the Arabians, two thirds of the population with less than 43% of the land. The area allotted to the Jewish State was the fertile land along the coast, while the places to the Arab State were mostly barren desolated plateaus and hills. Therefore, the resolution was rejected by the Arabians in Palestine and all Arab states, with the Palestinians resorting to armed revolts and the Arab League expressing the resolution to fight against the Partition Plan. They gained the support and compassion of Britain, while the United States sided with the Jewish people. The Arabians and the Jews were caught in all-out confrontation.

On 14 May 1948, the Jewish People's Council declared the establishment of a Jewish state in Eretz Israel (The Land of Israel), to be known as the State of Israel and David Ben-Gurion took up the posts of the Prime Minister and the Defense Minister. Soon after its declaration, the United States and the Soviet Union granted diplomatic recognition to the new country. Following the announcement of the independence of the state of Israel on May 14, 1948, the Arab-Israeli War of 1948 broke out when five Arab League nations, Egypt, Iraq, Lebanon, Syria and Transjordan invaded territory in the former Palestinian mandate in protests against the sacrifice of the Palestinian Arab population's interests for the establishment of the State of Israel. The war basically concluded by July, only sporadic battles continued until 1949. Israel signed Armistice Agreements with Egypt, Transjordan, Syria and Lebanon respectively from February to July in 1949. After this war, in addition to the UN-partitioned area allotted to the Jewish state, Israel captured and incorporated a further 6,700 km^2 land. Transjordan retained possession of a Palestinian area of 5,000 km^2 and Egypt took control of the 345 km^2 Gaza Strip. Jerusalem was divided, with Transjordan taking the eastern parts and Israel taking the western parts. The war turned almost a million of Palestinians into refugees.

The 1948 Arab-Israel War came to an end with the Arab countries being devastated, which brought about significant changes to Israel in its contrast with the Arab nations. It was the prelude to endless conflicts between the two sides on the question of Palestine and a situation-changer for the contention among Western countries in this region. The United States firmly supported and controlled Israel, forming the root of the continuous turmoil in this region; the United Kingdom took the opportunity to infiltrate Egypt, Iraq and Jordan; while France fought for Syria in the name of weapon supply. To guarantee their vested interests, the three countries in May 1950 on the London Council of Foreign Ministers issued a joint declaration, stating a full recognition of the current Arab-Israel Armistice Line and opposition against any disruption from any country.

5.5. Africa Began Its Independence Movement

5.5.1. Independence Movements in North Africa

When World War II concluded, only three African countries, Ethiopia, Liberia and Egypt were independent, while over 90% of the African continent were still under the control of Britain, France, Belgium, Portuguese and other long-established colonizers. After the war, independence movements witnessed unbalanced development across Africa. Generally speaking, in terms of the time of starting independence movements to gaining victory, North African countries ranked among the top, nations in West, East and Middle Africa came as the second, while South African ones lagged behind, but with some exceptions. This imbalance derived from the differences in politics, economy, social terms and colonial policies.

Located near the Eurasia, North Africa had a long history of fighting against colonizers and performed as a vital battlefield in the anti-fascist war during World War II, providing excellent practice for the people there. Therefore, the national independence movement in Africa initiated in North Africa.

Libya was the first country in Africa to gain its independence after the war. Before the war, it was colonized by Italy and became the battlefield for the fight between Britain, France and the US on the one side and Germany on the other. The long-term fight against Italian colonialism gave birth to a number of prestigious political organizations enjoying extensive mass base, including Senussi Muslim Order, Tripolitania National Congress and Pro-Progress Association. After the war, Britain and France successively set up military governments in Libya and the US established military base there. At the end of 1947, under the peace treaty with the Allies, Italy relinquished all claims on Libya. Later, Britain and Italy proposed the partition of Libya and be under the trusteeship of the United Nations. On May 7, 1949, Italy and Britain secretly signed the Bevin-Sforza Agreement, stating that Cyrenaica would fall under the trusteeship of Britain, Tripolitania under Italy and Fezzan under the trusteeship of France; and after ten years of trusteeship, Libya would be granted independence but only with the approval of the General Assembly of the United Nations[17]. This agreement received firm opposition from Libyan people of all circles. In May 1949, the Pro-Progress Association sent a telegram to the United Nations, demanding the establishment of an independent and unified Libya. In November, people in Tripolitania conducted a massive demonstration, chanting "Down with the British Imperialists" and "Long Live the Unified Libya". On November 21, 1949, the United Nations passed the resolution on Libya, which promulgated the handover of political power from the British and French military governments to the Libyan government andapproved the granting of independence to it. On December 24, 1949, Libya declared its independence as the United Kingdom of Libya, a constitutional and hereditary monarchy ruled by King Idris.

Tunisia was colonized by France in 1881. In the long fight against colonialism, the Tunisians formed a nationalist organization with the Neo-Destour Party as the core. After the war, under the leadership of the Neo-Destour Party, the Tunisians held conferences to fight for independence and conducted strikes across the nation, imposing great pressure on the French government. Initially, the French colonial government resorted to violent suppressions, but later shifted to deceptive "reforms". But the Tunisians stuck to struggles for absolute political independence. In January 1952, the fearless Tunisian patriots built guerrilla forces to conduct armed fights in the southeast and central regions. In 1954, the Neo-Destour Party led and organized the National Liberation Army for armed struggles as well. France was compelled to promise Tunisia independence. On March 20, 1956, after negotiations, France and Tunisia reached an agreement, acknowledging Tunisia as an independent country. April 1956 saw the establishment of an independent government in Tunisia. In July 1957, the monarchy was abolished and Tunisia proclaimed a Republic. But French garrison remained there.

Morocco, the French Protectorate, also witnessed fierce fights against the Imperialists. On March 30, 1921, France forced Morocco to accept the Treaty of Trez, which made Morocco a protectorate of France. The Moroccans set that day as a shameful day, on which grand demonstrations were hold annually to protest against French colonizers. After the war, Morocco nationalist parties, such as the Communist Party, the Independence Party and the Independence Democratic Party, all came up with slogans like "Abolishing the Protectorate System" and "Achieving National Independence". To deal with the independence movements, The French attempted to employ the means of division and demoralization. But before October 1954, Morocco witnessed national strikes and attacks on the warehouses and motor squadrons of the French colonial troops, capture of the Atlas Mountains in the central region and liberation of some towns and cities by the guerrilla forces organized by patriots. The Moroccans also won the support of the Sultans. The French colonial authorities

---

17   Lu, Tingen, and Kunyuan Peng, eds. *A History of Africa*. The Modern Volume. Shanghai: East China Normal University Press, 1995: 263.

were compelled to sign with the Morocco government in March 1956 the French-Morocco Agreement, declaring the independence of Morocco. But French continued to enjoy diplomatic and garrison privileges in Morocco.

The July Revolution in Egypt marked the most influential event on the African and Arab world of that period. The revolt led the United Kingdom government to declare Egypt's independence, but retained many privileges in Egypt. From 1945 to 1946, workers, farmers, intellectuals and national bourgeois conducted movements demanding the abolishment of the 1936 Anglo-Egyptian Treaty and complete withdrawal of the British troops. In 1948 during the first Middle East War, King Farouk and his treacherous group, proceeding from their self-interests, conveyed inferior arms and ammunitions to the front, causing crushing defeats for the Egyptian troops. This cast light on the fact that "the greatest battlefield was in Egypt"[18] and that complete independence would be impossible unless the pro-British feudal dynasty was overthrew for people with vision. In January 1950, Egypt saw the holding of the parliamentary election, in which the Wafd Party who maintained a great tradition of safeguarding the constitution proposed the guideline of monitoring the Anglo-Egyptian Treaty and demanding the complete withdrawal of British troops. The guideline gained popularity among the people and won the election for the Party. Driven by the Wafd Party, on October 15, 1951, the Egyptian Parliament declared the abolishment of the Anglo-Egyptian Treaty and the 1899 Anglo-Egyptian Sudan Agreement. These measures brought Egypt with all-rounded invasion from the British army, navy and air forces. Britain forced King Farouk to suppress the anti-Britain struggles of the Egyptian people as well. At this juncture of national survival, the Free Officers Movement founded during World War II and led by Gamal Abdel Nasser, on July 23,1952 conducted military uprising and overthrew the Farouk Dynasty. On June 18, 1953, the newly-founded government officially abolished the monarchy and declared the Egyptian Republic. It confiscated royal family's land and possessions, abrogated classes and noble titles, purged old national institutions and promulgated a decree on land reform at home. In dealing with foreign relations, the government unswervingly safeguarded the national sovereignty. In October 1954, Egypt signed with Britain the Anglo-Egyptian Agreement on Suez Canal Base Zone, demanding the complete withdrawal of the British troops no later than October 1956. Egypt later regained its sovereignty over the Suez Canal and nationalized foreign monopoly capital in Egypt. The struggle level of the Egyptian people symbolized the peak of post-war national liberation movements in Africa. Their victory exerted significant impacts on the national liberation movements in the world, particularly in other African countries.

---

18 Dakemejian, R. H. *Egypt under Nasser Rule*. London, 1978: 6.

5.5.2. The Awakening of Sub-Saharan Africa

Sub-Saharan Africa, when the war first ended, saw movements fighting for political independence in Gold Coast (now Ghana), Guinea, Senegal and Kenya. But generally speaking, the struggle level here was much lower than that of North Africa. In Sub-Saharan Africa, unified national awareness was not yet formed with various tribes, which rarely contacted each other and were governed by patriarchal clan system. Real national bourgeois and proletariats barely existed and the organizations of the independence movements were based on tribe relations and mainly led by petite bourgeoisie and intellectuals who received modern western education. Therefore, initially the most influential liberation thought was not nationalism but Pan-Africanism, which advocated the fight against racial discrimination and colonial rule and the liberation and great unity of all black people across the world. This thought had profound impact on many independence movement leaders in Sub-Saharan Africa (such as Francis Nwia Kwame Nkrumah in Ghana and Uhuru Kenyatta in Kenya).

When the war first concluded, there was no newly-independent country in Sub-Saharan Africa, only some nations, like Gold Coast, Nigeria and Uganda, witnessed large-scale strikes and mass movements but without any slogans of autonomy and independence. The climax of independence movements in this region did not come until the convening of the Asian-African Conference and the conduction of the decolonization campaign by Britain, France and other colonial metropolitan states. During this period, Kenya witnessed large-scale armed struggles-the Mau Mau Uprising starting in 1952. The not small number of white immigrants in Kenya took up a large quantity of fertile farmland, inducing fierce conflicts with the local people on the issue of land. Mau Mau was a secret anti-colonial organization formed by the Kenyan Kikuyu tribe and the Mau Mau Uprising lasted for our years. The British government spent as much as 160 million pounds on the 140,000 military guards to suppress the uprising, killing over 10,000 African residents and putting over 100,000 people in concentration camps[19]. The Mau Mau Uprising spread across the Central Province, Eastern Province, Rift Valley Province, and parts of Nyanza Province. The main force of the uprising was peasants and their major weapons against British colonial armies were home-made guns, cannons, bows and arrows, and lances. "The uprising, though it led to sickening excesses on both sides, did force the British to recognize the futility of attempting to follow a conciliatory policy in West Africa and a rigid one in the East".[20] The British released the outstanding Kikuyu leader, Uhuru Kenyatta, and the new type of independence movement leader who received classic British education won the majority in the general election and led Kenya towards independence in 1963.

19   Liang, Zhicheng, et al. *Before and After the British Empire Retreated from Hongkong*. Hongkong: Xintian Publishing House, 1993: 190.
20   Stavrianos, L. S. *The World since 1500: A Global History*. Prentice Hall, 1999: 597.

5.6. Situation in Latin America

Traditionally, Latin America was within the influence sphere of the United States, which considered Latin America as a chunk of meat for its exclusive consumption. During World War II, under the pretext of "mutual assistance and cooperation in defense", the United States signed bilateral or multilateral treaties with Latin American countries, thus pushing out British and French forces and enhancing its economic and political control over these countries. After the war, the United States signed new military alliance treaties on the one hand, including Latin America in its strategic plan; on the other hand, it shifted from direct plunder to new colonial approaches like "assistance", unequal trade and cultivating pro-America agents. Since these agents were mainly local exploiters carrying out treacherous policies and doctorial rule, the national democratic movements after the war in Latin America targeted at America monopoly capital and reactionary governments. The fight took on many forms but was dominated by strikes and demonstrations. Some countries and regions witnessed nationalization movements and even armed struggles against reactionary regimes. The national democratic movements in many countries were joined by communist parties to various extents.

After the war, with the start of the Cold War, the United States placed its priority of diplomatic strategy on opposing the Soviet Union and communist parties. In order to turn Latin America into its stable rear while seeking world hegemony and to better suppress the struggles of the Latin American people, the United States decided to piece together in Latin America a political military group under its control. On August 15, 1947, called together by America, 20 foreign ministers of Latin American countries gathered in Rio de Janeiro to hold the Inter-American Conference for the Maintenance of Peace. Pressed by the United States, September 2 saw the signing of the Inter-American Treaty of Reciprocal Assistance, promulgating that "an armed attack by any State against an American State shall be considered as an attack against all the American States and, consequently, each one of the said Contracting Parties undertakes to assist in meeting the attack in the exercise of the inherent right of individual or collective self-defense"[21]. This was the first treaty of regional military alliance nature signed by the United States in the post-war period.

America considered it urgent to enhance the inter-America system so as to strengthen the economic infiltration into and political and military control over Latin America. In March 1948, the Ninth Conference of the American States was held in Bogotá, the capital of Columbia, participated by the representatives from the United States and all 20 Latin American countries. This was the event that saw the birth of the Organization of American States replacing the Pan American Union, with the signature of the Charter of the Organization of American States. The Organization of American States is composed of an

---

21 World Affairs Press, ed. *Collections of International Treaties*. Beijing: World Affairs Press, 1961: 337-338.

Organization of American States General Secretariat, the Permanent Council, the Inter-American Council for Integral Development, and a number of committees. Since its birth, the council of foreign ministers and international conferences organized by the OAS had become the major mechanism for cooperation between the United States and Latin America. From 1952 to June 1955, the United States, through separate negotiations, concluded bilateral treaties for military reciprocal assistance with 12 Latin American states[22], thus establishing another significant mechanism for political and military cooperation with Latin American countries.

Nevertheless, Latin America did not cease and focused on sustaining national independence and sovereignty and fighting against American control and enslavement and its agents in Latin America. Thanks to such national democratic movements, from 1945 to 1948, Argentina, Brazil, Ecuador, Cuba and other countries nationalized major rail lines taken by foreign capital; Uruguay took back the transportation business and public utilities; Argentina its phone, coal gas and domestic air routes businesses; Chile its urban public transport companies and Bolivia its tin ore companies in the same period. In December 1947, the Panamanian people went on multiple massive strikes, compelling the Congress to reject the bill on prolonging the rent of the American military base and the United States to declare its withdrawal of the base and military facilities within the Canal Zone. On July 3, 1952, the mass rally of 50,000 people in the capital Santiago opposed the government's signing of the Chile-US Bilateral Agreement. In May 1954, Honduras saw the first strike by the workers in banana plantations, demanding United Fruit Company of the United States to increase salary and to improve medical conditions. In 1954, some business people in Mexico launched a campaign to protect the markets near the Mexico-US border and to oppose the smuggling of American products. On the Tenth Conference of the American States, the Mexico and Argentina representatives stuck together and refused to support the American operation of overthrowing the Arbenz government in Guatemala and to pass the declaration of opposing the threat of international communism. Armed struggles became increasingly important in Latin America. Since 1949, Columbian farmers organized guerilla forces to fight against dictatorial rule, among the six guerilla troops in the nation, four were led by the Communist Party. Farmers in Venezuela to seize land, held an uprising in 1952. Among these struggles, the most influential ones were the overthrow of the Arbenz government in Guatemala by the United States and the great uprising in Bolivia.

Guatemala, with an area of only 110,000 km^2 and a population of about 5 million, was a backward agrarian country being subject to colonial exploitation for a long time. In 1944, the national bourgeois led the people to conduct an uprising, which overthrew the pro-American dictatorial government. In

---

22 They are, in the order of signing agreements, Ecuador, Peru, Brazil, Cuba, Chile, Columbia, Uruguay, Dominica, Nicaragua, Honduras, Haiti, and Guatemala. Note by the author.

November 1950, Arbenz Guzmn, a nationalist was elected the president under the support of the Communist Party and other democratic parties. Satisfying people's demand, he carried forward a series of rather radical economic and social reforms, especially the land reform decree. The government expropriated land not only from the big landlords but also seized 4.07 million acres from the United Fruit Company of the United States. While vigorously stimulating the national economy and improving the treatment for workers at home, Arbenz adhered to independent diplomacy, withdrew from the Organization of Central American States controlled by the United States, refused to support America in its invasion in North Korea but presented goodwill to China. These measures intrigued America's extreme rancor. In June 1954, armed rebels trained by the Central Intelligence Agency of the United States entered Guatemala and over-threw the Arbenz government.

The uprising in Bolivia was another grand gesture in the 1950s history of liberation movements in Latin America. In 1950, with a population of about 5 million, Bolivia took agriculture and mining industry as the pillars of its national economy. But 80% of its farmland was in the hands of landlords and 80% of the tins were mined by three foreign companies including the Batano Mining Corporation of the United States[23]. On April 9, 1952, the Rojas military government submitted to America and was ready to send a troop of 30,000 to North Korea, thus intensifying the domestic conflict. Under the leadership of the Revolutionary Nationalist Movement and the Communist Party and its labor union, Bolivia witnessed an uprising, which overthrew the Rojas military government and organized a new government by the Revolutionary Nationalist Movement with Victor Paz Estenssoro as the president. The new government implemented a number of political and economic reforms, demobilizing the old army, organizing an army and militia for the new government and granting voting rights to its citizens aged over 20. On October 31, 1952, it passed the decree of nationalizing the tin ores and decided to nationalize the monopolistic companies. August 2, 1953 saw the pass of the land reform decree, derecognizing the land tenure. However, these measures encountered boycotts and obstructions from America monopolistic capital and large plantations, which paralyzed the tin mining business-the foundation of the national economy and caused a substantial decrease for the national income. The new government was pressed by the United States to compensate foreign-funded companies and to ensure the rights of American investors. And the land reform was put on hold since the new government dared not offend the big plantation owners. Politically, the government went rightward under domestic and foreign pressures and turned to persecute members of the Communist Party and democratic parties and to prohibit their participation in the politics. Although the national democratic revolution in Bolivia was incomplete, "the 1952 Revolution still marks a significant event in modern history of Bolivia since it brought about

---

23   See Barton, Robert. *A Short History of Bolivia*, Shenyang: Liaoning People's Publishing House, 1975: 375.

fundamental changes. Understanding the significance of this revolution is essential to understand the current Bolivia. It has fundamentally transformed the Bolivian economic structure, from a semi-colonial and dependent economy controlled by private capital with limitless privileges to an economy, wherein over 70% of it was controlled by the state"[24].

24 Li, Chunhui, et al. *A History of Latin America*. Vol. 3. Beijing: The Commercial Press, 1993: 509.

Chapter VI

The Making of the North-South Political Structure

6.1. The Awakening of the Third World

The 1950s and 1960s witnessed robust development in the national liberation activities in countries in Asia, Africa and America and the countries generally achieved political independence and awakening. And a number of Asian and African countries stepped on the historical stage as a member of the international society. However, even with the collapse of the old colonial system, the long-established colonizers still put up the last fight for their reluctance to give up the previous colonial interests; and the new world powers in every form possible strived to "fill up the vacuum" and encompass the newly-founded nations in their world strategic blueprint. Besides, the collapse of the old colonial system left the newly independent countries with negative impacts from the fight and invasion of the colonizers, which induced instability and border, ethnic and racial issues within or among the new countries. Therefore, under this circumstance, these nations had to not only safeguard political independence and live up to the urgent demand of developing national economies, but also strengthen unity and cooperation with each other in the area of fighting against foreign intervention so as to exert positive and significant influence on the international landscape as a whole and to realize common aspirations and demands.

The first independent countries pioneered this move. China and India, to resolve their border issues, in December 1953 in Beijing held a negotiation, in which former Chinese Premier Zhou Enlai proposed five principles for dealing with Sino-Indian border issues. In June 1954, Premier Zhou Enlai during his visits to India and Myanmar in the joint declarations with Indian and Burmese Prime Ministers officially put forward the Five Principles of Peaceful Coexistence, which provides for mutual respect for each other's territorial integrity and sovereignty; mutual non-aggression; mutual non-interference in each other's internal affairs; equality and cooperation for mutual benefit; and peaceful co-existence. The Sino-Indian Joint Declaration proposed that "these principles be applicable not only to relations between nations, but also to the general international relationship, and then indeed there would hardly be any conflict and certainly no war."[1] While the Sino-Myanmese Joint Declaration expressed the hope that "these principles be observed by all nations, so that the threat of and fear for invasion and intervention in domestic affairs would be replaced by security and mutual trust"[2]. This new type of principles for international relations received great attention and resonance among the Third World countries, which considered it as the Charter of Asia. The Five Principles of Peaceful Coexistence laid a solid foundation for the friendly cooperation among Asian and African countries.

6.1.1. The Asian-African Conference and the Bandung Spirit

Following the robust national liberation movements in Asia and Africa, the request for more extensive cooperation among countries in this region was brought up on the agenda. (The Asian-African Conference, also known as the Bandung Conference, was held in Bandung, Indonesia from 18 to 24 April, 1955.) In March 1954, the Indonesian Government proposed the convocation of an Asian-African conference. This proposition received active support from India, Burma, Indonesia, Pakistan and Ceylon at meetings participated by the Prime Ministers of the five countries in Colombo-the capital of Ceylon from April 2nd to May 2nd. In December of the same year, in order to discuss preparatory work for the conference, the five Prime Ministers held a conference in Bogor, Indonesia and reached an agreement on convening an Asian-African conference and decided that the conference would be jointly proposed by the five countries. The conference was attended by 29 Asian and African countries besides the five countries mentioned above, namely, Afghanistan, Cambodia, China, Egypt, Ethiopia, the Gold Coast (Ghana), Iran, Iraq, Japan, Jordan, Laos, Lebanon, Liberia, Libya, Nepal, the Philippines, Saudi Arabia, Sudan, Syria, Thailand, Turkey, the Vietnam Democratic Republic, South Vietnam (later reunified with the Democratic Republic of Vietnam) and Yemen (Republic of Yemen). It was decided that the conference would be a ministerial-level one.

---

1 "Joint Statement between Premier of the People's Republic of China and that of the Republic of India." *Xinhua Monthly* 7(1954): 52.
2 Ibid.: 53.

Being clearly written in the Joint Declaration and the invitation letters, the objectives of the conference include: "1. Promoting amicability and cooperation among nations in Asia and Africa, discussing and enhancing mutual and common interests and establishing and strengthening friendly and neighborly relationship; 2. Discussing the economic, social and cultural issues and relations of the attending nations; 3. Exploring issues of special interests to people in Asian and African countries, such as nationalism, racialism and colonialism; 4. Talking about the contributions made by Asian and African countries and their people to world peace and cooperation."[3]

The decision of convening this conference attracted worldwide attention. While people in Asia and Africa responded enthusiastically to and international progressive opinions cheered for it, Western countries were shocked and unsettled. They were in fear of the formation of a new and independent international force of Asia and African countries on the basis of mutual assistance and recognition. The newspaper, Saint Louis Postal Dispatch from the United States put it bluntly: "We wish that there would be no Asian-African Conference at all"[4]. To obstruct the conference, in April 1955, the former US president Eisenhower exploited economic aid to newly independent countries as the decoy to draw some of the participating countries over. The U.S. also sent a big contingent of so-called press delegation to Bandung in an attempt to manipulate the conference from outside and to split the conference. But none of these kept the Asian-African Conference from convening.

From April 18 to April 24, 1955, 340 representatives from twenty-nine governments of Asian and African nations gathered in Gedung Merdeka in Bandung, Indonesia to hold the First Asian-African Conference. Former Indonesian president Sukarno delivered an opening speech entitled "Let a New Asia and a New Africa be Born", which considered the conference as the "first intercontinental meeting participated by colored people in human history"[5] and appealed to the great number of Asian and African countries to enhance solidarity and cooperation in every aspect. The agenda of the conference consists of economic cooperation, human rights, self-governance, dependent states and promoting peace and cooperation. Most countries conducted full deliberation on the subjects of the conference, but the conference did not go all smoothly due to differences in social systems, ideologies and development levels of the attending countries, which led to divergences in opinions and viewpoints. And even more importantly, some Western powers tried to use the differences and the barrier caused by long-time colonial rule among these countries to alter the purpose and direction of the conference and to make sure no agreement comes out of it. For example, the representative of Iraq, Muhammad Fadhel al-Jamali with the support of Western powers indicated the end of colonialism and that

219

3   "Joint Communique of the Five Prime Ministers in South Asia." *Xinhua Monthly* 1955/1): 164.
4   "The Conspiracy of Spoilers of the Asian-African Conference." *People's Daily* 1 April 1955.
5   World Affairs Press, ed. *Collected Documents of the Asian-African Conference.* Beijing: World Affairs Press, 1955: 12.

the task of Asian and African countries was not fighting against colonialism but communism at the conference. Some countries even alluded to and attacked and condemned China and other countries which carried forward neutral foreign policies.

Faced with this situation, the delegations of China of many other countries worked together and made great contributions to settling differences and guaranteeing the conference purposes. In the afternoon of April 14, Premier Zhou Enlai delivered a speech, in which he put forward the celebrated principle of "seeking common ground while reserving differences". He clearly stated: The Chinese Delegation has come here to seek unity and not to quarrel, to seek common ground and not to create divergences. There exists common ground among the Asian and African countries the basis of which is that the overwhelming Asian and African countries and their peoples have suffered and are still suffering from the calamities of colonialism. All the Asian and African countries gained their independence from colonialist rule whether these countries are led by the communist or nationalists. We should seek to understand each other and respect each other, sympathize with and support one another[6]. During the Conference, the Chinese Delegation advocated the principle of seeking common ground while putting aside differences which not only won the support of an overwhelming number of delegates but also laid the ground for the success of the Conference.

April 24 saw successful conclusion of the conference and the adoption of a "Final Communiqué", the contents of which included economic cooperation, cultural cooperation, human rights and self-determination, the issue of people in dependent countries, other issues, promotion of world peace and cooperation as well as the adoption of the Declaration on Promotion of World Peace and Cooperation. In the declaration, for peaceful coexistence and friendly cooperation among all nations, ten principles were listed, which covers:

1. Respect for fundamental human rights and for the purpose and principles of the Charter of the United Nations;
2. Respect for the sovereignty and territorial integrity of all countries;
3. Recognize the equality of all races and the equality of all nations,
4. No-intervention in the internal affairs of other countries;
5. Respect for the right of each nation to defend itself singly or collectively, in conformity with the Charter of the United Nations.
6. (a) Abstention from the use of arrangements of collective defence to serve any particular interests of the big powers. (b) Abstention by any countries from exerting, pressures on other countries.
7. Refraining from acts or threats of aggression or the use of force against the territorial integrity or political independence of any countries.
8. Settlement of all international disputes by peaceful means, such as negotiation, conciliation, arbitration or judicial settlement as well as

---

6   *Xinhua Monthly* April 1955.

other peaceful means of the parties' own choice, in conformity with the Charter of the United Nations.

9. Promotion for mutual interest and cooperation.
10. Respect for justice and international obligation.

The Asian-African Conference, an unprecedented event, was the first international meeting without the participation of any western country. It symbolized the awakening and solidarity of the people in Asia and Africa, demonstrated the fruitful results of nationalist movements when the war first concluded and drove the fight for independence of Asian and African countries to a new climax. The period from 1956 to 1965 witnessed as many as 33 nations gained independence in Asia and Africa. The spirit of unity of the Asian and African people, opposing imperialism and colonialism, struggling for the defense of national independence and world peace and the promotion of friendship among the peoples as demonstrated at the Conference is known as the Bandung Spirit. The Conference imposed significant impact on the world economic and political landscape after the World War II. Not only did it clash the post-war bipolar structure, but also ushered in the new epoch of South-South Cooperation. The ideas and principles for economic cooperation among developing countries in Asia and Africa initiated at the conference were all put into practice in the subsequent South-South Cooperation.

After the Bandung Conference, the national movements in Asia and Africa became even more robust, creating more independent countries. The international situation underwent significant changes with the US and the Soviet Union confronting and struggling with each other in a global context. The wide regions of neutral zone turned into an important target of their fight, making the newly independent countries the object of threat or cozying up to world powers. But rather than being included in the power struggle between the political groups, most nations preferred solidarity and cooperation with each other and a peaceful and neutral foreign policy of non-alignment. It gave rise to the Non-aligned Movement.

6.1.2. The Rise and Development of Non-Aligned Movement

As early as in December 1949, the Vice President of the Socialist Federal Republic of Yugoslavia, Edward Kardelj, referring to its foreign policy, addressed the Parliament as follows: "Yugoslavia will neither join any military group nor take part in any invasion plans against any country." In March 1951, Indian Prime Minister Nehru in his address to the Parliament advocated non-aligned foreign policy and opposed alignment of any form. From the end of 1954 to the early 1955, the President of Yugoslavia, Josip Broz Tito, visited India and Burma and in an important speech to the Indian Parliament, proposed the idea of Non-aligned Movement. It was followed by the publication of a joint declaration by Nehru and Tito who announced to abide by "non-alignment policy" and pointed out that non-alignment was not a synonym to "neutral" or "neutralism", but "a positive and constructive policy with the objective of collective peace and only it can realize the objective". These efforts and the principles and the spirit of Bandung originated in the Bandung Conference laid solid foundation for the rise of Non-aligned Movement.[7]

From 18 July to 19 July 1956, the idea of non-alignment was further defined when the Yugoslavia President Tito, the Egyptian President Nasser and the Indian President Nehru met in Brijuni, Yugoslavia. The presidents also reached consensus with the Indonesian President Sukarno and the President of Ghana Nkrumah through negotiations. From February to April 1961, in his visit to nine African countries, Tito came up with the suggestion of holding a conference of heads of states of non-aligned countries. Subsequently, a preparatory meeting for the First NAM Summit Conference was held in Cairo, Egypt from 5 to 12 June 1961. At this meeting, participants discussed the goals of a policy of nonalignment, which were adopted as criteria for membership. These were as follows:

1. The country should have adopted an independent policy based on the coexistence of States with different political and social systems and on non-alignment or should be showing a trend in favor of such a policy;

2. The country concerned should be consistently supporting the Movements for national independence;

3. The country should not be a member of a multilateral military alliance concluded in the context of Great Power conflicts;

222 4. If a country has a bilateral military agreement with a Great Power, or is a member of a regional defense pact, the agreement or pact should not be one deliberately concluded in the context of Great Power conflicts;

5. If it has conceded military bases to a Foreign Power the concession should not have been made in the context of Great Power conflicts.

The first Conference of Non-Aligned Heads of State or Government of the Non-Aligned Movement, at which 25 countries[8] were represented, was convened at Belgrade in September 1961. The conference saw the adoption of the Declaration of the Heads of State or Government of Non-Aligned Countries, which considered that the non-aligned countries should fully support righteous struggles for gaining or safeguarding national independence since a lasting peace could only be achieved only if imperialism and colonialism in all there manifestations were radically eliminated, the only way to replace the Cold War and to avoid any possible comprehensive nuclear disaster was sticking to the principle of peaceful coexistence, non-aligned nations that adhered to independent and peaceful foreign policies were significant forces to the preservation of world peace and ease of international tensions, these countries should

---

7   Qtd. in Yuan, Changyao, ed. *Contemporary International Relations*. Nanjing: Jiangsu Education Press, 1993: 261.

8   They were Afghanistan, Burma, Cambodia, Ceylon (Sri Lanka), India, Indonesia, Iraq, Lebanon, Nepal, Cyprus, Saudi Arabia, and Yemen in Asia; Algeria, Ethiopia, Ghana, Guinea, Mali, Morocco, Somalia, Sudan, Tunisia, United Arab Republic, and Congo in Africa; Cuba in Latin America; and Yugoslavia in Europe. Note by the author.

actively participate in affairs regarding world peace and security, the widening gap between the developed and developing nations needed to be bridged, the participating countries of the conference should strengthen economic and commercial cooperation to boycott the stressful policies held by the large powers in international economic activities[9]. The convocation of the conference unveiled the Non-Aligned Movement with independence, non-alignment and non-group as the fundamental principles.

Subsequent summit conferences, being held every three years, act as the major form of organization and performance. Till 1998, twelve such conferences have been convened and participated by 113 countries. As the fight for winning and safeguarding national independence in the Third World moved forward and the international situation evolved, the contents and missions of the Non-aligned Movement kept enriching and progressing. At the 1961 Summit, the idea of holding a special General Assembly on disarmament was initiated. The 1964 Conference featured widespread condemnation of Western colonialism and the establishment of new international economic order for the first time. The 1970 Summit covered a denunciation of the arms race between the super powers and their intervention and subversion towards small countries and proposed the idea of breaking the old international economic order through "collective self-reliance" of the developing countries. And racial discrimination in South Africa was condemned in unequivocal terms at the 8th summit in 1986. The rise of the NAM symbolized the third world stepping onto the global stage as an independent political entity, which greatly crashed the post-war bipolar landscape. The Third World countries became the "third force" free from the confrontation between the super powers.

6.1.3.The Group of 77 and Its Fight for A New International Economic Order

In the atmosphere of solidarity and cooperation owing to the Asian-African Conference and the Non-Aligned Movement, the developing countries started a number of international economic organizations or leagues for beneficial cooperation and struggles against the old international economic order featuring inequality. These organizations comprise the International Tea Committee founded in 1955, the Organization of Petroleum Exporting Countries in September 1960, the Inter-African Coffee Organization with 17 African countries in December 1960, the Central American Common Market in December 1960 and the Association of Southeast Asian Nations in July 1961. Among them, the Group of 77 is the only significant international organization featuring the Third World countries as a whole resisting the economic hegemony of the developed nations, conducting North-South dialogue, pushing for South-South cooperation and fighting for a new global economic order that is favorable to them.

9   See "Declaration of the first Conference of Non-Aligned Heads of State or Government." *People's Daily* 7 September 1961.

At the initiative and promotion of the NAM countries, the General Assembly of the United Nations passed on December 8, 1963 the resolution of holding the Conference on Trade and Development. while the idea of having such a conference was being deliberated at the 18th General Assembly in 1963, 73 countries in Asia, Africa and Latin America, the Socialist Federal Republic of Yugoslavia and the New Zealand issued a declaration, vigorously advocating the holding of a conference on trade and development, thus the countries were then referred to as the Group of 75. At their request, the General Assembly at the end appointed the Economic and Social Council to take charge of the Conference on Trade and Development of the year next. From March to June in 1964, the first Conference on Trade and Development of the United Nations took place in Geneva. It was participated by 120 countries and dominated by the large number of developing nations. Their representatives strongly condemned the developed countries of the West for seizing and plundering their natural resources and sustaining an unreasonable system of prices in international trade, thus holding the developing countries in a disadvantaged position in international trade. Therefore, to enhance the force of struggling with the developed countries, on the basis of previous 75 developing countries, 77 developing countries[10] signed the Joint Declaration of the Seventy-Seven Developing Countries, which calls for the developing nations to dispense with the oppression, exploitation and plundering of colonizers and imperialists for their own economic development and to negotiate with the developed countries together. Its issuance symbolized the official formation of the Group of 77. With the efforts of G-77, the United Nations made at the end of 1964 the Conference on Trade and Development of the United Nations a permanent body of the General Assembly which holds every four years. Meanwhile, the United Nations Trade and Development Council was recognized as the executive body of the conference and its Secretariat was located in Geneva.

In October 1967, prior to the second Conference on Trade and Development of the United Nations, G-77 held the first "Ministerial Meeting, which adopted the Charter of Algiers and the slogan of "Establishing a New International Economic Order". In April 1974, the sixth Special Session of the United Nations passed the Declaration on the Establishment of a New International Economic Order and the Programme of Action on the Establishment of a New International Economic Order drafted by the G-77. The declaration pointed out that the new world economic order should be based on "equality, mutual benefit, equal sovereignty, mutual dependence, common interests and cooperation", while the action program determined a series of vital principles and goals for establishing a new international economic order, for example, every country enjoys the right of equally participating in resolving world economic issues and permanent sovereignty over its natural resources and economic activities, the monopoly in the international market should be broken to

---

10   There were formerly 75 countries, with the withdrawal of New Zealand and the Participation of Kenya, South Korea, and South Vietnam. Note by the author.

guarantee and stabilize the exporting price of primary goods , and the barriers obstructing technology transfer from the developed countries and their unreasonable relations with the developing nations should be eliminated. On their basis, in December 1974, the 29th General Assembly of the United Nations and the Conference of Developing Countries on Raw Materials in February adopted the Charter of Rights and Obligations of National Economies and the Dakar declaration respectively. Plus with the Declaration on the Establishment of a New International Economic Order and the Programme of Action on the Establishment of a New International Economic Order, these documents are guiding the developing nations in erecting a new international economic order. The allied struggle of the Group of 77 compelled the developed nations of the West to attach greater importance to the improvement of the North-South relationship and to be more proactive towards the North-South dialogue, thus safeguarding the legitimate rights and interests of the developing nations and making great contribution to international economic cooperation. After the long course of struggles and cooperation, the developing nations stuck closer and grew more mature. The influence and activity sphere went beyond the United Nations and covered other institutions with a surge of member states, which reached 132 by 1998, making it one of the largest international organizations only second to the United Nations.

The convocation of the Asian-African Conference, the rise of the Non-Aligned Movement and the birth of the Group of 77 signify the general awakening of the developing countries and the gradual formation of the Third World. This new force, rather than being arbitrarily dominated by developed countries as before, went from strength to strength through its fight with the world powers. It thoroughly transformed the old pattern dominated by the Western nations, heavily blew the bipolar landscape in the Cold War and elevated the North-South issue to a critical component of international relationship, thus the North-South landscape took shape.

6.2. The North-South Confrontation in Southeast Asia

6.2.1. The Infiltration into and Control over Southeast Asia by the United States

As with the confrontation between the two large groups headed by the Soviet Union and the United States respectively and the remnants of the old colonial forces, while Europe entered the Cold War and other areas in Asia and Africa just started nationalist activities, Southeast Asia became a hotspot for the two large ideologies to fight over. Under these circumstances, the Southeastern Asian nations, being reluctant to be manipulated by others, were the first to conduct allied struggles and cooperation. The highlights of which were the joint resistance against the US imperialism conducted by the people of the three nations of Indochina and the establishment of the Association of Southeastern Asian Nations.

After the founding of the People's Republic of China in 1949 and other socialist countries like Vietnam and North Korea, the US who took opposing "totalitarianism" and defending the free world as its responsibility listed Southeast Asia as a key region in its global strategy. In 1949, the National Security Council, NSC 48/1 of the US stressed: "the Western Powers are both unwilling and unable to assist in resisting Russian pressure, the psychological effect may be that local resistance is weakened, with the result that the process of undermining the systems of government in that region will succeed to the extent that eventually the whole of South East Asia will fall a victim to the Commnunist advance...."[11] As for Indochina, special attention should be paid to it, evaluating its strategic significance for Japan and India. On February 27, 1950, the National Security Council issued another report reading as follows: "[a] decision to contain communist expansion at the border of Indochina must be considered as a part of a wider study to prevent communist aggression into other parts of Southeast Asia."[12] On April 10, Chairman of the Joint Chiefs of Staff Omar Bradley presented to the Secretary of Defense a memorandum, which pointed out that "[t]he mainland states of Southeast Asia also are at present of critical strategic importance to the United States because" "Southeast Asia is a vital segment in the line of containment of communism stretching from Japan towards southward and around to the Indian Peninsula"[13]. And it was believed that the rule of communism in Asia posed serious threat to the security and interests of the United States and therefore it needed to strike firmly against China's "publicity attack"

226 towards Southeast Asia. The United States confirmed the strategy as exploiting the resurrection of France in Indochina and supporting France in suppressing the national liberation movements there to extend into the area and setting up a military association of Southeast Asian nations to arouse internal fight in Asia[14]. With the aim of putting its strategy in Southeast Asia into action, establishing the military league and obstructing the peace course of Indochina, the US conducted a great number of diplomatic activities prior to the Geneva Conference. During an April 7, 1954 news conference, the former American president Dwight D. Eisenhower put forward the Domino Theory as a threat against the nations in Southeast Asia. After stressing the importance of Indochina, he illustrated the necessity of America intervening in Indochina by referring to dominoes. He said this fight was of decisive significance. If France failed, "many human beings [would] pass under a dictatorship that is inimical to the free world", "that might follow what you would call the 'falling domino' principle".[15] However, the US couldnot get what it wanted at the Geneva Conference.

---

11   "Policy Planning Staff Paper on United States Policy toward Southeast Asia." *FRUS* VII (1949): 1135.
12   "Draft Report by the National Security Council." *FRUS*,VI(1950): 745.
13   "Indochina." *FRUS* VI (1950): 781.
14   See Wang, Zusheng, ed. *History of International Relations*,.Vol. 8. Beijing: World Affairs Press, (1995): 169-170.
15   Ambrose, Stephen. *Eisenhower Volume 2: The President*. New York: Simon & Schuster, 1984: 361. Trans. Wenquan Xu, et al. Beijing: China Social Sciences Press (1989): 180-181.

The purpose of the Geneva Conference (April 26 - July 20, 1954) was to find a way to settle outstanding issues on the Korean peninsula and discuss the possibility of restoring peace in Indochina. The Soviet Union, the United States, France, the United Kingdom, and the People's Republic of China were the participants. At the conference, no declaration was adopted on the issue of the Korean peninsula. While in terms of the Indochina issue, France dispensed with the influence of the US America and adopted a pragmatic policy after it had suffered great losses in the Dien Bien Phu Battle and encountering huge pressure from the French people opposing the war. The participating countries signed the Final Declarations of the Geneva Conference and the Agreement on the Cessation of Hostilities in Vietnam, Laos and Cambodia[16], which provided for ceasefire in Indochina, withdrawal of the French troops and the participating nations respecting the sovereignty, independence, unity and territorial integrity of Vietnam, Laos and Cambodia. After the adoption of the Geneva Accord, the national resistance-war against the French of the Vietnamese was basically over. The three countries won independence and the Vietnam part north of the "provisional military demarcation line" running approximately along the 17th Parallel was liberated.

However, rather than fulfilling the Geneva Accord, the United States vigorously propped up new governments in Vietnam, in an attempt to use South Vietnam as its springboard into North Vietnam and Southeast Asia.

After long-time preparation, a foreign minister's meeting in order to arrange the collective defense of Southeast Asia was convened in September 1954 in Manila, in the capital city of the Philippines. Seven countries were brought together by the US, including Britain, France, Australia, New Zealand, the Philippines, Thailand and Pakistan. Even though the participating nations were divided into three parties with Britain and France being one of them, the US as the second party and the Asian-Pacific countries the third party, naturally conflicts occurred among them, under threat and pressure, they agreed on setting up the Southeast Asia Treaty Organization, as an organization with obvious military nature with clear targets. The meeting saw the adoption of Southeast Asia Collective Defense Treaty, or Manila Pact, in which the parties agreed as follows:

1. Each Party recognizes that aggression by means of armed attack in the treaty area against any of the Parties or against any State or territory which the Parties by unanimous agreement may hereafter designate, would endanger its own peace and safety, and agrees that it will in that event act to meet the common danger in accordance with its constitutional processes.

2. As used in this Treaty, the "treaty area" is the general area of Southeast Asia, including also the entire territories of the Asian Parties, and the general area of the Southwest Pacific not including the Pacific area north of 21 degrees

---

16   The U.S. refused to sign the final declaration. However, the U.S. delegation issued a statement alone, announcing the U.S. would not impede the implementation of Geneva Agreement with force or threat of force.

30 minutes north latitude. The Parties may, by unanimous agreement, amend this Article to include within the treaty area the territory of any State acceding to this Treaty in accordance with Article VII or otherwise to change the treaty area.

3. The Parties undertake to strengthen their free institutions and to cooperate with one another in the further development of economic measures, including technical assistance, designed both to promote economic progress and social well-being and to further the individual and collective efforts of governments toward these ends[17].

With the Mutual Defense Treaty between the US and ROC was signed by the US and the Taiwan authorities in December, 1954, the Japan US Security Treaty in 1951 and the Mutual Defense Treaty between the USand the Philippines in 1953, the US established in East Asia and Southeast Asia a military alliance. The founding of the Southeast Asia Treaty Organization was sabotage to the Geneva Accord and intensified the situation in Southeast Asia which was initially improving after the ceasefire in Indochina. The US took the place of Britain and France and directly intervened in the affairs of Indochina, which forced the people there to conduct an allied fight against the American to save their country.

6.2.2. The Wars against the United States in Indochina

In October 1955, the Ngô Đình Diệm group supported by the United States overthrew emperor Bao Dai and founded the Republic of Vietnam in which Ngô Đình Diệm assuming the positions of the Prime Minister and president. The U.S. gained hold of the economic lifeline of Vietnam by means of "aid" and helped South Vietnam build an army of hundreds of thousands of men. It also supported the South Vietnam Government (GVN) to mercilessly persecute patriots in South Vietnam. From1954 to 1960, two hundred thousand people were arrested and imprisoned and over fifteen thousand people were killed. These practices of the GVN ignited the armed struggles against it. December 1960 witnessed the formal creation of the National Liberation Front (NLF, a.k.a. the Viet Cong). With it, America involved and intervened in the Vietnamese affairs.

The resistance war against America in Indochina, dominated by the Vietnam War, can be divided into three phases. The first phase was the Kennedy years from 1961 to 1963. In 1961 when J.F. Kennedy took the office, facing the revolution in South Vietnam, he waged the war conducted by Special Forces, namely the U.S. offered the fund, weapons, instructors and counselors to equip, train and command the Vietnamese troops, which attempted to suppress the guerilla forces of the people in South Vietnam. Guided by the strategy of conducting the war by Special Forces, America on the one hand strengthened the GVN and

---

17 "Southeast Asia Collective Defense Treaty." *Compilation of Documents on the Issue of Indochina*. Beijing: World Affairs Press, 1959.

its troops to exploit them as tools of the war, and on the other carried out the Strategic Hamlets Program to transfer rural peasants to strategic hamlets for concentrated management, attempting to isolate them from contact with and influence by the NLF. However, this strategy failed to tackle the wide-spreading guerilla forces in South Vietnam. In view of the corruption, inability and unpopularity of the Ngo Dinh Diem government, in November the US secret services instigated a coup and replaced the Ngo Dinh Diem regime. The following military governments were all highly vulnerable, short-lived and dependent on the full support of the U.S., making it difficult to pull out from Vietnam.

After this strategy frustrated seriously, the US had no alternative but to send more ground troops in an attempt to expand the war, thus entering the second phase, the Lyndon B. Johnson's Escalation from 1964 to 1968. Former President Johnson, succeeding Kennedy in the post, signed National Security Action Memorandum 273, which stressed that the reason for the failure of special warfare was that the north Vietnam gave support to the guerrilla forces in the south Vietnam so that the U.S. should spare no efforts in disrupting plots directed and supported by foreign countries. The memorandum agreed to scheme for special coups against the Democratic Republic of Vietnam[18]. In early August 1964, the U.S. plotted the Gulf of Tonkin Incident, using the excuse of its warships being attacked by North Vietnam to bombard the region and expand the war. The war by Special Forces escalated to partial war of "fighting in the south and bombarding in the north".

While expanding the Vietnam War, the U.S. spread the warfare across the Indochina area. Following the Geneva Conference, it propped up pro-American forces in Laos. The year 1956 witnessed the overthrow of the coalition government participated by the Lao Patriotic Front and the establishment of a pro-American government, which was toppled when Captain Kong Le carried out a coup in 1960. A new government implementing neutralist policies was founded by Prince Souvanna Phouma. In December of the same year, the Savannakhet regime plotted by the U.S. started offensives against the new government, marking the start of civil war in Laos. In April 1961, the military aid counseling group formed by regular troops of the U.S. was sent for direct involvement in the civil war. The Lao Patriotic Front, united with the neutralists headed by Kong Le and Souvanna Phouma, conducted courageous struggles, which forced the U.S. to compromise at the Geneva Conference on the issue of Laos. In July 1962, it reluctantly signed the Geneva Accord, which provided for a neutral standing on the situation in Laos. However, for the great strategic value of Laos in Indochina War, the U.S. was not ready to give up seeking control over it. In May 1964, America instigated another coup by the right-wing armed police and forced Prime Minister Phouma into restructuring the government multiple times. In May, the U.S. army involved. And in October, the Vietnam People's Army was founded by the Lao Patriotic Front

---

18 Qtd. in Ji, Shengli. *History of Post-War International Relation.* Harbin: Heilongjiang People's Publishing House, 2002: 130.

and neutral patriotic, unveiling the courageous resistance-war against America to save their country.

The government of the Kingdom of Cambodia led by Prince Sihanouk aroused dissatisfaction of the U.S. for safeguarding its sovereignty and vigorously supporting the resistance-war against the U.S. in Vietnam and Laos. To turn around its failing war in Vietnam, the U.S. instigated the Lon Nol group to plot a coup and establish a pro-American government while Prince Sihanouk was visiting abroad on March 18, 1970. In April 30 of the same year, it sent an army of 100,000 solders formed by the US and GVN troops to invade Cambodia. During his visit in china, Prince Sihanouk organized in Beijing the Royal Government of National Union of Kampuchea.

With the aim of coordinating the resistance war against the U.S. in the three countries, at the initiative of Prince Sihanouk, the Top Conference of Indochina People was convened in April 1970 and participated by leaders of four sides (North Vietnam, South Vietnam, Laos and Cambodia) from three countries. In the joint declaration after the conference, it was stated that "in line with the principle that liberation and defense of each country is its domestic affair, all parties are alleged to support each other according to the wishes of all parties concerned and on the basis of mutual respect"[19]. It signified the new phase of joint struggles against the U.S. by the three Indochina countries.

6.2.3. The Founding of the Association of Southeast Asian Nations

While the three Indochina nations united for struggles against the U.S., the newly-independent countries in Southeast Asia also moved towards coalition. On July 31, 1961, the Association of Southeast Asia (ASA) was founded at a conference in Bangkok participated by representatives from Malaya, Thailand and the Philippines but was later handicapped by the cut of diplomatic ties between Malaya and the Philippines for territorial disputes in Sabah. In September 1963, Malaya united with Singapore, North Borneo and Sarawak, with si being added to give the new country the name of the Federation of Malaysia. Less than two years later in August 1965, Singapore was expelled from the federation and became a republic. ASEAN was inaugurated on 8 August 1967, when foreign ministers of five countries, Malaysia, the Philippines, Singapore, Thailand and Indonesia held in Bangkok the first ministerial conference and signed the ASEAN Declaration, more commonly known as the Bangkok Declaration.

The factors leading to the establishment of the ASEAN can be explored internally and externally. The internal causes came first. The ASEAN area in the 1950s and 1960s was plagued by political struggles, resulting from the long-term colonial administration by the Western countries. The centuries-long contention here among the Netherlands, Britain, Spanish and the US erased the

---

19   Qtd. in Yuan, Changyao, ed. *Contemporary International Relations*. Nanjing: Jiangsu Education Press (1995): 132.

original local political entities, disrupted ethnical layout and reshaped the political landscape. Therefore, newly-independent nations were caught in a great number of territorial and ethnical disputes, such as the Muslim issue in four southern provinces in Thailand, the territorial dispute in North Borneo among Malaysia, the Philippines and Indonesia and the successive independence of Singapore and Brunei from Malaysia. These problems induced the severance of diplomatic relationship between Malaysia and the Philippines in September 1963 and the two-year military confrontation between Indonesia and Malaysia from 1964 to 1966. "From the perspective of the evolvement of the relationship among the member states, the primary goal of the ASEAN was easing the conflicts of interests of the member states to sustain a peaceful environment in the region. The reason for the emphasis on economic and cultural cooperation in the Bangkok Declaration was that the member states were more likely to reach consensus and less likely to oppose in these areas. And in the long term, only with the development of economic cooperation can the improvement of the harmonious political relationship in the region be guaranteed"[20].

Externally, limited by the decline of its national strength, Britain publicly announced the implementation of strategic contraction and the gradual withdrawal of its troops from Malaysia and Singapore in July 1967; the U.S. pressed by the Vietnam War attempted to persuade the Southeast Asian countries to share its war obligations and enhance their own defense; the nations in Southeast countries were also anxious about the turmoil in Indochina Peninsula would spread to the area after the exit of the forces of the powers. Therefore, nations in the region accelerated their regional cooperation.

Against the international backdrop, Cold War impacts on the ASEAN were inevitable. But its member states who recently gained national independence all aspired to break away from the control of Western powers, especially the U.S., and to implement diplomatic policies of independence. The joining of Indonesia, the pioneer of Non-Aligned Movement, exerted significant influences on the ASEAN marching towards independence, self-decision and collective self-reliance.

6.3. Enhancement of China's International Status

6.3.1. Diplomatic Strategy of "Leaning to One-Side" and the Sino-Soviet Split

Impacted by the Cold War and faced with the threat of being contained and toppled by the United States, the PRC's foreign policy initially focused on its solidarity with other socialist nations. With the transformations in the international situation, putting national interests in the first place in developing foreign relations, the PRC gradually formulated a peaceful foreign policy of

---

20   See Wang, Shengzu, ed. *The History of International Relations*. Vol. 9. Beijing: World Affairs Press (1995): 244-248.

independence as a large developing nation and exerted significant influence on the formation and evolvement of the North-South relationship.

On October 1, 1949, at the founding ceremony of the People's Republic of China, President Mao Zedong solemnly announced to governments across the world: "this government is the only legal government representing all citizens of the People's Republic of China. We are happy to establish diplomatic relationship with any foreign government that abides by the principles of equality, mutual benefit and mutual respect for territorial integrity and sovereignty"[21]. Since the Communist Party of China announced the foreign policy of "allying with the socialist countries", by early 1950, the PRC forged diplomatic ties with the Soviet Union and Eastern Bloc countries. The non-socialist countries that established foreign relations with the PRC can be divided into two types: one was the neighboring countries of China, including India, Burma, Nepal and Indonesia and the other type was those had barely any contact with China, such as Norway, Denmark, Finland, Switzerland and Sweden. By the end of 1955, the PRC has established ambassadorial level diplomatic ties with 23 countries[22]. Nevertheless, the PRC was still besieged by the capitalist camp headed by America and its trading partners were limited to countries in the socialist camp, the Soviet Union in particular.

The Sino-Soviet relationship went through twists and turns. On February 14, 1950, the Chinese Prime Minister Zhou Enlai signed with the foreign minister of the Soviet Union Vyshinsky the Sino-Soviet Treaty of Friendship, Alliance and Mutual Assistance and the Sino-Soviet Agreement on Changchun railway, Port Arthur and Dalian, which symbolized the inauguration of the alliance between the PRC and the Soviet Union. It had a great significance to the consolidation of the new regime of the PRC by foiling the imperialists' blockade and isolation against the PRC and speeding up the recovery and development of economy in China.

The Sino-Soviet relationship was characterized by friendliness from 1949 to 1957. In this period, the two countries cooperated in diplomacy and struggled together for the security of the socialist countries and peace in Asia and the world at large. Particularly, during the Korean War and the Resistance War against the US forces in Indochina, the two countries firmly supported the fights of the Korean and Indochina people and contributed to the resolution of restoring peace in Indochina at Geneva Conference in 1954. During the period short after the 20th Congress of the Communist Party of the Soviet Union witnessed the Hungarian Revolution of 1956, which led to tensions between the Soviet Union and some East European countries. In those days the leaders of the CPC visited the Soviet Union and the socialist countries in East

---

21 Chinese Foreign Ministry and Party Literature Research Center of CPC Central Committee, eds. *Mao Zedong on Diplomacy*. Beijing: Central Party Literature Press, 1994: 116.
22 Although the U.K. and Holland acknowledge the newly founded PRC, they only established charged'affaires level relations with China due to their anti-China stance. Note by the author.

Europe, assisting the former in properly dealing with the relationship among socialist nations. China, while condemning the chauvinism conducted by the Soviet Union, tried hard to strike a great balance between the healthy maintenance of solidarity among socialist countries and maintenance of the authority of the Soviet Union in the socialist camp. It led to the successful convocation and conclusion of the Moscow Conference by the 12 Communist and Workers Parties of Socialist countries, in Moscow in November 1957.[23]

In terms of economy and culture, China and the Soviet Union signed four agreements on the establishment of Sino-Soviet joint stock companies in March 1950 and July 1951 respectively.[24] And the Sino-Soviet Trade Agreement was forged in April 1950 in Moscow. In May 1953, during his visit to the Soviet Union, the former Vice-President Li Fuchun entered with the Soviet Union agreements and protocols concerning it aiding China in the development of the national economy. The Soviet Union promised to help China to build or rebuild 141 major projects, provide systematic economic and technological assistance and receive a large number of Chinese students and interns to study there. In October 1954, the two countries signed an agreement, which provided for the Soviet Union providing a long-term loan of 520 million roubles to China and helping China found 15 enterprises and provide more equipment to the previously established 141 companies. The assistance of the Soviet Union to China directly contributed to the smooth completion of the First Five-Year Plan and the primary establishment of a rather solid industrial foundation in People's Republic of China.

233

However, owing to the chauvinism carried forward by the Soviet Union in dealing with the relationship among the socialist countries and the communist parties and the shift in the attitude towards the history and theory of the international communist movements, China and the Soviet Union were caught in serious disputes in the relationship between the socialist countries and the communist parties in ideology and in national interests. At the Twentieth Congress of the Communist Party of the Soviet Union, the roadmap of "peaceful coexistence, peaceful transition and peaceful competition" was proposed for the management of foreign relations and the ideas of "a state of the entire people and a party of the entire people" and playing down class struggles were initiated. These propositions were referred to as "revisionism of the Soviet Union" by the Communist Party of China, which went on with a war of words with its Soviet Union counterpart for a decade from 1959 to 1969. Upon these, the Soviet Union demanded the establishment of "Long Wave Radio" and "Joint Fleet" in China and interfered in the Taiwan Question, jeopardizing China's sovereignty. The tensions between the two countries culminated on July16,

23   Representatives of 12 Communist and Workers Parties of Socialist countries, in Moscow for the celebration of the fortieth anniversary of the great October Socialist Revolution in Russia, met on November 14-16, 1957, and adopted a Declaration.
24   These joint-stock companies had been completely transferred to China since January 1955. Note by the author.

1960 when the Soviet Union government notified its Chinese counterpart about the withdrawal of all Soviet experts from China in one month, which symbolized the official split between China and the Soviet Union. The split had a direct bearing on the border issues. Disputes along the Sino-Soviet border continued form 1960 to 1969 with the two sides stationing large number of troops there. Tensions along the border escalated in March 1969, when armed clashes broke out on Damansky Island.

6.3.2. Flexible Diplomacy towards the Western Countries

Western countries represented by the United States, limited by their narrow ideology and national interests, imposed economic blockade on China and established military alliances with China's neighboring countries through the Southeast Asia Treaty Organization and collective defense treaties signed by the United States with the Philippines, South Korea and Taiwan or invaded them, such as North Korea and Vietnam, so as to besiege and contain China militarily. In response, China not only contended courageously by assisting the people in Vietnam and North Korea to fight against the American invaders and bombarding Jinmen, but also continued with its contacts with the Western countries, hoping to create a favorable international environment. China and the United States kept in touch as well. The Chinese ambassador to Poland and the American ambassador to Czechoslovakia held 136 meetings on Taiwan issue from August 1955 to February 1970. In spite of the different positions on the issue, the negotiation continued since neither side wished to break it off. It provided a channel for communication and contacts for the two great powers when they were in opposition and refused to recognize each other. Other than talking about their relationship, China and the Unites States exchanged views on international issues of mutual concern, which played a critical role in enhancing mutual understanding and laid a foundation for the improvement of Sino-US relationship.

Britain is worth mentioning as it was the first among the Western countries to recognize the People's Republic of China. To safeguard its interests in China, especially its status and interests in Hong Kong, after careful weighing, the British government on January 6, 1950 officially telegraphed the PRC government to announce its recognition of the central government of the People's Republic of China as the "legal government" and that it was ready to forge diplomatic ties on the basis of equality, mutual benefit and mutual respect for territorial integrity and sovereignty and to exchange ambassadors with the people's government of China[25]. It was followed by the negotiations on establishing diplomatic relations. Due to the factors like the understanding of "recognition" and positions of the two countries being different[26], Britain submitting to the

25   Ministry of Foreign Affairs of PRC. *Diplomatic Communique* 1950/11: 18.
26   The U.K. held that, in keeping with international practices, the exchange of notes between two countries meant they acknowledged the establishment of foreign relations while the newly founded PRC proposed to precede negotiations before establishing foreign relations due to its national conditions. Note by the author.

pressure from America in dealing with the issues of recognizing the PRC's seat in the UN, the airplanes of China Airlines and Central Airlines[27] and Britain sending troops to participate the Vietnam War, China and Britain maintained informal diplomatic ties in the form of agents until March 1972 when official diplomatic relations were forged between the two countries.

The establishment of the diplomatic ties between China and France marked a significant breakthrough in China's relationship with the Western nations in that period. After the founding of the PRC, France sided with the United States for a while. In 1955, the French government brought up the principle of "Joint Recognition", which provided for the issue of recognizing the PRC and forging diplomatic relations with it must be decided by Western countries all together. June 1958 saw the second rule of General De Gaulle, who vigorously carried forward independent foreign policies to escape the restraint and control of the Unites States and to play a positive role in dealing with major world issues. Since France detonated its first atomic bomb in1960, De Gaulle refused to sign the Partial Nuclear Test Ban Treaty for his belief in the independent nuclear deterrence as the guarantee and symbol of France as a major power. To force-fully challenge the bipolar system of the Unites States and the Soviet Union who were contending for hegemony, France needed to the support of China. De Gaulle as a realist politician believed national interests not ideologies as the de-terminer of national relations[28]. At the end of October 1963, he sent the Senate Speaker and former Premier Edgar-Jean Faure to conduct a semi-official visit to China bringing a letter written by him. During the visit, Edgar-Jean Faure found many identical or similar views on a great number of major international issues with his Chinese counterpart in the course of dialogs. He clearly pro-posed the idea of establishing diplomatic relations, which was highly valued by the Chinese government. The two sides reached agreement on three points[29]: first, France recognizes the People's Republic of China as the sole legal gov-ernment of the Chinese people; second, Frances supports the legitimate rights and position of the PRC in the United Nations; and last, after the establish-ment of Sino-French diplomatic relations and the voluntary withdrawal of the "diplomatic delegate" to France by the Taiwan authorities, France should call

---

27   Before its withdrawal from the mainland, the Kuomintang (KMT) carried China Airlines and Central Airlines and their major assets to Hongkong. On November 9, 1949, Jingyi Liu, General Manager of China Airlines, and Zhuolin Chen, General Manager of Central Airlines, led 11 planes to fly from Hongkong to Beijing, announcing the revolt of all the staff. Chinese government declared over 70 planes of the two airline companies detained in Hongkong to be the properties of the PRC and demanded the Hongkong British authorities to return the planes. Although the local court in Hongkong ruled that the PRC was entitled to the property rights of the planes, the U.K., yielding to the U.S. pressure, al-lowed the KMT authorities to sell these planes to the U.S. civil airlines. Note by the author.
28   Crozier, Brian. *De Gaulle*. Vol. 2. Trans. Songhao Cao. Beijing: The Commercial Press (1978): 667.
29   "Three Tacit Agreements Reached between Zhou Enlai and Edgar-Jean Faure." See *Compilation of Major Literatures on Four Decades of Sino-French Diplomatic Relations*. Eds. Haixing Liu and Feng Gao. Beijing: World Affairs Press, 2004: 91.

back its "diplomatic delegate" to Taiwan. Based on the three points, China and France swiftly entered negotiations for forging diplomatic ties. In January 1964, President Charles de Gaulle declared its severance of diplomatic relations with Taiwan. On the 27th of the same month, the governments of China and France simultaneously published the Joint Communiqué on the establishment of diplomatic relations: "the People's Republic of China and the Republic of France agreed unanimously to forge diplomatic relations. Therefore, the governments of the two countries decided to appoint ambassadors in three months"[30]. France was the first major Western country to establish foreign relations with China at the ambassador level, marking a breakthrough in China's history of diplomacy. It foiled the attempt of the United States of isolating China and accelerated the course of other Western countries improving their relationship with China.

6.3.3. Active Support Given to National Liberation Struggles and Economic Construction of the Third World Countries

As a large developing country, China shares the same history and destiny with other nations in the Third World. Ever since its foundation, the People's Republic of China has started to develop foreign relations with Asian and African countries, vigorously support their fight for national independence and sovereignty and actively pursue South-South cooperation and exchanges. The victory of Chinese revolution was viewed as a triumph of the Third World countries as well. Regardless of the policy of isolating China held by the United States, the countries in Asia and Africa forged diplomatic ties with China one after another. Burma was the first non-socialist country to recognize the PRC. It was followed by India, Pakistan, Indonesia, Ceylon, Nepal and Afghanistan. As other Asian and African countries gained independence at a later date or was then subject to the control and impact of Western countries, most of them did not establish diplomatic relations with the PRC until after the Asian-African Conference. In the course of dealing with the relations with neighboring countries, China initiated the idea of taking the Five Principles for Peaceful Coexistence as the basic code for managing national relations, which won wide acknowledgement from the neighboring countries and nations at the Asian-African Conference.

The PRC erected a favorable diplomatic image at the international stage at its birth. Ceylon, as for a severe food shortage, was in urgent need to increase foreign currency reserve for rice from 1951 to 1952. But its economy was put in a difficult position as the United States deliberately brought down the price of rubber exported by Ceylon. It resorted to China for assistance with the diplomatic relations un-established yet. On October 1952, on the basis of equality and mutual interests, China and Ceylon governments signed a five-year trade

---

30   "Joint Communique on the Establishment of Diplomatic Relations Between the People's Republic of China and the French Republic." See *Compilation of Major Literatures on Four Decades of Sino-French Diplomatic Relations*. Eds. Haixing Liu and Feng Gao. Beijing: World Affairs Press, 2004: 92.

agreement, which stipulated that China would import 50,000 tons of rubber from Ceylon each year, at a price slightly higher than that in the international markets[31] and in turn would export 270,000 tons of rice to Ceylon at a price slightly lower than that of the global market prices[32]. India was also caught in a food shortage from 1950 to 1951 and China provided India with a total of 660,000tons of rice. Later, at the Geneva Conference and Asian-African Conference, China established itself as a developing world power that held a peaceful foreign policy of independence and actively supported national liberation activities in Asian and African countries. These efforts of the PRC laid a solid foundation for the positive development of South-South cooperation and put the Asian and African countries in a more favorable position in the North-South landscape.

The period after the Asian-African Conference saw the climax of national liberation activities in Asia and Africa. China offered great compassion and support to the best of its ability to countries under colonial rule like Angola, Mozambique and Zimbabwe. It closely contacted national liberation organizations in many of these countries to help with their victory. As for those newly-independent ones, the Chinese government recognized them immediately, forged diplomatic relations with 15 countries including Ghana, Mali, Congo and Tanzania and signed friendly treaties and agreements for economic and technological cooperation with Guinea, Mali and Somalia.

In the course of promoting South-South cooperation, Premier Zhou Enlai's visit to Africa is a milestone. In order to enhance Sino-African relationship, from 13 December 1963 to 5 February 1964, Premier Zhou toured ten African countries[33]. During the tour, Premier Zhou put forward two critical principles: one being the five principles guiding China's relations with the Arab countries, and the other being the eight principles for China's aid to foreign countries. In brief, the five principles guiding China's relations with the Arab and African countries were as follows: a. China supports the Arab and African peoples in their struggle to oppose imperialism and old and new colonialism and to win and safeguard national independence. b. It supports the pursuance of a policy of peace, neutrality and non-alignment by the Governments of Arab and African countries. c. It supports the desire of the Arab and African peoples to achieve unity and solidarity in the manner of their own choice. d. It supports the Arab and African countries in their efforts to settle their disputes through peaceful consultations. e. It holds that the sovereignty of the Arab and African countries should be respected by all other countries and that encroachment and interference from any quarter should be opposed. The Premier put forward the following eight principles for China's aid to foreign countries: a. The Chinese Government always bases itself on the principle of equality and mutual benefit

31   It accounted for over a half of the rubber output in Ceylon.
32   It accounted for over 60% of imported rice in Ceylon.
33   They were the United Arab Republic (now Egypt and Syria), Algeria, Morocco, Tunisia, Ghana, Mali, Guinea, Sudan, Ethiopia, and Somalia. Note by the author.

in providing aid to other countries. It never regards such aid as a kind of uni-lateral alms but as something mutual. b. In providing aid to other countries, the Chinese Government strictly respects the sovereignty of the recipient countries, and never attaches any conditions or asks for any privileges. c. China provides economic aid in the form of interest-free or low-interest loans and extends the time limit for repayment when necessary so as to lighten the burden of the recipient countries as far as possible. d. In providing aid to other countries, the purpose of the Chinese Government is not to make the recipient countries dependent on China but to help them embark step by step on the road of self-reliance and independent economic development. e. The Chinese Government tries its best to help the recipient countries build projects which require less investment while yielding quicker results, so that the recipient governments may increase their income and accumulate capital. f. The Chinese Government provides the best-quality equipment and material of its own manufacture at international market prices. If the equipment and material provided by the Chinese Government are not up to the agreed specifications and quality, the Chinese Government undertakes to replace them. g. In providing any technical assistance, the Chinese Government will see to it that the personnel of the recipient country fully master such technique. h. The experts dispatched by China to help in construction in the recipient countries will have the same standard of living as the experts of the recipient country. The Chinese experts are not allowed to make any special demands or enjoy any special amenities. These eight principles fully give expression to the sincere desire of China in seeking to conduct economic and cultural cooperation with the newly-emerged countries of Asia, Africa and Latin America[34].

238

These principles were well-targeted and feasible since they were proposed proceeding from the real conditions of African and Arabian countries and were totally different from the foreign aid practices of the Unites States, the Soviet Union and other Western countries as they were based on quality, mutual benefit and mutual respect for sovereignty. Since their proposition, the Chinese government has been following the eight principles and providing economic assistance to developing countries in Africa and other regions. By 1967, China has entered assistance treaties with Guinea, Mali, Algeria, Somalia, Congo, United Arab (Egypt and Syria), Kenya, Uganda, Tanzania, Zambia and Mauritania. Besides providing regular materials (including grains) and cash, China mainly undertook projects. It was estimated that a total of 428 million dollars were offered to the above 12 countries by China from 1956 to 1966[35]. The absolute equality and great effects of the economic cooperation between China and these countries has made it a model for South-South cooperation among the developing countries.

---

34   See Wang, Shengzu, ed. *History of International Relations*. Vol. 8. Beijing: World Affairs Press, 1995: 350-351.
35   Albright, David E. *Communism in Africa*. London, 1986: 170-171.

At the end of 1950s and early 1960s, China addressed the issue of dual nationality of the Chinese in Indonesia and settled border disputes with Burma, Nepal, Pakistan and Afghanistan. But conflicts on the Sino-Indian border broke out in December 1962 due to several factors. The major one was that India stuck to the McMahon Line illegally created by the British colonizers and provoked in the border area. The other factor was that India stubbornly supported the separatist forces of Dalai Lama in Tibet for its narrow national interests. But after the victory of the Chinese defense battle, India went back to the border line as drew by China and voluntarily sent back the captives and seized weapons, which created a favorable atmosphere for the peaceful settlement if Sino-Indian border disputes.

In a word, by the end of 1960s, China already created a favorable international environment. It broke the isolation of the Western countries when it was initially founded by conducting economic cooperation and mutual political and diplomatic support with several countries in the West and the large number of developing countries in Asia and Africa. Although with limited capabilities, the PRC actively aided the righteous fight for national independence in Asian and African nations. These deeds not only contributed to the national independence, economic development and social progress of these countries but also elevated China's international status and prestige and laid a solid foundation for restoring the legitimate seat of the PRC in the United Nations.

6.4. North-South Confrontation in the Middle East

The prominent features of the situation in the Middle East in the 1950s and 1960s were the domination of the United States after taking the place of Britain and France and the accelerated entering of the Soviet Union. Being at a critical strategic position which connects the east and the west and boasting rich oil resources, the Middle East was one of the most critical regions to the Soviet Union and the United States in their fight for hegemony. The ongoing activities for national liberation in the region had to be conducted against the tough situation of the two great powers struggling with each other. The turn of the situation came after the Bandung Conference when the climax of the fight for national independence arrived in Asia and Africa and the shocking event of regaining the sovereignty over the Suez Canal, which triggered the Second Israel-Arab War. Therefore, North-South confrontation was extremely serious and out in the open in the Middle East.

6.4.1. Regaining the Sovereignty over the Suez Canal

The Suez Canal, being a critical international route connecting the Mediterranean Sea, the Red Sea, the Indian Ocean and the Atlantic Ocean, is of great strategic significance. It was opened in November 1869 after ten years of construction by Egyptian workers as commanded by the French colonizers. For the construction, Egypt spent eight million Egyptian dollars and sacrificed the lives of 120,000workers. The canal, since its opening, was under the control of a company owned by French and British colonizers, who held 96%of its stocks. After it occupied Egypt in 1882, Britain set up a military base with the stationing capacity of 100,000 soldiers in the canal area, making the area a "state within a state". In October 1954, the newly-independent Egyptian national government signed with the British government the Anglo-Egyptian Agreement providing for the withdrawal of the British troops from the canal area no later than June 12, 1956. But the Universal Suez Canal Ship Company was still in the grasp of British and French monopolists.

On July 26, 1956, at a mass meeting celebrating the fourth anniversary of the July Revolution, President Gamal Abdel Nasser promulgated a decree purporting to nationalize the Suez Canal which was a significant manifestation of Egypt's fight for sovereignty and accomplishment of national revolution. And the direct cause for its birth was that the developed countries in the West was discontented with the independent foreign policy implemented by the Egyptian government and therefore attempted to economically blockade Egypt and hinder its economic progress.

As early as in the autumn of 1952, the Egyptian government planned to construct in the middle reach of the Nile River the Aswan Dam, which would cost one billion dollars but bring Egypt with over10million mu of farmland, 1million kilowatt electric power and one fourth of the national income. Due to the large expense, the government asked loans from the World Bank and British and American banks. In December 1955, though with harsh terms, the British and American consented for loans to Egypt. However, due to dissatisfaction with Egypt participating the Asian-African Conference, forging diplomatic relations with the People's Republic of China in May 1956 and starting the Non-Aligned Movement after meeting president Tito and President Nehru, the United States went back on its commitment of providing economic assistance to Egypt, as followed by Britain and the World Bank. The Nasser government was forced to nationalize the Suez Canal, which would bring back the national sovereignty and revitalize the economy for independence.

The resolution of taking back the sovereignty over the Suez Canal shocked the Western world. On August 2, 1956, the United States, France and Britain published a joint declaration of three countries, which opposed nationalizing the canal and claimed it to be an international waterway and therefore its management should be international to ensure free sail. The three nations imposed economic sanctions on Egypt by putting pressure on it at international conferences, freezing Egyptian assets and canal fund in their countries and inciting foreign navigators to leave their posts and return homes. They also tried threat with forces by assembling fleets at the Mediterranean Sea and the mouth of the canal. When none of them worked, Britain and France allied with Israel to wage a war. But the three countries started the war with distinctive objectives with Britain wishing to regain the control over the canal, France hoping to undermine Egypt's support with military forces to the resistance force against the

French in Algeria and strengthen their traditional influences in Africa and the Middle East to resist the increasing American infiltration, and Israel attempting to seize the land of Egypt and other Arabian countries.

On October 29, 1956, with French and British support, Israel troops of 45,000 men invaded the Sinai Peninsula in four directions. On the 30, under the pretext of protecting the canal, Britain and France sent an ultimatum to Egypt, demanding a ceasefire and withdrawal of troops by Egypt and Israel and that the British and French troops be stationed in the canal area and Port Said. After these unreasonable demands being turned down by the Egyptian, on 31st, Britain and France founded a joint commanding headquarters for bombarding Cairo, Port Said and Alexander with a large number of airplanes, thus unveiling military invasion known as the Second Israel-Arab War or the Suez War.

After the war broke out, the Egyptian government mobilized the whole nation by calling for "a generalized war", sealing up British and French banks in Egypt and taking over their oil companies. The resistance war against the French, British and Israeli in Egypt won support from the countries in the Arab world and the Third World. Syria and Saudi Arabia announced the severance of diplomatic relations with Britain and France, Jordan cut it with France and the three countries mobilized the whole country and promised to put all their forces under Egypt's allocation. Iraq also ended its foreign relations with France. Syria, Lebanon and Jordan cut the oil pipes of the Iraq Oil Company controlled by the British, Saudi Arabia decided to temporarily stop providing the British and French with oil and the oil depots of the British troops in Libya were blew up. Sudan sent volunteer troops to Egypt and some Arabian countries forbade the British and French from using their military bases.

The British Prime Minister Anthony Eden "joined with so little hesitation and without even consulting Eisenhower in the French-Israeli plot to invade Egypt and overthrow Nasser. The world and half the British were aghast at the attack on Suez. Even Britain's few remaining Arab friends, who would privately have been glad to see Nasser removed, felt obliged to take anti-British measures. But what mattered far more was the extreme disapproval of the Americans. This was most effectively expressed by withholding their financial support for Britain, without which her economy and the convertibility of sterling were doomed."[36] As being expected, America was surprised and furious at Britain and French for invading Egypt and President Eisenhower, being busy with his election, publicly criticized the two nations after weighing pros and cons. To impose greater pressure, the United States cut oil supply lines in Latin America urgently needed by the French and British. The Soviet Union, after putting down the Hungarian incident, warned Britain and France that a "volunteer troop" would be sent and even long-distance missiles would be sent unless they withdrew their troops immediately. Both the U.S. and the Soviet Union

---

36 Brown, Judith M., and W.M. Rogers Louise, eds. *The Oxford History of the British Empire*. Vol. IV. Oxford: Oxford University Press, 1999: 510.

actively supported the United Nations to pass a resolution requiring an armistice in the Middle East and withdrawal of British and French troops.

The invasion war against Egypt put Britain and France in a tough spot both at home and abroad and with the United States and the Soviet Union refusing their support, the two countries were forced to declare a ceasefire on November the 6th and stated withdrawing their troops. Egypt not only reclaimed the ownership and management over the Suez Canal, but also nationalized foreign-funded companies in finance, trade, insurance and telecommunication on the back of a victory. During the war, the Arab World demonstrated great solidarity, which significantly undermined the ruling foundation of the colonizers in the region. In November 1956, Jordan abolished its alliance treaty with Britain; Egypt abrogated the Aglo-Egyptian Agreement of 1954 at the end of 1957; the Iraqi people overthrew the Faisal Dynasty and founded a republic in July 1958; the interim government of the Republic of Algeria was founded in September 1958. By the end of 1950s, the colonial rule of the British and French basically ended in the Middle East.

6.4.2. The Intervention of the United States in the Middle East

Exploiting the second Israel-Arab War, the United States got fully involved in the affairs of the region, attempting to fill up the "power vacuum" left by Britain and France after their defeat. It also enhanced its ties with Israel. And the Soviet Union, by siding with Egypt, gained voice and influence in the Middle East. In order to replace the traditional influences of Britain and France and resist the infiltration of the Soviet Union, America was in urgent need of a new Middle East policy.

On the New Year's Day of 1957, when meeting the leaders of the Democratic Party and the Republican Party, Dwight David Eisenhower and John Foster Dulles stated: "The existing vacuum in the Middle East must be filled by the United States before it is filled by Russia."[37] He believed that "the situation required that the United States negotiate agreements to help the Middle East countries economically and militarily" (ibid.).

On the 5th, within a "Special Message to the Congress on the Situation in the Middle East", President Eisenhower suggested that the Congress authorized the government to provide military assistance and carry out cooperation plans in the Middle East to fill up the vacuum and that the American armed troops could be used and economic aid was offered to Middle East countries for preserving their independence. He required the Congress to authorize the president with free allocation of 200 million dollars in this region each year in the fiscal years of 1958 and 1959[38]. This speech signified the birth of Eisenhower

---

37   Eisenhower, Dwight D. *The White House Years: Waging Peace 1956–1961*. New York: Doubleday, 1965: 178. Trans. Jianghai. Shanghai: Shanghai Joint Publishing Press, 1977: 200.

38   International Relations Institute, ed. *Compilation of Literature on the Issue of Middle East*. Beijing: World Affairs Press, 1958: 336-338.

Doctrine. Initially, only several pro-American countries declared acceptance of the doctrine. American special envoys were sent to lobby in the Middle East so as to promote the doctrine. By April 19, the American State Council published a report, which claimed: "up until now, Lebanon, Libya, Turkey, Iran, Pakistan, Afghanistan, Iraq and Saudi Arabia extended the will to participate the Middle East plan of the United States"[39]. As for the countries that rejected Eisenhower Doctrine, America resorted to intervention. On April 24, 1957, the United States plotted in Jordan a coup, in which the Nabulsi government that stood for national interests was overthrown, thus leading to domestic turmoil in Jordan. In May 1957, it instigated Turkish troops to build up on the Syrian border for military threats. However, ever since its inception, Eisenhower Doctrine encountered strong opposition from many Arabian countries and most Arabian people, especially Egypt and Syria. And in countries that accepted the doctrine, domestic turmoil of various magnitude occurred with the most serious ones being the revolution in Iraq and the internal struggles in Lebanon.

The Faisal Dynasty in Iraq proactively joined the Bagdad Pact[40] led by the USA in 1955 and announced acceptance of the Eisenhower Doctrine in 1957. The pro-Western dynasty was overthrown in July 1958 by Free Officers headed by Abd al-Karim Qasim under people's support and the Republic of Iraq was founded afterwards. In March 1959, the new government declared its withdrawal from the Bagdad Pact and the sterling area, implementation of a neutral and peaceful foreign policy and called for solidarity of the Arab World. At home, the new regime undertook measures to invigorate the economy and weaken the control of foreign capitals over its national economy and abolished some privileges enjoyed by foreign capitalists. The Iraqi revolution acted as a rather big blow to the military alliance system of the United States in the Middle East.

Around the same time, internal turmoil broke out in Lebanon, which is a small country in the Middle East. It was ruled by the Ottoman Empire before World War I and France after it. It is the only Arabic nation with two main religions, which are Christianity (the Maronite Church, the Eastern Orthodox Church, the Melkite Catholic Church, the Protestant Church, the Armenian Apostolic Church) and Islam (Shia and Sunni). There is also the Dürzi minority religion. When it gained independence in September 1943, the religious sects reached an agreement that political power would be allocated in line with the proportion of follower numbers of the two main religions. The proportion of Christians to Muslims was then 6 to 5. Lebanon's unwritten National Pact of 1943 required that its president be Maronite Christian, its speaker of the parliament to be a Shiite Muslim, its prime minister be Sunni Muslim, and the Deputy Speaker of

39   Wang, Shengzu, ed. *History of International Relations*. Vol. 8. Beijing: World Affairs Press, 1995: 369.
40   The Bagdad Pact was a military alliance in Middle East established by the U.S. in 1955 on the basis of the Command for the Middle East and the Northern Tier for the overall control over the Middle East, suppression of the local national independence movements, and blockage of the southward access of the former Soviet Union down to the Mediterranean, the Persian Gulf and the Indian Ocean. Note by the author.

Parliament and the Deputy Prime Minister be Greek Orthodox. The tenure of president would be 6 years and no president might hold office for two or more consecutive terms; the foreign policy should be neutral and not seek alliance, these clauses were also in the pact[41]. When the Christian Camille Chamoun was elected as the president in 1952, he held pro-Western policies. In February 1957, he became the first to accept the Eisenhower Doctrine. Meanwhile, he was attempting to modify the pact for a reelection, which aroused strong dissatisfaction among Muslims and other religious believers. In the parliamentary election held in June 1957, under the support of CIA special agents and dollars, Camille Chamoun created some illegal votes and divided electoral districts in an unfair manner. In the end, 53 of the 66 elected members of the Parliament stood firmly by Chamoun, more than the required number of the modified pact[42]. On May 8, 1958, Nasib Al-Matni, the celebrated anti-American personnel of the Telegraph, was murdered, which led to large scale demonstrations across Lebanon. On May 10, armed conflicts broke out between the demonstrators and the Police when the oil pipes of the Iraq Petroleum Company were damaged. The domestic turmoil gradually evolved into a civil war. By the end of June, most parts of Lebanon were seized by the opposition, who was joined by some Syrians crossing the border between Syria and Lebanon. The radio Cairo of Egypt encouraged the Lebanon people to stand up and fight against the Chamoun government. The Commander of the Lebanon Army—General Fuad Chehab who was a Christian refused to get involved in the political conflict and announced a neutral standing in fear of division for religions within the army. The Chamoun government turned to the U.S. for help. And since President Eisenhower worried about Lebanon following the steps of Iraq and the Domino Effect emerging in the Middle East after witnessing the military coup in Iraq on July 14, he decided to conduct military intervention. On July 15, the U.S Marine Corps composed nearly 10,000 troops invaded Lebanon being covered by 70 warships of the Sixth Fleet and 420 airplanes. This invasion made America the subject of wide condemnation around the world with demonstrations demanding its withdrawal cross Lebanon and powerful and dynamic anti-American movements in the Arab World. On July 16, the Soviet government issued a declaration supporting the fight of the Arabian people against the Western imperialists and reserving the right to necessary measures for preserving peace and security. The U.S. barely won any support in the world public opinions. On July 27, 1958, the speaker of the Lebanon Parliament wrote to the American president to criticize his military intervention in Lebanon. On July 31, the Commander of the Army Chehab who was a Christian was elected as the new president and demanded the withdrawal of the United States, who had no choice but oblige since it lost the excuse for intervention. On December 12, the new government declared its rejection of the Eisenhower Doctrine.

244

---

41   Little, Douglas. "His Finest Hour? Eisenhower, Lebanon, and the 1958 Middle East Crisis." *Diplomatic History* 20. 1 (1996): 27.
42   Ibid.: 35-36.

In spite of their resistance against the American hegemony to various degrees, the Middle East countries were still under its great influences. The strong presence of the United States in the region was predetermined by its great significance in the global strategy of America. For the same reason, the Middle East countries, voluntarily or not, had to accept the extension of the Soviet power. The fight between the Soviet Union and the United States in the Middle East complicated the relationship between countries in the region. After the Suez War, America was caught in the troubles of the Vietnam War. Taking this opportunity, the Soviet Union accelerated its extension in the Middle East by entering agreements for military and economic assistances with Egypt, Syria and Iraq. It gained the right to provide weapons to countries in the area and infiltrated into their major economic departments to various degrees. In response, the United States isolated Egypt and other pro-Soviet Arabian nations and fully equipped and supported Israel. While the fight between the two great powers and the Arab-Israeli conflict intensified, the Third Arab-Israeli War, or the June War or the Six-Day War broke out on June 5, 1967. Within 6 days, after conducting all-out offensives against Egypt, Syria and Jordan, Israel seized the Sinai Peninsula and the most parts of the West Bank and Golan Heights, totaling 65,700 km^2 and forcing the three countries to accept a cease-fire. On November 22, 1967, the Security Council of the United Nations passed the British proposal unanimously, requiring Israel to withdraw from the seized lands in the Six-Day War. But the resolution was rejected by Israel. Since then, although small-scale battles took place between Egypt and Israel from now and then, on the whole, the state of neither war nor peace maintained in the Middle East for the contention and compromises between the U.S. and the Soviet Union until the 1973 Arab-Israeli War.

6.5. Rise of Africa and Establishment of the Organization of African Unity (OAU)

While the convocation of the Asian-African Conference and the rise of the Third World propelled the nationalist movements in Africa, the struggles of Egypt to take back the Suez River drove them to climax. The long-established colonizers, Britain and France, after recognizing the irresistible trend of colonies gaining independence, shifted their policies in Africa from high-pressure armed suppression to voluntarily acknowledging the right to independent self-decision of the colony people. The extension of the United States and the Soviet Union complicated the fight for national independence. As for those countries that newly-gained independence, they went for joint development as influenced by Pan-Africanism.

6.5.1. North Africa Gaining Independence from Britain and France

National liberation movements in Africa were not equal-paced with those in North Africa moving faster due to subjective and objective factors. On November 1, 1954, the Algerians under the leadership of the Front de Liberation Nationale launched armed uprisings against French colonial rule. Till 1956, an armed force of over 100,000 men was founded and authorities were established in rural areas. The interim government of the Republic of Algeria was founded in September 1958. After controlling Algeria for over a hundred years, many large French families owned huge assets and over a million French descendents lived there. For a long time, the French authorities carried forward a policy to assimilate the non-French ethnic groups, which made the French ruling class regard Algeria as an integral part of France. After massive oil reserves being discovered there, the upper class in France praised Algeria as the cornerstone of the revitalization of French Empire. They were determined to pay every price to maintain the control over the country permanently. Therefore, the French government gave the toughest response to the Algerian war for national liberation. "When it comes to preserving the internal peace of a nation and the integrity of the republic, we will make no compromise…. Algerian residents separating from the local land is inconceivable… no parliament and no government shall ever concede in this fundamental principle."[43] Through long-term hard fights, the Algerian National Liberation Army foiled every encirclement and mop-up operation of the French. The De Gaulle government was forced to make the painful decision and announced to grant Algeria self-decision right on September 16, 1959. President Charles de Gaulle required Algeria to choose among three options: independence, Francization and integration with France but allowing a referendum four years after the ceasefire for the Algerians to decide on their own. Although through twists and turns, the French government and the interim government signed on March 18, 1962 the Evian Agreements, which provided for self-decision and independence of Algeria. On July 1 of the same year, a referendum was held in Algeria. July the 3rd saw the official declaration of independence and the establishment of the Republic of Algeria with Ben Bella as the president, which signifies the end of the 130-year-long French colonial administration. Making compromises, the Algerian government respected the French assets in Algeria and permitted the excavation of oil in Sahara and its use of the Mers el-Kébir military base for 15 years[44].

43   French Prime Minister Pierre Mendès-France's speech in National Assembly. Qtd. in *Post-War Diplomatic History of France*, by Xichang Zhang and Jianqing Zhou. Beijing: World Affairs Press, 1993: 84.
44   Watt, D.C. *Survey of International Affairs*. Trans. Compilation and Translation Committee of Shanghai Municipal CPPCC. Shanghai: Shanghai Translation Publishing House, 1983: 373.

Being inspired by national liberation activities in Algeria, people in Morocco and Tunis conducted fights against the French colonizers and the French government was forced to recognize both as independent countries. In 1956, the largest African country—Sudan became free from the British colonial rule. In the late 1950s, the trend for independence spread from North Africa to Sub-Saharan Africa, in which Ghana's independence is worth mentioning. Ghana, originally known as Gold Coast, was the most developed and prosperous British colony in Africa. The national independence movement in Ghana was led by the celebrated Pan-Africanism activist—Francis Nwia Kwame Nkrumah, who was an idealist and dedicated his whole life to the unity of Africa. As a practical revolutionist, he fully considered the evolvement of the post-war international environment, the social and economic conditions of British West Africa and the flexible British governing. On June 12, 1949, Nkrumah founded the Convention People's Party in Gold Coast demanding immediate self-administration with himself as the Party Secretary. The first point of the party program was: "To fight relentlessly by all constitutional means for the achievement of full 'Self-Government Now' for the chiefs and people of the Gold Coast."[45] But the British attempted to carry out autonomy under the colonial governor within the constitutional government system in line with Sir Alan Burns Constitution of Gold Coast of 1946. In the government election in February 1951, the CPP took 34 of the 38 seats. Nkrumah was appointed as the leader of the Gold Coast's government business. And later a new constitution of Gold Coast was promulgated after negotiating with the British government. In June 1954, a parliament through direct suffrage and a cabinet with all African members came into being, thus realizing autonomy under the governor. However, the trend of independence, once formed, could not be resisted. In July 1956, the legislative assembly authorized the Gold Coast government to submit the motion for independence within the Commonwealth to Britain, which was wisely passed by the British government. On March 6, 1957, Gold Coast officially became independent and was renamed as Ghana. It was the first Sub-Saharan African country to gain political independence after WWII. On July 1, 1960, Ghana became a republic with Nkrumah as the president and remained a member of the British Commonwealth.

On October 2, 1958, Guinea, under the leadership of the Democratic Party and Ahmed Sekou Toure freed from the French colonial rule and became the second Sub-Saharan country to gain independence. "[J]ust as the first post-war decade witnessed the liberation of Asia, so the second witnessed the liberation of Africa"[46]. In 1960 alone, the Year of Africa, 17 African countries gained independence. During the period from 1961 to 1969, 15 more African countries followed their steps, basically ending the colonial administration of

45   Nkrumah, Francis Nwia Kwame. *Ghana: The Autobiography of Kwame Nkrumah*. T. Nelson. 1957: 101. Beijing: World Affairs Press, 1960.: 105.
46   Stavrianos, L. S. *The World since 1500: A Global History*. Prentice Hall, 1999: 605. trans. Xiangying Wu and Chimin Liang. Shanghai: Shanghai Academy of Social Sciences Press, 1996: 825.

the French and British in Africa. From then on, the focus of decolonization in Africa shifted to the Portuguese colonies in the southern part of the continent, like Zimbabwe, Namibia and South Africa.

The approaches for gaining independence of the African countries can be classified as three types: one being armed struggles as represented by Algeria, the second type being the mixture of armed fights and political struggles with the former as the basis, peace treaties and universal suffrage as exemplified by Morocco and Tunis and the last one being non-violent struggles. The third type mainly had to do with the non-colonial policies of the colonial suzerains and was the choice of most African countries. The paths for independence, since they variously determined the internal integration degree of these countries and their relationship with the former suzerains, exerted great influences on their future development. Among the African countries, Congo went through the most twisted path for independence. "Belgium, however, was forced to leave the Congo in 1960. By then, the Congo faced independent states across most of its borders, an inspiration to and a haven for dissidents"[47].

6.5.2. The Congo Crisis

Congo, located at the heart of Africa, boasts rich mineral resources. It was a Belgian colony known as Belgian Congo[48]. After WWII, Congo witnessed vigorous activities for national independence with the birth of several nationalist parties and organizations, such as The Bakongos' Alliance, the Congolese National Movement, and African Solidarity Party. Among the parties, the most influential one was the Congolese National Movement led by Patrice Lumanba. In September 1951, Lumanba demanded independence in the capital at a mass gathering, at which hundreds of people were killed or wounded in the brutal suppression of the colonial authorities. It was followed by large-scale armed rebellions, which led to the Round Table Conference at the consent of the Belgian colonial authorities in January 1960. At the conference, considering countries surrounding Congo gained independence in succession, Belgium unexpectedly accepted Congo's demand for independence but forced it to enter Treaty of Friendly Assistance and Technical Co-operation, which provided for the control of Belgium over Congo troops after its independence and that Belgium would provide personnel for its administrative, judicial, military, cultural, scientific and educational fields and the Congo government would cooperate in foreign affairs.

---

47   Urwin, Derek W. *A Political History of Western Europe since 1945*. Trans. Dingzhao Xing. Beijing: China Translation and Publishing Corporation, 1985: 197.
48   It was named as the Republic of the Cong upon its independence in June 1960, renamed as the Democratic Republic of the Congo in August 1964, and called as Congo (Leo) for short due to its capital Leopoldville. In May 1966, its capital adopted its former name Kinshasa, it was also called as Congo (Kin) for short. It was again renamed as Republic of Zaire in October 1971. Note by the author.

In June 1960, Congo declared independence and established a republican government with Joseph Kasa-Vubu as the president, Patrice Lumumba as the premier and Antoine Gizenga as the vice premier. However, soldiers in the capital and other areas conducted a coup in July, refusing to take orders from Belgium officers and demanding the leadership of Congolese. Immediately, Belgium declared anarchy in Congo and deployed paratroopers there with the excuse of protecting Belgium citizens. Meanwhile, with the incitation of Belgium, CQNAKAT led by Moise Tshombe founded in Katanga the State of Katanga and the Luba ethnic group headed by Albert Kalonji established in Kasai the Mining State of South Kasai. The new regime was under the immediate threat of being invaded and toppled.

The Congo government turned to the United Nations for intervention. On July 14, the Security Council of the United Nations passed the resolution of deploying in Congo peacekeepers funded and commanded by America, who started to get involved in Congo. Shortly after its entering, the UN peacekeepers seized Congo rather than fighting the secessionists for the government. Frustrated, Lumumba turned to the Soviet Union, enabling the presence of the Soviet and Czech militants in Congo, and required the UN to withdraw its troops so that it could curb the insurgency on its own. As a result, Congo was controlled by three forces: the group led by Tshombe and Kalonji supported by Belgium, French and Britain, Kasa-Vubu and Cyrille Adoula side with the support of the United States and the party led by Lumumba and Gizenga backed up by the Soviet Union, China and other countries in Asia and Africa. The domestic affairs of Congo turned into an arena in which the new and old colonial forces contended and the Soviet Union and the United States fought for hegemony. And in this arena, the United States gained the upper hand.

On September 5, 1960, under the support of the UN and the USA, President Kasa-vubu announced the dismissal of the Premier Lumumba, who was house arrested by the UN peacekeepers. Later, the US CIA plotted the abduction of Lumumba and turned to him over to the Tshombe group for kill. But Antoine Gizenga announced to act as the Premier and relocated the government in Stanleyville, continuing to resist the forces backed up by America and Belgium. In February 1961, using expelling Belgium forces as the bait, America enticed the Soviet Union to make compromises by selling the national interests of Congo. The Soviet Union persuaded Gizenga to dissolve the government for a new election. In August 1961, a new government headed by Adoula was founded and Gizenga was deprived of actual power. From September 1961 to January 1963, the United States ordered the UN peacekeepers three times to assist the new government in exterminating the Tshombe group supported by Belgium, Britain and France, forcibly reunifying Congo.

The intervention of America in Congo irritated the Congolese. In January 1964, armed uprisings for national independence once again took place in Congo. The uprising troops swiftly seized provinces in the north and east, compelling the UN peacekeepers to withdraw from Congo and overthrowing the pro-American

Adoula government. In November, Belgium sent troops to suppress the Congolese resistance and re-foster the Tshombe group in Katanga. In November 1965, the pro-American Mobutu appointed himself as the President after a coup. With the support of the United States, he defeated the secessionists and gained control over the situation. In October 1971, he renamed the country as the Republic of Zaire. In the fierce struggles centering on Congo, America won the final victory.

6.5.3. The Founding of the Organization of African Unity

Though going through many twists and turns, the new Africa gradually moved onto the path of independence and development. With the birth of many independent African countries, the Pan-Africanism seeking the unification of Africa was advocated by leaders in the continent. Pan-Africanism, coming into being in the late 19th and early 20th century, was about uniting the African people to fight against colonial rule and racial discrimination and for the independence of Africa and its unification. The idea of fighting for the independence and unification of Africa was first coined as Pan-Africanism by the American black thinker—W.E.B. Du Bois, who set up the Pan-African Congress. The idea impacted many nationalist leaders who led fights for independence in African countries[49]. After Ghana gained independence in 1957, at the initiative of its leader Kwame Nkrumah, three All-African People's Conferences were convened from 1958 to 1961. At the conferences, the resolution of enhancing cooperation and solidarity among African nations was passed. Propelled by the spirit, Africa saw the inception of unions of nations in various forms. The first of the kind was the Union of African States, sometimes called the Ghana-Guinea-Mali Union, originally linked Ghana and Guinea in 1958 and then added Mali in 1960. But African countries differed significantly on how to realize union. At the end of 1960, 12 national leaders of Francophone Africa held in Brazzaville a conference, at which it was proposed to coordinate regional economic cooperation and diplomacy but not to rush for political integration. The participating nations were referred to as the Monrovian Group, which was the moderate side in the Pan-African movement. In early 1961, heads of states of Ghana, Mali, Morocco and Algeria, gathering in the capital of Morocco— Casablanca, advocated unified foreign activities, peaceful and neutral foreign policies featuring non-alignment, the establishment of Africa consultative conference, technology council and other political integrated institutions as soon as possible and vigorous support for the national liberation activities in Africa. The six countries were known as the Casablanca Group whose members were progressive states. The ideas of the two groups came near after the conciliation of Ethiopia and Libya. On May 22, 1963, the heads of states and governments and representatives of 31 African countries met in the capital of Ethiopia, Addis Ababa, and the leaders of national liberation movements in non-emancipated countries attended as observers. May 25 saw at the conference the adoption of the OAU Charter, the establishment of the Organization of African Unity and

49   See Fang, Lianqing, et al., eds. *History of Postwar International Relations*. Beijing: Peking University Press, 1999: 426.

the stipulation of May the 25th as African Liberation Day. In the charter, the purposes of the OAU were specified as: a. To promote the unity and solidarity of the African States; b. To coordinate and intensify their cooperation and efforts to achieve a better life for the peoples of Africa; c. To defend their sovereignty, their territorial integrity and independence; d. To eradicate all forms of colonialism from Africa; and e. To promote international cooperation, having due regard to the Charter of the United Nations and the Universal Declaration of Human Rights. The top institution of the OAU was the Assembly of Heads of State and Government, which held once a year.

The founding of the OAU transformed the landscape of Africa. All countries gained independence after its inauguration joined this organization, which had over 50 member states and boasted extensive representativeness and great appeal. It rapidly elevated the status and role of African countries in global politics. The OAU also played a crucial role in pushing forward the fight for absolute independence in the African continent. Its liberation council was in charge of planning and organizing independent African countries to provide assistance to nationalist movements in countries that were not yet independent. Its vigorous support led to the collapse of British, French, Belgium and Portuguese colonial systems in Africa, thus contributing to the active influence and role of the OAU played in North-South confrontation.

6.6. National Independence Struggles and Regional Integration Efforts in Latin America

Since early 1920s, Latin America has been within the sphere of influence of the United States. However, since 1950s, Latin people fought hard against the collusion between the United States and their own governments especially in Central America and the Caribbean Seas. And in the broad South America, the countries stated to unite together to break away from the shackles of various economic, political and military organizations imposed by the USA, to safeguard national interests and to conduct mutually beneficial cooperation as a whole. These actions and measures constituted significant parts of the formation and evolvement of the North-South relationship.

6.6.1. The Cuban Revolution and the Fight against the United States in Dominica

The victory of the Cuban Revolution marked the turn of the national independence movements in Latin America. Cuba, an island in the Caribbean Sea, was only 90 sea miles from the American soil. As a result, the United States brought Cuba under its control for a long time for its critical strategic and safety values. Even though America recognized Cuba as an independent country in 1902, it was still under the political and economic control of the neighbor. In 1952, in order to better ensure its interests, America plotted a coup in Cuba and supported pro-American Fulgencio Batista to become the president. But the

Batista government deeply disappointed the people, and with the double conflicts of national and class contradictions, a revolution broke out in Cuba. On July 26, 1953, the 26-year-old Fidel Castro led over 100 patriotic youngsters to attack barracks for weapons but failed due to the great disparity in strength. He was captured and sentenced to 15 years of imprisonment. At the court, he spoke in his defense, ending with the words "condemn me, it does not matter, history will absolve me". The speech became the revolutionary declaration of the Cuban people fighting for national liberation. After being released in 1955, Castro organized a revolutionary organization of the 26th of July Movement. At the night of November 25, 1956, he and the renowned revolutionist—Ernesto Che Guevara led 82 warriors, taking the yacht Granma, and headed for Cuba from Mexico. After failing to land on the Corolla Beach in the south of Cuba, they turned to conduct guerrilla warfare in the Sierra Maestra Mountains, where they set up, consolidated and expanded bases. In 1958, Castro's forces began their own offensive and seized the capital Havana on 1 January 1959, overthrowing the Batista regime.

On February 7, 1959, the United States recognized the new Cuban government. But the US-Cuban relationship cooled rapidly with the further development of the Cuban Revolution, especially after Castro declared the entering of the stage of socialist revolution in Cuba. Socialist economic reforms centering on land reforms and nationalization were conducted and as a result, American monopolists and Cuban plantation owners and bourgeois. In January 1961, the United States decided to curb the Cuban Revolution through economic blockades, diplomatic isolation and invasions with mercenaries, creating the famous assault on the Bay of Pigs. In April 1961, the CIA of America organized over 1,600 mercenaries to invade the Bay of Pigs in the southern sea of Cuba with the cover of airplanes and warships. The mercenaries landed on Giron Beach where they were exterminated by Cuban troops and civilians. In dealing with foreign relations, Cuba adopted the First Declaration of Havana (September 1960) and the Second Declaration of Havana (February 1962), which strongly condemned the invasion, plundering and intervention of the United States in Latin American countries and came up with the slogan that each sovereign country of Latin America should have the right to resolve its internal problems without foreign intervention.

The victory of the Cuban Revolution inspired the independence movements in Caribbean colonies. As early as 1930, the American fostered an autocratic government headed by Rafael Trujillo in Dominica. Trujillo by carrying out dictatorial rule and suppressing opponents gained the reputation of being "the little Caesar of the Caribbean". He also owned 55% of the lands and substantial properties, making him the largest landowner of Dominica, and controlled a great number of economic departments of the country. The man implemented pro-American foreign policies by handing the control over many critical economic sectors and raw materials to America and making Dominica a vital base for the United States to intervene other Latin American countries. In 1954, Trujillo participated in the subversion of Guatemala's left-wing government and the assistance of the Cuban dictator—Batista and plotted three invasions into Cuba following the triumph of the Cuban Revolution. In June 1959, the dictator was finally confronted with armed uprisings against him which spread across the nation before long. In January 1960, facing nationwide opposition, Trujillo was forced to resign. Shortly after, he was assassinated. During the confusion, the United States once ordered over 4,000Marines to land on Dominica. In 1962, Juan Bosch was elected as the president and adopted some policies to safeguard national interests and contain American capitals. In September 1963, America plotted another coup and established a pro-American military government, which was overthrown by patriotic Dominican soldiers and civilians in April 1965. On April 28, 1965, the Johnson government sent a troop of 35,000 men, over 380 aircrafts and more than 40 warships to strike attacks against Dominica. In the second half of December, the American troop entered the capital Santo Domingo where 40,000 Dominicans fought with the American for over four months. The United States tricked Francisco Caamaño to step down so as to found a pro-American government with Hector Garcia-Godoy as the head and to deceive the people around the world. In spite of the strong opposition of the Dominican people and the demonstrations around the world protesting against the invasion of the American troops, due to the weak strength compared with the American power, Dominican people were unable to change the situation.

Influenced by the Cuban Revolution and the anti-American struggles in Dominica, from 1961 to 1981, 12 former colonies in the Caribbean area gained independence. The political power of these newly-independent countries was in the grasp of their national bourgeoisie and intellectuals.

66.2. The Fight for the Sovereignty over the Panama Canal in Panama

Encouraged by the Cuban Revolution, the anti-American struggles in Dominica and the successful regaining of the sovereignty over the Suez Canal, people in Panama—once the most stable dependent state of the United States—started vigorous fights for the sovereignty over the Panama Canal. Cutting across the Isthmus of Panama, the Panama Canal is a golden waterway connecting the Atlantic Ocean and the Pacific Ocean, and therefore of critical military and economic values to America's Asia-Pacific strategy. In November 1903, the United States forced the new Panamanian government to sign a new treaty under similar terms to the Hay-Herran Treaty, which promulgated that America pay US $10million one-time and an annual of US $250,000 starting from the ninth year of the opening to the Panamanian government, which granted America rights to construct the canal, build and indefinitely administer the Panama Canal Zone covering 10miles on both banks and maintain the order of the Panama city and Cologne on the ends of the canal[50]. As a result, since its

50   World Affairs Press, ed. *Referential Materials on the Issue of Panama Canal.* Beijing: World Affairs Press, 1964: 36.

opening in 1914, the canal has been under the control of the US, who set up in the Canal Zone Southern Command stationing tens of thousands of militants. Both the governor and the general manager of the Canal Zone were appointed by the US President, US laws were carried out and American flags were hung in the zone, making it basically a colony of the United States.

The patriotic Panamanian people were greatly inspired by the triumph of the fight for the sovereignty over the Suez Canal. In May 1958, young students in Panama launched large-scale anti-American demonstrations. In November 1959, Panamanian people started a march for sovereignty. In November 1961, with the prerequisite of acknowledging the canal sovereignty, the Parliament of Panama demanded to sign a new treaty concerning the canal with America. In January 1963, the United States was compelled to approve to hang the national flag of Panama in the Canal Zone. But the American in the zone refused to comply with the agreement, thus arousing strong indignation among the Panamanian. On January 9, 1964, a Panamanian student entered the Canal Zone carrying a national flag of Panama and was shot by American force as he tried to raise the flag. The incident triggered nationwide anti-American storms. Over 30,000 Panamanians, holding banners with "Panama owns the sovereignty of the Panama Canal", demanded to raise their national flag in the Canal Zone. The long-prepared American forces suppressed them with gunshots, causing 22 dead and 325 wounded and creating a tragedy that shocked the whole world. The infuriated Panamanians attacked the US embassy to Panama, burned the news office of America. Many cities witnessed strikes and protests by suspending classes and businesses, demanding the recovery of the sovereignty over the canal. The Panama government cut its diplomatic relations with United States.

The anti-American riots in Panama shook the American government. It was warned by the American military that the Panama Canal was vulnerable to damages as it was supported by dams, ship locks and auxiliary power plants. Besides, the Canal Zone, located in marshes, hills and jungles, was cut out for guerilla warfare, which were hard to defend against. The canal would be difficult to control without the cooperation of the Panama government[51]. After weighing the pros and cons, the Johnson government decided to make compromises to Panama. In June 1967, the two countries reached three basic agreements after tough negotiations lasting three years. The agreements, though clearly abolished the 1903 agreement on the canal and recognized Panama's sovereignty over the canal and the Canal Zone, did not harm the privileges enjoyed by the United States in the Canal Zone or change its actual control over the canal. Therefore, the agreements received extensive criticism in Panama and the president presiding over the negotiations was impeached. In October 1968, General Omar Torrijos came to power through a coup. The new government disavowed the agreements, clearly demanded to recover the sovereignty over the canal and the American troops be withdrawn from the Canal Zone.

---

51   See Fang, Lianqing, et al., eds. *History of Postwar International Relations*. Beijing: Peking University Press, 1999: 431.

January the 1st was set as a National day of mourning to commemorate the sacrifices in the anti-American fights in 1964. The anti-American struggles for independence in Panama reached a new high point.

6.6.3. The New Stage of the United Struggles of Latin American Countries

As the United States attempted to include Latin America within its sphere of influence, countries in this region changed their foreign policies. They implemented independent foreign policies to break away from the tight control of America. On the one hand, these countries enhanced their contacts and cooperation with Asian and African countries; on the other hand, they stepped up economic cooperation and political consultation within Latin America.

Latin American countries in Mexico City officially signed the Treaty for the Prohibition of Nuclear Weapons in Latin America and the Caribbean on 21 February 1967. Its Additional Protocol II requires the world's declared nuclear weapons states to refrain from using or threatening to use nuclear weapons on signatories and to respect Latin America's aspiration for a nuclear free zone. After the meeting, the participatory countries started diplomatic activities to get every country with nuclear weapons to sign the second additional protocol.

In the economic fields, Latin American nations explored step by step the economic development path featuring solidarity, mutual assistance and independent development. In January 1960, Argentina, Brazil, Chile, Mexico, Paraguay, Peru and Uruguay signed the 1960 Treaty of Montevideo, deciding to found the Latin American Free Trade Association. In December 1960, Guatemala, El Salvador, Nicaragua and Honduras entered the General Treaty for Central American Economic Integration, which was also participated by Costa Rica two years later when the five countries officially decided to establish Central American Common Market. The general treaty provided for the abolishment of tariff barriers, free trade and the establishment of tariff alliance among the five countries and uniform tariffs on 95% imported commodities outside of the common market. Promoted by the series of economic cooperation, in October 1965, ten Latin American nations, including Argentina, Brazil, Mexico and Venezuela, organized the Association of Latin American State Petroleum Enterprises for Mutual Assistance to exchange petroleum mining experiences and technologies and to coordinate oil production policies. In February 1967, Caribbean nations held a meeting at which the decision of establishing the Caribbean Free Trade Zone was made. In April 1969, Argentina, Bolivia, Brazil, Paraguay and Uruguay signed the River Plate Basin Treaty for economic cooperation. In May 1969, heads of state of Bolivia, Columbia, Ecuador, Chile and Peru held a meeting in Cartagena of Columbia and officially announced the inauguration of the Andean Pact Organization, which intended to exploit local resources to the utmost to accelerate regional economic development and to enhance coordinating policies of the member states to better contend with industrial countries. The five countries promised to lift all tariffs against each other and to formulate common tariffs against other countries.

In terms of conducting South-South cooperation, sub-regional economic cooperation in Latin America was more profound and extensive than that of Asia and Africa. Meanwhile, Latin American countries were exploring the possibility of coordinating policies and conducting equal-footed dialogs with the United States as a whole. In August 1966, before the Summit of the Americas heads of state of Chile, Columbia, Venezuela, Ecuador and Peru, after careful deliberations, issued the Bogota Declaration, which elaborates viewpoints of Latin American countries on major political and economic issues at the global stage and advocates collective cooperation in Latin America. In May 1969, when they met in Chile, Latin American countries, putting aside the Special Coordinating Committee led by the United States, unanimously demanded that the US should reform its traditional economic and trade relations with them. This started a new stage for of the solidarity and mutual assistance among Latin American nations and their fight for independent development and opened a new chapter in the South-South cooperation and North-South confrontation in Latin America.

Chapter VII

Development of the North-South Relationship

7.1. Adjustment of Foreign Policies by the Major World Powers

The architecture of international relations after World War II, in general, was basically brought about by the fight and compromise between the US and the former Soviet Union. Not only did their relationship influence the Second World, but also permeated the struggle for national independence and efforts for solidarity and mutual aid of the Third World and played a complex role of mixed pros and cons. Nevertheless, by late 1960s and early 1970s, various political and economic forces had gone through over 2 decades of differentiation and alliance and the architecture of international relations formed new strategic trends, i.e. the emergence of great centers of the US, Soviet Union, West Europe, Japan and China. In particular, with the growing strength of their own, West Europe and Japan gradually began to free themselves of the shackles of America and identified their strategic guidelines toward countries of the South. These core countries were endeavoring to strengthen their relationships with the great number of developing countries, be it political, military or economic, either friendship and equality, or suppression and intervention, or even aggression. At the same time, developing countries were scaling new heights in fighting for and defending national independence, enhancing South-South

Cooperation, and improving their dialogue capacity with world powers. In a word, the South-North relationship during this period showed signs of diversification. These new situations and problems urged major world powers to adjust their international strategies.

7.1.1. Strategic Adjustments Made by the US and the USSR

Hit by several economic crises, engaged in military and economic confrontation and assistance for a long time, and mired deep in the Vietnam War, the post-war US already felt its strength fall short of ambitions in many international affairs and therefore had to somewhat restrain itself. The newly-elected US President Richard M. Nixon revised the US global strategy in a bid to maintain America's hegemony even when its power was relatively weakened. On February 8th, 1970, in the State of the Union message delivered to the Congress entitled America's Foreign Policy in the 70s: New Strategies for Peace, he advanced a conception for the US diplomatic strategies which was later called the Nixon Doctrine. The Nixon Doctrine, in a nutshell, meant that the United States would assist in the defense and developments of allies and friends, but would not undertake all the defense of the free nations of the world. The United States shall furnish assistance, when requested, to a nation allied with us or of a nation whose survival we consider vital to our security. When it came to the South-North relationship, the Nixon Doctrine implied that Japan and West Europe shall share the responsibility of Two Camps Confrontation and allies of America were pushed to the forefront so that the US withdrew from Indochina and focused on its scramble and rivalry against the Soviet Union in Europe and Middle East.[1] This is the America's global strategic guidelines of finite contraction.

The Soviet Union, however, presented a strategic posture of global attack during this period. Following the Nixon Doctrine, Leonid Brezhnev, on the one hand, adopted "détente policy" in handling the Soviet Union's relationships with the US and Europe. On the other hand, he stated that: first, "détente" must not be used to "interfere in the internal affairs of the Socialist countries", which was a warning to the US and West Europe from meddling in Eastern European affairs by taking advantage of "détente" policy; second, "détente" was by no means "giving up fight of ideology", nor "freezing the social and political realities"; and third, "détente" must not stand in the way of the Soviet Union's support for national liberation movements, progressive and democratic forces as well as forces of national independence.[2] In this way, when the power of the United States was relatively contracted, the Soviet Union, backed up with its military might, was actively promoting the strategy of southward attack and scrambling for the Third World under the cover of "détente". Leveraging the

1 Wang, Shengzu, ed, *The History of International Relations*, Vol.10, Beijing: World Affairs Press, 1995: 4-7.
2 "Leonid Brezhnev's Political Report at the 25th Communist Party Congress of the Soviet Union", See Selected Documents of the 25th Communist Party Congress of the Soviet Union. Qtd. in Fang, Lianqing, et al., eds. *The History of Post-war International Relations*. Beijing: Peking University Press, 1999: 469.

"détente" timing, the Soviet Union, under the banner of internationalism, expanded its sphere of influence and encroached on many strategically vital areas by means of extending economic and military assistance, practicing friendly diplomacy, signing treaties of friendship and waging battles via agents. In the meantime, the Soviet Union strengthened its relationship with Cuba and tried to develop its relationship with South American nations; it also intensified its permeation and expansion in South Asia and vigorously grew its strategic relationship with India; after the reunification of Vietnam, the Soviet Union supported Vietnam's expansion; in Africa, the Soviet Union actively involved in the internal disputes of the continent, such as stepping in the Angolan Civil War and the conflict between Ethiopia and Somalia as well as attempting to topple the Sadat Administration of Egypt; in 1979, the Soviet Union even sent out troops and occupied Afghanistan, etc.

7.1.2. Active Efforts by the European Community to Adjust Its South-North Relationship and Develop South-North Dialogue

The European Community of Western European countries achieved an overall economic take-off in the 1960s and began to compete with the United States. In diplomacy, the European Community began to "speak with one voice" and, by dint of favorable international situations, practiced a policy to the Third World with European characteristics. For a long time, Western European nations had been major targets of Asian and African nationalist movements. Under the impact of waves of national independence in vast regions of Asia and Africa, Western European nations all adopted pragmatic attitudes, allowing some countries to win political independence without many twists and turns. Against such backdrop, how to re-handle the relationship between the former colonizers and the ex-colonies that had recently gained independence became a vital task of diplomatic strategies for Western European countries. In March 1957, the six member countries of the European (Economic) Community signed the Treaty of Rome whose Article 131 provided and established the association system (Association Agreement). The system of Association Agreement incorporated 18 African ex-colonies in "particular" economic and political relationships with the six members of the European (Economic) Community into the sphere of "associates" and provided that the Community, same as the former colonizers, should be entitled to exploiting resources and labor force of "the associates". This is basically an arrangement made by colonialism.[3] Unilaterally instituted by Western European countries, the system of Association Agreement excluded the autonomous right of "the associates", and such provisions only served developed countries in their unfair economic exploitation. Therefore, the system met with universal opposition. By 1963, the Community agreed to improve the system of Association Agreement. Negotiations were held

3   Brown, William. "Restructuring North-South Relations: ACP-EU Development Cooperation in a Liberal International Order." *Review of African Political Economy* 27(2000): 370.

between the Community (Party A) and 18 African countries (Party B) and the two parties signed the Yaoundé Convention which had a validity period of 5 years. This time, the associates entered into negotiations and signed the convention in the identity of sovereign states, but the economic relations identified by both parties were not substantially changed. Furthermore, the associates were limited to African countries only, which also evidenced that the European Community was then in the midst of economic revitalization and integration and that it had not yet formulated a comprehensive system-wide policy toward the Third World.

Yet, significant changes took place in the 1970s. The 1973 Middle East War (or the 1973 Arab-Israeli War), the oil crisis it triggered as well as the world economic crisis in particular dawned on the Western European countries that they should not have blindly followed the US because their interests in the Middle East and other Third World regions were not consistent with that of the United States. They realized that the relationship between developed and developing countries should not be simply classified as that between the strong and the weak, but rather the North-South relationship as equally important as the East-West relationship. They also recognized that properly handling the North-South relationship was central to the long-term growth of Western European economy and the rise of their international status. Against this backdrop, in face of the North-South tension, the Western European countries formulated the guiding principle of "replacing confrontation with dialogue". On February 28, 1975, 9 countries of the then European Community (EC) signed the Lomé Convention with 46 developing African, Caribbean and Pacific Group of States (ACP countries), expanding the system of direct association to non-African developing countries. Compared with the previous Yaoundé Convention, Western European countries made many concessions to developing countries in the Lomé Convention. First, the former "trade reciprocity system" gave way to "one-way preferential system". The EC agreed that all industrial products and 94% of agricultural products of the ACP signatories could access the EC free of duty, whereas the exports of the EC countries to the ACP countries only enjoyed most-favored-nation treatment. Second, funded by the EC, Export Revenue Stabilization Fund was established to help the ACP associates stabilize foreign trade revenue. Third, the EC increased aid for developing countries. Fourth, the Community supported industrial development of developing countries and the two sides were engaged in broad economic and technical cooperation and set up Industrial Development Center for this purpose.[4] The Lomé Convention was executed smoothly and renewed every 5 years. At the end of 1979, when the second Lomé Convention was signed, the number of developing countries involved amounted to 63. The Lomé Convention set up good credit in South-North Cooperation. Following that, the EC entered into economic ties with other countries and intergovernmental economic organizations (e.g. ASEAN and the Andean Pact Organization) in succession.

4   Wang, Guishan. "Lomé Conventions and North-South Relationship." *Contemporary International Relations* 2,(1991): 56-57.

260

Also in the mid-70s, advocated by the then French President Valéry Giscard d'Estaing, 27 countries, including 7 countries and the EC of the North and 19 of the South, successively held two ministerial conferences in Paris. Although the two dialogues ended up in failure, they indicated that the European Community played a significant role in the promotion of North-South relationship.

7.1.3. Japan Began Adjusting and Developing Its Relationship with Southeast Asia

With its economic take-off, Japan became another pole on a par with the United States and the European Community. It began to seek an international political status compatible with its economic status. While readjusting its re-lationships with the United States, European Community, Soviet Union, and China, Japan cast eyes on the Southeast Asia Region. Japan first expanded its economic presence in Southeast Asia, and by 1967, it had replaced the United States as the leading trade partner of ASEAN. The 1973 Oil Crisis made Japan more clearly recognize the importance of ASEAN to itself: the sea area con-trolled by ASEAN, particularly the Strait of Malacca, constitutes the only route of trade between Japan and the Europe, Middle East, Near East, Africa, West Asia and South Asia and hence such a marine thoroughfare is a lifeline in-dispensable to Japan. Therefore, Japan set great store by the regional stabil-ity of Southeast Asia, which featured the self-stability of Southeast Asian na-tions and the stable relationship between Japan and Southeast Asian nations. Developing friendly political and economic relationships with ASEAN was a top priority of Japan in handling its relations with the Third World. In March 1977, Japan and ASEAN formally established the Japan-ASEAN Forum. On August 18th, 1977, Japanese Prime Minister Takeo Fukuda delivered a speech in Manila entitled "Our Foreign Policy towards Southeast Asia". The initiative introduced in the speech, known as the Fukuda Doctrine, comprised three prin-ciples: Japan, a country committed to peace, would never become a military power; Japan would foster "heart-to-heart" relationships of mutual trust with Southeast Asian states; and that Japan, as an equal partner, would cooperate positively with ASEAN and its member countries, and contribute positively to regional peace and prosperity.[5]

261

7.2. National Independence Struggles in Southeast Asia

In the late 1960s and early 1970s, the US assumed a strategic in its conten-tion for hegemony with the Soviet Union. The US had to make adjustments to its global strategies in an effort to find a way out of the stalemate of the Vietnam War as soon as possible and focus its attention on the Europe and Middle East. In consequence, people in Indochina (Vietnam, Cambodia and Laos) finally tri-umphed over resistance wars against America after years of hard struggle. But the Soviet Union saw this as an opportunity to meddle in the Southeast Asian

5   Yao, Wenli. "On Japan's Adjustment of Foreign Policies during the Cold War." *Japanese Studies* 1(1994): 13.

affairs and tried to fill the political vacuum left by the American withdrawal. This presented new destabilizing factors to the Southeast Asia region, where the countries were thus confronted with new tasks of fighting for and defending national independence and sovereignty.

7.2.1. Independence of Vietnam and Its Regional Hegemonism

In face of intense pressure both internally and externally, the newly-elected US President Richard Nixon, who considered America's withdrawal from the Vietnam War as the most vital part of its strategic adjustment, also wanted to achieve the so-called "peace with honor" and hoped to maintain South Vietnam regime. To this end, the Nixon administration meticulously designed the dual-track policy of alternating peace talks and military attacks. Negotiations were not interrupted and wars against North Vietnam were not ceased. America employed this delaying tactics aimed at achieving "Vietnamization". Started on May 13th, 1968, the US-Vietnam Peace Talks held in Paris lasted for 4 years and 8 months until a peace agreement was officially signed on January 27th, 1973. During the negotiations, North Vietnam insisted that the US Army and its coalition fully and unconditionally withdraw from Vietnam and give up support for South Vietnam, on which the United States disagreed.

To strengthen its negotiating position, the Nixon administration decided to expand the war in an attempt to achieve peace through military means. In April 1970, the US and ARVN (the Army of the Republic of Vietnam) forces launched an invasion into Cambodia, hoping to sabotage the NVA (North Vietnamese Army) and the Viet Cong sanctuaries and military supply bases in Cambodia. In February 1971, they invaded Laos in an attempt to cut off the Ho Chi Minh trail in Laos, a vital transit line linking the Viet Cong and North Vietnam. The invasions led to a joint resistance war against America by people of the three Indochina countries. The war escalation of the Nixon administration not only made itself politically and diplomatically isolated, but also failed to achieve desired military effects. In March 1972, North Vietnam launched the Easter Offensive to counterattack. Under the circumstances of setbacks in peace negotiations and warfare, the United States was forced to get down to peace talks which thereby entered into a substantive stage. In October 1972, North Vietnam proposed separating military affairs from political problems as a precondition for negotiation, and the peace talks made breakthrough. On January 27, 1973, all parties concerned signed the Paris Peace Accords on Ending the War and Restoring Peace in Vietnam. The main provisions of the agreement were: Beginning on 27 January 1973 at midnight, Greenwich Mean Time, there would be an in-place ceasefire. Once the ceasefire is in effect, U.S. troops would begin to withdraw, with withdrawal to be complete within sixty days. The United States and all other countries respect the independence, sovereignty, unity, and territorial integrity of Vietnam. There would be negotiations between the two South Vietnamese parties towards a political settlement that would allow the South Vietnamese people to decide themselves the political future of South Vietnam through genuinely free and democratic general elections. South and North Vietnam should reach an agreement through negotiations without external interference and reunification of Vietnam was to be carried out step by step through peaceful means. The United States and all other countries recognize and respect the basic national rights and neutrality of the peoples of Cambodia and Laos.

Yet, after the withdrawal of US troops, America continued to provide much assistance to South Vietnam and supported South Vietnam's refusal to honor the Paris Peace Accords. The United States firmly opposed the founding of a coalition government and the stay of North Vietnam Army in the south. The South Vietnam regime even launched armed attacks on liberated southern areas. But the South Vietnam regime that had already lost the support of its people could hardly fulfill the mission entrusted by the US — Vietnamization of the war. By March 1975, the Viet Cong (also known as the South Vietnamese National Liberation Front) aided by the People's Army of (North) Vietnam launched the general offensive against the South Vietnam regime. On May 1st of the year, the entire south was liberated and North and South Vietnam were officially reunified in June.

At the end of March 1975, the People's armed forces of Cambodia counter-attacked the pro-US Lon Nol's regime and soon achieved the control of the whole country. On January 5th, 1976, the Cambodian government issued a new constitution and changed the official name of the country to Democratic Kampuchea. In December 1975, the Pathet Lao, also known as the Lao People's Revolutionary Party, announced the abolishment of monarchy and the founding of a unified Lao People's Democratic Republic. Till then, the anti-US movement of Indochina national salvation saw a final victory.

Nevertheless, peace didn't fall on this war-torn land soon. Due to the acquiescence, political, economic and military assistance of the Soviet Union, the then newly-reunified Vietnam practiced regional hegemonism aimed at annexing Laos and Cambodia. In July 1977, Vietnam and Laos signed the 25-year Lao-Vietnamese Treaty of Friendship and Cooperation. The treaty legitimized the stationing of 50,000-odd Vietnamese soldiers in Laos, thousands of Vietnamese "advisers" serving at Party, political and military departments of Laos and large numbers of Vietnamese immigrating to Laos, which made Laos enslaved to Vietnam in various respects.

In late October 1979, Vietnam sent 100,000-odd troops to Cambodia and seized its capital Phnom Penh. In the wake of the occupation, Vietnam installed Heng Samrin's regime and controlled the domestic and foreign policies of Cambodia. Three Cambodian forces rose up against the Vietnamese invasion. They were Patriotic and Democratic Front of the Great National Union of Kampuchea (Cambodia) organized in August 1979 by Khieu Samphan, the president of the state presidium of Democratic Kampuchea, and the Khmer

People's National Liberation Front founded by Son Sann as well as National United Front for an Independent, Neutral, Peaceful and Cooperative Cambodia led by Prince Norodom Sihanouk in October 1979. In 1982, the three sides joined together and formed the Coalition Government of Democratic Kampuchea. The Cambodian people's national resistance against the Vietnamese invasion won widespread support and compassion of most countries, particularly the support of ASEAN countries and China. With the Soviet Union's retrenched global strategy and dwindling assistance to Vietnam in late 1980s, Vietnam suffered a domestic economic recession from the invasive war to Cambodia. Under continuous pressure from the international community, Vietnam announced in January 1989 to withdraw all troops from Cambodia.

7.2.2. The Rise of Neutrality Trend in Southeast Asia

The United States contracted its power in the Asia-Pacific region and publicly requested its Asian allies to gradually take responsibility for their own national security and military defense whereas the Soviet Union attempted to take the opportunity to permeate the Southeast Asia. In June 1969, Leonid Brezhnev conceived the idea of Asian Collective Security System and touted everywhere in Southeast and South Asia. The Soviet Union's support for Vietnamese invasion in Cambodia and its own direct aggression in Afghanistan in December 1979 constituted two vital links of its southward strategy. The Soviet Union's direct military presence in Indochina greatly enhanced its strategic situation in Southeast Asia, developed direct military confrontation with the US in the Philippines and other places, and gravely undermined the channels in the Pacific and Indian Ocean.

To safeguard their own security, all ASEAN countries claimed for neutrality of Southeast Asia. On November 26th and 27th, 1971, ASEAN held a special foreign ministers meeting in Kuala Lumpur and issued a declaration on the Zone of Peace, Freedom and Neutrality in Southeast Asia, or the Kuala Lumpur Declaration of 1971. To some extent, this reflected the separation of ASEAN from the US. Meanwhile, it manifested that ASEAN denied the program of Asian Collective Security System advocated by the Soviet Union and the claim for internationalization of the Strait of Malacca made by the Soviet Union and Japan. Malaysia, Singapore and Indonesia even announced that they would jointly manage the Strait of Malacca and the Singapore Strait. Confronted with the expansionary momentum of the Soviet Union and Vietnam as well as the economic crisis in the West, the ASEAN countries after the Indochina wars deeply recognized internal solidarity and unity as the foundation for maintaining their own international standing and resisting interventions of powers. Consequently, the five ASEAN countries held the first Summit meeting in Bali, in February 1976, and signed the Treaty of Amity and Cooperation in Southeast Asia and the Declaration of Concord of ASEAN. The main provisions of the treaty were: mutual respect for the independence, sovereignty, territorial integrity and national identity of all nations; non-interference in the internal affairs of one another; settlement of differences or disputes by peaceful means and maintenance of regional stability; closer cooperation among signatories in economy, social culture, science and technology as well as executive administration; regular contacts and consultations on international and regional issues.[6] In August 1977, the second ASEAN Summit, held in Kuala Lumpur, further coordinated the relations among member states. In particular, a compromise was reached between the Philippines and Malaysia on the territorial claim over Sabah. In terms of foreign relations, the five ASEAN members agreed to gradually strengthen their relations with Japan, the European Community, Australia and New Zealand. After Vietnamese occupation of Cambodia, they pushed the United Nations to pass a resolution that refused to recognize the Vietnam-backed Heng Samrin's regime and demanded Vietnam's unconditional withdrawal of troops from Cambodia. Such practices of ASEAN Countries constituted an integral part of the development of North-South relationship in the 1970s.

7.3. China's Role and Influence in the North-South Relationship

7.3.1 International Strategic Thinking of the "Three Worlds" by the PRC

In the late 1960s and early 1970s, international situation witnessed dramatic turns, bringing about major transformation to the strategic position of the PRC. The defeat of the US in the Vietnam War of Aggression, the advocacy of Nixon Doctrine, President Nixon's visit to Beijing, all contributed to relaxations in the overall global situation. One the one hand, China felt the national defense security of its southern border. On the other hand, tension rose between the PRC and the Soviet Union, which further triggered border clashes. The Soviet Union championed the conception of "Asian collective security" aimed at besieging China. In terms of worldwide political situations, the Soviet Union revealed its offensive, whereas the United States was on the defensive; the rising Western Europe and Japan increasingly unfolded diplomacy different from that of the US; thanks to their great number, unity and cooperation, the newly-independent Third World countries were beginning to play an important and independent role in the international arena. The world multi-polarization has already come into view, and the evolution of North-South relationship developed new features accordingly.

New international situation called for new thinking of China on the overall global strategy. Through long-term serious consideration, Chairman Mao Zedong formulated his theory on the Three Worlds, which held that international relations comprised three politico-economic worlds: the first world consisting of superpowers such as the United States and the Soviet Union, the third world consisting of developing countries and regions in Asia, Africa and Latin

---

6   Wang, Shilu, and Guoping Wang, eds. *Contemporary ASEAN*. Chengdu: Sichuan People's Publishing House, 1998: 304.

America, and the second world consisting of lesser powers such as developed countries other than the US and the USSR. Such a demarcation fully displayed the profound changes of China's diplomacy under new historical conditions. The strategic thinking of "Third Worlds" proceeded from the idea of China being a member of the Third World. The United States and the Soviet Union as two superpowers were considered as major adversaries of the Third World in the international arena; the large number of developing countries were believed to be major international forces standing by China, and the Third World could win the support of those developed countries in between in their fight against the oppression and threats of war waged by the superpowers.

Thanks to the guidance of such global strategic thinking, the 1970s marked China's return to the United Nations and witnessed major breakthrough in China's foreign relations. For one thing, China accomplished the normalization of its diplomatic relations with the United States and other Western countries. This not only served as a powerful strike to the bipolar structure of the Cold War era and a driving force behind the World diversification, but also presented significance to the maintenance of World peace and development. For another, China scaled new heights in its cooperation and mutual support with many developing countries.

7.3.2. China's Return to the UN and Normalization of Sino-US Relations

In June 1945, 282 representatives from 50 countries involved in drafting and signing the Charter of the United Nations in San Francisco, USA, proclaiming the establishment of the United Nations. China is a founding member of the UN and one of the five permanent members of the UN Security Council. Upon the founding of the People's Republic of China, the seat of the Republic of China in the United Nations was supposed to give way to the PRC. However, since the United States adopted a prolonged policy of isolation and hostility against the People's Republic of China, the PRC was, for a long time, deprived of its legitimate seat in the United Nations. Throughout the 50s, despite the proposals of resuming the New China's lawful seat made by the USSR and other friendly nations at every session of the UN General Assembly, the then UN, controlled by the United States, denied the resumption with a majority of veto votes in form. Fortunately, thanks to the PRC's continuously improved international standing and prestige, with the admission of newly-independent Asian, African and Latin American countries to the UN, the composition of the United Nations turned from being US-dominated to benefiting the break of the control of the US. In September 1960, 24 out of the 31 countries whose representatives addressed the 15th Session of the UN General Assembly placed the resumption of China's seat in the UN on the agenda of the Assembly. At the 25th Session of the UN General Assembly convened in September 1970, there were 51 in favor, 49 opposed and 25 abstentions in a voting on the resumption of China's representation. On October 25th, 1971, 23 countries including Albania and Algeria advanced a joint

motion on restoring all lawful rights of China in the United Nations and immediately expelling the Chiang Kai-shek bloc, and Resolution 2758 was passed at
the 26th Session of the UN General Assembly with an overwhelming majority,
with 76 affirmative votes, 35 veto votes and 17 abstentions. As such, the motion
of "dual representation" conceived by the US and Japan became invalid before
a voting. After about 2 decades of unremitting efforts, China finally returned to
the United Nations with the help of fellow countries of Asia, Africa and Latin
America. This was not only a significant victory in China's diplomacy, but also
a great triumph of the Third World in the efforts to oppose the US-USSR bipolar
supremacy and to step up South-South Cooperation. Marked by its reentry into
the UN, China's foreign relations opened up new vistas, beginning with the normalization of diplomatic relations with US-led Western countries.

In January 1969, Republican Richard Nixon took office in the White House.
At that time, the United States was in the midst of the most difficult and harsh-
est situation since the end of World War II. The heavy burden of the Vietnam
War, the deepening political, economic and social crisis domestically, all this
put the United States at a disadvantage in the rivalry for hegemony with the
Soviet Union. In the meantime, Nixon acutely sensed the falling supremacy of
the US, the strength of the PRC and its increasing influence among Asian and
African countries. Therefore, Nixon made the improvement of US-PRC relations a priority in his country's diplomacy. His confidence was further boosted
in March 1969 when a conflict over Zhenbao Island broke out between the
Soviet Union and the PRC. Soon afterwards, Nixon conveyed his wish of improving US-China relationship to the People's Republic of China through leaders of France and Pakistan. At a reception banquet held in late October, 1970
to welcome the Romanian President, US President Nixon, for the first time, officially and publicly used the term "the People's Republic of China." Besides,
he took a series of friendly measures to China, such as withdrawing destroyers
on patrol in the Taiwan Strait and lifting an embargo against China. Out of its
strategic concerns, China resisted the pressure from the Soviet Union and made
positive responses to Nixon. For example, at the end of 1969, China voluntarily
proposed to resume China-US ambassadorial talks that had suspended for two
years; on October 1, 1970, Chairman Mao invited the famous American jour-
nalist Edgar Snow and his wife to review the National Day parade; On April
6th, 1971, China invited the American Table Tennis Teams to visit China during
their stay in Japan for the World tournament. In July 1971, Dr. Henry Kissinger,
the US National Security Advisor under Nixon, made a secret visit to Beijing
and on July 16, he and the then Chinese Premier Zhou Enlai issued a joint announcement that shocked the whole world: "Knowing of President Nixon's expressed desire to visit the People's Republic of China, Premier Zhou Enlai, on
behalf of the Government of the People's Republic of China, has extended an
invitation to President Nixon to visit China at an appropriate date before May
1972. President Nixon has accepted the invitation with pleasure."[7]

---

7   *People's Daily* July 16, 1971.

On February 21, 1972, President Nixon and his party arrived in Beijing and paid a 7-day historic visit to China. On the 28th, the Chinese and the US sides signed the Joint Communiqué in Shanghai (also known as the Shanghai Communiqué), and stated: "That the United States and the People's Republic of China work toward the full normalization of diplomatic relations serves the interests of all countries." "Both sides desire to reduce the risks of international military conflicts." "Neither of the two countries should seek hegemony in the Asia-Pacific region and each is opposed to efforts by any other country or group of countries to establish such hegemony." "Neither party is prepared to negotiate on behalf of any third party nor is prepared to conclude an agreement or understanding with the other party directed against any other country." As to the Taiwan question, the United States made a statement that "The US acknowledges the PRC position that all Chinese on both sides of the Taiwan Strait maintain that there is only one China and that Taiwan is part of China. The United States does not challenge that position, and reaffirms its concern over a peaceful solution to the Taiwan question by the Chinese people themselves."[8] China and the United States realized the normalization of their diplomatic relations. Despite some twists and turns, the two countries issued the second Joint Communiqué dated December 16, 1978, and announced the decision to establish diplomatic relations as from January 1, 1979. In the third US-PRC Joint Communiqué dated August 17, 1982, the United States reiterated its stand on the Taiwan question. The three Joint Communiqués serves as a foundation for the United States and China to deal with their bilateral relations.

7.3.3. Fresh Progress in China's Diplomatic Relations

Upon the normalization of China-US relations, a flock of Western countries speedily established diplomatic relations with China, which was followed by the restoration of China-Japan diplomatic relations. On September 25, 1972, the new Japanese Prime Minister Kakuei Tanaka paid a visit to Beijing, China, and on the 29, issued a joint statement which says the two countries has decided to establish diplomatic relations as from September 29, 1972. At a press conference held on that very day, Japanese Foreign Minister Masayoshi Ohira declared the annulment of the Japan-ROC Treaty of Peace with the Taiwan authority. On August 12th, 1978, Japan and the People's Republic of China officially signed the Treaty of Peace and Friendship. Throughout the Western World, as of 1979 when Portugal and Ireland established diplomatic relations with China, almost all European countries had established ambassadorial relations with China, except for Andorra, Liechtenstein and Monaco. Australia and New Zealand established diplomatic ties with China in 1972, and the European Community did so in May 1975.

---

8   Group of Selecting and Editing Materials on the History of international Relation, the Editorial Office of Textbooks of Law, ed. *Selected Compilation of Materials on the History of International Relations.* Wuhan: Wuhan University Press, 1983: 570-573.

The 1970s also saw some breakthrough in China's relations with the Association of Southeast Asian Nations (ASEAN). With the improvement of China-US relations, the penetration of the Soviet Union and the escalation of China's international status, all ASEAN countries eased off their policies to China. At the foreign ministerial conference held in Manila, in July 1972, ASEAN set the guideline of establishing relations of peace and friendship with China. The Southeast Asia is adjacent to China's Southern border and has a major concentration of overseas Chinese and foreign citizens of Chinese race. Such a fact makes the political, economic development of ASEAN as well as national security closely linked to China. China's efforts of establishing and strengthening its relations with ASEAN became an integral part of its holistic policy towards the Third World. On May 31, 1974, the diplomatic tie between China and Malaysia was established; on June 9, 1975, China and the Philippines declared the establishment of foreign relations, and on July 1 of the same year, China-Thailand diplomatic relations was inaugurated.

Concurrently, China adhered to the implementation of the five principles of mutual relations and eight principles of foreign aid with Africa and Arab. With regard to the Mozambican and Angolan people's fight against Portuguese colonialism, and the South African, South West African (now Namibia) and Rhodesian (now Zimbabwe) people's anti-racism struggle, as well as Zambia's and Tanzania's resistance against political, economic pressure and military harassment of the white-led racist regimes in South Africa and Rhodesia, China provided enormous support in various forms, politically, materially, including military training. To those independent countries subjected to the influence of colonialism remnants, China offered much economic assistance. In the 70s, China signed aid agreements with 31 African countries that diplomatic ties were newly established with. Plus the 12 African countries that had signed aid agreements with China in the 60s, there were altogether 43 African countries having done so, making up over 90% of all African countries then. According to statistics, China's aid to the Africa from 1970 to 1977 amounted to US $1,825million.[9] According to the agreements, China's aid covered industry, agriculture, energy, transportation, culture and education, as well as public health, and programs of aid involved railways, farms, factories, water conservancy, hospitals, schools and office buildings. Basically, African countries are agrarian ones where prolonged colonial ruling and harsh natural conditions led to backward agriculture. Consequently, agricultural aid from China has always been very important. Almost every African country had China-aided agricultural projects, such as Tanzania's rice farms, Mali's tea plantations and Guinea's sugarcane farms, etc. China's aid has helped improve their agricultural productivity and unit output of grain, and hence has been widely popular with African countries.

269

---

9 *References on African Issues* 1(1979): 84.

Of all China's aid programs in Africa, the largest has been the Tazara Railway. In 1964, Tanzania and Zambia made requests to the World Bank, the United Nations, the Soviet Union, Britain and Canada on building a railway between Tanzania and Zambia. But they all declined to fund the project, with reasons being "not economically justified, uneconomical." Tanzanian President Julius Nyerere and Zambian President Kenneth Kaunda pursued the help of Chinese Premier Zhou Enlai respectively in 1965 and 1967, and were given an affirmative response. To build the railway, China supplied an interest-free loan of more than US$400 million. The construction was initiated in October 1970 and completed in July 1976, lasting for 5 years and 8 months. The completion of the Tazara Railway played a vital role in promoting the two countries' economic development and the Southeast African transportation. It also enabled foreign aid to successfully reach the forefront of struggles against Portuguese colonialists and South African racists, greatly boosting the morale of revolutionary forces. Above all, deep friendships were forged between the two countries and China since.

Concerning the fight against hegemonism, aggression and oppression, China supported the Vietnamese Resistance War Against America till 1973, aided the righteous struggles of the Cambodian and the Afghanistan people in the late 70s, and for a long time expressed support for the Palestinians and Arabians in their fight against Israeli expansionism, as well as opposed the two superpowers' scramble for the Middle East and their arbitrary manipulation of the destiny of local people.

In the mid-1970s, various Third World countries, encouraged by the victory of the Middle East Oil Struggle, stirred waves of movement to protect national resources, develop national economy and oppose the economic exploitation and predation of Western powers. The billowy nationalization movements in many Third World countries, the spring-up of organizations of raw material producers and regional economic cooperation organizations, and the Latin American countries' fight for 200-sea mile exclusive economic zone, all this converges to an extensive struggle for the establishment of a new international political and economic order. Regarding all these efforts, the Chinese delegates explicitly proclaimed to offer full support in a speech at the 6th Special Session of the UN General Assembly held in April 1974.

In terms of maintaining World peace, China actively supported the propositions of the Third World countries on the establishment of Zone of Peace and Nuclear-free Zone. In the 70s, many Third World countries demanded and proposed the establishment of Zone of Peace and Nuclear-free Zone. The advocacy of Nuclear-free Zone was directed against nuclear nations, while that of Zone of Peace was directed against any country that could possibly commit aggression against relevant regions. The call for establishing Nuclear-free Zone was first made by Some Latin American countries such as Mexico, and was later joined by South Asia, Middle East and Africa. For example, in September 1970, Prime Minister of Sri Lanka Sirimavo Bandaranaike made a proposition of making the Indian Ocean Zone of Peace; in September 1973, President of Algeria Houari Boumediene demanded the Mediterranean to be Zone of Peace; and in 1975, King Birendra of Nepal presented the proposal to recognize Nepal as a zone of peace. Since the oppositions of Zone of Peace and Nuclear-free Zone were conducive to regional peace and significant to peace in the world as a whole, China hence provided strong support for them. For instance, at the First Committee of the UN General Assembly dated November 11th, 1976, Chinese delegate Huang Hua, on behalf of the Chinese government, expressed support without exception toward the propositions on Zone of Peace and Nuclear-free Zone. In the meantime, he stressed that such propositions must have promises of superpowers otherwise it would be "merely nominal." More importantly, the Chinese government signed, on August 21st, 1973, the Additional Protocol II to the Treaty for the Prohibition of Nuclear Weapons in Latin America. Protocol II requires the world's declared nuclear weapons states to refrain from undermining in any way the nuclear-free status of the region, refrain from exporting any nuclear weapon and technology to any contracting party, and refrain from using or threatening the use of nuclear weapons against the contracting parties.[10] China is the first nuclear weapon state to sign the protocol.

With all the efforts, the New China (People's Republic of China) has established its own special and important position in East-West relationship and North-South relationship, opening up new vistas of Chinese diplomacy.

7.4. The North-South Relationship in the Middle East

In the 1970s, the United States gradually rid itself of the Vietnam War and practiced strategic contraction in Asia. Such strategy enabled the United States to concentrate its forces and intensify its contention in the Middle East with the Soviet Union. In particular, it succeeded in incorporating Egypt into its own sphere of influence. After the Suez Crisis (also known as the Israeli Aggression on Suez), the Soviet Union took measures of military and economic assistance and successfully established friendly relations with many Arab countries. The 1970s witnessed the most ferocious competition in the Middle East between the Soviet Union and the United States. Both countries, out of their own strategic needs, interfered in the internal, military and diplomatic affairs of the Middle East countries, causing new instability in the region and arousing strong antipathy and boycott of the Middle East countries against them. The Middle East countries joined up together and resisted against the US-USSR hegemonism in forms of the League of Arab States, Islamic fundamentalism, nationalization of oil supplies and OPEC (short for Organization of the Petroleum Exporting Countries).

---

10   Pan, Zhenqiang. *International Disarmament and Arms Control.* Beijing: The PLA National Defense University Press, 1996: 415.

7.4.1 The Fourth Middle East War and Oil Crisis

The rout of the Egypt–Syria–Jordan alliance in the June War (also known as the Third Arab-Israeli War) in 1967 outraged the entire Arab world and united various Arab countries. In the wake of the war, Egypt, Syria and Jordan began rearmament and set about plotting the Fourth Arab-Israeli War aimed at "erasing humiliation" and "recapturing lost territories". Their initiatives received full support of other Arab states. 12 Arab heads of state and government attended the Arab League Summit held in Khartoum and formulated the Khartoum Resolution, which was known as the "Three No's": No peace with Israel, no recognition of Israel, no negotiations with Israel. Given the political unity and growing military might of the Arab states, Israel, though having won a major victory in the June War, continued to carry out arms expansion and war preparations, and constantly launched military provocations. The 3-year "War of Attrition" was primarily fought between Israel and Egypt to deplete the economic and military strengths of Arab states. In addition, Israel contributed US$238 million to build a solid defensive line called the Bar Lev Line along the eastern coast of the Suez Canal. The line, which was named after Israeli Chief of Staff Haim Bar-Lev, spanned about 160 km and was flaunted by the Israeli as "an impregnable defensive chain".

While the Arab states and Israel were undergoing a new round of war preparations, the United States and the Soviet Union were creating a "no-war-no-peace" situation in the Middle East, aiming to control the peace and war process in the region. In this way, both Arab and Israel were militarily and diplomatically dependent on them, which facilitated the Unites States and the Soviet Union to expand their respective forces and influence. The Arab states could neither recapture lost territories by the use of force and restore the legitimate national rights of the Palestinian people, nor obtain a fair and just solution to the Middle East issue through serious negotiations. As a result, the "no-war-no-peace" situation presented much more pressure and difficulty to the Arab states and gravely hampered their initiatives. In May 1972, heads of the US and the USSR held talks and later issued a joint statement that proposed to achieve "military relaxation" in the Middle East. This allowed the Arab world to understand clearly the real purposes of the two superpowers. "Now it's time that the government should examine its excessive dependence on the Soviet Union."[11] The Arab states made up a decision to retrieve sovereignty on their own.

On July 8th, 1972, Egyptian President Anwar Sadat, during his meeting with the USSR ambassador, strongly condemned the Soviet Union's refusal of military support for Egypt and declared to terminate the mission of the Soviet military advisers and experts and take over the USSR military facilities and supplies in Egypt. Following this, Egypt and other Arab countries, Syria and Jordan in particular, agreed on the plan of joint military operations. On October 6th, 1973, Egypt concentrated its troops and launched a surprise attack against the Israeli forces that

11   Liu, Jing, et al. *The History of the Soviet Union-Middle East Relationship*. Beijing: China Social Sciences Press. 1987: 227.

stationed on the eastern coast of the Suez Canal. The Fourth Arab-Israeli War (also known as the October War[12]) broke out. Within the first week, Egyptian forces broke through the so-called impregnable Bar Lev Line and cleaned up all Israeli strong-points on the eastern coast, and Syria also retook part of its lost territories in the Golan Heights. Just as the Egyptian and Syrian forces gained an advantage in the warfare and popular morale was greatly boosted, the Egyptian leadership suddenly gave an order of halting the attack and consolidating the gains on October 10, leaving a "combat interval" to the western front. The key reason for such an act was that Anwar Sadat set the pre-war target of "limited defeat". In fact, the ideology of "limited war" was embodied in the entire attack plan and operation process of Egypt. With Egyptian advantages over Israel in the battlefield, Sadat hoped to involve the United States and the Soviet Union in an intermediation during the "combat interval" so that Arab and Israel could embrace political negotiations in favor of the Arab side. Yet, the subsequent truth proved that such one-sided wishful thinking resulted in Egypt's missing a critical opportunity of victory and Israel's catching a breath in the warfare. Soon the Israeli forces restored from the off-guard chaos and gained a favorable chance of counteroffensive so that they first contained the attack of the Syrian counterparts in the northern front and then took 30 km of the Syrian territory. Afterwards, the Israeli forces turned to counterattack in the western front. Particularly on October 16th, under the commander-ship of General Ariel Sharon, an armored division of the Israeli Army disguised as the Egyptian forces to take the West Bank of the Suez Canal by surprise. They opened up the western battlefield and besieged the principal Egyptian Army at the eastern bank. Brokered by the United States and the Soviet Union, the UN Security Council passed a Middle East ceasefire resolution which mobilized the United Nations Emergency Forces excluding the forces of the Permanent Members to take charge of supervising the ceasefire, which marked the end of the Fourth Arab-Israeli War.

The Fourth Arab-Israeli War was a military contest or rivalry of the largest scale between the Arab world and Israel since the World War II. "Judging from the end of the war, both the Arab and Israeli sides had their victories and defeats. Although Israel was at a military advantage, the Arab states reaped more political fruits. Through this war, the Arab states breached the obstruction of the United States and the Soviet Union, broke at one stroke the no-war-no-peace state of the Arab and the invincible mythology of Israel, and refreshed the national spirit of the Arabian people. The Arab world was unprecedentedly united as one. Iraq, Jordan, Saudi Arabia, Kuwait, Algeria and Libya, Tunisia, Morocco as well as Sudan...9 countries coordinated militarily in different degrees with Egypt and Syria. Besides, about 40 Third World countries issued statements during the war in support of the Arab countries and denounced Israel, and more than 20 nations severed diplomatic relations with Israel."[13]

12   The Fourth Arab-Israeli War is also known as the Yom Kippur War and the Ramadan War because October is the Ramadan (the month of fasting) of Islam and October 6th is the Yom Kippur (Day of Atonement) of the Jews. Note by the author.
13   Wang, Shengzu, ed. *The History of International Relations*.Vol.10. Beijing: World Affairs Press, 1995: 108.

Most notably, to coordinate military operations, the Arabic oil producers waged an earthshaking oil war (the 1973 Oil Embargo). On the very day of the outbreak, Syria first closed an oil pipeline within its sphere of territory. The following day, Iraq announced to nationalize all the oilfields and facilities in Basra which belonged to the Exxon Oil Corp and the Mobil Oil Corp of the United States. On October 17, a ministerial conference of the Organization of the Petroleum Exporting Countries passed a resolution of reducing the oil production in five percent increments, rating oil importers as friendly, neutral and hostile according to their respective attitudes toward the Arab-Israeli issue and determining respective amounts of oil supply accordingly, as well as imposing an oil embargo against countries in firm support for Israel, particularly the United States. On November 4 and 5, the OPEC again decided to cut the production of November to 25% of the September output, and in December, there was another 5% cut. The oil price had increased from the initial USD 3.001 per barrel to USD 11.651 per barrel.[14] The oil weapon of the Arab states was a heavy economic blow to western countries such as the United States, West Europe and Japan, precipitating the West into an economic crisis of long-term stagflation. This, to a large extent, led to a division of the Western Camp, which featured West Europe and Japan first showing amity to the Arab countries and finally the United States having to adjust its policy toward the Middle East.

Greece, France, Italy, the United Kingdom and Spain refused to allow the US airplanes committed to delivering arms and ammunition to Israel to stop or fly over their territories. On November 6th, 1973, the nine foreign ministers of the European Community issued a joint statement in Brussels urging Israel to strictly abide by the United Nations Security Council Resolution 338 and stressing that Arab-Israeli peace should be in conformity with the following principles. (1) Acquisition of land by force was not permitted. (2) Israel must end the occupation of the Arab territory as from the 1967 War. (3) The sovereignty, territorial integrity, independence of all countries in the Middle East and their right of living in peace within safe and universally acknowledged boundaries should be respected. (4) Concerning building up equitable and lasting peace, the legitimate rights and interests of the Palestinian people should be given into account.[15]

In order to ensure oil supply, Susumu Nikaido, chief cabinet secretary of the Liberal Democratic Party of Japan, issued a statement regarding the Middle East situation on November 22, explicitly demanding "Israel must withdraw from all the occupied territory during the 1967 war" and standing "to recognize and respect the legitimate rights and interests of the Palestinian people."[16]

---

14   See Fang, Lianqing, et al., eds. *The History of Post-war International Relations.* Beijing: Beijing University Press, 1999: 544-545.
15   Moore, John Norton. *The Arab-Israeli Conflict.* Vol. III. Princeton University Press, 1974: 1146. qtd. in Wang, Shengzu, ed. *The History of International Relations.* Vol. 10. Beijing: World Affairs Press, 1995: 116.
16   Japan's Kyodo News Agency October 22, 1973,

Confronted with a grave oil crisis in addition to continuous pressure from West Europe and Japan, the United States changed the conventional standpoint of supporting Israel in the late period of the Arab-Israeli War. This compelled Israel to give up the plan of encircling and annihilating the Third Army of Egypt and reach the first agreement of divorcing military contact with Egypt in early 1974.

The oil battle launched by the Arab states on the occasion of the War severely hit the West-dominated world economic order and improved their own economic power and say in international affairs. With the efforts of the Middle East countries, the 29th UN General Assembly admitted the Palestinian National Liberation Movement (abbr. PLO, i.e. El Fatah) as a formal observer of the United Nations. However, the oil battle of the Arab states was more than this. Following the oil nationalization of Iraq in 1974, the Arab oil producers such as Saudi Arabia, Kuwait, Algeria, Libya, Iran and the United Arab Emirates successively achieved nationalization of the petroleum industry through either oil and gas nationalization movement or stock holdings increase based on negotiations with Western oil companies. The oil pricing authority that had long been held by Western companies returned to the oil producing countries. From 1979 to 1981, the Organization of Petroleum Exporting Countries again decided to raise the price of crude oil whose record high was US $34 per barrel, bringing about the Second Oil Shock to Western countries. The price rise and control of petroleum mining right, in reverse, quickly transformed the economic look of the Arab countries by bringing enormous fortune to them and influenced the balance of power in the Middle East. Moreover, the successful battle of the Middle East oil producers greatly inspired other Third World raw material exporters and boosted the spring-up of organizations of raw material producing countries, thus presenting a new situation to the struggle for a new international economic order.

275

7.4.2. Egypt's Adjustment of Foreign Relations and Turbulent Situation in the Middle East

The October War served as an important turning point in the evolution of the Middle East situation, which mainly derived from Egypt's adjustment of foreign policy. As an influential large country in the Arab world and the Third World, Egypt has for a long time played a leading role in the Arab world's fight against Israel and constituted main force in wars against Israel. Egypt, accordingly, paid the heaviest cost. Clouded with prolonged state of war, Egypt hardly focused on developing its national economy. In the wake of the October War, President Anwar Sadat of Egypt found it impossible to regain the lost territory and restore the lawful national rights of the Palestinian people solely by force. "The United States held 99% of poke chips of solving the Middle East problem,"[17] whereas the role of the Soviet Union was limited. The Soviet

---

17   Shanghai Institute for International Studies, ed. *Survey of International Affairs.* Beijing: Encyclopedia of China Publishing House, 1982: 156.

Union simply took the Arab states as its tool of contesting with the United States in the Middle East. Only by making contacts with the United States and imposing pressure on Israel through it, could the Middle East problem be peacefully solved. Therefore, Egypt shifted its foreign policy from allying with the USSR to resist the US and oppose Israel to allying with the US to make peace with Israel and resist the USSR. Besides, the United States also strongly felt the need to cool down the anti-American sentiment of the Arab world, and in Israel, a strong anti-war wave emerged. The calls of "envisaging reality", "stopping war" and "exchanging territories for peace" are echoed in the upper class and ruling class of Israel. As such, Egypt and the US entered into peace talks.

In February 1972, Egypt and the United States restored their diplomatic relations. In June, the two sides signed the US-Egypt Relations and Mutual Cooperation Agreement. In October 1975, Egyptian President Anwar Sadat visited the United States. With the forceful matchmaking of the United States, Egypt and Israel signed <Second-stage Agreement on Canceling Military Contacts> on September 4th, 1975. In November 1977, Israeli Prime Minister Menachem Begin officially invited Egyptian President Anwar Sadat to visit Jerusalem. In September 1978, the US President Jimmy Carter, Egyptian President Anwar Sadat and Israeli Prime Minister Menachem Begin had talks at Camp David Presidential Villa and finally came to the Camp David Accords which hereby initiates what the Western media called "Middle East Peace Process at Camp David". According to the Accords, brokered by the United States, Egyptian President Anwar Sadat and Israeli Prime Minister Menachem Begin officially signed the Egypt-Israel Peace Treaty in March 1979. Subsequently, the Egypt-US Strategic Partnership saw a breakthrough. From 1979 to 1981, the United States extended a total of 5.5 billion US dollars of financial assistance and agreed to provide advanced weapons to Egypt. The US Army also began to hold joint military exercises with the Egyptian Forces. Egypt gradually became the most important ally of the United States in the Middle East.

These developments further complicated the situation in the Middle East, which was first reflected in the worsening of relations between Egypt and the Soviet Union. On March 15th, 1976, Egypt announced the abrogation of the 1971 Soviet-Egypt Treaty of Friendship and cleared away the Soviet forces in Egypt step by step. Second, Egypt was reduced to a state of isolation in the Arab world due to its sole reconciliation of Egypt with Israel. In December 1977, Libyan ruler Muammar Gaddafi called together heads of Syria, Algeria, South Yemen and other countries as well as the Palestinian Liberation Organization to convene in Tripoli and announced the formation of the Arab Steadfastness and Confrontation Front. On March 27, 1979, which was the next day after the signing of the Egypt-Israel Peace Treaty, the Arab League held a ministerial conference in Baghdad and passed a resolution of enforcing political and economic sanctions on Egypt. After the conference, 17 Arab states announced to sever diplomatic relations with Egypt. Many organizations under the Arab League canceled the membership of Egypt and the Arab League headquarters was moved from Cairo to Tunis. At the Egyptian military review marking the eighth anniversary of the October War on October 6, 1981, some extremists among the Egyptian Army who believed in Islamic fundamentalism shot President Sadat.

7.4.3. Iranian Revolution and Its Massive Influence

During this period, the major change in the Middle East situation was the breakout of the Islamic Revolution in Iran. To build Iran into the fifth power in the world and hegemony in the Persian Gulf, the Pro-US Pahlavi Dynasty underwent a so-called "White Revolution" in the early 1960s. In line with the Western modernization ideas, a series of large-scale reforms were carried out in politics, economy, society and culture of Iran. However, the capitalist ideology and Western lifestyle were a severe shock to the Islamic traditions and the original socio-economic structure, triggering strong dissatisfaction of some religious forces. In particular, regulations on land reform in the "revolution" posed huge losses to mosques and religious institutions that were in possession of 1/3 rural land of the country. Mohammad Reza Shah Pahlavi's ambition of making Iran the fifth power of the world and his practice of arbitrary expanding economic development plan led to vicious inflation of the Iranian economy. Worse still, the gap between the rich and the poor was enlarged increasingly and the royal class became even more corrupt. All this incurred the increasing dissatisfaction and opposition of the Iranian people. Eventually, in the massive rebel movement which broke out at the end of 1978, the Pahlavi royal family fled from the palace. In February 1979, an Islamic republic ruled by the Mullah group was established in Iran and Ruhollah Khomeini became the Supreme Leader of the Islamic Republic of Iran. "The Iranian revolution was the first made and won under the banner of religious fundamentalism and which replaced the old regime by a populist theocracy."[18] In foreign relations, the Islamic Republic of Iran chanted the slogans of "No west, no east, only Islam", practiced the policy of independence and non-alignment, and opposed hegemony of the two superpowers, while at the same time it preached the Islamic Revolution and made revolution exports overseas. It firmly denied Israel and claimed Zionism the sworn enemy of Islam.

The ruling of Ruhollah Khomeini in Iran made major changes against the United States to the strategic US-USSR situation. The United States not only lost a barrier to contain the Soviet Union, but also had to strengthen its own military presence in the Persian Gulf region as a result of the weak military might of pro-US countries such as Saudi Arabia and Oman. In contrast, though the Soviet Union didn't directly benefit from Iran, it took advantage of the situation and intensified its southward strategy. In October 1979, the Soviet

---

18   Hobsbawm, Eric. *The Age of Extremes: The Short Twentieth Century, 1914-1991.* London: Abacus, 1995: 455.

Union and the Yemen Arab Republic entered into a 20-year treaty of Friendship and Cooperation and acquired two military bases—Gulf of Aden and Socotra Island. In December 1979, the Soviet Army occupied Afghanistan. And before that, the Soviet Union had forged close military relations with Iraq and Syria. Another significant impact of the Iranian Revolution was that it drove the fast development of Islamic Fundamentalism Movement in the Middle East, of which the extreme organizations were Hizb ut-Tahrir of Tunisia, Hezbollah of Lebanon and Hamas of Palestine, etc. They gradually became important forces of influencing the Middle East situation. On how to treat Iran, the Arab states once again had divisions. Syria, Libya and PLO were friendly and partial to Iran. All this contributed to an even more complicated Middle East situation.

7.5. The North-South Relationship in Africa

In Africa from the 1960s to the 1980s, one the one hand, some countries like Portuguese African colonies were still involved in the anti-imperialism and anti-colonialism struggle for and maintenance of national sovereignty. On the other hand, in regions that gained or still fought for independence such as the Horn of Africa and Western Sahara, evil consequences as a result of prolonged colonial rule, such as disrupted national and tribal boundaries, religious and racial discrimination and chaotic boundaries, began to exert negative effects in and among new national states. In particular, these problems stood out in some "countries" and regions that had not yet enter a development stage of modern national states. These factors were often taken advantage of by world powers that thereby permeated their influence.

7.5.1. Libya-US Clash

Located in northern Africa, Libya is a country wherein Arabs form the majority of its population. On September 1, 1969, the Free Officers Movement led by Colonel Gaddafi overthrew King Idris's monarchy and proclaimed the founding of the Libyan Arab Republic. Libyan ruler Muammar Gaddafi constantly followed a political diplomacy of firmly opposing imperialism and Jewish Zionism and supporting the nationalist movement in his mind. This directly collided with the interests of Western countries, the USA in particular. Tension rose between the two sides. In the early 70s, Libya took back the US Air Force base in the country, and soon abrogated the military, economic and technical agreements signed between the former monarchy and the United States, reducing the bilateral relations to charged' affaires level. Later, the United States recalled its diplomatic institutions to Libya under the pretext of Libyan anti-Americanism, escalating confrontation between the two countries. In 1981, the United States shot down two Libyan fighters over the Gulf of Sirte, further escalating their bilateral relations from mutual antagonism to direct military confrontations. In January 1986, the Reagan Administration announced to enforce economic sanctions against Libya by claiming that Libya supported terrorism. On April 15th, by claiming that Libyan terrorists set off an explosion and bombed American military servicemen in a nightclub of the Federal Republic of Germany, the United States staged lots of fighters and bombed Capital Tripoli and second largest city Benghazi of Libya. In January 1989, the US fighters again shot down two Libyan planes over the Mediterranean.

7.5.2. Independence Course of Portuguese Colonies

Portuguese colonies in Africa, including Cape Verde, Guinea-Bissau, Angola and Mozambique, were among the oldest colonies of the European powers in Africa. The colonial policy of Portugal was the most backward and most barbarian, particularly so during the rule of Dictator António de Oliveira Salazar. Under such an institution, he practiced a policy of assimilation politically, strictly controlled local education through Catholic missionaries and followed a system a forced labor economically. The Salazar regime turned a blind eye to the national independence movement that was sweeping across Asia, Africa and Latin America after World War II. "In 1951, to perpetuate its stay in Africa, the Salazar regime amended the Constitution and categorized the Portuguese colonies in Africa as provincial-level administrations on a par with other parts of the Portugal territory. These practices and other measures obstructed the local development of national consciousness and resulted in the nationalist movement in Portuguese Africa relatively lagging behind."[19]

In the mid-1950s, inspired by the victories of national liberation struggles of the British and French colonial people, nationalist organizations were erected one after another in Portuguese colonies. Under their leadership, large-scale anti-colonialism parades and demonstrations were launched successively in three large colonies—Guinea-Bissau, Angola and Mozambique. After their peace struggles were suppressed by the Portuguese colonial authorities, the nationalist organizations moved onto the road of armed struggle. By 1973, armed forces in Guinea-Bissau had liberated two thirds of the nation's territory and 45% of its people. In September of the same year, the National People's Assembly of Guinea-Bissau was held to declare its independence, which was soon recognized by more than 70 countries. Engaged in the suppression of anti-colonialism movements for a long time, Portugal was now laden with heavy political and economic burdens. Against the backdrop of worsening colonial wars and the end of colonial rule in Africa of other European countries, there were domestic claims for embracing the tide of the times. In April 1974, a group of young Portuguese military officers staged a military coup, overthrew the Salazar regime that tried to maintain the colonial empire, and advocated the practice of "decolonization and democratization." The new Portuguese government began to have negotiations with nationalist organizations in various colonies on the issue of independence. "In the event it was revolution at home rather than in the colonies that destroyed the Portuguese empire".[20] In September 1974, the Republic of Guinea-Bissau was first recognized, and in

---

19 Zheng, Jiaxin. *The History of Colonialism: Africa*. Beijing: Peking University Press. 2000: 676.
20 Fieldhouse, D.K. *The Colonial Empires*. Ithaca: Cornell University Press, 1973: 408.

November 1975, Angola proclaimed independence from Portugal, making the termination of Portuguese colonial rule in Africa.

Nevertheless, out of their own strategic interests, the United States and the Soviet Union actively meddled in the internal affairs of these newly-independent countries, and above all, led to the long-term civil war in Angola. The National Liberation Movement of Angola was mainly led by three guerrilla groups, i.e. the National Front for the Liberation of Angola (FNLA), the National Union for the Total Independence of Angola (UNITA) and the People's Movement for the Liberation of Angola (MPLA). On January 30, 1975, a transitional government jointly ruled by the three groups was established in Angola. However, with the interference of the United States and the Soviet Union, the three groups fell into armed conflicts soon. The Soviet Union provided hundreds of millions of dollars worth of weapons and military equipment to MPLA, sent hundreds of military advisors and even helped Cuba to send thousands troops to fight for the victory of MPLA. While the United States supported the FNLA and UNITA and instigated South Africa to get involved in the Angolan Civil War by mobilizing thousands of servicemen. Since the US Congress was concerned about the birth of a second Vietnam, it passed the resolution of forbidding from extending assistance to Angola. In this way, the Soviet Union and Cuba gained the upper hand of the contention. By February 1976, MPLA routed FNLA and its troops, expelled UNITA from cities and basically took control of Angola. In December 1976, the Soviet Union and the MPLA government signed the Soviet-Angolan Treaty of Friendship and Cooperation and the CPSU-MPLA Cooperation Agreement. The UNITA that was expelled from cities, moved to jungles and rural areas in the middle and southern parts of the country to launch guerrilla warfare against the MPLA, Soviet and Cuban troops. On entering the 80s, with the worldwide ease-off of the US-USSR relations, Angola, Cuba and South Africa signed the Brazzaville Protocol, which marked reconciliation between the MPLA and the UNITA and the end of the Angolan Civil War.

7.5.3. Civil War in Africa and Intervention by Major Powers

During the same period, some hotspot regions also appeared in Africa. They mainly concentrated in Ethiopia and Somalia of the Horn of Africa, Libya and Chad of Northern Africa, and Morocco, Algeria, Mauritania of Northwest Africa. Owing to territory disputes, these newly-independent countries were engaged in large-scale border warfare or civil wars.

The Horn of Africa generally referred to the northeastern part of the African Continent, the part that was surrounded by the Red Sea, Gulf of Aden and the Indian Ocean, traditionally including three countries—Somalia, Ethiopia and Djibouti. Because it was situated in the artery of the Mediterranean Sea, Red Sea, the Indian Ocean and the Asian-African Continent, it was deeply valued by the United States and the Soviet Union. Ethiopia was, for a time, the African country that received the most assistance from America, whereas Somalia was constantly supported by the Soviet Union and, in July 1974, signed the Treaty of Friendship and Cooperation with the latter. In 1974, an anti-government campaign joined by all social classes took place in Ethiopia. A group of young army officers established a military government and controlled the state power. In September, they deposed Emperor Haile Selassie, practiced industrial and commercial nationalization, and launched land reforms and declared Ethiopia a socialist country. The US-Ethiopia relations tended to cool down, whereas the Soviet Union had a close relationship with Ethiopia. In May 1977, the Soviet Union and Ethiopia signed the Declaration on Mutual Relations and Cooperation and the Economic and Technical Cooperation Protocol, according to which the Soviet Union provided large quantities of weapons and military supplies to Ethiopia, military personnel of the Soviet Union and Cuba secretly accessed Ethiopia to train and command the Ethiopian government troops.

Right against such backdrop, however, the Ogaden War (i.e. the Ethio-Somali War) broke out between Ethiopia and Somalia. With an area of 380,000 square kilometers, Ogaden was located on the plateau where the two countries bordered each other. The territorial dispute was left over by the Western colonial rule. As early as the 1890s, the present-day Somalia region didn't have a unified government. When Britain, Italy and France was aggressing on and carving up the region, the independent Ethiopia government gradually took the Ogaden area so that the Western countries signed a border treaty with Ethiopia in line with this fact. After gaining independence in 1960, Somali refused to recognize the border treaty and included the recovery of the area into the Constitution. In 1963, the Western-Somalia Liberation Front (WSLF) operating in the Somali-inhabited Ogaden area claimed for national self-determination and independence, which thereby incurred the prolonged border clash between Ethiopia and Somalia. In 1972, scientific surveys discovered oil in the Ogaden area, resulting in increasing tension between the two countries. On July 23, 1977, Somalia sent out regular armed forces to initiate a lightning war against the Ogaden area and took 90% of the Ogaden area within 4 months. Yet, the Soviet Union denied the territorial claim of Somalia and sided with Ethiopia, resulting in Somalia's abrogation of the Soviet-Somalia Treaty of Friendship and Cooperation. With the strong help of the Soviet Union and Cuba, Ethiopia forced the Somali troops to withdraw from Ogaden in March 1978.

The Soviet Union and Cuba's involvement met with strong objections from many African countries and aroused concerns of Western countries, which feared the presence of the Soviet and Cuban troops in the Horn of Africa would threaten the marine oil supply line in the West and challenge the global strategies and economic interests of the United States and Europe. The Carter Administration of the USA was forced to adjust its strategy. In August 1980, the United States and Somalia signed a military agreement where the US Army obtained military bases in Somalia, and in exchange, the US agreed to provide within 2 years 40 million US dollars of military loans and 53 million US dollars of economic assistance to Somalia. Thus, the US and the USSR was in a tit-for-tat confrontation in the Horn of Africa.

Chad is situated in the crossroad of North Africa and Sub-Sahara, East and West Africa. It borders six countries and is strategically important. Throughout the country, there are 140-odd small and large tribes with a total population of over 4 million. Residents in its northern, central and eastern parts are Arabians believing in Islam, accounting for 45% of the total population, while the southern and southwestern parts are dominated by tribes of the Bantu languages believing in Christianity. In a word, Chad is a country of complex races, tribes and religions and multiple contradictions. Struggles for scrambling territories and control of the Central government were pretty intense in the past, which was the root cause of long-lasting Civil War after independence of Chad.

In 1960, Chad obtained independence and the government was controlled by the southern Chadian administrators. The government's discriminatory policy against the North resulted in the breakout of armed riots in northern and central regions of the country in 1965. The insurgents established the National Liberation Front of Chad (FROLINAT) and Chad was then mired in the Civil War. During the Chadian Civil War period, Libya gradually "islamized" Chad in order to expand its sphere of influence. In 1973, Libyan troops occupied the Aozou Strip in northern part of Chad and supported FROLINAT. Chad's former colonizer France, to maintain its traditional economic benefits and strategic interests, militarily intervened from August to November 1968 and gave a heavy blow to FROLINAT armed forces. However, by the early 1978, the FROLINAT People's Armed Forces had controlled half of Chad's territory. In November 1979, with the efforts of the Organization of African Unity (OAU), the 11 factions of Chad jointly signed a treaty and formed the Transitional Government of National Unity (GUNT), with Goukouni Oueddeï, Colonel Kamougué and Hissène Habré, who were leaders from three powerful factions, holding positions of President, Vice President and Defense Minister respectively. Disputes in the division of power between Goukouni Oueddeï and Hissène Habré triggered the second Chadian Civil War. To defeat Habré, Goukouni sought help from Libya. In November 1980, Libyan troops forced Habré to retreat to the border area between Chad and Sudan. Libya not only militarily and administratively controlled the Capital of Chad and four fifths of the Chad's territory, but also compelled Goukouni to sign Libya-Chad Merger Agreement, which aroused objections of the Chadian people and many African countries. Confronted with internal and external pressures, Libya was forced to withdraw from Chad in November 1981. Yet, the French-and-US-supported Habré launched a counter-offensive and by August 1983, a three-year military confrontation formed in Central Chad, with Libya-Goukouni as one side and France-Habré as the other. In October 1986, Goukouni expressed his will to stop the Civil War and have south-north peace talks and defected to Habré's government, which infuriated Libya. On December 20, 1986, Libya directly and unilaterally sent out troops and invaded Chad, and the nature of the war was changed. In the warfare of the next 2 years, the Chadian government Army not only recovered all lost territories, but also went more than 100 km deep into Libya. In May 1988, the Libyan President Muammar Gaddafi decided to end the war and agreed to achieve peaceful resolution of the Chadian question under the supervision of the Organization of African Unity.

Located in northwestern part of the African Continent, the Western Sahara faces the Atlantic Ocean to the west and is bordered by Morocco, Algeria and Mauritania. On the map, its borderlines with the three countries are parallel to the latitude and longitude lines. Such a division does not conform to geographic situations, nor allow for tribal distribution, which constitutes the principal cause of disputes over the Western Sahara. The disputed territory consists of southern and northern parts, Saguía el Hamra with an area of 170,000 square kilometers in the north and Río de Oro with an area of 90,000 square kilometers in the south. Mostly a semi-desert region, the Western Sahara is rich in phosphate ore and iron ore. After gaining independence in 1956, Morocco refused to recognize the borderline and claimed for the territory of Western Sahara. Mauritania and Algeria were also anxiously concerned about the ownership of the territory. Yet, Spanish colonizers didn't want to give up the region. In February 1958, Spain declared that Western Sahara was a province of Spain, which provoked the denunciation of local people and world opinion. In September 1970, Morocco, Algeria and Mauritania signed a Joint Declaration hoping to resolve the Western Sahara issue on the basis of the UN resolutions. On October 14th, 1975, the International Court of Justice at Hague issued its advisory opinion and pointed out that Western Sahara was not "an ownerless land"; its northern part was related to Morocco and had legally pledged allegiance to the Sultan of Morocco during the colonial period; and its southern part was connected to Mauritania. King Hassan II of Morocco interpreted this as confirming its rights to the disputed territory and called on over 300, 000 citizens to enter the Western Sahara and impose pressure on Spain. On November 13th, 1975, Spain signed a tripartite Madrid Accords with Morocco and Mauritania, ending Spanish presence in the Western Sahara. The territory was then taken over by Morocco and Mauritania. By April 1976, Morocco and Mauritania explicitly divided and occupied the northern and southern parts of the Western Sahara respectively.

However, the Popular Front for the Liberation of Saguia el-Hamra and Río de Oro (the Polisario Front) established in 1973 firmly opposed the partition of the Western Sahara by Morocco and Mauritania. With the support of Algeria, the Polisario Front proclaimed the Sahrawi Arab Democratic Republic (SADR). In May 1977, Morocco and Mauritania signed a mutual defense treaty and formed military alliance to jointly deal with Polisario. During the war, the Polisario Front concentrated its forces to attack Mauritania, and Mauritania suffered a heavy loss in manpower, material and financial resources. In August 1979, Mauritania signed a peace treaty with the Polisario Front, declaring to abandon its territorial claims over the Western Sahara. Nevertheless, Morocco sent out troops and conquered the entire territory of the Western Sahara. Morocco and the Polisario Front were involved in a 13-year conflict until the signing of a resolution on peaceful solution to the Western Sahara problem by both sides in 1989.

7.6. The North-South Relationship in Latin America

The 1960s was characterized by the US-USSR contention for hegemony and the rise of the European Community and Japan which led to diversified trends in the international architecture and that the Third World as a whole became the main force in the struggles against imperialism, colonialism and hegemonism. The 1960s also saw Latin fine achievements of Latin America in economy, politics and diplomatic cooperation as well as the United States' faltering economic and military influence in Latin America. These accordingly enhanced the international standing of Latin American countries. Under such favorable conditions, Latin American countries established their independent foreign policy of peace in succession. Two principal manifestations were: on the one hand, Latin American countries, for the first time, formulated independently the rules governing foreign economic relations and set off the nationalization of foreign capital and the culmination of the struggle for 200n mile maritime sovereignty; on the other hand, Latin American countries strove for the diversification of foreign relations and internally broke ideological barriers.

7.6.1. Efforts by the Latin American Countries for National Independence and Self-Reliance

For a long time, Latin America had a single economic structure of relying on the export of a few agricultural and mineral products due to prolonged attachment status in the international economic system. At the same time, thanks to its relatively good economic foundation and political stability, Latin America was the most important investment destination of the Western countries led by the United States in the Third World.

To cope with the economic control of developed countries over Latin America, in the late 60s and early 70s, Latin American countries initiated waves of nationalization one after another. At first, individual countries carried out nationalization independently in three ways. One, restricting and reclaiming leased land; two, gradually reclaiming part or all of equities of foreign-invested enterprises by means of stock sharing; and three, nationalizing foreign capital by means of redemption, expropriation and confiscation. Later, these countries began to take joint actions. One thing worth mentioning was that in December 1970, the Andean Pact Organization (APO) formulated the General Regulations on the Treatment of Foreign Investment, Trademarks, Patents, Licenses and Lease Charge (Resolution No.24) and set strict limitations on foreign investment. The main contents were:

Prohibit foreign investment in sectors such as public utility, commercial banking, insurance, domestic transport, newspapers and magazines, commercial radio and TV stations. Foreign Enterprises that have already made investments must sell at least 80% of its shares of stock to investors of the host country within 3 years.

Foreign investment must be approved in advance by relevant member countries and its operation activities must be subjected to the supervision and control of the government of the host country. As of 1971, foreign enterprises newly built in any one of the Andean Pact member countries must sell at least 51% of their shares of stock to investors from the host country within the set time.

The profit remitted by foreign-invested enterprises every year must not exceed 14% of the direct investment and their reinvestment with profit every year must not exceed 5% of the amount of profit.[21]

Nearly all members of the Andean Pact Organization adopted measures of nationalization before and after the promulgation of this ordinance. For example, Peru, from 1968 to 1975, confiscated or expropriated 17 foreign-funded enterprises and reclaimed 3100 leased mines and completed nationalization of fishery, etc. Influenced by the Andean Pact Organization, other Latin American countries such as Guyana, Mexico, Venezuela and Argentina followed suit in succession. "The nationalization movement in Latin America hit and weakened the power of US-dominated foreign monopoly capital. According to statistics, from 1960 to 1976, foreign enterprises nationalized by Latin American countries amounted to as many as over 200, including 158 US-funded companies and 8 British-funded ones."[22]

In the meantime, Latin American countries went a step further in promoting collective self-reliance in the region and strengthening South-South Cooperation. They put forward the slogan of Latin American economic integration. President Daniel Oduber Quirós of Costa Rica (in office between 1970 and 1978) explicitly pointed out: "Latin American countries must deal with industrial powers with one single voice. If Latin America cannot negotiate with American and Europe with one voice, our individual efforts of dealing with industrial powers will be in vain." He stressed that only with the accomplishment of Latin American economic integration, "Could we formulate common policies to deal with large countries or powers."[23] Following the Central American Common Market (1960), Organization of La Plata Basin (1969) and Andean Pact Organization (1969) established in the 1960s, 3 economic integration organizations were successively established in the 70s. In July 1973, Prime Ministers of Caribbean countries such as Barbados, Guyana, Trinidad and Tobago and Jamaica signed the Treaty of Chaguaramas and proclaimed the establishment of the Caribbean Community and Common Market. On October 7th, 1975, government representatives of 23 Latin American countries signed in

21   Hong, Yuyi. *An Outline History of International Relations in Latin America*. Beijing: Foreign Language Teaching and Research Press, 1996: 312.
22   Wang, Shengzu, ed. *The History of International Relations*. Vol. 10. Beijing: World Affairs Press. 1995: 226.
23   Xiao, Nan, et al., eds. *Political Trends of Contemporary Latin America*. Beijing: The Oriental Press, 1988: 28.

Panama City the Convenio Constitutivo de Panamá, proclaiming the establishment of Latin American Economic System (SELA). On July 3ʳᵈ, 1978, foreign ministers of eight countries at the Amazon River basin, i.e. Bolivia, Brazil, Columbia, Ecuador, Guyana, Peru, Surinam and Venezuela, signed the Treaty for Amazonian Cooperation and established the Amazonian Cooperation Treaty Organization. Besides, under the influence of the Oil Crisis, Latin American countries also set up some regional organizations of raw material production and export, such as Group of Latin American and Caribbean Sugar Exporting Countries (1973), Latin American Energy Organization-OLADE (1974) and Organization of Latin American Coffee Producers (1974), etc.

Latin American countries also tried a new form of struggle which was forming Latin American multinational companies. According to statistics, since December 1971 when the Andean Treaty Organization ratified the founding of "Andean Multinational Company", more than 170 Latin American multinational companies had been established as of the first half of Year 1977, including the Central American and Caribbean Soft Coffee Multinational Company and the Caribbean Food Company, etc. Such companies became a powerful weapon of Latin American countries to conduct economic cooperation and jointly respond to permeation of Western industrial powers as well as protect national economic rights and interests.

The nationalization movement of Latin American countries and their integration construction were, at first, met with objections of US-led developed countries. To deal with Latin American countries, the United States took various measures such as raising tariff, trimming quota, limiting import, halting loans, trade embargo, destroying production, imposing economic sanctions and exerting political and military pressures. Above all, the United States overthrew the Chilean President Salvador Allende's regime through the New Trade Act and economic blockade.

On January 3ʳᵈ, 1975, the U.S. President signed a congress-approved the Trade Act of 1974 (the New Trade Act). The New Trade Act stipulated a generalized system of preferences: the President of the United States of America had the authority to, according to Article No. 5, grant tariff-free treatment to any qualified commodity; the President also had the authority to determine, with administrative orders, which countries could be made as beneficiary countries of the Generalized System of Preferences. Besides stipulations of under what conditions some developing countries were deprived of preferential treatment,[24] the New Trade Act stipulated that the U.S. President had the authority to dispose the following three types of countries: (1) countries that

---

24　Author's Note: The three categories were: (1) the Communist countries in other than exceptional cases (2) members of the Organization of Petroleum Exporting Countries or any other foreign treaty organization involved in obstructing supply of important commodity resources in international trade or raising such commodity prices to unreasonable levels and (3) countries that grant other developed countries with preferences that harm the business interests of the United States.

confiscated properties belonging to a U.S. citizen; (2) countries that did not cooperate with the United States to prevent illicit drug trafficking; (3) countries that did not pay due compensation to a U.S. citizen by the rule.[25] According to this stipulation, most Latin American countries became objects of the US trade restriction and retaliation. The Trade Act of 1974 was met with collective oppositions of Latin American countries. For instance, the Latin American and Caribbean Exporters' Association composed of 24 countries issued a joint statement opposing the "new form of economic aggression" of the United States. Also, at the five sessions of the Congress of Organization of American States from 1975 to 1979, Latin American countries collectively condemned the U.S. New Trade Act. Subjected to the pressure from Latin American countries, the Carter Administration of the United States had to amend some of the discriminatory clauses therein on March 30, 1980.

In 1970, the Unidad Popular[26] (Popular Unity) led by Salvador Allende won the Chilean presidential election. Their campaign manifesto was: to nationalize industries of copper mining, saltpeter mining, iron mining, private banking, insurance, power, railway, air freight, maritime transport, petroleum and cement; to speed up the implementation of land reform; to take measures good for labor force in health, housing and education; and to establish diplomatic relations with all countries, regardless of political system.[27] As a large copper producer, Chile's 80% of tax revenue and 80% of hard currency revenue all come from copper. On July 11th, 1971, the National Congress of Chile passed a draft amendment to the Constitution on nationalizing mineral reserves. Later in November, the Allende Administration nationalized all mining industries originally in the possession of American capital and other foreign capitals, and, in the form of collection, take-over and expropriation, nationalized tens of domestic and foreign-funded enterprises and banks. July 11th was also celebrated as the Day of National Dignity. Allende's government went on to carry out radical land reform and socio-economic reform with socialist nature according to his presidential campaign program. These reforms affected the interests of the right wing forces, the Chilean military and the US. Actively supported by the United States Central Intelligence Agency, the Chilean military waged a coup d'état on September 11th, 1973 and killed Salvador Allende, and overthrew the left wing government, as well as canceled the nationwide reform measures taken by Allende's government. The Chilean military regime even withdrew from the Andean Treaty Organization.

25   Wang, Shengzu, ed. *The History of International Relations*. Vol. 10. Beijing: World Affairs Press. 1995: 229-230.
26   Author's Note: It was a coalition of left wing, the Socialist Party, the Communist Party, the Radical Party, the Social Democratic Party, etc.
27   Volsky, V., ed. *A Survey of Latin America*. Trans. Shiming Sun. Beijing: China Social Sciences Press, 1987: 776.

7.6.2. Struggle for Maritime Sovereignty of 200n Miles

In the economic field, to seize advantageous position in the process of North-South contact, Latin American countries waged a struggle to defend the maritime sovereignty of 200 sea miles and made great success in opposing maritime hegemony of superpowers, which is of significant historic meaning. Except for Paraguay and Bolivia, all Latin American states are coastal ones with abundant fishery and mineral resources in their maritime space. In the 1960s and 1970s, large areas of oil and gas field were successively discovered in coastal Latin America. Ocean exploitation and development thus became an important pillar of national economic development in Latin America. However, at the first United Nations Conference on the Law of the Sea held in Geneva, February 1958, the US-led Western countries insisted on 3n mile maritime domain, and the Soviet Union only recognized the maritime rights of 12n miles. This was purely subject to the need of maritime supremacy of powers and facilitated maritime powers' predation of marine resources. As early as 1947, Chile and Peru took the lead to propose the expansion of maritime jurisdiction to 200 sea miles. By the 70s, this issue had aroused increasing attention of Latin America and the Third World. In May 1970, Chile, Peru, El Salvador, Ecuador, Nicaragua, Argentina, Panama, Uruguay and Brazil signed the Montevideo Declaration on the Law of the Sea. In August that year in Lima-Peru, 20 Latin American countries held the Conference on the Law of the Sea and issued the Declaration of Latin American countries on the Law of the Sea. As such, jointly promoted by Latin American states and other Third World countries, the 25th Session of the United Nations General Assembly passed the Declaration of Principles Governing the Seabed, Ocean Floor and Subsoil thereof Beyond the Limits of National Jurisdiction on December 17th, 1970 and established the principle that "the seabed, ocean floor and subsoil and resources thereof beyond the limits of national jurisdiction are properties commonly inherited by all mankind", laying a foundation for the birth of the United Nations Convention on the Law of the Sea (UNCLOS).

In the struggle for the 200 nautical mile maritime rights, many Latin American countries constantly enforced their own coast defense building, actively implemented coastal patrols and took measures of arrest and fine against those foreign ships that infringed their 200 nautical mile sea demarcation lines, international organizations of developing countries, such as the Group of 77 and Organization of African Unity also responded to and supported, in the form of resolutions or declarations, the struggle waged by Latin American countries to defend 200n mile maritime right.

The 3rd United Nations Conference on the Law of the Sea, which lasted 9 years, began in December 1973 and ended on December 10, 1982, consisting of 11 sessions attended by 167 countries in total. The Conference finally worked out the signing of the United Nations Convention on the Law of the Sea (UNCLOS). The Convention stipulated 12n mile maritime domain and defined the system of 200n mile exclusive economic zone.

7.6.3. Diversification of Foreign Relations and Reinforcement of Internal Cohesion

To change the attachment status in the world system, Latin American countries endeavored to diversify foreign relations and break ideological boundaries inside Latin America while struggling for and defending national sovereignty. This was mainly shown in the following aspects:

First, Latin American countries made much headway in their relations with West Europe and Japan. For one thing, the rapid economic development of West Europe and Japan required Latin American raw materials and market. For another, to extricate themselves from one-way attachment to the United States, Latin America was also in dire need of the capitals, technologies and markets of West Europe and Japan. Mutual needs drove the fast development of Latin American economic and trade relations with West Europe and Japan. "From 1968 to 1978, Latin American import from and export to the 10 countries of the European Community increased respectively from 2.71 billion and 3.45 billion US dollars to 11.67 billion and 12.1 billion US dollars. Latin American export to Japan increased from 279 million US dollars in 1951 to 4.52 billion US dollars in 1979, and its import from Japan increased from less than 0.1 billion US dollars in 1951 to 8.917 billion US dollars in 1980. Latin America attracted a total of 15 billion US dollars of investment from the European Community and Japan in 1981, rising by 2 times of that of 1969."[28]

Second, Latin American countries restored and developed their relationships with socialist countries. During the period of bipolar confrontation, Latin American countries were basically incorporated into the global strategy system of the United States. A few Latin American states echoed the American theory of "ideological boundaries" and adhered to the opposite standpoint against the socialist countries. In the wake of the victory of the Cuban Revolution, most of them followed the United States by severing diplomatic relations with Cuba and got involved in collective sanctions against Cuba. By the 1970s, with the ease of international situations, Cuba abandoned the practice of "guerrilla-ism" in Latin America. Latin American states all broke through ideological boundaries and drastically adjusted their relations with socialist countries. In November 1970, Chile was the first to restore diplomatic relations with Cuba, and by 1975, a total of 16 Latin American countries had restored or established diplomatic relations with Cuba. Moreover, the number of Latin American countries that established diplomatic relations with the Soviet Union increased from 9 in 1970 to 17 in 1980. Some Latin American countries with strong nationalist sentiment, such as Chile and Peru, not only accepted massive economic assistance from the Soviet Union, but also purchased lots of arms and ammunitions from the latter. Between 1970 and 1980, 13 Latin American and Caribbean countries established diplomatic relations with China. Latin America's improvement of relations with these countries strengthened their capacity to get rid of their attachment status.

---

28   Li, Chunhui, et al., eds. *A History of Latin America*. Vol. 3. Shanghai: The Commercial Press, 1993: 102.

Third, Latin American states strengthened relations with developing countries in Asia and Africa and began to play an active part in the Non-Aligned Movement. For a long time, the evolution of Latin America had been different from that of Asian and African countries. They, particularly those economically developed countries, often boasted themselves a part of the Western world or fantasied to be in the "Club of Rich Countries." Yet, harsh realities dawned on them that they, the same as many Asian and African countries, were fettered by unequal international political and economic order. In the 70s, some influential personage of Latin America acknowledged that Latin America belongs to the Third World. For example, Mexican President Echeverria Alvarez advocated Third-Worldism; President Juan Peron of Argentina advanced the Third Position; and President Ernesto Geisel of Spain declared Spain a Western and Third World Country. On the issues of fighting for 200n mile maritime sovereignty and changing the unequal international political and economic order, Latin American countries stood together with other Third World countries. At the same time, many Latin American countries began to break the alliance with the United States and increasingly participate in the Non-Aligned Movement (NAM). In 1961, the only Latin American member of the Non-Aligned Movement was Cuba. By 1970, Guyana, Jamaica, Trinidad and Tobago also became NAM members, and by 1979, Argentina, Panama and Peru also joined it as members, in addition to 8 Latin American observers.[29] During this period, Latin American foreign relations were characterized by the conversion from the West to the South, from alliance to non-alignment, and enhanced cooperative relations with Asian and African developing countries.

290

Last but not least, in terms of fighting for and defending national sovereignty, it's worth mentioning that the sovereign dispute of the Panama Canal was successfully addressed. For one thing, this was a result of prolonged struggle of the Panamanian people and joint support of fellow Latin American countries. For another, this was also attributed to the America's restlessness toward the meddling of the Soviet Union. The United States had learned the historical lesson that all the Third World countries with anti-Americanism would turned to the Soviet Union for help. As a consequence, the Carter Administration of the United States signed with General Omar Torrijos of Panama in September 1977 a new Panama Canal Treaty and the Treaty Concerning the Permanent Neutrality and Operation of the Panama Canal. The treaties provided that: Panama would gain full control of the Panama Canal after 1999, ending the U.S. privilege of permanent appropriation of the Canal Zone; Judicial organs, immigration agencies and customs that had been set up in the Canal Zone would be handed over from the United States to Panama; before 1999, the Canal would be managed by a joint committee comprised of US and Panama authorities; and as from 12:00 on December 31, 1999, Panama would assume full control of the Canal operations and management authority, and the U.S. Army would fully withdraw from the Canal Zone.

29　Author's Note: They were Barbados, Bolivia, Spain, Venezuela, Grenada, Columbia, Mexico, and Ecuador.

Chapter VIII

The North-South Relationship in the 1980s

8.1. USA and USSR Adjust Their Third World Policies

In the early 1980s, faced with the aggressive expansionist polices of the Soviet Union targeting the Third World, the United States began to adopt increasingly tougher policies against the Soviet Union. Previously, the Iranian regime change and the Soviet direct invasion of Afghanistan gravely challenged the United States. Iran was a strategic base of the United States to prevent the expansion of the Soviet Union in the Middle East. In February 1979, the Pro-US Iranian regime was toppled and a religious leader named Ruhollah Moosavi Khomeini seized the power. Khomeini's regime was strongly against America, and later in November, the staff of the American Embassy in Teheran was held as hostages, an event that rapidly exacerbated the bilateral relations of the two countries. Political situation change in Iran constituted a heavy blow to the American efforts of containing the Soviet southward development. In December 1979, the Soviet Union directly sent troops to encroach Afghanistan. It soon occupied the entire territory of Afghanistan, and established the Babrak Karmal's regime which was under its direct control.

The Soviet direct encroachment of Afghanistan and the changes of Iranian political situation incurred strong reactions from the United States. On January 4, 1980, President Jimmy Carter of the United States announced in his nationally televised address that the United States would take a series of measures, such as stopping selling cutting-edge technologies to the Soviet Union, postponing cultural and economic exchange programs between the two countries and providing military equipment and food assistance to Pakistan, and "cannot allow the Soviet to get away with such an act."[1] On January 22, President Carter sent mails to heads of government of 100-odd countries, asking them to support his suggestion of not holding the Olympic Games in Moscow.[2] On January 23, 1980, President Carter delivered an important State of the Union Address to the congress. He said "the implications of the Soviet invasion of Afghanistan could pose the most serious threat to the peace since the World War II." "The Soviet Union must pay a concrete price for their aggression." And the American government took a series of measures to this end. He explicitly warned "an attempt by any outside force to gain control of the Persian Gulf region will be regarded as an assault on the vital interests of the United States of America, and such an assault will be repelled by any means necessary, including military force." This is what was later called Carter Doctrine. In the meantime, President Carter recognized that "it demands collective efforts" and "the expansion of sphere of friendship" in the Third World to meet the threats from the Soviet Union. To this end, the United States continued to grow its ties with developing countries, and "ready to cooperate with all Moslem countries", and hoped to "develop a new type of mutually beneficial relationship with Iran."[3]

The Carter Administration also set about reinforcing armament. One the one hand, the United States established quick response troops so as to make strong response to military crisis in areas of major and tangible interests to itself. On the other hand, the United States increased military expenditure by a large margin and raised military assistance to pro-US forces.

Nevertheless, the emergency policy of the Carter Administration was too late to dispel the discontent of the American people due to its previously weak policy to the Soviet Union. In the 1980 Presidential election, Jimmy Carter was defeated by Republican Ronald Reagan who initiated an 8-year Reagan Era in the history of the United States.

On January 20, 1981, conservative Ronald Reagan was elected the 40th President of the United States of America. After taking office, he adopted an offensive anti-Soviet policy and seizing strategic control of the Third World became one of the basic strategies of this policy. Confronted with the Soviet worldwide permeation and expansion, particularly in the Third World, Reagan proposed to subsidize and support anti-communist activities across the world by means of economic, military and technological assistance.

1   *People's Daily* January 6, 1980.
2   *People's Daily* January 24, 1980.
3   *People's Daily* January 25, 1980.

In the course of scrambling for the Third World with the Soviet Union, the United States practiced "the rollback strategy" by fighting "low-intensity warfare" so as to "roll back" the Soviet Union out of expanded sphere of influence. "Low-intensity conflict" refers to "special warfare" waged by the United States to avoid direct military conflict with the Soviet Union in their scramble for spheres of influence in the Third World, to suppress struggles of the Third World people by means of political subversion, prop-up of agents, penetration and counter-insurgency, and to keep the warfare at low intensity.[4]

Soon afterwards, by means of "low-intensity conflict" and other measures, the United States unfolded scramble with the Soviet Union in Asia, Africa and Central America. In Asia, the United States proactively supported Pakistan and made it a frontier country against the Soviet Union. In the meantime, the United States continued to support resistance forces in Afghanistan to strike a blow to the Soviet control of the situation in Afghanistan. The Middle East was a region of strategic importance to the American efforts of stopping the Soviet southward expansion. The Reagan Administration, on the one hand, vigorously prop up Israel, establish "strategic cooperation" ties with it and made it an agent of the United States in the Middle East. On the other hand, the Reagan Administration hooked in some key Middle East countries such as Egypt and Saudi Arabia to reach a "strategic consensus" on preventing the Soviet power expansion. The United States reinforced its military presence in the Middle East and directly struck adversaries through "low-intensity conflict". It also sought to confine the opportunities of the Soviet expansion in the Middle East by promoting the Middle East peace process. In Africa, the United States provided some countries with political and economic support and also directly supplied them with massive military assistance. "During the 5-year period from 1981 to 1985, the Reagan Administration provided a total of 6.7296 billion US dollars of military assistance to Africa, 160% more than that of 19 years before 1981."[5] In Central America which the United States regarded as its own "backyard", the United States waged a head-on and tit-for-tat scramble with the Soviet Union. The United States took military, political and economic means to compress the Soviet expansion space in the Central America. Not only did the United States meddle in the civil wars of Nicaragua, EI Salvador and Guatemala, but also sent troops and invaded countries like Grenada.

During Reagan's second term, his policy towards the Soviet Union was changed. His administration practiced a policy of "seeking peace with strength" and carried out dialogues on some regional conflicts in the Third World. This was attributed to, on the one hand, slow progress of the U.S. "rollback strategy" as a result of the Soviet resistance, and on the other hand, new changes in the Soviet policy following the change of the Soviet leadership. After all, thanks to relative détente of the US-USSR relationship, some regional hotspot issues in the Third World began to cool off.

---

4   Gu, Guanfu, et al., eds. *The History of International Relations*. Vol. 11. Beijing: World Affairs Press, 2004: 14.
5   Ibid.: 16-17.

In 1989, George Herbert Walker Bush (George Bush Senior) was elected the new president of the United States, and he came up with a new strategy to deal with the Soviet Union, i.e. "beyond containment". The strategy of "beyond containment" required active expansion of cooperation with the Soviet Union, promotion of "liberalization" in the Soviet Union and the integration of the Soviet Union into "the international community". The strategy intended to force the Soviet to make political concessions by keeping the powerful military situation versus the Soviet Union, and to lure the Soviet Union to agree on the U.S. Claims by means of economic assistance in a view to implementing peaceful evolution of the Soviet. The strategy of "beyond containment" objectively eased the US-USSR scramble in the Third World and, to some extent, mitigated the North-South relationship.

In face of the American increasingly tough policy against the Soviet and its offensive of global attack in the early 80s, the Soviet Union, as the other superpower, did not weaken its expansion at the very beginning, but adopted the policy of confronting the tough with toughness and comprehensively counterbalancing.

During the terms of Leonid Brezhnev, Yuri Andropov and Konstantin Chernenko, the relations between the Soviet Union and the United States can be depicted as "tit-for-tat". Both countries spared no efforts in arms expansion and hardly gave up their respective sphere of influence and vested interests in the Third World. Because the Soviet and America refused to make any compromise, their bilateral relations in the first half of the 80s were characterized by: fierce arms race extending to space, mutual criticism and assault, suspension of high-level official mutual visits; not even one top-level talk has occurred in the first 4 years of the Reagan Administration.[6]

But the tough expansionist policy of the Soviet Union gradually fell short of its ambitions. The Soviet expansion in the Third World was met with dual dilemmas, both internal and external. Domestically, the economic development had shown signs of noticeable stagnation. Worse still, massive military expenditure needed for its expansion in the Third World became more and more unaffordable to the Soviet Union. Internationally, the Soviet invasion of Afghanistan not only provoked sanctions from Western countries, but also severely harmed its own image in the Third World.

At a time when the country was plagued by internal and external troubles, Mikhail Gorbachev took up the post of general secretary of the CPSU Central Committee. After Gorbachev took office, he put forward his "New Thinking" in estimating the trend of world development and treating international relations. In his book entitled Perestroika: New Thinking for Our Country and the World, he wrote, "A new way of thinking is not an improvization, nor a mental exercise. It is a result of serious reflections on the realities of today's world,

---

6   Fang, Lianqing, et al., eds. *History of Postwar International Relations*. Beijing: Peking University Press, 1999: 710.

of the understanding that a responsible attitude to policy demands scientific susstantiation, and that some of the postulates which seemed unshakable before should be given up".[7] "New Thinking" covered a wide range. On foreign policy, Gorbachev believed that in an era of nuclear confrontation, there would not be winners in nuclear wars; human survival was above all else and peaceful coexistence was the only condition of survival of all mankind in the nuclear era. He also believed that security was universal, mutual and inseparable, and the only path to security was the path of political solution, of disarmament. He stressed that no country or group of countries had the right to intervene into the internal affairs of any other countries or to impose its own political system, economic pattern or ideology upon any other countries through military and economic means.

Under domestic and international pressure and under the guidance of "New Thinking" on diplomatic relations, the Soviet Union advanced an arms control centered global détente strategy and spontaneously underwent considerable strategic retreat, began to give up the 1970s strategy of aggressive expansion in the Third World, and withdrew part of its troops from hotspot regions of the Third World. Driven by the Soviet Union, Vietnam announced on May 26th, 1987 to withdraw troops from Cambodia. On April 14, 1988, an agreement was reached on political solutions to the Afghanistan issue. In 1988, the Soviet Union proclaimed that it would withdraw part of its troops from Mongolia, particularly those stationed at border areas between Mongolia and China, and that the withdrawal of most of the Soviet troops stationed in Mongolia would be completed within two years. At the same time, the Soviet Union suspended and cut military and economic assistance to some southwest African and Central American countries in hotspot regions. The Soviet strategic retreat eased the tensions in hotspot regions in the Third World.

In the Cold War era, the United States and the Soviet Union dominated the evolution of global pattern. Many Third World countries and regions were under their direct control or indirect influence. Therefore, the major adjustments that the US and the Soviet Union made to their foreign strategies, particularly their policies to the Third World, inevitably exerted profound implications on the North-South relationship.

---

7   Gorbachev, Mikhail Sergeyevich. *Perestroika: New Thinking for Our Country and the World.* New York: Harper & Row, Pub. 1987: 145.

8.2. New Situation of the North-South Relationship in East & Central Asia

8.2.1. The Rise of East Asia

In the early 1980s, a group of Third World countries in East Asia rose economically which both affected the Third World and the North-South relationship.

The economic rise of East Asia mainly referred to the rapid economic growth of ASEAN, China and the four Asian tigers. And their economic scale was continuously expanding. For example, the economic scale of South Korea (ROK) reached 236.4 billion US dollars in 1990, up by 79 times than that of 1965.[8] With the efforts of East Asian countries, by the end of the 80s, the overall economic scale of East Asia could be put on a par with those of North America and East Europe. East Asian countries not only had their economic aggregates grow by a large margin, but also improved their economic structures. In the entire national economy, the proportion of agriculture fell and that of manufacturing rose by a large margin. And East Asian countries continuously strengthened their competitiveness in the World economy.

Different from East Asian countries, many Third World countries in South Asia, Africa and Latin America were challenged by many economic problems such as debt crisis, irrational economic structure, backward agriculture and food shortage. With economic difficulties on the rise, their development was faced with numerous resistances. Compared with Third World counties in other regions, East Asian economy was outstanding in the 1980s. On the economic front, a large division happened to Third World countries.

The division of Third World countries on the economic front led to an adversary political consequence. Different levels of development caused the cohesion inside the Third World to weaken and the separation tendency to deepen. Due to different levels of economic development, the Third World countries hardly kept consistency on the major issue of fighting for the establishment of a new international political and economic order, and thus weakened the overall strength of the Third World in the North-South relationship. But the rise of East Asian economy in the 80s was like, for the Third World, "advantages outweighed disadvantages" on the whole. As a part of the Third World, the rise of Third World countries in East Asia showed other Third World countries a path of catching up with developed countries, which was significantly meaningful to the development of the North-South relationship.

---

8   Gu, Guanfu, et al., eds. *The History of International Relations*. Vol. 11. Beijing: World Affairs Press, 2004: 239.

8.2.2. Progress of the Situation in the Korean Peninsula

At the same time when the East Asian economy was on the rise, the situation in the Korean Peninsula saw new progress. Entering the 80s, world powers such as the USA and the Soviet actively adjusted their policies toward the Korean Peninsula. The United States continued to promote the conception of "cross recognition" of South Korea (ROK) and North Korea (DPRK). The Reagan Administration unfolded "serial smiling diplomacy" and a series of contact with North Korea (DPRK), including such measures as allowing South Korean people to pay academic visits to America and instructing expatriate staff to make contacts with North Korean diplomats. The Soviet Union continued to strengthen its relationship with North Korea (DPRK) and at the same time, gradually engaged in contacts with South Korea (ROK) in an attempt to minimize the influence of the United States in the Korean Peninsula. "All in all, the Korean Peninsula was subjected to dual external influence in the 80s. On the one hand, policy adjustments of powers provided some favorable conditions for Inter-Korean Dialogue. On the other hand, rivalry of world powers in the Korean Peninsula became an important factor of capricious situations in the Peninsula."[9]

The bilateral relations between South and North Korea in the 80s were marked by the coexistence of zigzag and development. In January 1980, North Korea (DPRK) proposed to hold talks between the Premier of DPRK and his ROK counterparts. From February to June 1980, the two sides held 9 work-level delegates meetings in Panmunjom to discuss relevant issues about the talks. The meetings worked out an agreement on issues such as direct dialing telephone and the meeting place of the DPRK and ROK Prime Ministers. But later the suppression of the Chun Doo-hwan authorities over the Gwangju popular uprising (Gwangju Massacre) resulted in the suspension of bilateral work-level delegates meetings. In October 1983, when South Korean President Chun Doo-hwan was paying a visit to Rangoon, Myanmar, he was the target of a failed assassination attempt during which 17 of Chun's entourage, South Korean senior officials, were bombed. Myanmar accused North Korea of plotting the bombing and tensions on the Korean Peninsula rose again.

In 1984, South Korea suffered heavy loss from severe inundations. North Korea provided abundant supplies such as grain, medicine and cement to South Korea via the Red Cross, which eased the tension of mutual confrontation. The two sides conducted multi-level dialogues and exchanges hereafter. Economically, the two sides held economic talks from November 1984 to November 1985. The talks reached consensus on many issues such as economic cooperation and interflow of commodities, laying a foundation for subsequent economic cooperation and exchanges. In 1989, founder of Hyundai Corporation Chung Ju-yung visited North Korea, which greatly promoted bilateral economic cooperation between ROK and DPRK. Politically, the two

---

9   Ibid.: 276.

sides held the preparatory meeting of South and North Korean Congress Talks. In July 1987, North Korea proposed to sign a Joint Declaration on Mutual Non-Aggression with South Korea and put forward the proposal of disarmament of the two sides in three stages. But the DPRK-ROK dialogue was obstructed because of a large-scale ROK-USA joint military exercise. In February 1989, South and North Korea restored the preparatory meeting of Prime Ministerial Meeting, paving the way for direct dialogue between the two sides and, to a certain extent, easing their bilateral relations.

8.2.3. The Detente Trend in the Southeast and Central Asia

In the 1980s, the situations in Southeast and Central Asia unfolded tendencies of detente. This was mainly reflected in the Vietnamese withdrawal of troops from Cambodia pushed by the Soviet Union and the Soviet withdrawal of troops from Afghanistan.

In the early 80s, under the full support of the Soviet Union, Vietnam stepped up its aggression against Cambodia. The Cambodian people quickly launched anti-aggression righteous struggle. Resistance forces in Cambodia gradually worked toward joint efforts. On July 9, 1982, the Democratic Kampuchea, the Movement for the National Liberation of Kampuchea (MOULINAKA) and the Khmer People's National Liberation Front (KPNLF) formed the Coalition Government of Democratic Kampuchea, with Prince Norodom Sihanouk as the President. By 1987, the anti-Vietnam armed forces under the leadership of the Coalition Government of Democratic Kampuchea had over 70,000 guerrillas. Because of resistance of the Cambodian people, Vietnam cannot take full control of the situation in Cambodia by any means. The Soviet support of Vietnamese invasion of Cambodia not only made the USSR laden with heavy economic burdens, but also aggravated the Soviet relations with ASEAN and China.

In Central Asia, the Soviet occupation of Afghanistan not only brought about huge loss of the Soviet Union, but also resulted in its isolation in the international community. Despite the Soviet continuous increase of troops, it cannot fully defeat the resistance forces of Afghanistan. Throughout the 8-year aggressive war, the Soviet casualty reached 35,000 and the cost amounted to 40-odd billion US dollars. The invasion of Afghanistan became an increasingly heavy burden on the Soviet Union. The United States had been supporting Afghan resistance groups and claimed that the Afghanistan issue had an effect on the growth of the American-Soviet relations and was even "a key factor" as to whether the Intermediate-Range Nuclear Forces Treaty (INF) could be signed or not.

The Soviet invasion of Afghanistan and its support of Vietnamese invasion of Cambodia not only caused heavy economic burdens on the Soviet Union with declining strength, but also provoked the indignation and denunciation of people of all countries in the world as well as worsened the international environment of the Soviet Union. The anti-hegemony and anti-aggression struggles of Afghan and Cambodian people received extensive support of the international community, particularly Third World countries. Western powers actively put down the Soviet expansion, and the Third World countries were also on the alert against it. The alliance of countries of the South played an important role in supporting and assisting the anti-aggression struggles of people of the two countries. The Summit of Non-Aligned Countries, Islamic Summit Conference, ASEAN and China as well as other Third World countries and organizations all requested the Soviet withdrawal of troops from Afghanistan and a political solution to the Afghanistan issue. The Association of Southeast Asian Nations (ASEAN) not only provided Cambodia with political and moral support, but also took practical actions to increase arms, military supplies and material assistance to Cambodia. And China consistently offered valuable support for the peoples of Afghanistan and Cambodia.

After Mikhail Gorbachev assumed the post of secretary general of the (Communist Party of the Soviet Union) CPSU Central Committee, under the guidance of "new thinking" in foreign relations, the Soviet Union practiced a strategy of retreat in Asia and set about withdrawing from Afghanistan and changing the previous policy of supporting Vietnamese invasion of Cambodia. In May 1988, the Soviet Union began to withdraw troops from Afghanistan. The full withdrawal was completed on February 15, 1989, marking the end of 9-year-long Soviet invasion of Afghanistan. Driven by the Soviet Union, Vietnam announced on May 26, 1987 to withdraw its troops from Cambodia. In September 1989, Vietnam proclaimed that all its troops had withdrawn from Cambodia.

The Soviet withdrawal of troops from Afghanistan and its promotion of Vietnamese withdrawal of troops from Cambodia symbolized the falling tide of the Soviet hegemony in Asia and promoted relaxation and stability of situations in East and Central Asia, which exerted a positive impact on the evolution of the North-South relationship.

8.3. New Changes in North-South Relationship across the Middle East

Due to its important strategic position and rich oil reserve, the Middle East has always been one of the key regions contended by the United States and the Soviet Union. The two superpowers have held strong influence to the Middle East since World War II so that their contention and policy change in the Middle East since the 1980s have contributed to the complexity and volatility of the regional situation.

Due to the Camp David Accords and the Egyptian-Israeli Peace Treaty, the Arab states fell into a state of split and division and the United States further enhanced its status in the region. With the support of the United States, Israel was at an advantage over the Arab states in terms of military and security. The

Soviet Union, though had its influence weakened, sought interest in the Persian Gulf area by interfering in the Iran-Iraq War and other means.

In the second half of the 80s, against the backdrop of the Soviet strategy of global strategic withdrawal, Mikhail Gorbachev advanced its policy towards the Middle East, featuring peace, solidarity, and cooperation. He stressed a peaceful solution to the Middle East issues which was in essence "exit strategy". Under the guidance of Gorbachev's idea of comprehensive and universal security system, the Soviet Union attempted to avoid the rise of tension in the Middle East and worked proactively towards political reconciliation between Arab states and Israel. The Soviet policy change, to some extent, benefited the detente of the Middle East situation, but its exit strategy also facilitated the American expansion in the region.

Different from the Soviet strategic defensive in the Middle East, the United States intensified its offensive in the region and seized the chance to expand its influence. The United States actively interfered in the regional conflicts and continuously consolidated its status in the Middle East so as to ensure the oil interest of its own and its allies. By vigorously supporting Israel, the United States made the former its strategic base in the region; and by promoting the Middle East Peace Process, it strove to maintain the regional stability and reduce and contain the influence of the Soviet Union. Numerous contradictions between countries in the Middle East and constant conflicts and warfare served as pretexts of the United States and the Soviet Union to meddle in the regional affairs, which was clearly manifested in the Iran-Iraq War.

8.3.1. Iran-Iraq War

The Iran-Iraq War was an armed conflict between Iran and Iraq lasting from September 1980 to August 1988. The war caused heavy losses to both sides and became a chance for the Western powers to meddle in the Middle East affairs.

Contradictions between Iran and Iraq have been long-standing and intricate and the major causes attributed to the war were territorial, national and religious disputes between the two countries. Iraq and Iran shares a boundary of 1,280 km and on the southern boundary where the two countries were separated by the Shatt al-Arab, the disputes have been particularly striking. The Shatt al-Arab is the only marine outfall of Iraq to the Gulf and an important passageway of Iranian oil tankers. As a consequence, contention for this golden waterway between the two countries has led to multiple armed conflicts. As far as religion is concerned, the state power of Iran was in the hands of Shia Islam that accounted for the majority of the Iranian people, whereas Iraq was in the hands of Sunni Islam that accounted for the minority of the Iraqi people. After Khomeini took power in Iran, the bilateral relations became even worse.

Nevertheless, the interference of world powers on the Iran-Iraq issue was also a major cause of the breakout of the Iran-Iraq War. After the Islamic Revolution, the international community, major powers in particular, began to be alienated from Iran. Iraq thought it a best opportunity to seek hegemony in the Gulf area and Saddam Hussein resolved to take the chance and struck a blow to Iran. The United States considered the Iran after the Iranian Revolution as a huge threat to its expansion of sphere of influence in the Middle East. In the hope of containing and hitting the Khomeini regime of Iran from expanding influence in the Gulf region, the United States acquiesced in the provocation of Iraq against Iran.

Driven by domestic and international factors, on September 22, 1980, the Iraqi Air Force staged a preemptive surprise attack on 7 Iranian Air Force bases and 15 cities, the Tehran Airport included. Iran immediately returned fire and the Iran-Iraq war broke out. The two sides fought hard in the course of the war. At first it was Iraq that seized upon the initiative of the war. But Iran began to counterattack after it managed to hold its ground, and recovered almost all lost territory As from October 1982, the belligerent sides entered into a stage of strategic stalemate where now one side and then the other is on the offensive.

To bring the United States and other western oil consuming countries to intervene in the war, Iraq tried every means possible to expand the scope of the war to the entire Persian Gulf region. On August 15, 1982, Iraq announced to attack any oil tankers entering the surrounding waters of the Kharg Island of Iran. Such an act was aimed at sabotaging oil export of Iran. To this, Iran immediately issued a statement that if Iraq took this action, Iran would close the Strait of Hormuz. Soon afterwards, the two sides waged intense contention on oil importers. Because oil tankers coming in and going out of Kuwait were attacked by Iran, Kuwait turned to the international community for help.

The United States and the Soviet Union seized upon the timing of the Iran-Iraq War and jockeyed for influence in the Middle East. After Kuwait petitioned protection, the Soviet Union proclaimed in early April to lease 3 tankers to Kuwait. The United States, in order to prevent the Soviet Union from expanding influence, immediately announced to support Kuwait by permitting Kuwaiti tankers to fly the U.S. flag and even sending its warships to escort Kuwaiti tankers. But Iran continued to attack the oil tankers and, deployed large numbers of naval mines in the Gulf waters to stop oil tankers from passing through. After the US-escorted tanker Sungari and the US-flagged tanker Sea Isle City were hit by Iran, the United States launched devastating attacks against two Iranian oil drilling platforms. In 1988, after the U.S. frigate Samuel Roberts knocked into the naval mine, the United States announced to expand the scope of convoy and provided protection to merchant ships of neutral countries. Hereafter, Iran which was in no mood for escalation of the situation didn't ever attack any U.S. frigate fleet, marking the end of the Iran-US conflict.

Because of the US and the Soviet interventions in the Iran-Iraq War, the war moved towards international orientation and the situation in the Persian Gulf Region became increasingly tense. To ease off the tension, the United Nations Security Council passed on July 20, 1987, resolution No 598 that called for a ceasefire between Iran and Iraq. The resolution requested, as the first step of settling disputes through negotiations, that the two sides at war immediately cease fire, stop all military operations by air, land and sea, and immediately withdraw all troops to the international border. The resolution also appealed to the Secretary-General of the United Nations for sending a team of the UN observers to confirm and monitor Iran-Iraq ceasefire and withdrawal of troops, for making necessary arrangements on the basis of negotiations with the two sides as well as for submitting a report to the Security Council; it urged the two sides to, upon stopping initiative hostile actions against each other, immediately release and repatriate prisoners of war according to the Third Geneva Convention dated August 12,1949. The resolution requested both Iran and Iraq to cooperate with the UN Secretary General in terms of execution of the resolution and mediation so that comprehensive, rational and decent solutions acceptable to both parties can be reached on all pronounced problems in accordance with the principles set forth in the Charter of the United Nations. It also requested that all other states try hard to restrain themselves from getting engaged in any actions that could possibly lead to further escalation and expansion of the conflict so that the resolution could be successfully executed.[10] At the beginning, Iran did not acknowledge the resolution. Iranian Foreign Minister Ali Akbar Velayati thought "Iran believes that the draft resolution is unacceptable."[11] But, in 1988, Iraq launched frequent offensives and fought on the territory of Iran, with the latter gradually reduced to a passive position in the battlefields. Under the pressure of domestic economic difficulties and war-weariness of the people brought about by years of war as well as the International community's push for its acceptance of the UN resolution 598, Iran officially announced to accept the UN ceasefire resolution on July 18, 1988. Brokered by the United Nations, Iran and Iraq officially achieved full ceasefire on August 20, 1988. By now, the 8-year-long Iran-Iraq War that brought untold sufferings to the peoples of the two countries was concluded.

8.3.2. The Fifth Middle East War

At a time when Iraq and Iran were at war, a state of disintegration and disunity again took on among the Arab states. In face of such a favorable situation, Israel was determined to seize upon the chance to eliminate the threat from Lebanon to the security of north Israel.

After 1970, major Palestinian armed forces relocated from Jordan to Lebanon, and attacked targets in the Israeli territory from Southern Lebanon. Lebanon is a country where Muslims and Christians live in compact communities. The 60% of the Lebanese were Muslims in favor of the Palestinian armed forces while the rest of the population was Christians who opposed them. As a consequence, the Lebanese Civil War broke out in the mid-1970s. In the name of mediating the war, Syria sent troops to Lebanon in May 1976. But the

---

10 *People's Daily* July 20, 1987.
11 *People's Daily* July 21, 1987.

Syrian troops did not withdraw even after the end of the Lebanese Civil War, and instead, permanently stationed in Lebanon in the name of the Arab peace-keeping troops.

Israel conceived the Palestinian operations in Lebanon and Syria's military presence in Lebanon as a threat to its security, and decided to wage a military attack against Lebanon. On June 4, 1982, Israel used the attempted assassination of Shlomo Argov, Israel's ambassador to the United Kingdom as a pretext and launched an air strike against the base of PLO (Palestine Liberation Organization). On June 6, with coordinated strikes of Israeli Air and Naval Forces, 20,000 Israeli Army attacked Southern Lebanon on all fronts, and soon pushed towards Beirut, capital of Lebanon where a fierce battle was fought between the Israeli forces and thousands of PLO soldiers stationed in the headquarters west of Beirut. The Israeli Army also fought fiercely against the Syrian Army stationed in the Bekaa Valley. The fifth Middle East War erupted all out. By virtue of its military superiority, Israel soon gained the initiative in the war. On June 11, Israel and Syria reached a ceasefire agreement in which Israel requested the PLO to evacuate from Lebanon and give up the use of force as well as turn into a purely political organization. Having lost support of all other Arab states, the PLO had to compromise and agreed to withdraw from Beirut.

After the outbreak of the war, the United States sent Philip Habib, Special Envoy of the President, to visit the region on August 6 on a mediation mission. On the 19th, Israel, Lebanon and Palestine reached a ceasefire agreement. According to the agreement, the Palestine Liberation Organization evacuated from Lebanon and spread in 8 Arab states; Multinational forces were deployed in Lebanon to prevent from another burst of the war. Nevertheless, Israel still occupied parts of the Lebanese territory and refused to withdraw its troops. It even compelled the Lebanese Government to agree to cede southern Lebanon as the security zone of Israel. Brokered by the United Nations, Lebanon and Israel began the negotiations of withdrawal in 1983. It was not until June 1985 that the Israeli forces finally evacuated from Lebanon. Under the pretext of protecting security in its northern parts, Israel had set up a "security zone" of 850 square kilometers in southern Lebanon. The Israeli security zone was administered by pro-Israeli personages and the Israeli Army was engaged in patrol in the zone. But the security zone was not secure at all. On the contrary, it led to subsequently continuous conflicts between the two sides.

As a result of the fifth Middle East War, Israel attained its ends of expelling the PLO (Palestine Liberation Organization) and compelling Syria to withdraw troops from Lebanon. But the war also led to consequences that Israel did not expect. After the PLO was hard hit, radical faction of the PLO that was inclined to terrorism rose to power and terrorist events targeted at Israel and Western countries were significantly on the rise, presenting more hardships and obstructions to the Middle East Peace Process.

8.3.3. Efforts for Reconciliation on the Middle East Issues and the PLO Assuming a New Strategy

In the mid-1980s, with the gradual relaxation of the US-Soviet relations, the Middle East issues had possibilities of reconciliation. In the early 1988, the United States advanced the "George Shultz Solution" to the Middle East issues, which proposed an international convention for Peace in the Middle East attended by the five permanent UNSC members and various parties concerned in the Middle East and concurrently, three bilateral direct negotiations between Jordan and Israel, between Syria and Israel, as well as between Palestine and Israel. However, the international convention couldn't either engage in the bilateral negotiations or oppose or reject agreements reached through the bilateral negotiations.[12] The Shultz Solution signified the U.S. change of previously consistent partiality policy for Israel in the Middle East.

In the wake of the fifth Middle East War, the tactics of struggle of the Palestine Liberation Organization (PLO) underwent changes. After retreating from Lebanon, the PLO was determined to return to West Bank of the Jordan River and the Gaza Strip. In September 1988, King Hussein of Jordan ordered to sever legal and executive connections with the West Bank and let the Palestine Liberation Organization to be in charge of the area. On November 15, the 19th extraordinary session of the Palestine National Council, the highest Palestinian legislative authority, passed the Palestinian Declaration of Independence and the Political Communique. In the Declaration of Independence, "the Palestine National Council, in the name of the Palestinian Arab People, hereby proclaims the establishment of the State of Palestine on our Palestinian territory with its capital Jerusalem (Al-Quds Ash-Sharif)". The Declaration of Independence proclaimed the acceptance of the United Nations General Assembly Resolution 181 of 1947 on partitioning Palestine into separate Jewish and Arab states. The Political Communique accompanying the Palestinian Declaration of Independence expressed the wish to, on the basis of the UNSC Resolutions 242 and 338, have negotiations with Israel on multinational conferences, and politically solve the Palestine-Israeli Conflict. This was seen as the Palestinian acquiescence in the existence of the State of Israel. The Political Communique also stressed the solution to disputes by international conventions for peace in the Middle East.[13] On December 15, 1988, the United National General Assembly passed a resolution on accepting the State of Palestine as an UN observer. Subsequently, 100-odd countries in the world have proclaimed recognition of the legitimacy of the State of Palestine.

The establishment of the State of Palestine symbolized a new stage where the Palestinian struggle for restoration of national rights shifted from armed resistance to political and diplomatic means.

---

12   Fang, Lianqing, et al., eds. *History of Postwar International Relations*. Beijing: Peking University Press, 1999: 697.

13   *People's Daily* November 6, 1988

In light of the policy change of the PLO, the United States adjusted its policy to Palestine. On December 16, 1988, Robert Pelletreau, the United States ambassador to Tunisia, held the first talk with the PLO delegation in the city of Tunis. In 1989, after George H. W. Bush took office in the White House, the United States began to proactively advance dialogue and peace talks between Israel and Palestine. With its efforts, the Middle East in the late 1980s did embrace a transient hope of peace. Nevertheless, the Middle East Peace Process did not see much headway thereafter, which was attributable to the great power of hardline faction in Israel and radical forces in Arab states.

8.4. Turbulence in Africa and Its Implications on the North-South Relationship

In the 1980s, Africa remained the most chaotic and turbulent region in the world. During this period, there were more than 30 major armed conflicts in a global context. And 11 out of them took place in Africa, making Africa the top of all regions worldwide.[14] However by the late 1980s, the situation in the Africa had made some headway along with the mitigation of the US-USSR relations.

Throughout the 1980s, the turbulent situation of Africa was marked with interventions of world powers. It was their contention in Africa that further intensified turmoil in the region. In particular, the tension in Africa was exacerbated by the US-Soviet new round of scramble for Africa, continuous increase of their military presence in the region and expanded interference in internal affairs of African countries in the early 1980s. The Reagan Administration considered Africa as a key region to carry out "the limited rollback strategy" and contend against the Soviet Union for the Third World. Not only did the United States took measures of military assistance and cooperation to expand its sphere of influence in Africa, but also engaged in a tit-for-tat rivalry with the Soviet Union through "low intensity warfare". Likewise, not reconciled to give up its own sphere of influence, the Soviet Union scaled up military assistance to Africa and supported pro-Soviet forces to measure swords with the United States in various areas of the region.

Direct interferences or indirect support from the United States and the Soviet Union existed in the unrests of Zimbabwe, Chad and Angola as well as Namibia. In a manner of speaking, changes of the African situations in the 1980s almost completely manifested how the strategy adjustment and changing relations of the United States and the Soviet Union influenced the region.

---

14   Gu, Guanfu, et al., eds. *The History of International Relations*. Vol. 11 (1980-1989). Beijing: World Affairs Press. 2004: 316.

8.4.1. Zimbabwe's Policy Towards the North-South Relationship

In February 1980, Zimbabwe held, for the first time, a parliamentary election attended by people of many races. The election campaign was mainly between the United African National Council and the Zimbabwe Patriotic Front which consisted of the Zimbabwe African People's Union (ZAPU) and the Zimbabwe African National Union-Patriotic Front (ZANU-PF). Thanks to long-term anti-colonialism struggle, the Patriotic Front had built up a high prestige and later won 77 seats out of the 80 African seats. Among the 77 seats, the Zimbabwe African National Union-Patriotic Front (ZANU-PF) won 57 seats and there-fore, its leader Robert Mugabe took up the post of the first Prime Minister of the Zimbabwe Government. On April 18, 1980, Zimbabwe officially pro-claimed its independence in the name of the Republic of Zimbabwe.

Upon its independence, Zimbabwe set anti-colonialism, anti-racism and anti-imperialism as the core of its foreign policy and strived to promote the resolution of the Namibia issue. It appealed to the international community for comprehensive sanctions against the white racist regime of South Africa, thus becoming a fresh and vital force among countries of the South. In September 1986, Zimbabwe hosted a Summit meeting of the Non-Aligned Movement (NAM) and R. Mugabe was elected as the rotating chair of the Movement.[15] During the session, Mugabe strongly called on the United States and the Soviet Union to listening attentively to the voices of the NAM and halt arms race as well as fierce scramble for spheres of influence. On the issue of South Africa, he even advised members of the NAM to impose mandatory sanctions on South Africa.

After Zimbabwe gained independence, the United States and the United Kingdom took precautions against the Soviet penetration into Zimbabwe in the form of providing a great multitude of assistance to Zimbabwe and establish-ing close economic relations with it. However, Zimbabwe could hardly reach a consensus with them on the issue of imposing sanctions on the white rac-ist regime of South Africa. The reason why the United States and the United Kingdom were reluctant to enforce comprehensive sanctions on South Africa was that South Africa was strategically vital for containing the Soviet expan-sion of sphere of influence in Southern Africa. And because of the irrecon-cilable divergence on the South African issue, Zimbabwe witnessed tensions in relations with the United States and the United Kingdom as well as other Western powers. Mugabe turned to the Soviet Union for support. In December 1985, the two countries signed multiple military and economic agreements on Mugabe's successful visit to the Soviet Union. Apparently, Western powers such as the United States and the United Kingdom would not like Zimbabwe to take sides in the Soviet Union, and consequently, voluntarily mitigated their relations with Zimbabwe by showing a somewhat positive attitude on the ques-tion of Southern Africa.

15 Gu, Guanfu, et al., eds. *The History of International Relations*. Vol. 11. Beijing: World Affairs Press, 2004: 344.

The founding of the Republic of Zimbabwe substantially changed the balance of power in Southern Africa and enhanced the strength of the Third World countries in the region. What's more, upon its independence, Zimbabwe has consistently adhered to justice and actively pursued the interests of the Third World countries by making full use of the contradictions among the major world powers. Zimbabwe has played a significant role in the affairs of Southern Africa region affairs and actively promoted the Non-Aligned Movement.

8.4.2. The North-South Relationship during the Chadian Civil War in the 1980s

Chad is a country located in the central part of the African continent. In 1960, Chad gained its independence from the colonial rule of France. After that, Chad was for a long time beset with the Civil War which was attributed to the complicated races, tribes and religions at home. Domestic rivalry served as a pretext for interventions of external forces. France wanted to maintain its interest in Central Africa; the pro-soviet Libya constantly sought to expand its power in Sub-Saharan Africa by holding Chad in hand, which apparently was something the United States did not wish to see. As a result, Chad became a hot spot region where powerful countries contended for sphere of influence.

In March 1980, President Goukouni Oueddei and Defense Minister Hissène Habré of the Transitional Government of National Unity (GUNT) of Chad had been on bad terms, which led to fierce combat of armies of the two sides. Under the circumstances when it seemed hardly possible to defeat Hissène Habré, President Goukouni Oueddei signed the Treaty of Friendship, Alliance and Mutual Aid with Libya and invited Libyan troops to Chad. By virtue of these, Goukouni Oueddei succeeded in beating down Hissène Habré. Yet, Libya seized upon the chance and forced Goukouni Oueddei to sign a treaty on establishing Chad-Libyan political alliance and demanding "merger" of the two countries. This aroused vigilance of the United States, France and other African countries against expansion of Libya. In January 1981, France strengthened its military presence in Central Africa on the grounds of preventing from Libyan southward expansion. The United States provided a large quantity of military assistance to Hissène Habré through Egypt and Sudan. Under enormous pressure from the international community, the Libyan troops withdrew from Chad in November 1981. Taking advantage of the opportunity, Hissène Habré launched an offensive and in June 1982, had the capital under control. Later in October, Hissène Habré announced himself the President of Chad.

Reluctant to give up the strategy of expanding its power to the Sub-Saharan Africa by controlling Chad, Libya twice supported the army of Goukouni Oueddei to counterattack the army of Hissène Habré, one in June 1983, and the other in February 1986. However, the two attacks all ended up in failure due to France's direct military strike.

Just at this time, the United States gave birth to "the Reagan Doctrine" and was actively staging "low-intensity warfare" and contending with the Soviet Union for sphere of influence in the Third World. The expansion of the pro-Soviet Libya in Chad perfectly matched the condition of launching "low-intensity wars". At the same time, the United States deemed Libya as a behind-the-scenes backer of the Middle East terrorist activities which gravely threatened its interest in the region. Therefore, supporting Habré's government became one of the means taken by the United States to contain the Libyan power expansion from the South. The United States thereby began to explicitly support the Habré's government and provided it with countless military assistance and even sent military advisors. In this connection, the balance of triumph began to swing to the Habré's government. In November 1986, Goukouni Oueddei announced to recognize the lawful headship of Hissène Habré, and the troops under Habré's command were incorporated to the government troops, marking a conclusion of the Civil War. In May 1988, Libya decided to recognize the Chadian Government led by Hissène Habré and resume the bilateral diplomatic relations. In October, the two countries signed a joint communique on the restoration of diplomatic relations, and the bilateral relations have turned for the better.

8.4.3. Clashes and Peace in Southwestern Africa

After the independence of Zimbabwe in 1980, Namibia was still under the colonial rule of South Africa, making it the last colonial African country. Namibia's South West African People's Organization (SWAPO) and other national liberation organizations led the Namibian people in launching armed struggle against the South Africa.

Upon entering the 80s, South Africa restored its tough policy on Namibia. By initiating successive rounds of military attack against the South West African People's Organization, the South African Army inflicted heavy losses on it. It's true that South Africa's adoption of such a tough policy was driven by domestic interests. But it was also closely connected to the US strategy adjustment. The Reagan Administration followed a strategy of "limited rollback" in the Third World, which was an approach to oppose the Soviet Union by supporting pro-Western forces in a bid to resolutely "roll back" the influence of the Soviet Union in the Third World. Because armed forces of the South West African People's Organization had received the Soviet and Cuban military training and weapons in Angola, they were considered by the United States as pro-Soviet forces. On the Namibia issue, the United States thus showed partiality for South Africa and the latter attempted to continue its colonial rule in Namibia with the help of the former. With the U.S. support, South Africa put forward a scheme of pegging South Africa's withdrawal of troops from Namibia to Cuba's pulling back troops from Angola as a solution to the issues of Southern Africa, which made the issues all the more complicated.

Angola also used to be a country featuring fierce scramble between the United States and the Soviet Union. Supported by the Soviet Union and Cuba, the People's Movement for the Liberation of Angola (MPLA) seized political power in the country. After that, the United States began to implement the "limited rollback strategy" toward Angola. Against the backdrop of ineffective "pegging scheme" in Namibia, the United States turned to overt support for the anti-government armed forces in Angola called the National Union for the Total Independence of Angola (UNITA). In 1986, the United States provided UNITA more than 10 million US dollars worth of secret military assistance, and in 1987, another 27 million US dollars worth of military assistance.[16] Endorsed by the United States and South Africa, the UNITA witnessed a dramatic increase of its military strength and was engaged in more and more ferocious contention with the MPLA-led government. Confronted with hard pressure from the United States and South Africa, the MPLA-led government of Angola sought help from the Soviet Union by importing weapons from the latter. And Cuba also enlarged its station troops in Angola. All this contributed to a peak of the contention between the UNITA and the MPLA.

Fortunately, the situation in Angola did not grow worse afterwards. With the appearance of detente in bilateral relations, the United States and the Soviet Union began to move from confrontation to cooperation on the issue of regional conflicts. In May 1988, four-party negotiations were held by Angola, Cuba, the United States and South Africa. After 11 rounds of tough negotiations, the four sides reached a consensus on key issues. On December 22, 1988, Angola, Cuba and South Africa signed in the UN headquarters the South-West Africa Peace Accords—an agreement on the independence of Namibia and the withdrawal of Cuban troops from Angola. With attention and assistance from the international community, the Constituent Assembly elections of Namibia were completed in November 1989 and the South West African People's Organization won 41 out of the 72 seats. On March 21, 1990, Namibia proclaimed its independence, marking the end of colonial rule in Africa.

It is observed that conflicts and peace in South-West Africa coincided with the strategy adjustment of the United States and the Soviet Union in the Third World. Therefore, "it is reasonable to say that every single progress in the South-West Africa peace process was bound up with the general circumstances of the US-Soviet relations back then."[17]

---

16   Gu, Guanfu, et al., eds. *The History of International Relations*. Vol. 11. Beijing: World Affairs Press, 2004: 357.
17   Fang, Lianqing, et al., eds. *History of Postwar International Relations*. Vol.2. Beijing: Peking University Press, 1999: 710.

8.5. The North-South Relationship in Latin America in the 1980s

8.5.1. Debt Crisis of Latin American Countries

In the 1980s, Latin America was faced with substantial challenges in economy and regional security. On the economic front, the 1980s was referred to as the Lost Decade of Latin America, featuring a severe debt crisis and unprecedented economic recession.

Radical worsening of economic situations in Latin American countries was mainly represented in two aspects: one, fast rise of external debts, and two, rapid drop of debt solvency. In August 1982, Mexico was the first Latin American country to announce insolvency of matured debts, followed by Brazil, Argentina and Chile. An unprecedented debt crisis finally broke out.

Let's take Mexico and Brazil of 1982 as an example. Total external debts owed by Mexico amounted to 86.019 billion US dollars. The principle and interest repaid of the year was 15.684 billion US dollars, accounting for 56.8% of total exports of goods and services in that very year. Foreign debts owed by Brazil in 1982 came to 92.221 billion US dollars, while the principle and interest repaid of the year was 19.078 billion US dollars, registering as much as 81.3% of total exports of that very year.[18] The debt crisis quickly spread to 15 countries, including Argentina, Venezuela, Chile and Peru. The Latin American economy was in a comprehensive emergency.

A debt crisis is more than an economic problem, but also a political one. The Latin American debt crisis resulted in political unrests in Latin American countries and destabilized the international political situation, as well as had a significant effect on the international relations, particularly the North-South relationship. For countries of both the South and the North, it was a daunting challenge to address this foreign debt crisis. If properly handled, it would be set as a classic example of countries of the South and North working hand in hand to tackle an international crisis; if failed, it would not only jeopardize economic development and social stability of countries of the South, but also inevitably damage the North-South relationship.

The foreign debt crisis of Latin America resulted from both domestic and international factors. Therefore, to solve the problem called for economic adjustments of Latin American countries and cooperation and support from creditor countries. However, the US-led creditor countries wanted to keep themselves from the financial crisis and hence took a tough stance on Latin American countries, asking them to promptly pay back the debts in the early stage of the debt crisis.

---

18   Hong, Yuyi, ed. *An Outline History of International Relations in Latin America.*
Beijing: Foreign Language Teaching and Research Press, 1996: 417.

Through negotiations with Western creditors, Latin American countries came to realize that the only way to make creditor countries and organizations change their attitude and share the responsibility of overcoming the debt crisis is stepping up mutual solidarity and cooperation and taking joint actions. As from 1984, Latin American countries began to strengthen regional cooperation and coordination and demand direct political dialogues with Western creditor countries to address debt problem. On January 12, 1984, 30-odd Latin American countries held the Latin American Economic Conference in Quito, capital of Ecuador. The conference stressed that concerted actions must be taken by Latin American countries to tackle regional debt issue. The Latin American Economic Conference held in Quito was the first joint effort made by Latin American debtor countries in response to the foreign debt crisis. The conference marked the formation of political will among Latin American countries to solve the debt crisis by working in unison. In June, 11 Latin American nations held a foreign ministers' and financial minister's conference in Cartagena, Columbia. The conference expressed strong discontent toward policies adopted by some countries of the North in response to the Latin American debt crisis, and came up with its own suggestions and requirements. The 11 countries participated in the meeting were called the Cartagena Group and began to have dialogues with creditor countries in the form of a collective mechanism and address the debt crisis by political means. The Cartagena Group underlined that debt problems involved many a sector such as politics, economy and diplomacy and could only be addressed through "direct political dialogues" between debtors and creditors. In the 1980s, the Group held five ministerial conferences where main debtors of Latin America explicitly expressed their aspiration for proper solution to the debt crisis. In a nutshell, the Cartagena Group played a positive role in promoting political dialogues between debtor and creditor countries.

With diplomatic efforts of Latin American nations, the US-led creditor countries and international financial institutions gradually changed their strategies of dealing with the debt crisis. In the early stage of the outbreak, creditor countries practiced a tightened economic policy requiring Latin American countries to repay the debt as soon as possible. In September 1985, the U.S. Secretary of the Treasury James A. Baker came up with the Baker Plan which featured the idea of promoting debt repayment with development. The Baker Plan was meant to enhance the debt repayment capability of debtor countries through recovering their economic growth.[19] In March 1989, the U.S. Secretary of the Treasury Nicholas F. Brady brought forward the Brady Plan featuring debt reduction and interest reduction for debtor countries.[20]

Thanks to diplomatic efforts and political appeal of Latin American countries, the debt crisis was alleviated to certain extent. In the course of combating the debt crisis, unity and cooperation among Latin American countries were enhanced, which later contributed to region cooperation in Latin America.

---

19   Ibid.: 425.
20   Ibid.: 426.

8.5.2. The Crisis in Central America as a Result of the US-Soviet Rivalry and Collective Efforts of Latin American Countries

In the 1980s, out of their respective needs of global hegemony strategy, the two superpowers—the United States and the Soviet Union—staged a series of military, political, economic and diplomatic rivalries in Central America and the Caribbean with a view to seizing upon control of the region and Latin America as a whole. Such rivalries gave rise to prolonged political unrest, economic recession and social turmoil in some Central American countries. At the same time, owing to involvement of some countries of Western Europe and Latin America, issues that belonged to internal affairs of some Latin American countries gradually evolved into the "Central American Crisis" that had impact on international relations. The Central America thus became one of the hotspot regions throughout the 1980s.

Nicaragua, the largest country in Central America, was the match that set off the outbreak of the Central American Crisis. In 1979, the Sandinista National Liberation Front (FSLN) overthrew the pro-US dictatorship of the Somoza family and founded the Government Junta of National Reconstruction of Nicaragua. The Junta of National Reconstruction of Nicaragua was proactively dedicated to developing bilateral relations with the Soviet Union. In March 1980, Nicaragua and the Soviet Union signed multiple agreements on bilateral economic and trade cooperation as well as cooperation between political parties. According to statistics, the Soviet Union had provided over 2 billion US dollars' worth of military assistance to the Junta of National Reconstruction of Nicaragua. In addition, Nicaragua was also vigorously developing its relations with Cuba at that time and in return, Cuba also supplied Nicaragua with plenty of economic and military assistance. Both the Soviet Union and Cuba had sent large numbers of military advisors to engage in extensive military cooperation with Nicaragua.

The evolution of the situation in Nicaragua featured not only the rise of a pro-Soviet regime, but also important implications on the situation in the region and Latin America as a whole. The victory of Junta of National Reconstruction of Nicaragua greatly inspired guerrilla combats in El Salvador, Guatemala and Honduras. In El Salvador, the Farabundo Marti National Liberation Front (FMLN) established in October 1980 announced to launch a general offensive against the government and gave successive heavy blows to the Government Army. The Salvador military regimes suffered several coups and ministerial crisis. In Guatemala, guerrilla troops of different factions formed the Guatemalan National Revolutionary Unity (URNG) in 1982. After that, the guerrilla forces continuously expanded and guerrilla operations took place in the vast majority of provinces of the country. At one time, the URNG controlled the entire western highlands and parts of northern cross-sectional areas. In addition, Honduras embraced the emergence of the People's Liberation Movement Guerrillas

Grenada is a country situated in the southeastern Caribbean Sea with an area of 344 square kilometers. It is in a very important strategic position because it holds the marine channel between the Caribbean Sea and the Atlantic Ocean. In 1974, Grenada gained its indepdence from the Britain colonial rule and began to forge close relations with the United States. However later in 1979, Maurice Bishop, leader of the New Jewel Movement (NJM) toppled the then pro-US regime and turned to follow a pro-Soviet policy. In 1982, Maurice Bishop signed economic, cultural and scientific cooperation agreements with the Soviet Union on his visit to the country. Cuba sent military advisors to Grenada and helped with the construction of airports. With regard to the pro-Soviet policy of the government of Bishop, the US President Ronald Reagan claimed many times to "teach him a lesson" and took manifold political, economic and military means to contain the Soviet expansion in Central America.

The first step taken by the Reagan Administration was to vigorously support the pro-US forces in Central America and striking the pro-Soviet forces through them. Military assistance extended by the United States to the Salvadoran government jumped from 35.6 million US dollars in 1981 to 243 million US dollars in 1984. The United States also helped EI Salvador with military training to strengthen strikes on guerrilla forces.[21] In addition, the US gave full support to the anti-government armed forces in Nicaragua by providing them military and economic aid which amounted to with 100 million US dollars, in 1986 approved by the US Congress. As from 1983, the United States held joint military exercises with Honduras, had the US troops stationed in Honduras and supported Honduras to constantly provoke border clashes with Nicaragua. The second step taken by the Reagan Administration was to politically and economically put down the pro-Soviet regimes and rope in the pro-US forces. Not only did the United States politically isolate Nicaragua and Grenada, but also enforced economic sanctions on them. In May 1985, the US announced a comprehensive economic sanctions against Nicaragua. To the pro-American forces, on the contrary, the United States gave energetic support and help. In alliance with Canada, Mexico and Venezuela, the United States formed the Nassau Group to make concerted assistance to the Central America. In 1982, President Reagan of the United States initiated the Caribbean Basin Initiative, scaling up economic assistance to many Central American and Caribbean countries other than Cuba, Nicaragua and Grenada. The third step of the Reagan Administration's diplomacy in Latin America was to directly send troops and interfere in the regional affairs. In October 1983, Grenada was reduced to a state of political turmoil. On the 19th of the month, the Prime Minister Maurice Bishop was captured and later executed by the army in favor of the Deputy Prime Minister Bernard Coard. On the 20th, General Hudson Austin of the People's Revoluntionary Army took over power and the national situation was acutely volatile and turbulent, which was taken by the United States as a pretext and opportunity of

21   Fang, Lianqing, et al., eds. *History of Postwar International Relations*. Vol. 2. Beijing: Peking University Press, 1999: 710.

its interference. On the 25ᵗʰ, under the pretexts of helping Grenada restore the order and protecting the 1000-odd U.S. citizens in Grenada, 1900 U.S. soliders and 400 soliders sent by six Caribbean countries began to invade Grenada. To prompt victory of the quick battle, the United States added more soliders so that by the 26ᵗʰ, the size of U.S. ground troops reached as many as 6000 soliders, with an evident military superiority. In contrast, Grenada was a small country with weak military forces. On the 28ᵗʰ, the U.S. Army occupied the entire country. The Governor General of Grenada, under the control of the United States, proclaimed to break off the diplomatic relations with the Soviet Union. On November 2, the United Nations passed a resolution requesting the United States to evacuate its troops from Grenada. On December 19, a general election was held in Grenada, but the United States had already established its military control over this country.

In an effort to hasten the solution of the Central American Crisis and realize regional peace and stability, Latin American countries set about vigorous pursuit of ways to put an end to the Crisis. In January 1983, foreign ministers of Mexico, Columbia, Venezuela and Panama held a conference in Contadora Island, Panama, discussing ways to address the crisis. After the talks, a press communique was released, claiming a deep discomfort to foreign direct or indirect interference in Central African conflicts and a proposition of requesting foreign countries to stop supplying or delivering weapons to the Central America. The four countries involved in the talks were called the Contadora Group. The Group, which was named after the Island, was the first political coordination group set up for the resolution of Central American Crisis. Through painstaking efforts, the Contadora Group contributed to the five-party talks among Nicaragua, EI Salvador, Honduras, Guatemala and Costa Rica and a detente of the tension in the region. Nevertheless, the Group was met up with constant obstruction from the United States that refused to give up its sphere of influence in the region. Against the backdrop of setbacks of the Group, in July 1985, Peru, Argentina, Brazil and Uruguay formed the Lima Group (or the Contadora Support Group) in clear-cut support of mediation efforts of the Contadora Group. In December 1986, foreign ministers of the countries that belonged to the two groups convened in Rio de Janeiro, Brazil, and decided to establish a Standing Body of Negotiations and Political Consultations. The decision led to the official founding of the Rio Group.[22] The founding of the Rio Group symbolized a new stage in the Latin American countries' solution to the Central American Crisis by means of the group coordination mechanism.

In the meantime, the international factors in the late 1980s began to be conducive to the settlement of the Central American Crisis. By then, the Soviet Union began to implement strategic withdrawal in Latin America in the form of voluntary reduction and suspension of economic and military assistance to some Latin American countries. As far as the United States is concerned,

314

---

22   Liu, Qingjian. *A New Approach to Contemporary International Relations*. Beijing: Tsinghua University Press, 2004: 101.

its tough policies in Central America incurred more and more resistance and objections from Latin American countries. Continuous impediment from the United States to the Central America peace process would be detrimental to its international image and hence impar its interest. In light of the strategic withdrawal of the Soviet Union in Central America, the United States catered to the requests of countries in the region and softened its policies. In August 1987, leaders of five Central American nations signed the Procedures for the Establishment of a Firm and Lasting Peace in Central America, i.e. the Central American Peace Accords, which represented substantive progress in the Central American peace process.

8.5.3. The Falkland Islands War and Its Implications on the North-South Relationship

Latin America of the 1980s also witnessed the outbreak of a war that had significant implications on the North-South relationship—the Malvinas Islands War. The Malvinas Islands War, or the Falkland Islands War, was a war fought between Argentina and Britain from April 2 to June 14, 1982 on the claim of territorial sovereignty of the Malvinas Islands and ended up with the victory of Britain.

The Malvinas Islands are located in the South Atlantic Ocean, 510 kilometers away from the southern coast of Argentina and about 13,000 kilometers away from the mainland of the United Kingdom. Because of a controversy over who first discovered and effectively occupied the islands, both Argentina and Britain claimed sovereignty over the Malvinas Islands. In 1965, the 20th United Nations General Assembly passed the Resolution 2065 stating a controversy in the sovereignty of the Islands and urging the two sides concerned to resolve the territorial dispute in a peaceful manner.

In the 80s, Argentina fell into an economic difficulty. General Leopoldo Galtieri, head of the then Argentine government, decided to shift the general people's discontent sentiment by recovering the Malvinas Islands. On April 2, 1982, Argentina sent about 4,000 soldiers out of the Air, Sea and Land forces to occupy the islands. The British army stationed on the islands was forced to surrender. Soon afterwards, Argentina declared reclamation of the sovereignty of the islands to be the 24th province of the nation.

The United Kingdom found itself difficult to accept the fact that Argentina had taken the islands by force, and therefore the British Parliament, requested by the Prime Minister Madam Thatcher, decided on the next day of the war to immediately mobilize the naval task force to seize the islands. After a long-distance travel, the British force launched an attack on April 25. Having taken back the foothold, the British force was engaged in naval combat with its Argentine counterpart, with wins and losses on each side. On May 21, the British Army made landing operations and after about 20 days of fierce battle, the Argentine defending troops finally surrendered to Britain on June 14.

The Falkland Islands War had a far-reaching impact on the North-South relationship. For one thing, it estranged the North-South relationship. During the war, countries of the North such as the United States and member countries of the European Economic Community were in favor of Britain, whereas countries of the South represented by Latin American countries supported Argentina and stood for peaceful settlement of the Malvinas Islands territorial dispute. Countries of the South and the North have conspicuously forged two camps, and American and British images in the Third World further dropped. For another, the war intensified solidarity among Latin American nations. In the course of joint opposition to the US and the UK, Latin American nations strengthened their awareness of unity and cooperation and further stepped up South-South Cooperation, laying a solid political foundation for the North-South politics.

8.6. North-South Dialogue and South-South Cooperation in the 1980s

8.6.1. New Conditions in the North-South Relationship

In the 1980s, the Third World movements of fighting for the establishment of new international political and economic order were met with even greater difficulties, for which both the Northern countries and the Southern countries were responsible. On the one hand, the Northern countries were unwilling to fundamentally change the present economic order. On the other hand, many Third World countries and regions witnessed internal divisions. Some countries in the South had worsening situations of national economy and numerous hardships in the course of development. While some other less developed countries made remarkable economic achievements. Different economic development of countries in the South resulted in their inconsistent requirements in the struggle for new international political and economic order and the weakened internal cohesion and collective strength in the Third World.

By the second half of the 1980s, with the detente of the US-Soviet relationship, Third World countries and regions had shown unbalanced economic development, and the North-South relationship centered on economic development had increasingly become a key issue of concerns to the International Community. Growing the South-North Dialogue and establishing a new international political and economic order once again drew the attention of countries of the North and the South. Further progress was made in the South-North Dialogue. The United States set up the North America Free Trade Area (NAFTA) which involved the US, Canada and a developing country—Mexico in. The European Community signed with African, Caribbean and Pacific countries the Third and Fourth Lomé Convention respectively in 1984 and 1989, which became an important fruit of the South-North Dialogue and the most wide-ranging South-North cooperation agreement. The European Community and many regional economic organizations of the South established relatively effective and rewarding dialogue and cooperation organizations. Japan continuously adjusted its Asia-Pacific policy in a bid to play a dominant role in the Asia-Pacific economic circle. As such, the South-North Dialogue made considerable headway through regional South-North Cooperation. "Regional economic integration or conglomeration was a manifestation of economic scramble developed countries made in the Third World, but created opportunities for South-North Dialogue and Cooperation and served as an important means of South-North Cooperation."[23]

8.6.2. New Characteristics of South-South Cooperation

At the same time when South-North Dialogue and Cooperation were carried out, South-South Cooperation also saw much headway after decades of development after World War II. When countries of the South were confronted with greater financial difficulties and external pressures in the 80s, they also paid greater attention to mutual cooperation.

In May 1981, the Group of 77 inaugurated the High-level Conference on Economic Cooperation among developing countries. In March 1983, the 7th Summit of Non-Aligned Countries was held, and in April, a ministerial conference of the Group of 77. On these meetings, the promotion of South-South Cooperation was unanimously stressed to propel the South-North Dialogue.

In the 80s, prosperous development of regional cooperation in the Third World became another great characteristic of South-South Cooperation. In Asia, ASEAN countries strengthened internal political and economic cooperation and expanded its cooperation and exchanges with other regions. 7 countries in South Asia adopted the Declaration on South Asian Association Regional Cooperation and the Integrated Program of Action in 1983, and held the Summit of South Asian Association for Regional Cooperation for many times. 6 countries in the Gulf region founded the Gulf Cooperation Council (GCC) in 1981 and strengthened political, military and economic cooperation. In Africa, the Organization of African Unity (OAU) Summit meeting held in 1980 passed the Lagos Plan of Action and brought forward specific programs and measures for economic cooperation. In Latin America, along with the official establishment of Latin American Integration Association (LAIA) in March 1981, the trend of regional cooperation was further strengthened.

Still, the South-South Cooperation among Third World countries was challenged by many hardships. First of all, in an effort to guarantee their vested interests, developed countries took various measures to obstruct South-South Cooperation. At the same time, factors such as unbalanced economic development among Third World countries, change of political stand and their contradictions made it difficult for the Third World to carry out extensive cooperation in a global context. Therefore, for the South-South Cooperation in the 1980s, strengthening solidarity and cooperation became all the more important.

23   Peng, Shuzhi, and Qianyun Huang. *Historical Process of the Third World*. Beijing: China Youth Publishing House, 1999: 383.

8.6.3. The Role of China

In the 80s, China made important contributions to the promotion of South-North Dialogue and South-South Cooperation. In Asia, China set store by developing good neighborly and amicable relations with neighboring countries. Not only did China further develop its friendly relations with countries of traditional friendship such as the DPRK, Pakistan, Cambodia and Myanmar, but also improved bilateral relations with India. In Africa, China strengthened friendly and cooperative relations with African countries, actively supported African countries' struggle for economic independence, and firmly opposed racism of the South African authorities as well as endorsed the righteous independence and anti-apartheid struggles of African people in the southern part. In Latin America, China reinforced exchanges and cooperation in all areas with Latin American countries and supported their rational proposition of addressing debt crisis and their righteous fight for national independence and state sovereignty.

China's responsible policies in regard to international issues has enhanced the status of the Third World in South-North dialogues and significantly promoted the peace and development trend across the world.

Chapter IX

The North-South Relationship
in the Post-Cold War Era

9.1. New Changes in the North-South Political Relationship in the Post-Cold War Era

9.1.1. New Challenges to the Third Worldin the Post-Cold War Era

In the late 1980s and early 1990s, with the fall of socialist regimes in the Eastern Europe and the dissolution of the Soviet Union, the protracted Cold War status after World War II came to an end. In the wake of the end of the Cold War, the global political pattern was drastically changed, entering a stage of transition from the old to the new. Major powers in the world adjusted their own strategies and policies one after another, and the standing of the Third World in the international arena also underwent changes. The transformation of the international situation presented daunting challenges to the Third World countries.

First of all, following the end of the Cold War, the Third World countries were no longer, in the conventional sense, "intermediate regions" contended by the two superpowers. Having lost the leeway of going between the East and the West, the Third World countries' strategic position was on the decline. In the midst of the Cold War, the Third World countries were opposed to the hegemonism and power politics of world powers and proactively sought political and economic independence, becoming the "intermediate regions" beyond the bipolarity of the United States and the Soviet Union. To fight for spheres of influence in the "intermediate regions", both the US and the USSR paid much attention to the Third World. However, after the Cold War, the Third World no longer had the strategic position of being "intermediate regions". On the issue of the North-South relationship, countries of the North had more converging interests and often joined up against developing countries, putting the Third World at a disadvantage.

Second, interferences made by developed countries, particulary countries of the North, got even worse. By means of "human rights diplomacy" and the promotion of democratization, the US-led developed countries imposed some Western values, ideology and the social system on the Third World countries. On the economic front, the former put various kinds of pressure on the latter. In the military field, the US-led developed countries limited the increase of national strength in the Third World through arms control and interfered in the internal affairs of the Third World countries with the threat or even direct use of force.[1]

Third, the development of economic globalization gravely challenged the Third World countries. For one thing, economic globalization made the Third World countries confronted with a serious problem of "national vulnerability", i.e. their national sovereignty was challenged. Against the backdrop of economic globalization, regional grouping and economic integration have made great headway. In the course of regional grouping and economic integration, countries had to release part of rights of exercising economic sovereignty in a bid to ensure coordination of regional economic actions and facilitate common economic growth. Compared with developed countries, however, it was a bigger challenge for the Third World countries to earnestly protect their own interests while transferring part of rights of exercising economic sovereignty. Besides, in the course of economic globalization, international economic organizations and multinational companies also constrained the Third World countries' exercising of sovereignty. For another, economic globalization posed a threat to the economic security of the Third World countries. Owing to economic globalization, the Third World countries' capabilities of protecting their own markets and industries were substantially weakened, leaving important domestic economic sectors possibly subject to the control of multi-national corporations. International financial capital, particularly venture capital in large amounts, is prone to give significant shocks to the incomplete financial order in the Third World. This has been best illustrated by the 1994 Mexican Financial Crisis and the 1997 Southeast Asian Financial Crisis. Economic

1 Liu, Qingjian. *A New Approach to Contemporary International Relations.* Beijing: Tsinghua University Press, 2004: 27-29.

globalization also widened the polarization and weath gap between the North and the South. Because of the leading role of developed countries dominated by those of the North in the economic globalization, the Third World could hardly enjoy the benefits of economic globalization on a par with developed countries. Furthermore, economic globalization increasingly expanded the gap between developing countries. Some of them had been actively involved in economic globalization and had the momentum of catching up with developed counterparts. In contrast, many with weak economic foundation and backward economy were faced with risks of "marginalization."[2]

Last but not least, even inside the Third World, there were numerous contradictions. Continuous aggravation of imbalanced economic development and territorial, ethnic and religious conflicts gave rise to the discretion of the overall political interests of the Third World and its declining role in the North-South Dialogue. Since the end of the Cold War, some countries and regions with resource advantages have actively participated in international competition and started to be open to the outside world earlier than the rest, such as some Middle East countries, Four Asian Tigers. They have made remarkable achievements in economic development. Nevertheless, for most of the Third World countries, some Latin American and African nations in particular, their economic growth was beset with countless hardships. Such economic differentiation in the Third World resulted in differentiation on the political front. Owing to disparity in economic growth, some Third World countries had diverse views toward international affairs, which weakened their interior political solidarity. Other countries that were rather backward in economic development featured deepening economic dependence and hence increasing political reliance on Western countries. When it came to international affairs, they tended to follow the will of developed countries in the West. In addition, as a result of backward economic growth, some Third World countries were not confident enough about independent development and blindly promoted the Western formula for democracy, only to result in national political turmoil and even civil wars which further crippled the overall strength of the Third World.[3] After the end of the Cold War, the Third World saw more and more outstanding state-to-state territorial, ethnic and religious conflicts under the cover of the old pattern. At the same time, some large countries took advantage of the post-cold war power "vacuum" and began to seek regional hegemony and expansionism, leading to serious regional conflicts. For example, Iraqi invasion of Kuwait triggered the Gulf War, offering an opportunity for Western countries to meddle in the internal affairs of the Persian Gulf states.

---

2   Ibid.: 114-116.
3   Lin, Limin, and Fan Yang. "The Third World and International New Order in the 21st Century". *Perspectives of the Contemporary Third World*. Ed. China Institutes of Contemporary International Relations. Beijing: Current Affairs Press, 2001: 35-36.

9.1.2. Opportunities for the Third World in the Post-Cold War Era

In spite of daunting challenges, the Third World has also embraced positive trends and rare opportunities for development. If the opportunities were seized, the Third World countries could make a difference. After all, the Third World still holds an important standing in the global pattern after the Cold War. Economic development in the Third World countries has also become vital sources of global economic growth. Some Third World countries rose rapidly and became a driving force behind the process of world multi-polarization. Besides, the Third World countries have important resource advantages. Thanks to the need of cooperation with the Third World nations on major issues such as economic development, security and arms control, developed countries dominated by countries of the North have attached greater importance to them in the form of adjusting relevant foreign policies and seeking to forge new-type cooperative relations with them.

Regional cooperation between the Third World countries has made further progress and the South-South Cooperation has taken on a new look. In the post-Cold War era, the Third World countries have become aware that against the backdrop of economic globalization and complex and volatile international situations, the only way to enhance the status in the world pattern and North-South Dialogue is to follow the course of joint self-improvement among countries of "the South" and step up regional cooperation. In Asia, ASEAN, short for the Association of Southeast Asian Nations, has strengthened alliance among Southeast Asian countries and actively developed cooperation with China, Japan and South Korea with an aim to establishing the East Asia Free Trade Area. In Africa, the Organization of African Unity (OAU) proclaimed the founding of the African Union (AU)on the basis of the OAU at the 37th Summit in 2001. The AfricanUnion will follow the example of the European Union and be dedicated to greatly promoting political and economic integration among African states. In the Americas, the countries have been vigorously advancing the plan of the America Free Trade Zone which will cover the 34 American countries except Cuba and become a trade zone on a par with the EU and the AU. Thanks to regional cooperation, the Third World countries have maintained powerful cohesion which still plays a positive role in maintaining world peace and promoting worldwide development.

9.1.3. New Developments in the North-South Dialogue

With the policy adjustment by the countries of the North and alongside with new changes in the Third World in the post-Cold War era, the North-South relationship has taken on eye-catching changes. This has been reflected in two aspects as follows.

One, the North-South conflicts have a more outstanding position in the international relations than ever before. In the Cold War period, the North-South conflicts had been in a subordinate position while the East-West conflicts held the dominate position. After the end of the Cold War, however, the North-South conflicts have become more and more pronounced in international relations notwithstanding the dominate position. On the economic front, economic conflicts between countries of the North and the South have shown a trend of intensification. Developed countries, which are mainly countries of the North, often tried to weaken the competitiveness of countries of the South by means of their economic might. In the meantime, they tended to set the protection of "human rights", the implementation of "democratization", "multi-party system" and "market economy" as preconditions of extending economic assistance so as to implant their political systems and values to the Third World, which resulted in contradictions and conflicts between the South and the North.

Two, mutual dependence between countries of the South and the North has deepened while their contradictions have become more outstanding. Increasingly vibrant regional North-South cooperation has become a notable characteristic of the North-South cooperation in the post-Cold War era.

In the early 1980s, worldwide North-South Dialogue came to a deadlock, but regional North-South relationship continued to grow further. Thanks to the development of world economic integration, economic growth and security of the North and the South became more closely interconnected. On the one hand, to contend for natural resources, commodity markets and expand influence, countries of the North that are economically developed need develop bilateral relations with some countries of the South. On the other hand, countries of the South that were in urgent need of capital and technologies were willing to enter into cooperation with countries of the North. Nevertheless, owing to intensified development imbalance in the Third World since the 1980s, different countries of the South may have diverse objectives of cooperation. As a result, countries of the North prefer to address their own urgent problems by way of mutual regional cooperation. Both sides have carried out a series of regional North-South Cooperation and achieved remarkable success. The founding of APEC (Asia-Pacific Economic Cooperation), NAFTA (North-America Free Trade Area) and regional cooperation between the EU and the Third World countries have indicated deepening mutual reliance between the North and the South. Moreover, regional North-South cooperation will become a major form of North-South cooperation in the current period of time. Cooperation in such a form will make a significant difference to the future political and economic development in the world.[4]

4   Chang, Zheng, and Fengjun Chen, eds. *Transformations and Revolutions in the Third World*. Beijing: China Renmin University Press, 1997: 387-391.

9.2. New Trends in the North-South Relationship in East and Central Asia

9.2.1. Korean Peninsula Dispute and the New Hopes during the Six-Party

As far as the North-South relationship is concerned, the hotspot issue in East Asia lies in the Korean Peninsula. As the frontier of contention among world powers in the Cold War era, the North Korea (or the DPRK) has taken on new tendencies after the end of the Cold War.

In September 1990, the North Korean Premier and South Korean Prime Minister held the first talks in Seoul. Although the talks failed to make substantive progress in improving the bilateral relations, it enhanced mutual understanding between North and South Korea. In September 1991, the two sides reached an agreement on simultaneously joining the United Nations. Later on December 13, the North Korean Premier and South Korean Prime Minister officially signed the Agreement on Reconciliation, Mutual Non-Aggression, Exchanges and Cooperation between North and South. The Agreement stated that South and North Korea promised mutual recognition and respect of the system of each other and non-interference in each other's internal affairs; both sides guaranteed non-use of force against each other and peaceful resolution of differences of views and disputes through dialogue and negotiation; both sides agreed to engage in joint development of resources, cooperation and investment as well as exchanges on culture, education and sports, and permit free correspondence and mutual visits between dispersed family members and other relatives.[5] At the end of 1991, President of South Korea (Republic of Korea, or ROK) Roh Tae-Woo issued a declaration on nuclear-free Korean Peninsula, declaring the complete evacuation of all U.S. tactical nuclear weapons deployed in South Korea. During this period, North-South talks on the Korean Peninsula made great progress, and both South and North Korea improved their relations with relevant world powers.

Nevertheless, it has been a turtuous path to realized peace in the Korean Peninsula. Early in 1993, the United States requested a special inspection of two sites near Yongbyon possibly used for storing raw materials of nuclear weapons. North Korea declined the U.S. request and declared in three months to officially withdraw from the Nuclear Nonproliferation Treaty. Soon afterwards, International Atomic Energy Agency (IAEA) sent an ultimatum requesting North Korea to accept an inspection within one month. Also, the United States warned the enforcement of economic sanctions and even the use of force against North Korea should it refused to accept the inspection as scheduled. Since the United States and South Korea resumed the joint military exercise, North Korea gave tit for tat by declaring the whole country in a quasi-wartime military state. The two sides on the Korean Peninsula were both set for a showdown and a crisis was on the verge of breaking out.

---

5   *People's Daily* December 14, 1991.

Brokered by China, the United States and the Democratic People's Republic of Korea (North Korea) had 3 major negotiations and on October 21, 1994, they finally signed in Geneva the "Agreed Framework" on the resolution of North Korean Nuclear Issues. North Korea agreed to accept the inspection of International Atomic Energy Agency (IAEA) and freeze its existing nuclear programs. North Korea agreed to freeze nuclear fueling to the 5 MW(e) experimental reactor and the construction of two graphite-moderated reactors, clost its nuclear fuel reprocessing plants. The United States agreed to help the DPRK to build in about 10 years a 2,000 MW(e) or two 1000 MW (e) light-water reactor (LWR) power plants, and from October 21 till the completion of the LWRs, provide heavy oil as energy compensation.[6] In June 1995, the United States and North Korea formed a concrete scheme to implement the Geneva Agreed Framework. The tension in the Korean Peninsula was relaxed temporarily.

From June 13 to 15, 2000, the state leader of DPRK Kim Jong II and President of ROK Kim Dae-Jung had a meeting in Pyongyang, capital of DPRK. This was the first historic meeting between leaders of South and North Korea for half a century after the division of the Korean Peninsula. The meeting reached positive results in that the two sides issued the North-South Joint Declaration. Both sides believed that the reunification issue should be independently resolved by North and South Korea through negotiations. In addition, they agreed on mutual exchange of visits by delegations of dispersed family members and other relatives, as well as bilateral cooperation and exchange in fields such as economy, society and culture and so on.

After George Walker Bush came into power, the United States began to practice tough policies on North Korea. Because of the outbreak of the September 11 Terrorist Attacks in 2001, the United States perceived terrorism and nuclear proliferation as the greatest threats.[7] In January 2002, George W. Bush called North Korea, Iraq and Iran Axis of Evil. Triggered by a severe sense of insecurity toward the new policy of the United States, North Korea condemned that the U.S. blockade and hostile policy against it gravely threatened its sovereignty and right of survival. The peace process in the Korean Peninsula was hence met with setbacks again.

Following the outbreak of the Iraqi War in 2003, North Korea no longer resolutely declined the multi-party talks proposition of the United States. With the Chinese efforts, from August 27 to 29, 2003, the first Round of Six-Party Talks attended by delegates from China, North Korea, America, South Korea, Japan and Russia was held at Diaoyutai State Guesthouse, Beijing, China. The talks reached a consensus that all parties were willing to dedicate themselves to peacefully resolve the North Korean nuclear issues through negotiations and agreed to continue the process of Six-Party Talks. From February 25 to 28, 2004, the second round of Six-Party Talks was again held in Beijing, China.

---

6   *People's Daily* October 22, 1994.
7   *People's Daily* September 12, 2001. Note: The September 11 Attacks were a series of terrorist incidents happened in the United States on September 11, 2001.

The talks issued the first common document entitled Chairmen's Declaration on the Second Round of Six-Party Talks since the launch of the Six-Party Talks and decided on the establishement of a work group to institutionalize the Six-Party Talks. From June 23 to 26, 2004, the Third Round of Six-Party Talks was held. Centering on the peaceful resolution of North Korean nuclear issue, relevant parties put forward their respective proposals, suggestions and conceptions and identified the progressive way and the principle of mouth-to-mouth and action-to-action.[8] The Six-Party Talks aim to promote resolution of international issues through peaceful negotiations and direct a peaceful path for achieving peace in the Korean Peninsula at an early date, playing an important role in relaxing the tension in the Peninsula.

Peace talks are the right solution to the North Korean issue. However, due to historical and realistic reasons, the final resolution of the issue remains to be seen.

9.2.2. The Afghanistan Civil War and "Reconstruction" of Afghanistan by the US

In Central Asia, peace and stability did not befall to Afghanistan after the withdrawal of the Soviet troops. On the occasion of the Soviet withdrawal of troops, Afghanistan resistance groups in different factions were all racing to control small and medium towns and besiege large cities such as Kandahar and Jalalabad. Resistance groups demanded the Kabul regime be handed over immediately after the Soviet withdrawal. But the Kabul regime declared the entire nation entering a state of emergency, tenaciously defended many other large cities by virtue of arms and refused to hand over the power to resistance groups.

Above all, the United States and the Soviet Union did not abide by the Geneva Agreement on politically solving the Afghanistan issue. They did not suspend military assistance to the fighting parties. On the contrary, they accelerated the dispatch weapons to Afghanistan. For one thing, the Soviet Union left the pro-Soviet Kabul regime various weaponry which amounted to 1 billion US dollars after its withdrawal. For another, the United States alleged not to suspend military assistance to resistance groups as long as the Soviet Union continued to support the Kabul regime. As a consequence, Afghanistan could not enjoy peace after the Soviet Union evacuated its troops, rather the country was soon engulfed in the civil war.

Against the backdrop of the protracted and dragged-on war, the proposition of seeking political solutions to the Afghanistan issue return to be the upper hand. In September 1991, the foreign Ministers of the Soviet Union and the United States issued a joint declaration that, by the year 1992, the two countries would cease supplying arms to the two rival parties of Afghanistan.[9] At the same time, the Kabul regime decided to practice unilateral ceasefire. In

---

8   See *People's Daily* August 30, 2003, February 29, 2004 and June 27, 2004.
9   Fang, Lianqing, et al., eds. *History of Postwar International Relations*. Beijing: Peking University Press, 1999: *913*.

early 1992, President Mohammad Najibullah of the Kabul regime asserted his willingness to hand over the power to the coalition government composed by multiple parties. But on April 16, he suddenly announced to resign, making the situation even more chaotic. Brokered by the United Nations, various resistance guerrilla groups of Afghanistan reached an agreement in the border city of Pakistan called Peshawar on forming an interim committee to take over the state power. But the establishment of the interim committee failed to effectively prevent contention for power among various factions of Afghan guerrilla troops who began to snatch strategic strongholds from one another. According to the Peshawar Accord, leader of Hizb-e-Islami Gulbuddin Hekmatyar was appointed Prime Minister of the Interim Government; leader of Jamiat-e Islami Burhanuddin Rabbani was appointed President of the Interim Government and responsible for organizing the general elections; and Professor Rabbani should hand over the power to the Afghanistan Decision-Making Council by October, 1992. Nevertheless, Rabbani did not hand over the power on time, but manipulated the presidential election and elected himself as the President. Hizb-e-Islami could hardly tolerate Rabbani's behaviors and launched a fierce battle in Kabul, which again put Afghanistan to a civil war.

While various parties in Afghanistan were engaged in fierce rivalries for power, a Islamic student movement armed force called the Taliban began to rise quickly under the leadership of Mullah Mohammed Omar and soon controlled most provinces of Afghanistan. Taliban claimed to dismantle armament of all groups and establish a stringent Islamic system, making the situation in Afghanistan even more complicated. Confronted with aggressive offensive of Taliban, other factions began to bury the hatchet. They have formed anti-Taliban alliances for 4 times and engaged in a four-year warfare with Taliban. However, Taliban was always on the upper hand. As a result, other factions had to hide in border areas to continue to fight with Taliban.

One important factor of fast rise of Taliban was the energetic support of the United States. "In order to establish a pro-US regime in Afghanistan, expand the American permeation in Central Asia and acquire the newly-discovered rich oil and gas resources in the Caspian Sea region, the United States stopped support for other Afghan factions and turned to financially assist Taliban."[10]

However, facts have proven the move made by the United States was like cherishing a snake in the bosom. After Taliban rose to power, it not only practiced religious extremism at home, but also endorsed foreign Islamic extremism forces and national separatists. Taliban's support for terrorists led to a large increase of terrorist incidents in the international community. Worse still, Taliban provided shelter to Osama Bin Laden, an international terrorist leader and founder of al-Qaeda. In this way, Afghanistan under the rule of Taliban became a vital base of Islamic Fundamentalism terrorists worldwide.

---

10   Wu, Shuhu. "Insights into Taliban." *Contemporary World* 5(2001): 23. Qtd. in Liu, Qingjian. *A New Approach to Contemporary International Relations*. Beijing: Tsinghua University Press, 2004: 154.

In face of the surge of worldwide Islamic revival movement, the United States began to contain it and no longer supported these Islamic armed forces. Such move of America infuriated a number of extremist terrorists who began to direct its spearhead against the United States. On September 11, 2001, terrorists hijacked two large commericial passenger aircrafts and flew into the twin towers of the World Trade Center in New York. A third aircraft was also hijacked to fly into the Pentagon, the headquarters of the United States Department of Defense. The fourth hijacked aircraft crashed near Pittsburgh. At the same time, terrorists also set off explosions near the State Department building and the U.S. Capitol.[11] This whole series of terrorist attacks were known as the September 11 Attacks. The incidents caused over 3,000 casualties and were the most severe terrorist attacks ever in the U.S. history. Subsequently, the United States concluded that the September 11 Attacks were orchestrated by Osama bin Laden and that the Afghan Taliban regime had refuged him. In response to the attacks, on October 8, the United States began to launch large-scale airstrikes against Afghanistan and ground search for Osama bin Laden and Mullah Mohammad Omar, leader of Taliban. In the meantime, the United States supported anti-Taliban Northern Alliance Troops of Afghanistan in their attacks against the Taliban. Because of the onslaught of the U.S. Army, Taliban finally evacuated from the last stronghold Kandahar on December 7, with the Taliban regime collapsed accordingly. On December 22, 2001, the Afghan Interim Administration was established and Hamid Karzai was appointed Chairman of the Interim Administration.

328

In an effort to thoroughly eradicate terrorism and establish a peaceful and stable Afghanistan, the International Conference on Reconstruction Assistance to Afghanistanwas concluded on January 22, 2002, in Tokyo, Japan. On the meeting, relevant countries pledged to donate a total of 4.5 billion US dollars as aid fund for reconstruction of Afghanistan.[12] On December 17, 2002, International Conference on Assistance to Afghanistan was held in Oslo, capital of Norway. The conference decided to continue assistance to Afghanistan and the amount of assistance in 2003 to Afghanistan reconstruction would reach 1.7 billion euros.[13] Because Afganistan is a major country of opium planting and illicit drug production and its domestic situation is far from stable, post-war reconstruction of Afghanistan has been confronted with considerable difficulties.

9.3. The Implications of the Middle East Turbulence on the North-South Relationship

9.3.1. The Gulf War

After the end of the bipolar structure, powerful forces and radical nationalist forces in the Middle East were on the rise, posing threats to the U.S. interest in the region. Following the end of the Cold War, the United States became the

---

11 *People's Daily* September 12, 2001.

12 *People's Daily* (Overseas Edition), January 23, 2002.

13 *People's Daily* December 20, 2002.

sole super power in the world and endeavored to strengthen its leading role in the Middle East. Russia, however, wanted to restore its position as a powerful country. It not only actively participated in the Middle East peace process, but also paid much attention to resuming traditional friendly relations with Iran, Syria and Iraq. By this means, Russia has strengthened its influence in the region. Countries like the UK, France, Germany and Japan either followed the United States or advanced their independent policies to the Middle East in a bid to protect and expand their own interests in this strategically vital region. In this connection, the outbreak of the Gulf War created favorable conditions for these powerful countries to get involved in the Middle East affairs.

On August 2, 1990, Iraq suddenly mobilized 100,000 soldiers and made a massive invasion to its neighbor Kuwait. Kuwait could not withstand a single blow and soon the whole country was occupied by the Iraqis. On August 8, Iraq announced to annex Kuwait and named it the 19th Province.

Immediately, the United States responded strongly to the Iraqi acts of aggression. On the day when the Iraq-Kuwait war broke out, the United States declared to freeze the huge amounts of assets of Iraq and Kuwait in the United States in no time and enforce sanctions against Iraq. In the meantime, the United States made proactive diplomatic efforts so as to isolate and apply sanctions on Iraq. Allies of the US and parts of the Persian Gulf countries also issued statements supporting the United States to send troops to the Gulf area. Iraq was reduced to extraordinary isolation in the international community.

Despite the tremendous pressure from the international community, Iraq refused to evacuate from Kuwait. When the peaceful efforts seemed hopeless, chances of military solution became greater and greater. On November 29, 2000, the United Nations Security Council passed the Resolution 678, with 12 affirmative votes, 2 veto votes and 1 abstentions. The resolution authorized the UNSC members to use all necessary means to uphold and execute relevant resolutions and restore peace and security in the Gulf area if Iraq refused to implement relevant UNSC resolutions of requesting Iraq to withdraw its troops from Kuwait by January 15, 1991. The resolution offered Iraq one last chance to fully abide by the Resolution 660 and all other relevant resolutions on Iraq immediately and unconditionally withdrawing from Kuwait and resuming Kuwait's sovereignty, independence and territorial integrity and specified the deadline. On November 30, Iraq declined the resolution requesting it to withdraw forces from Kuwait within 15 days. The Iraqi Revolution Command Council said in a statement that voting on this resolution was "illegal and futile" because some countries casted affirmative votes under the pressure of the United States.[14] The UNSC Resolution 678, in effect, acquiesced in military operations against Iraq. At that time, the US-led multinational forces swept into the Gulf area. Some Gulf states, Japan and Germany provided a total of 54 billion US dollars of war funding and the United States prepared for a war.

---

14 *People's Daily* December 1, 1990

On January 17, 1991, the US-led coalition forces enforced the military operation code-named Operation Desert Storm and the Gulf War broke out. The multi-national forces first launched an aerial bombardment against Iraq that lasted for more than one month. Following effectively hitting the Iraqi commande system and logistic supply system, on February 24, the multinational forces waged a ground assault code-named Desert Saber. On the 26th, Iraq announced full withdrawal from Kuwait. On the 27th, Iraq proclaimed unconditional acceptance of the UNSC resolutions on the Kuwait issue and pleaded for a ceasefire. By far, the 42-day Gulf War ended up with the Iraqi failed venture to seize regional hegemony.

The victory of the Gulf War helped the United States further build up its dominant position in the Middle East. By this time, the United States hoped to promote peace in the region to guarantee stable oil supply. On the one hand, in the wake of the Gulf War, the Arab states furthered internal differentiation and the joint forces against Israel was accordingly weakened. On the other hand, Israel has boasted great military advantages, but Arab-Israeli conflicts have never ceased and the Israeli people have never obtained peace and stability. They began to show willingness to "conditionally" negotiate with the Arab world to realize peace. Above all, through decades of armed confrontation, both Arab and Israel have come to the awareness that their differences and conflicts can not be solved by violence and that only peaceful negotiations were the only correction solution.

9.3.2. The Tortuous Road to Palestine-Israeli Peace

On October 30, 1991, with concerted efforts from relevant parties, the Middle East Peace Conference was held in Madrid, Spain. The Madrid Conference clarified the basic principle of Arab-Israeli negotiations—"land for peace". According to this principle, Israel should return its occupied territories during the previous Middle East Wars to the Arabians to exchange for peaceful coexistence with them. This principle became the foundation of Palestine-Israeli negotiations and the Middle East Peace Process as a whole. In 1992, Yitzhak Rabin served as the Prime Minister of Israel. He accepted the United Nations Security Council resolutions on realizing peace in the Middle East. Promoted by Yitzhak Rabin and Yasser Arafat, the Palestinian-Israeli peace talks made fast headway. In 1994, the two sides signed the Gaza-Jericho Agreement on a partial Israeli withdrawal from Gaza and Jericho and the founding of Yasser Arafat-led self-governance regime of Palestine. In 1994, Jordan and Israel signed a peace treaty marking the normalization of the state-to-state relations and the establishment of their diplomatic relations. Because of his hard efforts for the Middle East peace process, Yitzhak Rabin won people's respect and admiration. And in 1994, Rabin was awarded the Nobel Peace Prize together with Arafat and Shimon Peres. However, Rabin's efforts also incurred hatred from domestic extremist forces. On November 4, 1995, Rabin was assassinated that night in Tel Aviv by an Israeli Jewish ultra-Rightist. At a crucial moment when the Israeli-Palestinian peace process began to enter the second stage, the assassination of Rabin inevitably added political pressure and psychological burden of leaders of Israel, Palestine and the Arab states who were engaged in negotiations. As a consequence, it brought about negative impacts on the Middle East peace process.[15]

In July, 1996, the Likud party seized power in Israel. Its chairman Benjamin Netanyahu renounced the principle of "land for peace" and stressed "security for peace". He adopted a hard line towards the Arab-Israeli peace talks, entangling the Middle East peace process into plights.

In May 1999, the Israeli Labor Party returned to power and Ehud Barak was elected Prime Minister of the new government. Israel and Palestine conducted negotiations and signed the Sharm el-Sheikh Memorandum. Due to serious differences plus deliberate delay of Israel, the memorandum was useless like an empty shell. In July 2000, the U.S. President Bill Clinton presided over the Palestinian-Israeli Summit at Camp David. He urged leaders of Palestine and Israel to make give-and-take compromise on the issues of the standing of Jerusalem, Jewish settlements, boundary division and return of Palestinian refugees. But the talks ended up in failure. Since September 28, 2000, large-scale sanguinary conflicts broke out successively between Palestine and Israel, making the negotiation bogged down.

In March 2001, Ariel Sharon was elected Prime Minister of Israel. He enforced a tough policy toward Arab states and stressed to spare no efforts, including the use of force to guarantee safety of the Israeli people. Sharon practiced the policy of "targeted elimination" to assassinate radical leaders of Palestine, which stirred up strong anti-Israeli sentiment of the Palestinian people and the Arab world. Presently, radical groups of Palestine organized a series of bombing attacks targeted at the Israeli people. The Middle East peace process was again reduced to plights.

In 2003, the United States won the victory in the Iraqi War. At this time, Palestine appointed Mahmoud Abbas as the new Prime Minister. There came an opportunity to solve the Palestinian-Israeli conflicts. The United States attempted to play a dominate role in the Middle East peace process and on April 30, published the Roadmap plan for peace in the region. Implementation of the Roadmap consisted of two stages. The first stage was from December 2002 to May 2003. During this stage, on the one hand, Palestine was requested to take substantive measures to counter and curb all violence and terrorist activities against Israel and enforce an all-round political reform; on the other hand, Israel was required to withdraw from all occupied territory that belonged to Palestine before September 28, 2000 and freeze all activities at settlements. The second stage was from June 2003 to December 2003. During this period, Palestine was required to hold general elections to firmly identify the democratic system and, with the help of the international community, build an independent

---

15 *People's Daily* November 7, 1995

self-governing interim Authority in Palestine with sovereign powers. The third stage was from 2004 to 2005. Both Palestine and Israel were requested to, on the basis of the UNSC resolution 242, resolution 338 and resolution 1397, has addressed the issues such as the territorial boundaries, final status of Jerusalem, refugees and settlements by means of negotiations and work to ensure fair, reasonable and practical resolution of the Palestinian-Israeli conflicts in the end as well as promote solution of left-over problems between Israel and Lebanon, between Israel and Syria. The ultimate goal of the plan was to put an end to the Palestinian-Israeli conflicts and help with the establishment of the state of Palestine.[16] Brokered by the United States, the Roadmap plan won recognition of Palestine and the Sharon government of Israel.

However, radical forces of Palestine did not aknowledge the Roadmap plan. The Hamas-led radical group took repeated revenges and was opposed to Israeli occupation of Palestinian territory. Without a sign of weakness, the Sharon government began to build Separation Barrier near Israeli-Palestinian border and limit commute of the Palestinian people. It also continued to implement the policy of "targeted elimination" and killed in succession the spiritual leader of Hamas Sheikh Ahmed Yassin and his successor Abdel Aziz Rantisi.

On November 11, 2004, President of Palestine Yasser Arafat passed away in Paris, France. Arafat was the only Palestinian leader that had absolute authority over the past 4 decades. It is said that Arafat has become a symbol with special meaning and a key word when it comes to the Middle East, Palestine and Israel. The editorial of Associated Press on that day said, "The death of Yasser Arafat opened a door. No one knows what's hidden behind the door, perhaps peace or perhaps chaos. All this depends on whether Arafat's successor has the ability to have the situation under control; it depends on whether Israel can resume negotiations with Palestine."[17]

9.4. The North-South Relationship in Africa and Latin America in the Post-Cold War Era

In the post-Cold War era, the overall political situation in Africa moved towards stability and detente. In particular, peace in Southern Africa and the birth of a new democratic South Africa brought new hope to Africa. Nevertheless, there were some countries and regions in Africa where unrests and conflicts broke out from time to time due to economic problems, international factors and internal contradictions. This cast a shadow over the prospect of Africa. In Latin America, the post-Cold War Latin American international relations have undergone enormous changes. In view of substantially declining strength of the Soviet Union (Russia) in Latin America, the United States who had all along regarded Latin America as its own "backyard" naturally would not miss the

16   Liu, Qingjian. *A New Approach to Contemporary International Relations*. Beijing: Tsinghua University Press, 2004: 208-209.
17   *People's Daily* November 12, 2004

chance of controlling the region. Besides, the United States attempted to create a stable "backyard" by promoting democratization process in Latin American nations.

9.4.1. Worsening Situation in Africa

Africa was increasingly at a disadvantage in the world economy. Economic crises in many African countries brought about turmoil of political situations which in turn stood in the way of revitalization of social economy, causing a vicious circle. After the end of the Cold War, both the Soviet Union and the United States substantially reduced assistance to Africa. Conditions for trade deteriorated and prices of primary commodities continued to fall. Most of African countries had a further dwindling export capacity. It was a long and uphill task for them to achieve economic independence.

Politically, since the Soviet Union implemented the strategy of getting away from Africa in the wake of the Cold War, some African countries that were supported and influenced by the Soviet Union thereby took a big hit. Opposition factions in some countries seized the chance and launched attacks, causing uninterrupted warfare and chaos in these countries. For example, in Angola, the Angolan government and the National Union for the Total Independence of Angola (UNITA) began negotiations on ending the civil war after the Soviet and Cuban withdrawal. In May 1991, the two sides reached an agreement on the conclusion of the civil war. In September 1992, a general election was held in Angola. But when the exit poll showed the People's Movement for the Liberation of Angola (MPLA) won the election, the UNITA condemned the MPLA for cheating in the election and refused to accept the results of the election. The UNITA began to launch turf wars which triggered a second civil war. Thanks to the efforts of the international community, the two sides finally reached a peace agreement in 1994. In May 1995, President of the Angolan government José Eduardo dos Santos and the leader of the UNITA Jonas Savimbi had direct negotiations and the peace process made some headway. However, due to deep grudge and a lack of trust, the conflict was not resolved in the end and the peace process could hardly proceed forward. In late May, 1997, their disputes were again intensified. At first, the Angolan government forces launched an attack against the UNITA armed forces in Lunda Norte Province. Soon afterwards, armed forces of the two sides had a seesaw battle featuring alternation of occupation and counteroffensive in some strategically important places of the region. In mid-November 1998, the Angolan government forces initiated an onslaught against the political and economic centers of the UNITA located in the Central part of the country. They were met with strong resistance and counter attack of the UNITA by tanks, missiles and long-range artilleries. A third Civil War broke out in Angola. The UNITA suffered one defeat after another in the battlefield. On February 22, 2002, leader of the UNITA Jonas Savimbi was shot dead by the government army, which became a turning point of the Angolan situation. After a series of negotiations, the utterly routed

UNITA forces finally reached an agreement with the government army on the conclusion of the Civil War. On April 4, 2002, the Angolan government and the UNITA officially signed a ceasefire agreement at the National Assembly Hall of Luanda, capital of Angola and proclaimed the end of the Civil War and resumption of the 1994 Lusaka Peace Agreement. This marked that the war-torn African country bid farewell to the 27 years of chaos and resumed the path of peace and development.[18]

Moreover, the developed countries, predominantly countries of the North, endeavored to promote the multi-party system and "democratization" in Africa after the end of the Civil War. Nevertheless, the Western values and political models did not suit the politically and economically backward Africa. Instead, the multi-party system and democratization highlighted the hidden internal contradictions within some African countries and even caused riots and civil wars, such as inter-tribal revengeful murders in Rwanda and Burundi. In Rwanda, the government of the Hutus who had a majority of population spared no efforts to cracking down on the Tutsis' activities, which further intensified the contradictions between the two large tribes. In Burundi, after enforcing the multi-party system, the Tutsis that had been in power for many years stepped down from office, but they still controlled economic and military power of the country. The Tutsis were deeply concerned about the Hutus regime. In April 1994, Presidents of the two countries were assassinated at the same time, which incurred mutual slaughter between the two tribes in the countries. According to relevant statitics, simply in Rwanda, more than 500,000 people died and 4 million people became refugees within three months while the total population of the country was merely 7 million.[19]

9.4.2. Peace in Southern Africa and the Deepening of African Integration

One thing worth mentioning is that in spite of problems and even crises in the political process of Africa, the birth of the new South Africa state in 1994 contributed to peace and development of the African continent.

After Namibia gained independence,the white racist rule of South Africa was subjected to more austere denunciation from the international community. In 1989, F.W. de Klerk assumed office of President of South Africa. In February 1990, the de Klerk-led government proclaimed the removal of ban on African National Congree (ANC), Pan Africanist Congress (PAC) and South African Communist Party (SACP) and the release of famous leader of black people anti-apartheid movement Nelson Mandela, which created favorable conditions for peace negotiations between the white regime and the black opposition party. In December 1991, the de Klerk administration and the ANC-led 19 political

---

18 *People's Daily* (Overseas Edition) April 8, 2002.
19 Fang, Lianqing, et al., eds. *History of Postwar International Relations*. Beijing: Peking University Press, 1999: 903.

parties and organizations held the Convention for a Democratic South Africa (CODESA) and conduct negotiations on the constitutional framing mechanism and the composition of a transitional government as well as other issue. After hard negotiations, in June 1993, a session of the South African Multi-party Negotiations Committee approved that the first multi-racial universal elections would be held the next April. In April 1994, South Africa held the first universal elections ever in its history and the African National Congress (ANC) under the leadership of Nelson Mandela won the elections. On May 9, Nelson Mandela was elected the first black President of South Africa.

The new South Africa has not only realized internal peace but also actively played its role as a regional power. Domestically, South Africa has abundant resources, a fast-growing economy and peace as well as social stability. Internationally, South Africa has been a member of the Non-Aligned Movemnet (NAM) and Organization of African Unity (OAU). In addition, South Africa actively played its role in regional affairs. It contributed to the reconciliation in Angola and helped the elective government of Lesotho return to power, playing a sound role in promoting regional stability.

Almost at the same time, some hotspot regions in Africa have gradually achieved peace. In 1994, Libya and Chad reached an agreement on the issue of Aouzou Strip that Libya recognized the Chadian sovereignty over the area. Chad also resolved the long-standing domestic issue of anti-government armed forces to achieve national reconciliation. Apart from these, Zimbabwe and Algeria held national elections and their national situations began to stabilize.

Moreover, the African regional integration process accordingly made further progress. Since the 1960s, the Organization of African Unity (OAU) has been a significant organization dedicated for cooperation between African countries. At the 32nd Session of the OAU Summit held in 1996, the task of realizing regional economic integration was proposed. At the 36th Session of the OAU Summit held in July 2000, the Constitutive Act of the African Union was approved because the conference believed that a more powerful African Union must be founded to help all African countries respond to challenges of economic globalization. At the Special OAU Summit held in early March 2001, the 53 members of the Oranization of African Unity (OAU) signed the Constitution Act of the African Union in Sirte, a port city of Libya, proclaiming the founding of African Union (AU). This symbolizes the African countries set foot on the road of self-imrpovement in alliance.

9.4.3. The US Policy of "Democratization" in Latin America

In the wake of the Cold War, the United States has shifted the focus of its policy towards Latin America, there occurred a change from anti-communist expansion to emphasizingeconomic interests and benefits and regional stability. Previously, the United States flaunted "democracy", but it choose the subjects of support more often than not whether they supported or acted in coordination with the U.S. diplomatic strategies. Since the 1990s, with the purpose of maintaining regional stability, the United States shifted to support those governments which was elected by the people of the countries. Such a practice has, to some extent, promoted the process of democratization in Latin America.

In Nicaragua, the United States began to endorse the right-wing forces to seize the regime through political elections. The United States actively facilitated the conservatives and the liberals who were against the regime of the Sandinista National Liberation Front to forge the National Opposition Union and take part in the 1990 national elections as well as provided funds for election campaigning. The elections which ended up with the victory of the National Opposition Union of Nicaragua were a practical example of "democratization" under the control of the United States.

However, it is worth pondering that the United States often resorted to the use of force when advancing the process of "democratization" in some countries like Haiti. The Haitian soldiers staged a coup in September 1991 in which the democratically-elected President Jean-Bertrand Aristide was deposed and deported. When the peace efforts and sanctions of international organizations such as the Organization of American States (OAS) and the United Nations did not work, the United Nations Security Council (UNSC) consented to guarantee the enforcement of sanctions by force. The United States decided to use force to compel the military regime of Haiti to step down from office. According to the authorization of the 1994 UNSC resolution 940, the United States immediately sent troops to Haiti along with troops of other 5 Central American states. Under the strong military pressures from the United States, the military regime of Haiti agreed to hand over power. In October 1994, Jean-Bertrand Aristide returned to Haiti and resumed power, but he left office only one year later because of expiration of the term of office. Later, Jean-Bertrand Aristide founded the La Fanmi Lavalas and continued to involve in political contention with the new President René Préval, making the political situation of Haiti in turmoil. In 2000, Jean-Bertrand Aristide took office again, but cannot truly address the political and economic crises of the country. In February 2004, armed opposition forces besieged Port-au-Prince, capital of Haiti. Jean-Bertrand Aristide was forced to step down from office on February 29 and was again in exile overseas.[20] The people-elected government established under the support of foreign military forces did not properly solve the political and economic problems of Haiti.

9.4.4. The US Sanctions on Cuba and Cuba's Flexible Diplomacy

In the region of the Caribbean Sea, Cuba was confronted with daunting economic and political challenges after the dissolution of the Soviet Union and the fall of Communism in Eastern Europe. On the economic front, because the Soviet Union and the Eastern Europe were busy enough with their own affairs, they substantially cut economic assistance to Cuba. Bilateral trade

---

20   *People's Daily* March 1, 2004.

relations almost passed out of existence, which caused great troubles to Cuba whose economy was heavily dependent on the Council of Mutual Economic Assistance. According to statistics, from 1990 to 1993, Cuba's GNP fell by 34%.[21] Taking this opportunity, the United States reinforced economic blockade against Cuba in an attempt to overthrow the Cuban socialist regime. The United States had all along enforced economic sanctions against Cuba. The 1992 Torricelli Amendment (or, Cuban Democracy Act) not only banned U.S. companies and their overseas subsidiaries from conducting trade with Cuba, but also banned any foreign countries from trading with it by providing that any foreign ships that have been to Cuba were banned from entry into ports of the United States in six months. In May 1996, the United States proclaimed the implementation of the Helms-Burton Act (or, Cuban Liberty and Democratic Solidarity Act). The Act banned any officials and entrepreneurs trading with Cuba as well as their family members from entry into the United States, and authorized U.S. companies whose property had been confiscated by Cuba to file suit in U.S. courts claiming for 3 times of compensation against any foreign companies that may be trafficking in that property.[22] Politically, Cuba was confronted with mounting pressures. On the one hand, the change of the Soviet global strategies lowered the strategic position of Cuba. In September 1991, without prior negotiation with Cuba, the Soviet Union unilaterally announced a withdrawal of the Soviet troops from Cuba. On the other hand, the U.S. economic blockade presented heavy pressure for Cuba to adhere to socialism.

In face of the austere situation brought about by changes of the post-Cold War international situations, Cuba began to adjust its own foreign policy. Since the U.S. Torricelli Amendment aroused unviversal discontent of the international community, Cuba seized upon the opportunity to actively launch diplomatic activities in a bid to overcome the U.S. blockade. While taking advantage of the contradictions between Western countries to develop its economic and trade relations with the EU countries and Canada, Cuba also paid great attention to developing friendly relations with developing countries such as China and Vietnam. On the basis of diversified foreign relations, Cuba placed top priority on its relations with Latin American states. Latin American states supported the Cuban efforts of overcoming the U.S. blockade and, in spite of the threats of the Torricelli Amendment, continued to develop economic relations with Cuba. The Latin American Integration Association (LAIA) accepted Cuba to join the cultural, education, scientific and technological cooperation agreements. President of Venezuela Hugo Chavez, regardless of the U.S. objection, invited the Cuban President Fidel Alejandro Castro to make a state visit to Venezuela. During the state visit, Hugo Chavez signed a bilateral cooperation agreement with Fidel Alejandro Castro and decided to sell petroleum to Cuba. "Such a move caused new waves in the American continent and deeply hurt

21　Xu, Shicheng. "A Decade of the Cuban Reform and Opening-up: Achievements and Problems." *Annual Report on Latin America and the Caribbean, 2002-2003*. Beijing: Social Sciences Academic Press, 2003.
22　*People's Daily* October 30, 2004.

the prestige and interests of the US."[23] In 1994, Mexican President Ernesto Zedillo visited Cuba at the invitation of Castro. The two sides signed some economic cooperation agreements. Exchange between the two countries has, to a large extent, reflected the effect and impact of South-South Cooperation. This is of significant international influence and historic implications in that it strengthened ties between the Third World countries, helped them get rid of irrational international economic order and further improved their own political and economic systems.

23 *Global Times* March 30, 2001.

References

Albright, David E. Communism in Africa. London, 1986.

Ambrose, Stephen. Eisenhower Volume 2: The President. New York: Simon & Schuster, 1984. Trans. Wenquan Xu, et al. Beijing: China Social Sciences Press, 1989.

Bacon, Francis. Novum Organum. Book 1. 1620.

Baran, P. The Political Economy of Growth. New York: Monthly Review Press, 1957.

Beaud, Michel. History of Capitalism: 1500-1980. New York: Monthly Review Press, 1983. Trans. Aimei Wu, et al. Beijing: Oriental Press, 1987.

Benedict, Ruth. Race: Science and Politics. Rev. ed. New York: Viking Press, 1943.

"Biography of Great Yuan." Historical Records.

"Biography of Zhang Qian." History of the Former Han Dynasty.

M.N. Pokrovsky. Collected Essays on Russian Diplomacy and Wars in the 19th Century. Trans. Zhangheng Bei. Beijing: The Commercial Press, 1994.

Bontekoe, William Ysbrantsz. Memorable Description of the East Indian Voyage: 1618-25. London: Routledge, 1929. Trans. Nan Yao. Beijing: Zhonghua Book Company, 1982.

V.P. Potemkin. History of World Diplomacy. Vol.3. Trans. Dake. Beijing: The 50's Press, 1950.

British Parliamentary Papers, 1831-1832. vol. 11, p. 10. Qtd. in Mingnan Ding, et al. History of the Imperialist Invasion of China. Vol.1. Beijing: Science Publishing House, 1958.

Brown, Judith M., and W.M. Rogers Louise, eds. The Oxford History of the British Empire. Vol. IV. Oxford: Oxford University Press, 1999.

Brown, William. "Restructuring North-South Relations: ACP-EU Development Cooperation in a Liberal International Order." Review of African Political Economy 27(2000): 367-383.

Carrera, Antonio. "Research on Slave Trade in Portugal." In Slave Trade in Africa from 1500 to 1900. UNSCO. Trans. Nian Li, et al. Beijing: China Translation and Publishing House, 1984.

"Chang Lai's Memorial to the Throne". Collection of Documents. 17th Collection.

Chang, Zheng, and Fengjun Chen, eds. Transformations and Revolutions in the Third World. Beijing: China Renmin University Press, 1997.

Chen, Yong. Commodity Economy and the Dutch Modernization. Wuhan: Wuhan University Press, 1990.

Chinese Foreign Ministry and Party Literature Research Center of CPC Central Committee, eds. Mao Zedong on Diplomacy. Beijing: Central Party Literature Press, 1994.

Chinese Foreign Ministry and Party Literature Research Center of CPC Central Committee, eds. Zhou Enlai on Diplomacy. Beijing: Central Party Literature Press, 1990.

G.E. Skorba. French Imperialism in West Africa. Trans. Ren Lu. Beijing: World Affairs Press, 1958

Clavijo, Ruy González de. Narrative of the Embassy of Ruy González de Clavijo to the court of Timour, at Samarcand, A.D. 1403–6. New York: Cambridge University Press, 2009. Trans. Zhaojun Yang. Beijing: The Commercial Press, 1985.

Britannica Concise Encyclopedia. Vol. 8. Beijing: Encyclopedia of China Publishing House, 1986.

"La Conference Africaine Brazaville." Qtd. in CKOPOB. T. E. French Imperialism in West Africa. Beijing: World Affairs Press, 1958.

Crozier, Brian. De Gaulle. Vol. 2. Trans. Songhao Cao. Beijing: The Commercial Press, 1978.

Curzon, George Nathaniel. Persia and the Persian Question. Vol.2. London, 1892.

Dai, He, and Zhang Yingli. "The Export of Chinese Silk and the 'Wild' Silk." History-Geography of Northwest 1(1986).

Dai, Yi. China and the World in the Eighteenth Century. Introductory Volume. Shenyang: Liaohai Publishing House, 1999.

Dai, Yi. History of Qing Dynasty. Vol. 2. Beijing: People's Publishing House, 1984.

Dakemejian, R. H. Egypt under Nasser Rule. London, 1978.

Davidson, Basil. Africa in Modern History. Harmondsworth, Middlesex: Penguin Books, 1978. Trans. Zhan Shu, et al. Beijing: China Social Sciences Press, 1989.

Ding, Mingnan et al. History of Imperialist Invasion of China. Vol. 1. Beijing: Science Publishing House, 1958.

"Die Grosse Politik der Europaischen Kabinnette". B. XI. No. 2610. S. pp. 31-32. In History of World Diplomacy, by V.P. Potemkin. Vol.3. Beijing: The 50's Press.

Eisenhower, Dwight D. The White House Years: Waging Peace 1956–1961. New York: Doubleday, 1965. Trans. Jianghai. Shanghai: Shanghai Joint Publishing Press, 1977.

Emmanuel, A. Unequal Exchange: A Study of the Imperialism of Trade. Trans. Brian Pearce. New York: Monthly Review Press, 1972.

Fang, Lianqing, et al., eds. History of Postwar International Relations. Beijing: Peking University Press, 1999.

Fieldhouse, D.K. The Colonial Empires. Ithaca: Cornell University Press, 1973.

Fieldhouse, D. K. "'Imperialism': A Historiographical Revision." The Economic History Review 14.2(1961): 187-208.

Fieldhouse, D.K. The West and the Third World: Trade, Colonialism, Dependence and Development. Oxford: Wiley-Blackwell, 1991.

Flint, J. "Planned Decolonization and Its Failure in British Africa," in Colonialism and Nationalism in Africa. Vol. 3. Ed. G. Maddox and T. K. Welliver. New York, 1933.

Frank, Andre Gunder. ReOrient: Global Economy in the Asian Age. Berkeley: University of California Press, 1998.

Frank, Andre Gunder. Capitalism and Underdevelopment in Latin America. New York: Monthly Review Press, 1969.

Furber, H. Rival Empires of Trade in the Orient 1600-1800. Minneapolis: University of Minnesota Press, 1976. Gallager, J., and R. Robinson. "The Imperialism of Free Trade." Economic History Review 6.1 (1953): 1-15.

Gao Dai, and Zheng Jiaxin. General Introduction to Colonialism. Beijing: Peking University Press, 2003.

Gorbachev, Mikhail Sergeyevich. Perestroika: New Thinking for Our Country and the World. New York: Harper & Row, Pub. 1987. trans. Qun Su. Beijing: Xinhua Publishing House, 1987.

Group of Selecting and Editing Materials on the History of international Relation, the Editorial Office of Textbooks of Law, ed. Selected Compilation of Materials on the History of International Relations. Vol. 2. Wuhan: Wuhan University Press, 1983.

Gu, Guanfu, et al., eds. The History of International Relations. Vol. 11. Beijing: World Affairs Press, 2004.

A.A. Gromyko, and B.N. Ponomarev, eds. History of the Soviet Union's Foreign Policies. Vol. 2. Trans. Zhengwen Han, et al. Beijing: China Renmin University Press, 1989.

"The General Act of African Conference". in Selections of Modern World History Materials. Vol. 2. Beijing: The Commercial Press, 1964: 212-213.

Han, Jijiang, and Xing Hu, eds. Economics of Development. Beijing: China Agriculture University Press, 2003.

He, Fangchuan. "Reforms by the Upper Class in the East in the mid-19th Century." Journal Historical Studies, 1981/4.

Hilferding, Rudolf. "The Inevitability of History and the Inevitable Policy". in The Second International Revisionists' Fallacy on Imperialism. Ed. Translation and Edition Group of Selected Collection of Opportunist and Revisionist Writings. Shanghai: Shanghai Joint Publishing House, 1976.

Hinsley, F. H., ed. Material Progress and World-Wide Progress: 1870-1898. The New Cambridge Modern History. Vol. 11. Cambridge: Cambridge University Press, 1962. Trans. World History Institute of Chinese Academy of Social Sciences. Beijing: China Social Sciences Press, 1987.

Ho, Pong-ti. Studies on the Population of China, 1368-1953. Cambridge, Mass.: Harvard University Press, 1959.

Hobsbawm, Eric. The Age of Extremes: The Short Twentieth Century, 1914-1991. London: Abacus, 1995. Trans. Mingxuan Zheng. Nanjing: Jiangsu People's Publishing House, 1999.

Hobson, J. A. Imperialism: A Study. London: Unwin Hyman, 1938.

Holborn, Louise W. War and Peace, Aims of the United Nations 1943-1945. Vol. 12. Boston: World Peace Foundation, 1948.

Hong, Yuyi, ed. An Outline History of International Relations in Latin America. Beijing: Foreign Language Teaching and Research Press, 1996.

Hugo, Victor. "Letter to Captain Butler". In The Old Summer Palace in the Eyes of Westerners. Beijing: University of International Business and Economics Press, 2000.

Hull, Cordell. The Memoirs of Cordell Hull. Vol. 2. New York: Macmillan Co., 1948. Qtd. in World History in the 20th Century. Ed. Zhizhan Li. Wuhan: Hubei Education Press, 1998.

International Relations Institute, ed. Compilation of Literature on the Issue of Middle East. Beijing: World Affairs Press, 1958.

International Relations Institute, ed. Referential Materials on the Issue of Palestine. Beijing: World Affairs Press, 1960.

Ji, Shengli. History of Post-War International Relation. Harbin: Heilongjiang People's Publishing House, 2002.

Jiang, Mengyin. Collected Essays of Jiang Mengyin. Nanjing: Nanjing University Press, 1995.

Kennedy, Paul. The Rise and Fall of the Great Powers: Economic Change and Military Conflict from 1500 to 2000. New York: Vintage Books, 1987.

Kissinger, Henry. Diplomacy. New York: Simon & Schuster, 1994. Trans. Shuxin Gu and Tiangui Lin. Haikou: Hainan Publishing House, 1997.

Lenin, Vladimir. Imperialism, the Highest Stage of Capitalism. New York: International Publishers, 1939. Beijing: People's Publishing House, 1974.

Lenin, Vladimir. Selected Works. Vol. 2. Beijing: People's Publishing House, 1972.

Lerner, Robert E., Standish Meacham, and Edward McNall Burns. Western Civilization: Their History and Their Culture. New York: Norton, 1988. Trans. Juefei Wang, et al. Vol. 1. Beijing: China Youth Press, 2003.

Lewin, Pierre Joye et Rosine. Les trusts au Congo. Bruxelles, 1961.

Li, Anshan. "The Collapse of the British Empire." Study of History 1(1995): 169-186.

Li, Chunhui, et al., eds. A History of Latin America. Vol. 3. Shanghai: The Commercial Press, 1993.

Liang, Zhicheng, et al. Before and After the British Empire Retreated from Hongkong. Hongkong: Xintian Publishing House, 1993.

Liang, Zhiming, ed. A History of Colonialism in Southeast Asia. Beijing: Peking University Press, 1999.

Lin, Chengjie. A History of India under Colonial Rule. Beijing: Peking University Press, 2004. p. 462.

Lin, Chengjie. "Some Issues Concerning the British and Indian Opium Trade with China." Peking University Historiography 5(1998).

Lin, Limin, and Fan Yang. "The Third World and International New Order in the 21st Century". Perspectives of the Contemporary Third World. Ed. China Institutes of Contemporary International Relations. Beijing: Current Affairs Press, 2001.

Little, Douglas. "His Finest Hour? Eisenhower, Lebanon, and the 1958 Middle East Crisis." Diplomatic History 20. 1 (1996).

Liu, Haixing, and Feng Gao, eds. Compilation of Major Literatures on Four Decades of Sino-French Diplomatic Relations. Beijing: World Affairs Press, 2004.

Liu, Jing, et al. A History of the Soviet Union-Middle East Relationship. Beijing: China Social Sciences Press, 1987.

Liu, Qingjian. A New Approach to Contemporary International Relations. Beijing: Tsinghua University Press, 2004.

Longrigg, S. H. Iraq: 1900-1950. Trans. Group of Translation on Iraq, Beijing Normal University. Beijing: Beijing People's Publishing House, 1977.

Louis, Roger. Imperialism. New York: New Viewpoints, 1976.

Lu, Tingen, and Kunyuan Peng, eds. A History of Africa. The Modern Volume. Shanghai: East China Normal University Press, 1995.

Luo, Rongqu, ed. Selected Readings of Colonial Theories. Beijing, Peking University Press, 1995.

Luxemburg, R. The Accumulation of Capital. London: Routledge, 1951.

Luxemburg, R. The Accumulation of Capital. London: Routledge, 1951. Trans. Zuoshun Peng and Jixian Wu. Shanghai: Shanghai Joint Publishing Corporation, 1959.

Madariaga, Salvador de. The Rise of Spanish-American Empire. London: Hollis & Carter, 1947. Qtd. in History of Latin American Countries by Chunhui Li. Vol. 1. Beijing: The Commercial Press, 1973.

Mantoux, Paul. The Industrial Revolution in the Eighteenth Century: An Outline of the Beginning of the Modern Factory System in England. Trans. Marjorie Vernon. New York: Routledge, 2005.

Marriott, J. A. R. Modern England 1885-1945. London, 1948.

Marx, Karl. Capital. Vol.1. Beijing: China Social Sciences Press, 1983.

Marx, Karl, and Fredrick Engels. Collected Works. Vol. 5. New York: International Publishers, 1975.

Marx, Karl, and Fredrick Engels. Collected Works. Vol. 6. New York: International Publishers, 1976.

Marx, Karl, and Fredrick Engels. Collected Works. Vol. 16. New York: International Publishers, 1980.

Marx, Karl, and Fredrick Engels. Collected Works. Vol. 12. New York: International Publishers, 1979.

Marx, Karl, and Fredrick Engels. Collected Works. Vol. 28. New York: International Publishers, 1986.

Marx, Karl, and Fredrick Engels. Collected Works. Vol. 17. New York: International Publishers, 1981.

Marx, Karl, and Fredrick Engels. Collected Works. Vol. 27. New York: International Publishers, 1990.

Marx, Karl, and Fredrick Engels. Collected Works. Vol. 39. New York: International Publishers, 1983.

Marx, Karl, and Fredrick Engels. Collected Works. Vol. 35. New York: International Publishers, 1996.

Marx, Karl, and Fredrick Engels. Collected Works. Vol. 37. New York: International Publishers, 1998.

Marx, Karl, and Fredrick Engels. Selected Works. Vol. 4. Beijing: People's Publishing House, 1972.

Mill, J. S. Principles of Political Economy. London, 1898.

Mcevedy, C. and R. Jones. Atlas of World Population History. New York: Facts on File, 1979. Trans. Haitao Chen and Wentao Liu. Beijing: Oriental Press, 1992.

Moore, John Norton. The Arab-Israeli Conflict. vol. III. Princeton University Press, 1974.

Morse, H. B. The International Relations of the Chinese Empire. Vol. 1. Shanghai, 1910.

Morton, A. L. A People's History of England. London: Lawrence and Wishart Ltd., 1951.

Needham, Joseph. Science and Civilization in China. Cambridge: Cambridge University Press, 1971.

Nkrumah, Francis Nwia Kwame. Ghana: The Autobiography of Kwame Nkrumah. T. Nelson. 1957. Beijing: World Affairs Press, 1960.

D.A. Olderogge, and I.I. Potemkin. Peoples in Africa. Shanghai: Shanghai Social Sciences Press, 1960.

Pan, Zhenqiang. International Disarmament and Arms Control. Beijing: The PLA National Defense University Press, 1996.

Park, Jeffrey. The Times Illustrated History of the World. New York, 1995.

Peng, Shuzhi, and Qianyun Huang. Historical Process of the Third World. Beijing: China Youth Publishing House, 1999.

References on African Issues 1(1979).

References on Cultural Relics 1(1953).

Report of the Royal Commission on Opium 7(1894):37. Qtd. in Mingnan Ding, et al., History of Imperialist Invasion of China. Vol. 1. Science Publishing House, 1958.

Ricardo, David. Principles of Political Economy and Taxation. 1817 ed. London: M. P. Fortarty, 1969.

Robinson, R. E., and J. Gallagher. "The Partition of Africa." Material Progress and World-Wide Progress: 1870-1898. Ed. F. H. Hinsley. The New Cambridge Modern History. Vol. 11. Cambridge: Cambridge University Press, 1962: 593-640. Trans. World History Institute of Chinese Academy of Social Sciences. Beijing: China Social Sciences Press, 1987.

Ronan, Colin. The Shorter Science and Civilization in China, An Abridgement of Joseph Needham's Original Text. Vol. 3. Cambridge: Cambridge University Press, 1986.

Rose, J. H. William Pitt and the Great War. London: G. Bell and Sons, 1911.

Ruth Benedict, Race: Science and Politics, rev. ed., Viking Press, 1943.

"The World War II." Encyclopedia of China-Foreign History. Encyclopedia of China Publishing House, 1990. p. 235.

Shanghai Institute for International Studies, ed. Survey of International Affairs. Beijing: Encyclopedia of China Publishing House, 1982.

Smelser, Neil J., and Paul B. Baltes. International Encyclopedia of the Social & Behavioral Sciences. Oxford: Elsevier, 2001.

Smith, Adam. An Inquiry into the Nature and Causes of the Wealth of Nations. New York: Modern Library, 1964.

Smith, Adam. An Inquiry into the Nature and Causes of the Wealth of Nations. New York: Modern Library, 1964.

Trans. Dali Guo and Yanan Wang. Beijing: The Commercial Press, 1983.

"Southeast Asia Collective Defense Treaty." Compilation of Documents on the Issue of Indochina. Beijing: World Affairs Press, 1959.

349 A.Y. Shpirt. Africa in the World War II. Trans. Xin He. Beijing: World Affairs Press, 1960.

Strandes, Justus. The Portuguese Period in East Africa. Trans. Jean F. Wallwork. Ed. J. S. Kickman. Nairobi: East African Literature Bureau, 1968.

Stavrianos, L. S. Global Rift: The Third World Comes of Age. New York: William Morrow & Co, 1981. trans. Chi Yue, et al. Beijing: The Commercial Press, 1993.

Stavrianos, L. S. The World since 1500: A Global History. Prentice Hall, 1999. trans. Xiangying Wu and Chimin Liang. Shanghai: Shanghai Academy of Social Sciences Press, 1996.

Stavrianos, L. S. The World since 1500: A Global History. Prentice Hall, 1999. Trans. Xiangying Wu and Chimin Liang. Vol. 2. Beijing: Peking University Press, 2006.

Tan, Chongtai, ed. The New Development of Economics of Development. Wuhan: Wuhan University Press, 2002.

Tarling, Nicholas. The Cambridge History of Southeast Asia. Vol. 2. New York: Cambridge University Press, 1999. Trans. Shilu Wang, et al. Kunming: Yunnan People's Publishing House, 2003.

S.A. Tyushkevich. History of the World War II, 1939-1945. Vol. II. Vol.12. Shanghai: Shanghai Translation Publishing House, 1989.

Urwin, Derek W. A Political History of Western Europe since 1945. Trans. Dingzhao Xing. Beijing: China Translation and Publishing Corporation, 1985.

Van Loon, Hendrik Willem. The Fall of the Dutch Republic. Houghton Mifflin Co., 1913. Trans. Ziyi Zhu. Beijing: Beijing Publishing House, 2001.

Volsky, V., ed. A Survey of Latin America. Trans. Shiming Sun. Beijing: China Social Sciences Press, 1987.

Wakefield, E. G. A View of the Art of Colonization. Oxford: Claredon Press, 1914.

Wallerstein, Immanuel. The Modern World-System: Capitalist Culture and the Origins of the European World-Economy in the Sixteenth Century. New York: Academic Press, 1974. Trans. Dan Lv. Beijing: Higher Education Press, 1998.

Wang, Guishan. "Lomé Conventions and North-South Relationship." Contemporary International Relations 2,(1991).

Wang, Shengzu, ed. The History of International Relations. Vol. 8. Beijing: World Affairs Press, 1995.

Wang, Shengzu, ed. The History of International Relations.Vol.9. Beijing: World Affairs Press, 1995.

Wang, Shengzu, ed. The History of International Relations.Vol.10. Beijing: World Affairs Press, 1995: 108.

Wang, Shilu, and Guoping Wang, eds. Contemporary ASEAN. Chengdu: Sichuan People's Publishing House, 1998. Watt, D.C. Survey of International Affairs. Trans. Compilation and Translation Committee of Shanghai Municipal CPPCC. Shanghai: Shanghai Translation Publishing House, 1983.

Webster, Andrew. Introduction to the Sociology of Development. Hampshire: Macmillan, 1984.

Williams, E. Capitalism and Slavery. New York: Capricorn Books, 1966.

Willoughby, Westel W. Foreign Rights and Interests in China. Baltimore: Johns Hopkins Press, 1927. trans. Shangfang Wang. Shanghai: Shanghai Joint Publishing Press, 1957.

World Affairs Press, ed. Collections of International Treaties. Beijing: World Affairs Press, 1961.

World Affairs Press, ed. Referential Materials on the Issue of Panama Canal. Beijing: World Affairs Press, 1964.

Wu, Shuhu. "Insights into Taliban." Contemporary World 5(2001): 23. Qtd. in Liu, Qingjian. A New Approach to Contemporary International Relations. Beijing: Tsinghua University Press, 2004.

V.M. Rostov. History of Diplomacy. Vol. 2. Shanghai: Shanghai Joint Publishing Press, 1979.

Xiao, Nan, et al., eds. Political Trends of Contemporary Latin America. Beijing: The Oriental Press, 1988.

Xu, Dixin, and Chengming Wu. Development History of Chinese Capitalism. Vol. 1. Beijing: People's Publishing House, 1985.

Xu, Shicheng. "A Decade of the Cuban Reform and Opening-up: Achievements and Problems." Annual Report on Latin America and the Caribbean, 2002-2003. Beijing: Social Sciences Academic Press, 2003.

Yan, Xiaofei. An Introduction to Development Economics. Beijing: Economic Science Press, 2000.

Yao, Wenli. "On Japan's Adjustment of Foreign Policies during the Cold War." Japanese Studies 1(1994).

Ye, Jingyi. Economics of Development. Beijing: Peking University Press, 2005.

Yuan, Changyao, ed. Contemporary International Relations. Nanjing: Jiangsu Education Press, 1993.

Zhang, Xichang, and Jianqing Zhou. Post-War Diplomatic History of France. Beijing: World Affairs Press, 1993.

Zheng, Jiaxin. The History of Colonialism: Africa. Beijing: Peking University Press, 2000.

www.ingramcontent.com/pod-product-compliance
Lightning Source LLC
Chambersburg PA
CBHW020431130626
46549CB00001B/89

* 9 7 8 6 0 5 9 9 1 4 7 0 3 *